Dodge
Grand Caravan
Chrysler
Town & Country
Automotive
Repair Manual

by Jeff Killingsworth
and John H Haynes
Member of the Guild of Motoring Writers

Models covered:

Dodge Grand Caravan and
Chrysler Town & Country
2008 through 2012

Includes Caravan Cargo models

*Does not include information specific to all-wheel drive
or diesel engine models*

(30014 - 1S1)

ABCDE
FGHIJ
KLMNO
PQRS

Haynes Publishing Group
Sparkford Nr Yeovil
Somerset BA22 7JJ England

Haynes North America, Inc
861 Lawrence Drive
Newbury Park
California 91320 USA

Acknowledgements

Wiring diagrams provided exclusively for Haynes North America, Inc.
by Bosch Automotive Service Solutions.

A book in the Haynes Automotive Repair Manual Series

Printed in the U.S.A.

ISBN-13: 978-1-62092-044-2
ISBN-10: 1-62092-044-1

Library of Congress Control Number: 2013941194

Contents

Haynes mechanic and photographer with a 2012 Dodge Grand Caravan

About this manual

Its purpose

The purpose of this manual is to help you get the best value from your vehicle. It can do so in several ways. It can help you decide what work must be done, even if you choose to have it done by a dealer service department or a repair shop; it provides information and procedures for routine maintenance and servicing; and it offers diagnostic and repair procedures to follow when trouble occurs.

We hope you use the manual to tackle the work yourself. For many simpler jobs, doing it yourself may be quicker than arranging an appointment to get the vehicle into a shop and making the trips to leave it and pick it up. More importantly, a lot of money can be saved by avoiding the expense the shop must pass on to you to cover its labor and overhead

costs. An added benefit is the sense of satisfaction and accomplishment that you feel after doing the job yourself.

Using the manual

The manual is divided into Chapters. Each Chapter is divided into numbered Sections, which are headed in bold type between horizontal lines. Each Section consists of consecutively numbered paragraphs.

At the beginning of each numbered Section you will be referred to any illustrations which apply to the procedures in that Section. The reference numbers used in illustration captions pinpoint the pertinent Section and the Step within that Section. That is, illustration 3.2 means the illustration refers to Section 3 and Step (or paragraph) 2 within that Section.

Procedures, once described in the text, are not normally repeated. When it's necessary to refer to another Chapter, the reference will be given as Chapter and Section number. Cross references given without use of the word "Chapter" apply to Sections and/or paragraphs in the same Chapter. For example, "see Section 8" means in the same Chapter.

References to the left or right side of the vehicle assume you are sitting in the driver's seat, facing forward.

Even though we have prepared this manual with extreme care, neither the publisher nor the author can accept responsibility for any errors in, or omissions from, the information given.

NOTE

A **Note** provides information necessary to properly complete a procedure or information which will make the procedure easier to understand.

CAUTION

A **Caution** provides a special procedure or special steps which must be taken while completing the procedure where the Caution is found. Not heeding a Caution can result in damage to the assembly being worked on.

WARNING

A **Warning** provides a special procedure or special steps which must be taken while completing the procedure where the Warning is found. Not heeding a Warning can result in personal injury.

Introduction to the Dodge Caravan, Grand Caravan and Chrysler Town & Country

The Dodge Caravan, Grand Caravan, Chrysler Town & Country and Lancia Grand Voyager are front engine, front wheel drive mini-van models. These models feature transversely mounted V6 engines equipped with electronic multi-port fuel injection. The engine drives the front wheels through a four-speed or six-speed automatic transaxle

via independent driveaxles.

The fully-independent front suspension consists of coil spring/strut units, and lower control arms with stabilizer bar links connecting the stabilizer bar. The rear suspension uses a beam axle, trailing arms, shock absorbers and spindle/hub units supported by coil springs. A track bar locates the beam axle,

and is connected between the beam axle unit and the vehicle body. A rear stabilizer bar is installed on some models.

The power-assisted rack-and-pinion steering unit is mounted behind the engine.

Front brakes and rear brakes are disc-type. Power brake assist is standard with an Antilock Brake System (ABS) optional.

Vehicle identification numbers

Modifications are a continuing and unpublicized process in vehicle manufacturing. Since spare parts manuals and lists are compiled on a numerical basis, the individual vehicle numbers are essential to correctly identify the component required.

Vehicle Identification Number (VIN)

This very important identification number is stamped on a plate attached to the left side of the dashboard just inside the windshield on the driver's side of the vehicle (see illustration). The VIN also appears on the Vehicle Certificate of Title and Registration. It contains information such as where and when the vehi-

cle was manufactured, the model year and the body style.

VIN year and engine codes

Two particularly important pieces of information located in the VIN are the model year and engine codes. Counting from the left, the engine code is the eighth digit and the model year code is the 10th digit.

On the models covered by this manual the engine codes are:

    H........3.3L, 2008 only
    E........3.3L, 2009 - 2010 (EGV)
    P........3.8L, 2008 only
    1 ....3.8L, 2009 - 2010 (EGL)
    G ....3.6L, 2011 and later (ERB)
    X........4.0L, 2008 - 2010 (EGQ)

On the models covered by this manual the model year codes are:

    8.............2008
    9.............2009
    A.............2010
    B 2011
    C 2012

Equipment identification plate

This plate is located on the inside of the hood. It contains valuable information concerning the production of the vehicle as well as information on all production or special equipment.

Safety Certification label

The Safety Certification label is affixed to the left front door (see illustration). The plate contains the name of the manufacturer, the month and year of production, the Gross Vehicle Weight Rating (GVWR) and the safety certification statement. This label also contains the paint code. It is especially useful for matching the color and type of paint during repair work.

Engine identification number

The engine identification number on all engines is stamped into the rear of the engine block, below the cylinder head.

Transaxle identification number

The ID number on the automatic transaxle is stamped into the left front corner of the transaxle (see illustration).

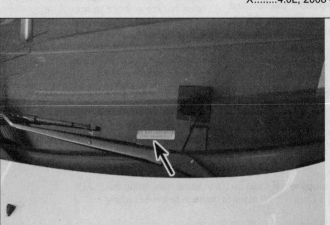

The VIN plate is visible from outside of the vehicle, through the driver's side of the windshield

The Vehicle Safety Certification label is affixed to the end of the driver's door

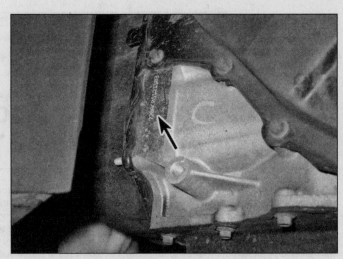

Automatic transaxle identification number location

Recall information

Vehicle recalls are carried out by the manufacturer in the rare event of a possible safety-related defect. The vehicle's registered owner is contacted at the address on file at the Department of Motor Vehicles and given the details of the recall. Remedial work is carried out free of charge at a dealer service department.

If you are the new owner of a used vehicle which was subject to a recall and you want to be sure that the work has been carried out, it's best to contact a dealer service department and ask about your individual vehicle - you'll need to furnish them your Vehicle Identification Number (VIN).

The table below is based on information provided by the National Highway Traffic Safety Administration (NHTSA), the body which oversees vehicle recalls in the United States. The recall database is updated constantly. For the latest information on vehicle recalls, check the NHTSA website at www.nhtsa.gov, www.safercar.gov or call the NHTSA hotline at 1-888-327-4236.

Recall date	Recall campaign number	Model(s) affected	Concern
2/5/2009	09V046000	2009 Dodge Grand Caravan and Chrysler Town & Country	On some models, unused electrical connectors for the blind spot detection system may become corroded and could short circuit, which can cause a variety of conditions. If the fuse for this circuit does not blow, the connectors could overheat and potentially catch fire.
6/3/2010	10V235000	2008, 2009 Dodge Grand Caravan and Chrysler Town & Country	Some models may have been built with an improperly routed wire harness that may have a condition where the lower sliding door hinge bracket can make contact and wear through the wire insulation. A short circuit could occur inside the sliding door, overheating the latch, possibly resulting in a fire.

Recall date	Recall campaign number	Model(s) affected	Concern
12/8/2010	10V611000	2008 Chrysler Town & Country and Dodge Grand Caravan	Some models may experience a heating and air conditioner (HVAC) condensate leak from the HVAC drain grommet onto the occupant restraint control (ORC) module, which can lead to the illumination of the airbag warning light and a potential inadvertent airbag deployment without warning. An inadvertent airbag deployment could result in injury to the seat occupant in front of the deploying airbag and/or a vehicle crash.
3/1/2011	11V139000	2010, 2011 Chrysler Town & Country and Dodge Grand Caravan	Some models may experience inadvertent ignition key displacement from the run to accessory position while driving causing the engine to shut off. Engine shut off while driving could increase the risk of a crash.
6/8/2011	11V315000	2011 Dodge Grand Caravan and Chrysler Town & Country	Some models may have been built with a missing or incorrectly installed steering column pivot rivet. A missing or incorrectly installed rivet could compromise the ability of the steering column to support the occupant loads in the event of a frontal crash, decreasing the effectiveness of the frontal impact safety system. As a result, the condition may increase the potential for injury in a frontal crash.
8/3/2011	11V394000	2008 Chrysler Town & Country and Dodge Grand Caravan	Some models may experience a heating and air conditioner (HVAC) condensate leak from the HVAC drain grommet onto the occupant restraint control (ORC) module, which can lead to the illumination of the airbag warning light and a potential inadvertent airbag deployment without warning. An inadvertent airbag deployment could result in injury to the seat occupant in front of the deploying airbag and/or a vehicle crash.

Recall date	Recall campaign number	Model(s) affected	Concern
9/29/2011	11V487000	2012 Chrysler Town & Country and Dodge Grand Caravan	On some models equipped with 3.6L engines, the engine may experience connecting rod bearing failure due to debris inside the engine block. Connecting rod failure may lead to engine seizure which may increase the risk of a crash.
4/3/2012	12V141000	2012 Chrysler Town & Country and Dodge Grand Caravan	Some models may be equipped with right rear hub and bearing assemblies that were not fully machined. This could result in a decrease in durability, which may lead to wheel separation, increasing the risk of a crash.
5/2/2012	12V191000	2012 Chrysler Town & Country and Dodge Grand Caravan	Some models may be equipped with a right side liftgate pinch sensor that does not function properly. As a result, increased force may be required in order to stop the power liftgate during final closing stages. The power liftgate door may close on an appendage, increasing the risk of injury.

Buying parts

Replacement parts are available from many sources, which generally fall into one of two categories - authorized dealer parts departments and independent retail auto parts stores. Our advice concerning these parts is as follows:

Retail auto parts stores: Good auto parts stores will stock frequently needed components which wear out relatively fast, such as clutch components, exhaust systems, brake parts, tune-up parts, etc. These stores often supply new or reconditioned parts on

an exchange basis, which can save a considerable amount of money. Discount auto parts stores are often very good places to buy materials and parts needed for general vehicle maintenance such as oil, grease, filters, spark plugs, belts, touch-up paint, bulbs, etc. They also usually sell tools and general accessories, have convenient hours, charge lower prices and can often be found not far from home.

Authorized dealer parts department: This is the best source for parts which are

unique to the vehicle and not generally available elsewhere (such as major engine parts, transmission parts, trim pieces, etc.).

Warranty information: If the vehicle is still covered under warranty, be sure that any replacement parts purchased - regardless of the source - do not invalidate the warranty!

To be sure of obtaining the correct parts, have engine and chassis numbers available and, if possible, take the old parts along for positive identification.

Maintenance techniques, tools and working facilities

Maintenance techniques

There are a number of techniques involved in maintenance and repair that will be referred to throughout this manual. Application of these techniques will enable the home mechanic to be more efficient, better organized and capable of performing the various tasks properly, which will ensure that the repair job is thorough and complete.

Fasteners

Fasteners are nuts, bolts, studs and screws used to hold two or more parts together. There are a few things to keep in mind when working with fasteners. Almost all of them use a locking device of some type, either a lockwasher, locknut, locking tab or thread adhesive. All threaded fasteners should be clean and straight, with undamaged threads and undamaged corners on the hex head where the wrench fits. Develop the habit of replacing all damaged nuts and bolts with new ones. Special locknuts with nylon or fiber inserts can only be used once. If they are removed, they lose their locking ability and

must be replaced with new ones.

Rusted nuts and bolts should be treated with a penetrating fluid to ease removal and prevent breakage. Some mechanics use turpentine in a spout-type oil can, which works quite well. After applying the rust penetrant, let it work for a few minutes before trying to loosen the nut or bolt. Badly rusted fasteners may have to be chiseled or sawed off or removed with a special nut breaker, available at tool stores.

If a bolt or stud breaks off in an assembly, it can be drilled and removed with a special tool commonly available for this purpose. Most automotive machine shops can perform this task, as well as other repair procedures, such as the repair of threaded holes that have been stripped out.

Flat washers and lockwashers, when removed from an assembly, should always be replaced exactly as removed. Replace any damaged washers with new ones. Never use a lockwasher on any soft metal surface (such as aluminum), thin sheet metal or plastic.

Fastener sizes

For a number of reasons, automobile manufacturers are making wider and wider use of metric fasteners. Therefore, it is important to be able to tell the difference between standard (sometimes called U.S. or SAE) and metric hardware, since they cannot be interchanged.

All bolts, whether standard or metric, are sized according to diameter, thread pitch and length. For example, a standard 1/2 - 13 x 1 bolt is 1/2 inch in diameter, has 13 threads per inch and is 1 inch long. An M12 - 1.75 x 25 metric bolt is 12 mm in diameter, has a thread pitch of 1.75 mm (the distance between threads) and is 25 mm long. The two bolts are nearly identical, and easily confused, but they are not interchangeable.

In addition to the differences in diameter, thread pitch and length, metric and standard bolts can also be distinguished by examining the bolt heads. To begin with, the distance across the flats on a standard bolt head is measured in inches, while the same dimension on a metric bolt is sized in millimeters (the same is true for nuts). As a result, a standard wrench should not be used on a metric bolt and a metric wrench should not be used on a standard bolt. Also, most standard bolts have slashes radiating out from the center of the head to denote the grade or strength of the bolt, which is an indication of the amount of torque that can be applied to it. The greater the number of slashes, the greater the strength of the bolt. Grades 0 through 5 are commonly used on automobiles. Metric bolts have a property class (grade) number, rather than a slash, molded into their heads to indicate bolt strength. In this case, the higher the number, the stronger the bolt. Property class numbers 8.8, 9.8 and 10.9 are commonly used on automobiles.

Strength markings can also be used to distinguish standard hex nuts from metric hex nuts. Many standard nuts have dots stamped into one side, while metric nuts are marked with a number. The greater the number of

dots, or the higher the number, the greater the strength of the nut.

Metric studs are also marked on their ends according to property class (grade). Larger studs are numbered (the same as metric bolts), while smaller studs carry a geometric code to denote grade.

It should be noted that many fasteners, especially Grades 0 through 2, have no distinguishing marks on them. When such is the case, the only way to determine whether it is standard or metric is to measure the thread pitch or compare it to a known fastener of the same size.

Standard fasteners are often referred to as SAE, as opposed to metric. However, it should be noted that SAE technically refers to a non-metric fine thread fastener only. Coarse thread non-metric fasteners are referred to as USS sizes.

Since fasteners of the same size (both standard and metric) may have different

strength ratings, be sure to reinstall any bolts, studs or nuts removed from your vehicle in their original locations. Also, when replacing a fastener with a new one, make sure that the new one has a strength rating equal to or greater than the original.

Tightening sequences and procedures

Most threaded fasteners should be tightened to a specific torque value (torque is the twisting force applied to a threaded component such as a nut or bolt). Overtightening the fastener can weaken it and cause it to break, while undertightening can cause it to eventually come loose. Bolts, screws and studs, depending on the material they are made of and their thread diameters, have specific torque values, many of which are noted in the Specifications at the beginning of each Chapter. Be sure to follow the torque recommendations closely. For fasteners not assigned a

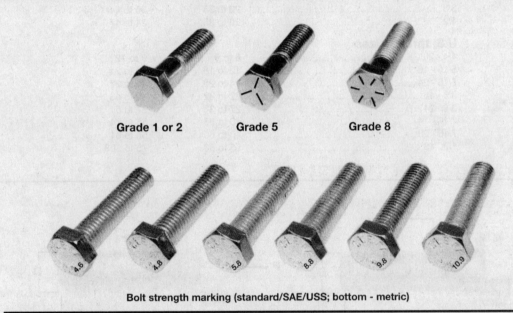

Grade 1 or 2   Grade 5   Grade 8

Bolt strength marking (standard/SAE/USS; bottom - metric)

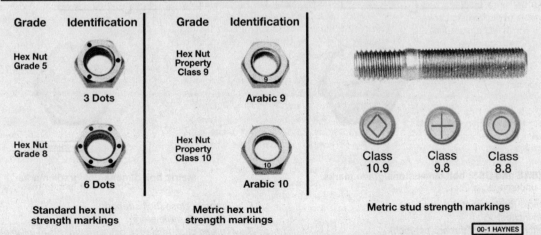

Grade	Identification
Hex Nut Grade 5	3 Dots
Hex Nut Grade 8	6 Dots

Standard hex nut strength markings

Grade	Identification
Hex Nut Property Class 9	Arabic 9
Hex Nut Property Class 10	Arabic 10

Metric hex nut strength markings

Class 10.9   Class 9.8   Class 8.8

Metric stud strength markings

00-1 HAYNES

specific torque, a general torque value chart is presented here as a guide. These torque values are for dry (unlubricated) fasteners threaded into steel or cast iron (not aluminum). As was previously mentioned, the size and grade of a fastener determine the amount of torque that can safely be applied to it. The figures listed here are approximate for Grade 2 and Grade 3 fasteners. Higher grades can tolerate higher torque values.

Fasteners laid out in a pattern, such as cylinder head bolts, oil pan bolts, differential cover bolts, etc., must be loosened or tightened in sequence to avoid warping the component. This sequence will normally be shown in the appropriate Chapter. If a specific pattern is not given, the following procedures can be used to prevent warping.

Initially, the bolts or nuts should be assembled finger-tight only. Next, they should be tightened one full turn each, in a criss-cross or diagonal pattern. After each one has been tightened one full turn, return to the first one and tighten them all one-half turn, following the same pattern. Finally, tighten each of them one-quarter turn at a time until each fastener has been tightened to the proper torque. To loosen and remove the fasteners, the procedure would be reversed.

Component disassembly

Component disassembly should be done with care and purpose to help ensure that

Metric thread sizes	Ft-lbs	Nm
M-6	6 to 9	9 to 12
M-8	14 to 21	19 to 28
M-10	28 to 40	38 to 54
M-12	50 to 71	68 to 96
M-14	80 to 140	109 to 154

Pipe thread sizes		
1/8	5 to 8	7 to 10
1/4	12 to 18	17 to 24
3/8	22 to 33	30 to 44
1/2	25 to 35	34 to 47

U.S. thread sizes		
1/4 - 20	6 to 9	9 to 12
5/16 - 18	12 to 18	17 to 24
5/16 - 24	14 to 20	19 to 27
3/8 - 16	22 to 32	30 to 43
3/8 - 24	27 to 38	37 to 51
7/16 - 14	40 to 55	55 to 74
7/16 - 20	40 to 60	55 to 81
1/2 - 13	55 to 80	75 to 108

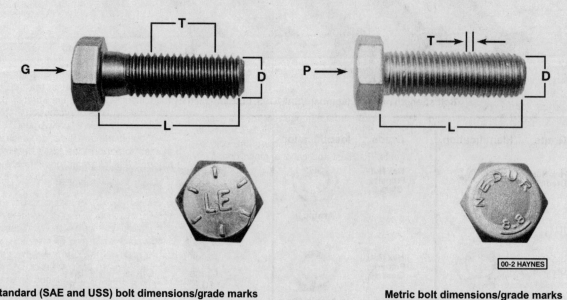

Standard (SAE and USS) bolt dimensions/grade marks

G	Grade marks (bolt strength)
L	Length (in inches)
T	Thread pitch (number of threads per inch)
D	Nominal diameter (in inches)

Metric bolt dimensions/grade marks

P	Property class (bolt strength)
L	Length (in millimeters)
T	Thread pitch (distance between threads in millimeters)
D	Diameter

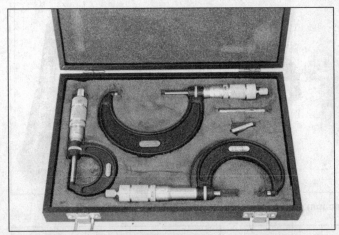

Micrometer set

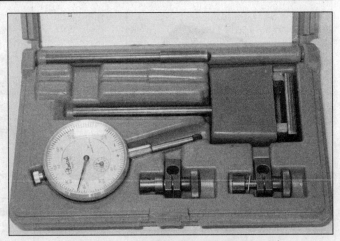

Dial indicator set

the parts go back together properly. Always keep track of the sequence in which parts are removed. Make note of special characteristics or marks on parts that can be installed more than one way, such as a grooved thrust washer on a shaft. It is a good idea to lay the disassembled parts out on a clean surface in the order that they were removed. It may also be helpful to make sketches or take instant photos of components before removal.

When removing fasteners from a component, keep track of their locations. Sometimes threading a bolt back in a part, or putting the washers and nut back on a stud, can prevent mix-ups later. If nuts and bolts cannot be returned to their original locations, they should be kept in a compartmented box or a series of small boxes. A cupcake or muffin tin is ideal for this purpose, since each cavity can hold the bolts and nuts from a particular area (i.e. oil pan bolts, valve cover bolts, engine mount bolts, etc.). A pan of this type is especially helpful when working on assemblies with very small parts, such as the carburetor, alternator, valve train or interior dash and trim pieces. The cavities can be marked with paint or tape to identify the contents.

Whenever wiring looms, harnesses or connectors are separated, it is a good idea to identify the two halves with numbered pieces of masking tape so they can be easily reconnected.

Gasket sealing surfaces

Throughout any vehicle, gaskets are used to seal the mating surfaces between two parts and keep lubricants, fluids, vacuum or pressure contained in an assembly.

Many times these gaskets are coated with a liquid or paste-type gasket sealing compound before assembly. Age, heat and pressure can sometimes cause the two parts to stick together so tightly that they are very difficult to separate. Often, the assembly can be loosened by striking it with a soft-face hammer near the mating surfaces. A regular hammer can be used if a block of wood is placed between the hammer and the part. Do not hammer on cast parts or parts that could be easily damaged. With any particularly stubborn part, always recheck to make sure that every fastener has been removed.

Avoid using a screwdriver or bar to pry apart an assembly, as they can easily mar the gasket sealing surfaces of the parts, which must remain smooth. If prying is absolutely necessary, use an old broom handle, but keep in mind that extra clean up will be necessary if the wood splinters.

After the parts are separated, the old gasket must be carefully scraped off and the gasket surfaces cleaned. Stubborn gasket material can be soaked with rust penetrant or treated with a special chemical to soften it so it can be easily scraped off. **Caution:** *Never use gasket removal solutions or caustic chemicals on plastic or other composite components.* A scraper can be fashioned from a piece of copper tubing by flattening and sharpening one end. Copper is recommended because it is usually softer than the surfaces to be scraped, which reduces the chance of gouging the part. Some gaskets can be removed with a wire brush, but regardless of the method used, the mating surfaces must be left clean and smooth. If for some reason the gasket surface is gouged, then a gasket sealer thick enough to fill scratches will have to be used during reassembly of the components. For most applications, a non-drying (or semi-drying) gasket sealer should be used.

Hose removal tips

Warning: *If the vehicle is equipped with air conditioning, do not disconnect any of the A/C hoses without first having the system depressurized by a dealer service department or a service station.*

Hose removal precautions closely parallel gasket removal precautions. Avoid scratching or gouging the surface that the hose mates against or the connection may leak. This is especially true for radiator hoses. Because of various chemical reactions, the rubber in hoses can bond itself to the metal spigot that the hose fits over. To remove a hose, first loosen the hose clamps that secure it to the spigot. Then, with slip-joint pliers, grab the hose at the clamp and rotate it around the spigot. Work it back and forth until it is completely free, then pull it off. Silicone or other lubricants will ease removal if they can be applied between the hose and the outside of the spigot. Apply the same lubricant to the inside of the hose and the outside of the spigot to simplify installation.

As a last resort (and if the hose is to be replaced with a new one anyway), the rubber can be slit with a knife and the hose peeled from the spigot. If this must be done, be careful that the metal connection is not damaged.

If a hose clamp is broken or damaged, do not reuse it. Wire-type clamps usually weaken with age, so it is a good idea to replace them with screw-type clamps whenever a hose is removed.

Tools

A selection of good tools is a basic requirement for anyone who plans to maintain and repair his or her own vehicle. For the owner who has few tools, the initial investment might seem high, but when compared to the spiraling costs of professional auto maintenance and repair, it is a wise one.

To help the owner decide which tools are needed to perform the tasks detailed in this manual, the following tool lists are offered: *Maintenance and minor repair, Repair/overhaul* and *Special*.

The newcomer to practical mechanics should start off with the *maintenance and minor repair* tool kit, which is adequate for the simpler jobs performed on a vehicle. Then, as confidence and experience grow, the owner can tackle more difficult tasks, buying additional tools as they are needed. Eventually the basic kit will be expanded into the *repair and overhaul* tool set. Over a period of time, the experienced do-it-yourselfer will assemble a tool set complete enough for most repair and overhaul procedures and will add tools from the special category when it is felt that the expense is justified by the frequency of use.

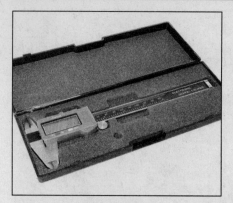

Dial caliper

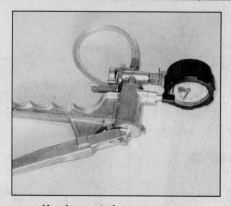

Hand-operated vacuum pump

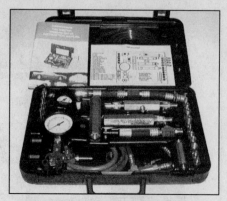

Fuel pressure gauge set

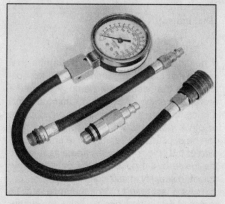

Compression gauge with spark plug hole adapter

Damper/steering wheel puller

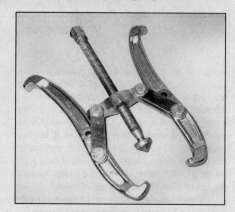

General purpose puller

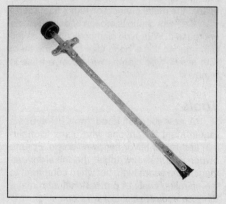

Hydraulic lifter removal tool

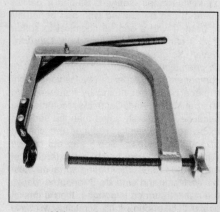

Valve spring compressor

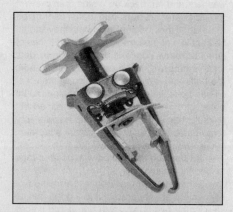

Valve spring compressor

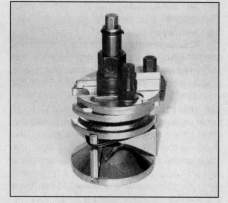

Ridge reamer

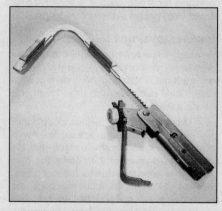

Piston ring groove cleaning tool

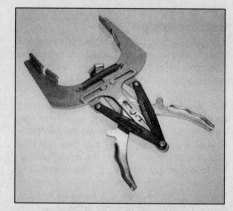

Ring removal/installation tool

Ring compressor

Cylinder hone

Brake hold-down spring tool

Torque angle gauge

Clutch plate alignment tool

Tap and die set

Maintenance and minor repair tool kit

The tools in this list should be considered the minimum required for performance of routine maintenance, servicing and minor repair work. We recommend the purchase of combination wrenches (box-end and open-end combined in one wrench). While more expensive than open end wrenches, they offer the advantages of both types of wrench.

Combination wrench set (1/4-inch to 1 inch or 6 mm to 19 mm)
Adjustable wrench, 8 inch
Spark plug wrench with rubber insert
Spark plug gap adjusting tool
Feeler gauge set
Brake bleeder wrench
Standard screwdriver (5/16-inch x 6 inch)
Phillips screwdriver (No. 2 x 6 inch)
Combination pliers - 6 inch
Hacksaw and assortment of blades
Tire pressure gauge
Grease gun
Oil can
Fine emery cloth
Wire brush
Battery post and cable cleaning tool
Oil filter wrench
Funnel (medium size)
Safety goggles
Jackstands (2)
Drain pan

Note: *If basic tune-ups are going to be part of routine maintenance, it will be necessary to purchase a good quality stroboscopic timing light and combination tachometer/dwell meter. Although they are included in the list of special tools, it is mentioned here because they are absolutely necessary for tuning most vehicles properly.*

Repair and overhaul tool set

These tools are essential for anyone who plans to perform major repairs and are in addition to those in the maintenance and minor repair tool kit. Included is a comprehensive set of sockets which, though expensive, are invaluable because of their versatility, especially when various extensions and drives are available. We recommend the 1/2-inch drive over the 3/8-inch drive. Although the larger drive is bulky and more expensive, it has the capacity of accepting a very wide range of large sockets. Ideally, however, the mechanic should have a 3/8-inch drive set and a 1/2-inch drive set.

Socket set(s)
Reversible ratchet
Extension - 10 inch
Universal joint
Torque wrench (same size drive as sockets)
Ball peen hammer - 8 ounce
Soft-face hammer (plastic/rubber)
Standard screwdriver (1/4-inch x 6 inch)

Standard screwdriver (stubby - 5/16-inch)
Phillips screwdriver (No. 3 x 8 inch)
Phillips screwdriver (stubby - No. 2)
Pliers - vise grip
Pliers - lineman's
Pliers - needle nose
Pliers - snap-ring (internal and external)
Cold chisel - 1/2-inch
Scribe
Scraper (made from flattened copper tubing)
Centerpunch
Pin punches (1/16, 1/8, 3/16-inch)
Steel rule/straightedge - 12 inch
Allen wrench set (1/8 to 3/8-inch or 4 mm to 10 mm)
A selection of files
Wire brush (large)
Jackstands (second set)
Jack (scissor or hydraulic type)

Note: *Another tool which is often useful is an electric drill with a chuck capacity of 3/8-inch and a set of good quality drill bits.*

Special tools

The tools in this list include those which are not used regularly, are expensive to buy, or which need to be used in accordance with their manufacturer's instructions. Unless these tools will be used frequently, it is not very economical to purchase many of them. A consideration would be to split the cost and use between yourself and a friend or friends. In addition, most of these tools can be obtained from a tool rental shop on a temporary basis.

This list primarily contains only those tools and instruments widely available to the public, and not those special tools produced by the vehicle manufacturer for distribution to dealer service departments. Occasionally, references to the manufacturer's special tools are included in the text of this manual. Generally, an alternative method of doing the job without the special tool is offered. However, sometimes there is no alternative to their use. Where this is the case, and the tool cannot be purchased or borrowed, the work should be turned over to the dealer service department or an automotive repair shop.

> *Valve spring compressor*
> *Piston ring groove cleaning tool*
> *Piston ring compressor*
> *Piston ring installation tool*
> *Cylinder compression gauge*
> *Cylinder ridge reamer*
> *Cylinder surfacing hone*
> *Cylinder bore gauge*
> *Micrometers and/or dial calipers*
> *Hydraulic lifter removal tool*
> *Balljoint separator*
> *Universal-type puller*
> *Impact screwdriver*
> *Dial indicator set*
> *Stroboscopic timing light (inductive pick-up)*
> *Hand operated vacuum/pressure pump*
> *Tachometer/dwell meter*
> *Universal electrical multimeter*
> *Cable hoist*
> *Brake spring removal and installation tools*
> *Floor jack*

Buying tools

For the do-it-yourselfer who is just starting to get involved in vehicle maintenance and repair, there are a number of options available when purchasing tools. If maintenance and minor repair is the extent of the work to be done, the purchase of individual tools is satisfactory. If, on the other hand, extensive work is planned, it would be a good idea to purchase a modest tool set from one of the large retail chain stores. A set can usually be bought at a substantial savings over the individual tool prices, and they often come with a tool box. As additional tools are needed, add-on sets, individual tools and a larger tool box can be purchased to expand the tool selection. Building a tool set gradually allows the cost of the tools to be spread over a longer period of time and gives the mechanic the freedom to choose only those tools that will actually be used.

Tool stores will often be the only source of some of the special tools that are needed, but regardless of where tools are bought, try to avoid cheap ones, especially when buying screwdrivers and sockets, because they won't last very long. The expense involved in replacing cheap tools will eventually be greater than the initial cost of quality tools.

Care and maintenance of tools

Good tools are expensive, so it makes sense to treat them with respect. Keep them clean and in usable condition and store them properly when not in use. Always wipe off any dirt, grease or metal chips before putting them away. Never leave tools lying around in the work area. Upon completion of a job, always check closely under the hood for tools that may have been left there so they won't get lost during a test drive.

Some tools, such as screwdrivers, pliers, wrenches and sockets, can be hung on a panel mounted on the garage or workshop wall, while others should be kept in a tool box or tray. Measuring instruments, gauges, meters, etc. must be carefully stored where they cannot be damaged by weather or impact from other tools.

When tools are used with care and stored properly, they will last a very long time. Even with the best of care, though, tools will wear out if used frequently. When a tool is damaged or worn out, replace it. Subsequent jobs will be safer and more enjoyable if you do.

How to repair damaged threads

Sometimes, the internal threads of a nut or bolt hole can become stripped, usually from overtightening. Stripping threads is an all-too-common occurrence, especially when working with aluminum parts, because aluminum is so soft that it easily strips out.

Usually, external or internal threads are only partially stripped. After they've been cleaned up with a tap or die, they'll still work. Sometimes, however, threads are badly damaged. When this happens, you've got three choices:

1) *Drill and tap the hole to the next suitable oversize and install a larger diameter bolt, screw or stud.*

2) *Drill and tap the hole to accept a threaded plug, then drill and tap the plug to the original screw size. You can also buy a plug already threaded to the original size. Then you simply drill a hole to the specified size, then run the threaded plug into the hole with a bolt and jam nut. Once the plug is fully seated, remove the jam nut and bolt.*

3) *The third method uses a patented thread repair kit like Heli-Coil or Slimsert. These easy-to-use kits are designed to repair damaged threads in straight-through holes and blind holes. Both are available as kits which can handle a variety of sizes and thread patterns. Drill the hole, then tap it with the special included tap. Install the Heli-Coil and the hole is back to its original diameter and thread pitch.*

Regardless of which method you use, be sure to proceed calmly and carefully. A little impatience or carelessness during one of these relatively simple procedures can ruin your whole day's work and cost you a bundle if you wreck an expensive part.

Working facilities

Not to be overlooked when discussing tools is the workshop. If anything more than routine maintenance is to be carried out, some sort of suitable work area is essential.

It is understood, and appreciated, that many home mechanics do not have a good workshop or garage available, and end up removing an engine or doing major repairs outside. It is recommended, however, that the overhaul or repair be completed under the cover of a roof.

A clean, flat workbench or table of comfortable working height is an absolute necessity. The workbench should be equipped with a vise that has a jaw opening of at least four inches.

As mentioned previously, some clean, dry storage space is also required for tools, as well as the lubricants, fluids, cleaning solvents, etc. which soon become necessary.

Sometimes waste oil and fluids, drained from the engine or cooling system during normal maintenance or repairs, present a disposal problem. To avoid pouring them on the ground or into a sewage system, pour the used fluids into large containers, seal them with caps and take them to an authorized disposal site or recycling center. Plastic jugs, such as old antifreeze containers, are ideal for this purpose.

Always keep a supply of old newspapers and clean rags available. Old towels are excellent for mopping up spills. Many mechanics use rolls of paper towels for most work because they are readily available and disposable. To help keep the area under the vehicle clean, a large cardboard box can be cut open and flattened to protect the garage or shop floor.

Whenever working over a painted surface, such as when leaning over a fender to service something under the hood, always cover it with an old blanket or bedspread to protect the finish. Vinyl covered pads, made especially for this purpose, are available at auto parts stores.

Booster battery (jump) starting

Observe the following precautions when using a booster battery to start a vehicle:

a) *Before connecting the booster battery, make sure the ignition switch is in the Off position.*
b) *Turn off the lights, heater and other electrical loads.*
c) *Your eyes should be shielded. Safety goggles are a good idea.*
d) *Make sure the booster battery is the same voltage as the dead one in the vehicle.*
e) *The two vehicles MUST NOT TOUCH each other.*
f) *Make sure the transaxle is in Park.*
g) *If the booster battery is not a maintenance-free type, remove the vent caps and lay a cloth over the vent holes.*

Connect the red jumper cable to the positive (+) terminals of each battery.

Connect one end of the black cable to the negative (-) terminal of the booster battery. The other end of this cable should be connected to a good ground on the engine block **(see illustration)**. Make sure the cable will not come into contact with the fan, drivebelts or other moving parts of the engine.

Start the engine using the booster battery, then, with the engine running at idle speed, disconnect the jumper cables in the reverse order of connection.

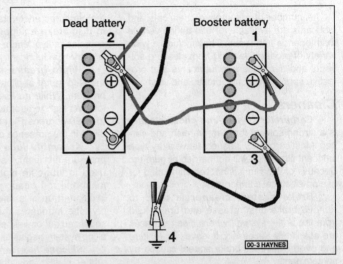

Make the booster battery cable connections in the numerical order shown (note that the negative cable of the booster battery is NOT attached to the negative terminal of the dead battery)

Jacking and towing

Jacking

The jack supplied with the vehicle should only be used for raising the vehicle for changing a tire or placing jackstands under the frame. **Warning:** *Never crawl under the vehicle or start the engine when the jack is being used as the only means of support.*

All vehicles are supplied with a scissors-type jack. When jacking the vehicle, it should be engaged with the rocker panel flange, between the two cutouts **(see illustration)**.

The vehicle should be on level ground with the wheels blocked and the transmission in Park. Pry off the hub cap (if equipped) using the tapered end of the lug wrench. Loosen the lug nuts one-half turn and leave them in place until the wheel is raised off the ground.

Place the jack under the side of the vehicle in the indicated position. Use the supplied wrench to turn the jackscrew clockwise until the wheel is raised off the ground. Remove the lug nuts, pull off the wheel and install the spare.

With the beveled side in, install the lug nuts and tighten them until snug. Lower the vehicle by turning the jackscrew counterclockwise. Remove the jack and tighten the nuts in a diagonal pattern to the torque listed in the Chapter 1 Specifications. If a torque wrench is not available, have the torque checked by a service station as soon as possible. Install the hubcap by placing it in position and using the heel of your hand or a rubber mallet to seat it.

Towing

As a general rule, the vehicle should be towed with the front (drive) wheels off the ground or, preferably, on a flat bed car carrier. If the front wheels can't be raised or a carrier isn't available, place them on a dolly. The ignition key must be in the ACC position, since the steering lock mechanism isn't strong enough to hold the front wheels straight while towing.

In emergency situations the vehicle can be towed from the front with all four wheels on the ground, provided that speeds don't exceed 40 mph and the distance is not over 100 miles. Before towing, check the transaxle fluid level (see Chapter 1). If the level is below the HOT mark on the dipstick, add fluid.

Towing equipment specifically designed for this purpose should be used and should be attached to the main structural members of the vehicle, not the bumper or brackets.

Safety is a major consideration when towing and all applicable state and local laws must be obeyed. A safety chain system must be used for all towing.

While towing, the parking brake must be released and the transmission must be in Neutral. The steering must be unlocked (ignition switch in the Off position). Remember that power steering and power brakes will not work with the engine off.

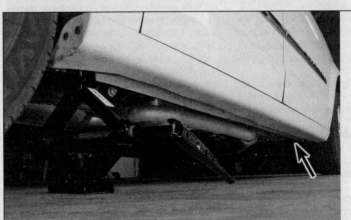

The jack fits over the rocker panel flange (there are two jacking points on each side of the vehicle)

Automotive chemicals and lubricants

A number of automotive chemicals and lubricants are available for use during vehicle maintenance and repair. They include a wide variety of products ranging from cleaning solvents and degreasers to lubricants and protective sprays for rubber, plastic and vinyl.

Cleaners

Carburetor cleaner and choke cleaner is a strong solvent for gum, varnish and carbon. Most carburetor cleaners leave a dry-type lubricant film which will not harden or gum up. Because of this film it is not recommended for use on electrical components.

Brake system cleaner is used to remove brake dust, grease and brake fluid from the brake system, where clean surfaces are absolutely necessary. It leaves no residue and often eliminates brake squeal caused by contaminants.

Electrical cleaner removes oxidation, corrosion and carbon deposits from electrical contacts, restoring full current flow. It can also be used to clean spark plugs, carburetor jets, voltage regulators and other parts where an oil-free surface is desired.

Demoisturants remove water and moisture from electrical components such as alternators, voltage regulators, electrical connectors and fuse blocks. They are non-conductive and non-corrosive.

Degreasers are heavy-duty solvents used to remove grease from the outside of the engine and from chassis components. They can be sprayed or brushed on and, depending on the type, are rinsed off either with water or solvent.

Lubricants

Motor oil is the lubricant formulated for use in engines. It normally contains a wide variety of additives to prevent corrosion and reduce foaming and wear. Motor oil comes in various weights (viscosity ratings) from 0 to 50. The recommended weight of the oil depends on the season, temperature and the demands on the engine. Light oil is used in cold climates and under light load conditions. Heavy oil is used in hot climates and where high loads are encountered. Multi-viscosity oils are designed to have characteristics of both light and heavy oils and are available in a number of weights from 0W-20 to 20W-50.

Gear oil is designed to be used in differentials, manual transmissions and other areas where high-temperature lubrication is required.

Chassis and wheel bearing grease is a heavy grease used where increased loads and friction are encountered, such as for wheel bearings, balljoints, tie-rod ends and universal joints.

High-temperature wheel bearing grease is designed to withstand the extreme temperatures encountered by wheel bearings in disc brake equipped vehicles. It usually contains molybdenum disulfide (moly), which is a dry-type lubricant.

White grease is a heavy grease for metal-to-metal applications where water is a problem. White grease stays soft under both low and high temperatures (usually from -100 to +190-degrees F), and will not wash off or dilute in the presence of water.

Assembly lube is a special extreme pressure lubricant, usually containing moly, used to lubricate high-load parts (such as main and rod bearings and cam lobes) for initial start-up of a new engine. The assembly lube lubricates the parts without being squeezed out or washed away until the engine oiling system begins to function.

Silicone lubricants are used to protect rubber, plastic, vinyl and nylon parts.

Graphite lubricants are used where oils cannot be used due to contamination problems, such as in locks. The dry graphite will lubricate metal parts while remaining uncontaminated by dirt, water, oil or acids. It is electrically conductive and will not foul electrical contacts in locks such as the ignition switch.

Moly penetrants loosen and lubricate frozen, rusted and corroded fasteners and prevent future rusting or freezing.

Heat-sink grease is a special electrically non-conductive grease that is used for mounting electronic ignition modules where it is essential that heat is transferred away from the module.

Sealants

RTV sealant is one of the most widely used gasket compounds. Made from silicone, RTV is air curing, it seals, bonds, waterproofs, fills surface irregularities, remains flexible, doesn't shrink, is relatively easy to remove, and is used as a supplementary sealer with almost all low and medium temperature gaskets.

Anaerobic sealant is much like RTV in that it can be used either to seal gaskets or to form gaskets by itself. It remains flexible, is solvent resistant and fills surface imperfections. The difference between an anaerobic sealant and an RTV-type sealant is in the curing. RTV cures when exposed to air, while an anaerobic sealant cures only in the absence of air. This means that an anaerobic sealant cures only after the assembly of parts, sealing them together.

Thread and pipe sealant is used for sealing hydraulic and pneumatic fittings and vacuum lines. It is usually made from a Teflon compound, and comes in a spray, a paint-on liquid and as a wrap-around tape.

Chemicals

Anti-seize compound prevents seizing, galling, cold welding, rust and corrosion in fasteners. High-temperature ant-seize, usually made with copper and graphite lubricants, is used for exhaust system and exhaust manifold bolts.

Anaerobic locking compounds are used to keep fasteners from vibrating or working loose and cure only after installation, in the absence of air. Medium strength locking compound is used for small nuts, bolts and screws that may be removed later. High-strength locking compound is for large nuts, bolts and studs which aren't removed on a regular basis.

Oil additives range from viscosity index improvers to chemical treatments that claim to reduce internal engine friction. It should be noted that most oil manufacturers caution against using additives with their oils.

Gas additives perform several functions, depending on their chemical makeup. They usually contain solvents that help dissolve gum and varnish that build up on carburetor, fuel injection and intake parts. They also serve to break down carbon deposits that form on the inside surfaces of the combustion chambers. Some additives contain upper cylinder lubricants for valves and piston rings, and others contain chemicals to remove condensation from the gas tank.

Miscellaneous

Brake fluid is specially formulated hydraulic fluid that can withstand the heat and pressure encountered in brake systems. Care must be taken so this fluid does not come in contact with painted surfaces or plastics. An opened container should always be resealed to prevent contamination by water or dirt.

Weatherstrip adhesive is used to bond weatherstripping around doors, windows and trunk lids. It is sometimes used to attach trim pieces.

Undercoating is a petroleum-based, tar-like substance that is designed to protect metal surfaces on the underside of the vehicle from corrosion. It also acts as a sound-deadening agent by insulating the bottom of the vehicle.

Waxes and polishes are used to help protect painted and plated surfaces from the weather. Different types of paint may require the use of different types of wax and polish. Some polishes utilize a chemical or abrasive cleaner to help remove the top layer of oxidized (dull) paint on older vehicles. In recent years many non-wax polishes that contain a wide variety of chemicals such as polymers and silicones have been introduced. These non-wax polishes are usually easier to apply and last longer than conventional waxes and polishes.

Conversion factors

Length (distance)

Inches (in)	X	25.4	= Millimeters (mm)	X 0.0394	= Inches (in)
Feet (ft)	X	0.305	= Meters (m)	X 3.281	= Feet (ft)
Miles	X	1.609	= Kilometers (km)	X 0.621	= Miles

Volume (capacity)

Cubic inches (cu in; in³)	X	16.387	= Cubic centimeters (cc; cm³)	X 0.061	= Cubic inches (cu in; in³)
Imperial pints (Imp pt)	X	0.568	= Liters (l)	X 1.76	= Imperial pints (Imp pt)
Imperial quarts (Imp qt)	X	1.137	= Liters (l)	X 0.88	= Imperial quarts (Imp qt)
Imperial quarts (Imp qt)	X	1.201	= US quarts (US qt)	X 0.833	= Imperial quarts (Imp qt)
US quarts (US qt)	X	0.946	= Liters (l)	X 1.057	= US quarts (US qt)
Imperial gallons (Imp gal)	X	4.546	= Liters (l)	X 0.22	= Imperial gallons (Imp gal)
Imperial gallons (Imp gal)	X	1.201	= US gallons (US gal)	X 0.833	= Imperial gallons (Imp gal)
US gallons (US gal)	X	3.785	= Liters (l)	X 0.264	= US gallons (US gal)

Mass (weight)

Ounces (oz)	X	28.35	= Grams (g)	X 0.035	= Ounces (oz)
Pounds (lb)	X	0.454	= Kilograms (kg)	X 2.205	= Pounds (lb)

Force

Ounces-force (ozf; oz)	X	0.278	= Newtons (N)	X 3.6	= Ounces-force (ozf; oz)
Pounds-force (lbf; lb)	X	4.448	= Newtons (N)	X 0.225	= Pounds-force (lbf; lb)
Newtons (N)	X	0.1	= Kilograms-force (kgf; kg)	X 9.81	= Newtons (N)

Pressure

Pounds-force per square inch (psi; lbf/in²; lb/in²)	X	0.070	= Kilograms-force per square centimeter (kgf/cm²; kg/cm²)	X 14.223	= Pounds-force per square inch (psi; lbf/in²; lb/in²)
Pounds-force per square inch (psi; lbf/in²; lb/in²)	X	0.068	= Atmospheres (atm)	X 14.696	= Pounds-force per square inch (psi; lbf/in²; lb/in²)
Pounds-force per square inch (psi; lbf/in²; lb/in²)	X	0.069	= Bars	X 14.5	= Pounds-force per square inch (psi; lbf/in²; lb/in²)
Pounds-force per square inch (psi; lbf/in²; lb/in²)	X	6.895	= Kilopascals (kPa)	X 0.145	= Pounds-force per square inch (psi; lbf/in²; lb/in²)
Kilopascals (kPa)	X	0.01	= Kilograms-force per square centimeter (kgf/cm²; kg/cm²)	X 98.1	= Kilopascals (kPa)

Torque (moment of force)

Pounds-force inches (lbf in; lb in)	X	1.152	= Kilograms-force centimeter (kgf cm; kg cm)	X 0.868	= Pounds-force inches (lbf in; lb in)
Pounds-force inches (lbf in; lb in)	X	0.113	= Newton meters (Nm)	X 8.85	= Pounds-force inches (lbf in; lb in)
Pounds-force inches (lbf in; lb in)	X	0.083	= Pounds-force feet (lbf ft; lb ft)	X 12	= Pounds-force inches (lbf in; lb in)
Pounds-force feet (lbf ft; lb ft)	X	0.138	= Kilograms-force meters (kgf m; kg m)	X 7.233	= Pounds-force feet (lbf ft; lb ft)
Pounds-force feet (lbf ft; lb ft)	X	1.356	= Newton meters (Nm)	X 0.738	= Pounds-force feet (lbf ft; lb ft)
Newton meters (Nm)	X	0.102	= Kilograms-force meters (kgf m; kg m)	X 9.804	= Newton meters (Nm)

Vacuum

Inches mercury (in. Hg)	X	3.377	= Kilopascals (kPa)	X 0.2961	= Inches mercury
Inches mercury (in. Hg)	X	25.4	= Millimeters mercury (mm Hg)	X 0.0394	= Inches mercury

Power

Horsepower (hp)	X	745.7	= Watts (W)	X 0.0013	= Horsepower (hp)

Velocity (speed)

Miles per hour (miles/hr; mph)	X	1.609	= Kilometers per hour (km/hr; kph)	X 0.621	= Miles per hour (miles/hr; mph)

Fuel consumption*

Miles per gallon, Imperial (mpg)	X	0.354	= Kilometers per liter (km/l)	X 2.825	= Miles per gallon, Imperial (mpg)
Miles per gallon, US (mpg)	X	0.425	= Kilometers per liter (km/l)	X 2.352	= Miles per gallon, US (mpg)

Temperature

Degrees Fahrenheit = (°C x 1.8) + 32   Degrees Celsius (Degrees Centigrade; °C) = (°F - 32) x 0.56

*It is common practice to convert from miles per gallon (mpg) to liters/100 kilometers (l/100km),
where mpg (Imperial) x l/100 km = 282 and mpg (US) x l/100 km = 235

DECIMALS to MILLIMETERS

Decimal	mm	Decimal	mm
0.001	0.0254	0.500	12.7000
0.002	0.0508	0.510	12.9540
0.003	0.0762	0.520	13.2080
0.004	0.1016	0.530	13.4620
0.005	0.1270	0.540	13.7160
0.006	0.1524	0.550	13.9700
0.007	0.1778	0.560	14.2240
0.008	0.2032	0.570	14.4780
0.009	0.2286	0.580	14.7320
		0.590	14.9860
0.010	0.2540		
0.020	0.5080		
0.030	0.7620		
0.040	1.0160	0.600	15.2400
0.050	1.2700	0.610	15.4940
0.060	1.5240	0.620	15.7480
0.070	1.7780	0.630	16.0020
0.080	2.0320	0.640	16.2560
0.090	2.2860	0.650	16.5100
		0.660	16.7640
0.100	2.5400	0.670	17.0180
0.110	2.7940	0.680	17.2720
0.120	3.0480	0.690	17.5260
0.130	3.3020		
0.140	3.5560		
0.150	3.8100		
0.160	4.0640	0.700	17.7800
0.170	4.3180	0.710	18.0340
0.180	4.5720	0.720	18.2880
0.190	4.8260	0.730	18.5420
		0.740	18.7960
0.200	5.0800	0.750	19.0500
0.210	5.3340	0.760	19.3040
0.220	5.5880	0.770	19.5580
0.230	5.8420	0.780	19.8120
0.240	6.0960	0.790	20.0660
0.250	6.3500		
0.260	6.6040		
0.270	6.8580	0.800	20.3200
0.280	7.1120	0.810	20.5740
0.290	7.3660	0.820	21.8280
		0.830	21.0820
0.300	7.6200	0.840	21.3360
0.310	7.8740	0.850	21.5900
0.320	8.1280	0.860	21.8440
0.330	8.3820	0.870	22.0980
0.340	8.6360	0.880	22.3520
0.350	8.8900	0.890	22.6060
0.360	9.1440		
0.370	9.3980		
0.380	9.6520		
0.390	9.9060	0.900	22.8600
0.400	10.1600	0.910	23.1140
0.410	10.4140	0.920	23.3680
0.420	10.6680	0.930	23.6220
0.430	10.9220	0.940	23.8760
0.440	11.1760	0.950	24.1300
0.450	11.4300	0.960	24.3840
0.460	11.6840	0.970	24.6380
0.470	11.9380	0.980	24.8920
0.480	12.1920	0.990	25.1460
0.490	12.4460	1.000	25.4000

FRACTIONS to DECIMALS to MILLIMETERS

Fraction	Decimal	mm	Fraction	Decimal	mm
1/64	0.0156	0.3969	33/64	0.5156	13.0969
1/32	0.0312	0.7938	17/32	0.5312	13.4938
3/64	0.0469	1.1906	35/64	0.5469	13.8906
1/16	0.0625	1.5875	9/16	0.5625	14.2875
5/64	0.0781	1.9844	37/64	0.5781	14.6844
3/32	0.0938	2.3812	19/32	0.5938	15.0812
7/64	0.1094	2.7781	39/64	0.6094	15.4781
1/8	0.1250	3.1750	5/8	0.6250	15.8750
9/64	0.1406	3.5719	41/64	0.6406	16.2719
5/32	0.1562	3.9688	21/32	0.6562	16.6688
11/64	0.1719	4.3656	43/64	0.6719	17.0656
3/16	0.1875	4.7625	11/16	0.6875	17.4625
13/64	0.2031	5.1594	45/64	0.7031	17.8594
7/32	0.2188	5.5562	23/32	0.7188	18.2562
15/64	0.2344	5.9531	47/64	0.7344	18.6531
1/4	0.2500	6.3500	3/4	0.7500	19.0500
17/64	0.2656	6.7469	49/64	0.7656	19.4469
9/32	0.2812	7.1438	25/32	0.7812	19.8438
19/64	0.2969	7.5406	51/64	0.7969	20.2406
5/16	0.3125	7.9375	13/16	0.8125	20.6375
21/64	0.3281	8.3344	53/64	0.8281	21.0344
11/32	0.3438	8.7312	27/32	0.8438	21.4312
23/64	0.3594	9.1281	55/64	0.8594	21.8281
3/8	0.3750	9.5250	7/8	0.8750	22.2250
25/64	0.3906	9.9219	57/64	0.8906	22.6219
13/32	0.4062	10.3188	29/32	0.9062	23.0188
27/64	0.4219	10.7156	59/64	0.9219	23.4156
7/16	0.4375	11.1125	15/16	0.9375	23.8125
29/64	0.4531	11.5094	61/64	0.9531	24.2094
15/32	0.4688	11.9062	31/32	0.9688	24.6062
31/64	0.4844	12.3031	63/64	0.9844	25.0031
1/2	0.5000	12.7000	1	1.0000	25.4000

Safety first!

Regardless of how enthusiastic you may be about getting on with the job at hand, take the time to ensure that your safety is not jeopardized. A moment's lack of attention can result in an accident, as can failure to observe certain simple safety precautions. The possibility of an accident will always exist, and the following points should not be considered a comprehensive list of all dangers. Rather, they are intended to make you aware of the risks and to encourage a safety conscious approach to all work you carry out on your vehicle.

Essential DOs and DON'Ts

DON'T rely on a jack when working under the vehicle. Always use approved jackstands to support the weight of the vehicle and place them under the recommended lift or support points.

DON'T attempt to loosen extremely tight fasteners (i.e. wheel lug nuts) while the vehicle is on a jack - it may fall.

DON'T start the engine without first making sure that the transmission is in Neutral (or Park where applicable) and the parking brake is set.

DON'T remove the radiator cap from a hot cooling system - let it cool or cover it with a cloth and release the pressure gradually.

DON'T attempt to drain the engine oil until you are sure it has cooled to the point that it will not burn you.

DON'T touch any part of the engine or exhaust system until it has cooled sufficiently to avoid burns.

DON'T siphon toxic liquids such as gasoline, antifreeze and brake fluid by mouth, or allow them to remain on your skin.

DON'T inhale brake lining dust - it is potentially hazardous (see *Asbestos* below).

DON'T allow spilled oil or grease to remain on the floor - wipe it up before someone slips on it.

DON'T use loose fitting wrenches or other tools which may slip and cause injury.

DON'T push on wrenches when loosening or tightening nuts or bolts. Always try to pull the wrench toward you. If the situation calls for pushing the wrench away, push with an open hand to avoid scraped knuckles if the wrench should slip.

DON'T attempt to lift a heavy component alone - get someone to help you.

DON'T *rush or take unsafe shortcuts to finish a job.*

DON'T allow children or animals in or around the vehicle while you are working on it.

DO wear eye protection when using power tools such as a drill, sander, bench grinder, etc. and when working under a vehicle.

DO keep loose clothing and long hair well out of the way of moving parts.

DO make sure that any hoist used has a safe working load rating adequate for the job.

DO get someone to check on you periodically when working alone on a vehicle.

DO carry out work in a logical sequence and make sure that everything is correctly assembled and tightened.

DO keep chemicals and fluids tightly capped and out of the reach of children and pets.

DO remember that your vehicle's safety affects that of yourself and others. If in doubt on any point, get professional advice.

Steering, suspension and brakes

These systems are essential to driving safety, so make sure you have a qualified shop or individual check your work. Also, compressed suspension springs can cause injury if released suddenly - be sure to use a spring compressor.

Airbags

Airbags are explosive devices that can **CAUSE** injury if they deploy while you're working on the vehicle. Follow the manufacturer's instructions to disable the airbag whenever you're working in the vicinity of airbag components.

Asbestos

Certain friction, insulating, sealing, and other products - such as brake linings, brake bands, clutch linings, torque converters, gaskets, etc. - may contain asbestos or other hazardous friction material. Extreme care must be taken to avoid inhalation of dust from such products, since it is hazardous to health. If in doubt, assume that they do contain asbestos.

Fire

Remember at all times that gasoline is highly flammable. Never smoke or have any kind of open flame around when working on a vehicle. But the risk does not end there. A spark caused by an electrical short circuit, by two metal surfaces contacting each other, or even by static electricity built up in your body under certain conditions, can ignite gasoline vapors, which in a confined space are highly explosive. Do not, under any circumstances, use gasoline for cleaning parts. Use an approved safety solvent.

Always disconnect the battery ground (-) cable at the battery before working on any part of the fuel system or electrical system. Never risk spilling fuel on a hot engine or exhaust component. It is strongly recommended that a fire extinguisher suitable for use on fuel and electrical fires be kept handy in the garage or workshop at all times. Never try to extinguish a fuel or electrical fire with water.

Fumes

Certain fumes are highly toxic and can quickly cause unconsciousness and even death if inhaled to any extent. Gasoline vapor falls into this category, as do the vapors from some cleaning solvents. Any draining or pouring of such volatile fluids should be done in a well ventilated area.

When using cleaning fluids and solvents, read the instructions on the container carefully. Never use materials from unmarked containers.

Never run the engine in an enclosed space, such as a garage. Exhaust fumes contain carbon monoxide, which is extremely poisonous. If you need to run the engine, always do so in the open air, or at least have the rear of the vehicle outside the work area.

The battery

Never create a spark or allow a bare light bulb near a battery. They normally give off a certain amount of hydrogen gas, which is highly explosive.

Always disconnect the battery ground (-) cable at the battery before working on the fuel or electrical systems.

If possible, loosen the filler caps or cover when charging the battery from an external source (this does not apply to sealed or maintenance-free batteries). Do not charge at an excessive rate or the battery may burst.

Take care when adding water to a non maintenance-free battery and when carrying a battery. The electrolyte, even when diluted, is very corrosive and should not be allowed to contact clothing or skin.

Always wear eye protection when cleaning the battery to prevent the caustic deposits from entering your eyes.

Household current

When using an electric power tool, inspection light, etc., which operates on household current, always make sure that the tool is correctly connected to its plug and that, where necessary, it is properly grounded. Do not use such items in damp conditions and, again, do not create a spark or apply excessive heat in the vicinity of fuel or fuel vapor.

Secondary ignition system voltage

A severe electric shock can result from touching certain parts of the ignition system (such as the spark plug wires) when the engine is running or being cranked, particularly if components are damp or the insulation is defective. In the case of an electronic ignition system, the secondary system voltage is much higher and could prove fatal.

Hydrofluoric acid

This extremely corrosive acid is formed when certain types of synthetic rubber, found in some O-rings, oil seals, fuel hoses, etc. are exposed to temperatures above 750-degrees F (400-degrees C). The rubber changes into a charred or sticky substance containing the acid. *Once formed, the acid remains dangerous for years. If it gets onto the skin, it may be necessary to amputate the limb concerned.*

When dealing with a vehicle which has suffered a fire, or with components salvaged from such a vehicle, wear protective gloves and discard them after use.

Troubleshooting

Contents

This section provides an easy reference guide to the more common problems which may occur during the operation of your vehicle. Various symptoms and their possible causes are grouped under headings denoting components or systems, such as Engine, Cooling system, etc. They also refer to the Chapter and/or Section that deals with the problem.

Remember that successful troubleshooting isn't a mysterious art practiced only by professional mechanics. It's simply the result of knowledge combined with an intelligent, systematic approach to a problem. Always use a process of elimination, starting with the simplest solution and working through to the most complex - and never overlook the obvious. Anyone can run the gas tank dry or leave the lights on overnight, so don't assume that you're exempt from such oversights.

Finally, always establish a clear idea why a problem has occurred and take steps to ensure that it doesn't happen again. If the electrical system fails because of a poor connection, check all other connections in the system to make sure they don't fail as well. If a particular fuse continues to blow, find out why - don't just go on replacing fuses. Remember, failure of a small component can often be indicative of potential failure or incorrect functioning of a more important component or system.

Engine and performance

1 Engine will not rotate when attempting to start

1 Battery terminal connections loose or corroded (Chapter 1).
2 Battery discharged or faulty (Chapter 1).
3 Automatic transaxle not completely engaged in Park (Chapter 7).
4 Broken, loose or disconnected wiring in the starting circuit (Chapters 5 and 12).
5 Starter motor pinion jammed in flywheel ring gear (Chapter 5).
6 Starter solenoid faulty (Chapter 5).
7 Starter motor faulty (Chapter 5).
8 Ignition switch faulty (Chapter 12).
9 Transmission Range (TR) sensor faulty (Chapter 6).
10 Starter pinion or driveplate teeth worn or broken (Chapter 5).

2 Engine rotates but will not start

1 Fuel tank empty.
2 Battery discharged (engine rotates slowly) (Chapter 5).
3 Battery terminal connections loose or corroded (Chapter 1).
4 Leaking fuel injector(s), fuel pump, pressure regulator, etc. (Chapter 4).
5 Fuel not reaching fuel injection system (Chapter 4).
6 Broken timing belt or chain (Chapter 2A or 2B).
7 Ignition system problem (Chapter 5).
8 Defective crankshaft sensor or camshaft sensor (Chapter 6).

3 Engine hard to start when cold

1 Battery discharged or low (Chapter 1).
2 Fuel system malfunctioning (Chapter 4).
3 Emissions or engine control system malfunctioning (Chapter 6).

4 Engine hard to start when hot

1 Air filter clogged (Chapter 1).
2 Fuel not reaching the fuel injection system (Chapter 4).
3 Corroded battery connections, especially ground (Chapter 1).
4 Emissions or engine control system malfunctioning (Chapter 6).

5 Starter motor noisy or excessively rough in engagement

1 Pinion or driveplate gear teeth worn or broken (Chapter 5).
2 Starter motor mounting bolts loose or missing (Chapter 5).

6 Engine starts but stops immediately

1 Insufficient fuel reaching the fuel injectors (Chapter 4).
2 Vacuum leak at the gasket between the intake manifold/plenum and throttle body (Chapters 1 and 4).
3 Restricted exhaust system (most likely the catalytic converter) (Chapters 4 and 6).

7 Oil puddle under engine

1 Oil pan gasket and/or oil pan drain bolt seal leaking (Chapters 1 and 2).
2 Oil pressure sending unit leaking (Chapter 2).
3 Rocker arm cover gaskets leaking (Chapter 2).
4 Engine oil seals leaking (Chapter 2).

8 Engine lopes while idling or idles erratically

1 Vacuum leakage (Chapter 4).
2 Leaking EGR valve or plugged PCV valve (Chapter 6).
3 Air filter clogged (Chapter 1).
4 Fuel pump not delivering sufficient fuel to the fuel injection system (Chapter 4).
5 Leaking head gasket (Chapter 2).
6 Camshaft lobes worn (Chapter 2).

9 Engine misses at idle speed

1 Spark plugs worn or not gapped properly (Chapter 1).
2 Faulty coil(s) or spark plug wires (Chapter 5).
3 Vacuum leaks (Chapters 1 and 4).
4 Uneven or low compression (Chapter 2C).

10 Engine misses throughout driving speed range

1 Fuel filter clogged and/or impurities in the fuel system (Chapter 4).
2 Low fuel pressure (Chapter 4).
3 Faulty or incorrectly gapped spark plugs (Chapter 1).
4 Leaking spark plug wires (Chapter 1).
5 Faulty emission system components (Chapter 6).
6 Low or uneven cylinder compression pressures (Chapter 2).
7 Weak or faulty ignition system (Chapter 5).
8 Vacuum leak (Chapter 2).

11 Engine stumbles on acceleration

1 Spark plugs fouled (Chapter 1).
2 Fuel injection system problem (Chapter 4).
3 Fuel filter clogged (Chapter 4).
4 Intake manifold air leak (Chapter 4).
5 Problem with emissions/engine control system (Chapter 6).

12 Engine surges while holding accelerator steady

1 Intake air leak (Chapter 4).
2 Fuel pump faulty (Chapter 4).
3 Problem with the fuel injection system (Chapter 4).
4 Problem with the emission or engine control system (Chapter 6).

13 Engine stalls

1 Fuel filter clogged and/or water and impurities in the fuel system (Chapter 4).
2 Faulty emissions or engine control system components (Chapter 6).
3 Faulty or incorrectly gapped spark plugs (Chapter 1).
4 Faulty spark plug wires (Chapter 1).
5 Vacuum leak (Chapter 2).

14 Engine lacks power

1 Faulty or incorrectly gapped spark plugs (Chapter 1).
2 Restricted exhaust system (most likely the catalytic converter (Chapters 4 and 6).
3 Fuel injection system malfunctioning (Chapter 4).
4 Faulty coil(s) (Chapter 5).
5 Brakes binding (Chapter 9).
6 Automatic transaxle fluid level incorrect (Chapter 1).
7 Fuel filter clogged and/or impurities in the fuel system (Chapter 1).
8 Emission control system not functioning properly (Chapter 6).
9 Low or uneven cylinder compression pressures (Chapter 2).

15 Engine backfires

1 Emissions system not functioning properly (Chapter 6).
2 Fuel injection system malfunctioning (Chapter 4).
3 Vacuum leak at fuel injectors, intake manifold or vacuum hoses (Chapter 4).
4 Valves sticking (Chapter 2).
5 Timing chain worn (Chapter 2).

16 Pinging or knocking engine sounds during acceleration or uphill

1   Incorrect grade of fuel.
2   Fuel injection system malfunctioning Chapter 4).
3   Improper or damaged spark plugs (Chapter 1).
4   Worn or damaged ignition components (Chapter 5).
5   Faulty emissions or engine control system (Chapter 6).
6   Vacuum leak (Chapter 2).

17 Engine runs with oil pressure light on

1   Low oil level (Chapter 1).
2   Short in wiring circuit (Chapter 12).
3   Faulty oil pressure sender (Chapter 2).
4   Oil viscosity too low or oil diluted.
5   Worn engine bearings and/or oil pump (Chapter 2).

18 Engine continues to run after switching off

1   Excessive engine operating temperature (Chapter 3).
2   Excessive carbon deposits on valves and pistons.
3   Leaking fuel injector(s).

Engine electrical system

19 Battery will not hold a charge

1   Drivebelt or tensioner defective (Chapter 1).
2   Battery terminals loose or corroded (Chapter 1).
3   Alternator not charging properly (Chapter 5).
4   Loose, broken or faulty wiring in the charging circuit (Chapter 5).
5   Internally defective battery (Chapters 1 and 5).

20 Voltage warning light fails to go out

1   Faulty alternator or charging circuit (Chapter 5).
2   Drivebelt or tensioner defective (Chapter 1).
3   Alternator voltage regulator inoperative (Chapter 5).

21 Voltage warning light fails to come on when key is turned on

1   Warning light bulb defective (Chapter 12).
2   Fault in the printed circuit, dash wiring or bulb holder (Chapter 12).

Fuel system

22 Excessive fuel consumption

1   Dirty or clogged air filter element (Chapter 1).
2   Emissions or engine control system not functioning properly (Chapter 6).
3   Fuel injection system malfunctioning (Chapter 4).
4   Low tire pressure or incorrect tire size (Chapter 1).

23 Fuel leakage and/or fuel odor

1   Leak in a fuel feed or vent line (Chapter 4).
2   Tank overfilled.
3   Evaporative emissions control canister defective (Chapter 6).
4   Fuel injector seals faulty (Chapter 4).

Cooling system

24 Overheating

1   Insufficient coolant in system (Chapter 1).
2   Drivebelt or tensioner defective (Chapter 1).
3   Radiator core blocked or grille restricted (Chapter 3).
4   Thermostat faulty (Chapter 3).
5   Electric cooling fan blades broken or cracked (Chapter 3).
6   Radiator cap not maintaining proper pressure (Chapter 3).
7   Faulty water pump (Chapter 3).

25 Overcooling

Incorrect (opening temperature too low) or faulty thermostat (Chapter 3).

26 External coolant leakage

1   Deteriorated/damaged hoses or loose clamps (Chapters 1 and 3).
2   Water pump seal defective (Chapter 3).
3   Leakage from radiator core (Chapter 3).
4   Engine drain or water jacket core plugs leaking (Chapter 2).

27 Internal coolant leakage

1   Leaking cylinder head gasket (Chapter 2).
2   Cracked cylinder bore or cylinder head (Chapter 2).

28 Coolant loss

1   Too much coolant in system (Chapter 1).
2   Coolant boiling away because of overheating (Chapter 3).
3   Internal or external leakage (Chapter 3).
4   Faulty radiator cap (Chapter 3).

29 Poor coolant circulation

1   Inoperative water pump (Chapter 3).
2   Restriction in cooling system (Chapters 1 and 3).
3   Drivebelt or tensioner defective or out of adjustment (Chapter 1).
4   Thermostat sticking (Chapter 3).

Automatic transaxle

Note: *Due to the complexity of the automatic transaxle, it's difficult for the home mechanic to properly diagnose and service this component. For problems other than the following, the vehicle should be taken to a dealer service department or a transmission shop.*

30 Fluid leakage

1   Automatic transmission fluid is a deep red color. Fluid leaks should not be confused with engine oil, which can easily be blown by airflow to the transaxle.
2   To pinpoint a leak, first remove all built-up dirt and grime from the transaxle housing with degreasing agents and/or steam cleaning. Drive the vehicle at low speeds so air flow will not blow the leak far from its source. Raise the vehicle and determine where the leak is coming from. Common areas of leakage are:

    a)   *Fluid pan*
    b)   *Fluid cooler lines (Chapter 7)*
    c)   *Vehicle Speed Sensor (Chapter 6)*

31 Transaxle fluid brown or has a burned smell

Transaxle overheated. Change fluid (Chapter 1).

32 General shift mechanism problems

1   Chapter 7 deals with checking and adjusting the shift linkage on automatic transaxles. Common problems which may be attributed to a poorly adjusted linkage are:
a) Engine starting in gears other than Park or Neutral.
b) Indicator on shifter pointing to a gear other than the one actually being used.
c) Vehicle moves when in Park.
2   Refer to Chapter 7 for the shift linkage adjustment procedure.

33 Engine will start in gears other than Park or Neutral

Transmission Range (TR) sensor malfunctioning (Chapter 6).

34 Transaxle slips, shifts roughly, is noisy or has no drive in forward or reverse gears

There are many probable causes for the above problems, but the home mechanic should be concerned with only one possibility - fluid level. Before taking the vehicle to a repair shop, check the level and condition of the fluid as described in Chapter 1.

Correct the fluid level as necessary or change the fluid and filter if needed. If the problem persists, have a professional diagnose the probable cause.

Driveaxles

35 Clicking noise in turns

Worn or damaged outer CV joint. Check for cut or damaged boots (Chapter 1). Repair as necessary (Chapter 8).

36 Knock or clunk when accelerating after coasting

Worn or damaged CV joint. Check for cut or damaged boots (Chapter 1). Repair as necessary (Chapter 8).

37 Shudder or vibration during acceleration

1   Worn or damaged CV joints. Repair or replace as necessary (Chapter 8).
2   Sticking inner joint assembly. Correct or replace as necessary (Chapter 8).

Brakes

Note: Before assuming that a brake problem exists, make sure . . .
a) The tires are in good condition and properly inflated (Chapter 1).
b) The front end alignment is correct (Chapter 10).
c) The vehicle isn't loaded with weight in an unequal manner.

38 Vehicle pulls to one side during braking

1   Incorrect tire pressures (Chapter 1).
2   Front end out of alignment (have the front end aligned).
3   Unmatched tires on same axle.
4   Restricted brake lines or hoses (Chapter 9).
5   Sticking caliper or wheel cylinder piston (Chapter 9).
6   Loose suspension parts (Chapter 10).
7   Contaminated brake pad material (Chapter 9).

39 Noise (grinding or high-pitched squeal) when the brakes are applied

1   Disc brake pads worn out. Replace pads with new ones immediately (Chapter 9).

40 Brake roughness or chatter (pedal pulsates)

1   Excessive brake disc lateral runout.
2   Parallelism of disc not within specifications (Chapter 9).
3   Defective brake disc (Chapter 9).

41 Excessive pedal effort required to stop vehicle

1   Malfunctioning power brake booster (Chapter 9).
2   Partial system failure (Chapter 9).
3   Excessively worn pads (Chapter 9).
4   One or more caliper or wheel cylinder pistons seized or sticking (Chapter 9).
5   Brake pads contaminated with oil or grease (Chapter 9).
6   New pads or shoes installed and not yet seated. It will take a while for the new material to seat.

42 Excessive brake pedal travel

1   Partial brake system failure (Chapter 9).
2   Insufficient fluid in master cylinder (Chapters 1 and 9).

3   Air trapped in system (Chapter 9).
4   Faulty master cylinder (Chapter 9).

43 Dragging brakes

1   Master cylinder pistons not returning correctly (Chapter 9).
2   Restricted brake lines or hoses (Chapters 1 and 9).
3   Incorrect parking brake adjustment (Chapter 9).
4   Defective brake calipers (Chapter 9).

44 Grabbing or uneven braking action

Contaminated brake pads (Chapter 9).

45 Brake pedal feels spongy when depressed

1   Air in hydraulic lines (Chapter 9).
2   Master cylinder mounting bolts loose (Chapter 9).
3   Master cylinder defective (Chapter 9).

46 Brake pedal travels to the floor with little resistance

Little or no fluid in the master cylinder reservoir caused by leaking caliper, or loose, damaged or disconnected brake lines (Chapter 9).

47 Parking brake does not hold

Parking brake cables improperly adjusted (Chapter 9).

Suspension and steering systems

Note: Before attempting to diagnose the suspension and steering systems, perform the following preliminary checks:
a) Check the tire pressures and look for uneven wear.
b) Check the steering universal joints or coupling from the column to the steering gear for loose fasteners and wear.
c) Check the front and rear suspension and the steering gear assembly for loose and damaged parts.
d) Look for out-of-round or out-of-balance tires, bent rims and loose and/or rough wheel bearings.

48 Vehicle pulls to one side

1 Mismatched or uneven tires (Chapter 10).
2 Broken or sagging coil springs (Chapter 10).
3 Wheel alignment incorrect.
4 Front brakes dragging (Chapter 9).

49 Abnormal or excessive tire wear

1 Front wheel alignment incorrect.
2 Sagging or broken springs (Chapter 10).
3 Tire out-of-balance (Chapter 10).
4 Worn strut or shock absorber (Chapter 10).
5 Overloaded vehicle.
6 Tires not rotated regularly.

50 Wheel makes a "thumping" noise

1 Blister or bump on tire (Chapter 1).
2 Improper strut or shock absorber action (Chapter 10).

51 Shimmy, shake or vibration

1 Tire or wheel out-of-balance or out-of-round (Chapter 10).
2 Worn wheel bearings (Chapter 10).
3 Worn tie-rod ends (Chapter 10).
4 Worn balljoints (Chapter 10).
5 Excessive wheel runout (Chapter 10).
6 Blister or bump on tire (Chapter 1).

52 Hard steering

1 Balljoints, tie-rod ends or steering gear worn (Chapter 10).
2 Front wheel alignment incorrect.
3 Low tire pressure (Chapter 1).

53 Steering wheel does not return to center position correctly

1 Balljoints or tie-rod ends worn (Chapters 1 and 10).
2 Defective rack-and-pinion assembly (Chapter 10).
3 Front wheel alignment problem.

54 Abnormal noise at the front end

1 Balljoints or tie-rod ends worn (Chapter 1).
2 Loose upper strut mount (Chapter 10).
3 Worn tie-rod ends (Chapter 10).
4 Loose stabilizer bar (Chapter 10).
5 Loose wheel lug nuts (Chapter 1).
6 Loose suspension bolts (Chapter 10).

55 Wander or poor steering stability

1 Mismatched or uneven tires (Chapter 10).
2 Balljoints or tie-rod ends worn (Chapters 1 and 10).
3 Worn struts or shock absorbers (Chapter 10).
4 Broken or sagging springs (Chapter 10).
5 Front wheel alignment incorrect.
6 Worn steering gear clamp bushing (Chapter 10).

56 Erratic steering when braking

1 Wheel bearings worn (Chapter 10).
2 Broken or sagging springs (Chapter 10).
3 Leaking caliper (Chapter 9).
4 Warped brake discs (Chapter 9).
5 Worn steering gear clamp bushing (Chapter 10).
6 Wheel alignment incorrect.

57 Excessive pitching and/or rolling around corners or during braking

1 Loose stabilizer bar (Chapter 10).
2 Worn struts/shock absorbers or mounts (Chapter 10).
3 Broken or sagging coil springs (Chapter 10).
4 Overloaded vehicle.

58 Suspension bottoms

1 Overloaded vehicle.
2 Worn struts or shock absorbers (Chapter 10).
3 Incorrect, broken or sagging springs (Chapter 10).

59 Cupped tires

1 Front wheel alignment incorrect.
2 Worn struts or shock absorbers (Chapter 10).
3 Wheel bearings worn (Chapter 10).
4 Excessive tire or wheel runout (Chapter 10).
5 Worn balljoints (Chapter 10).

60 Excessive tire wear on outside edge

1 Inflation pressures incorrect (Chapter 1).
2 Excessive speed in turns.
3 Wheel alignment incorrect (excessive toe-in or positive camber). Have professionally aligned.
4 Suspension arm bent (Chapter 10).

61 Excessive tire wear on inside edge

1 Inflation pressures incorrect (Chapter 1).
2 Wheel alignment incorrect (toe-out or excessive negative camber). Have professionally aligned.
3 Loose or damaged steering components (Chapter 10).

62 Tire tread worn in one place

1 Tires out-of-balance.
2 Damaged wheel.
3 Defective tire (Chapter 1).

63 Excessive play or looseness in steering system

1 Wheel bearings worn (Chapter 10).
2 Tie-rod end loose or worn (Chapter 10).
3 Steering gear loose (Chapter 10).

64 Rattling or clicking noise in steering gear

1 Steering gear mounting bolts loose (Chapter 10).
2 Steering gear defective (Chapter 10).

Chapter 1
Tune-up and routine maintenance

Contents

Specifications

Recommended lubricants and fluids

Engine oil	
Type	API "Certified for gasoline engines"
Viscosity	
3.3L and 3.8L engines	SAE 5W-20
4.0L engines	SAE 10W-30
3.6L engines	SAE 5W-30
Automatic transaxle fluid	Mopar® ATF +4 automatic transmission fluid or equivalent
Power steering fluid	Mopar® ATF +4 automatic transmission fluid or equivalent
Brake fluid	DOT type 3 brake fluid
Engine coolant	50/50 mixture of Mopar® 5 year/100,000 mile Formula (MS-9769) antifreeze/coolant with HOAT (Hybrid Organic Additive Technology) and water*
Door and liftgate latch	Multi-purpose grease
Fuel filler door remote control latch mechanism	Multi-purpose grease
Hood, door and liftgate hinge lubricant	Engine oil
Key lock cylinder lubricant	Graphite spray
Parking brake mechanism grease	Mopar Spray White Lube or equivalent

*These vehicles are filled with a 50/50 mixture of Mopar 5 year/100,000 mile coolant that shouldn't be mixed with other coolants. Refer to the coolant reservoir label under the hood to determine what type coolant you have. Always refill with the correct coolant.

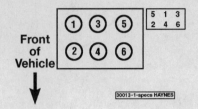

Cylinder and coil terminal location diagram -
3.3L and 3.8L engines

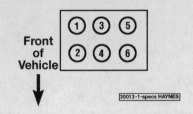

Cylinder location diagram - 3.6L and 4.0L engines

Capacities*

Engine oil (including filter)

3.3L and 3.8L engines	5.0 quarts
3.6L engines	6.0 quarts
4.0L engines	5.5 quarts

Automatic transaxle (drain and refill)**

42TE (4-speed)	4.0 quarts
62TE (6-speed)	5.5 quarts

Cooling system***

3.3L and 3.6L engines	13.4 quarts
3.8L and 4.0L engines	16.3 quarts

   * All capacities approximate. Add as necessary to bring to appropriate level.
   ** The best way to determine the amount of fluid to add during a routine fluid change is to measure the amount drained. It's important to not overfill the transaxle.
   *** Includes heater and coolant reservoir.

Brakes

Disc brake pad wear limit (minimum)	1/16 inch (1.5 mm)

Ignition system

Spark plug type and gap

Type

3.3L and 3.8L engines	RE14PLP5
3.6L engine	RER8ZWYCB4
4.0L engine	ZFR5LP-13G

Gap

3.3L, 3.8L and 4.0L engines	0.050 inches (1.27 mm)
3.6L engine	0.040 inches (1.0 mm)
Firing order	1-2-3-4-5-6

Torque specifications   Ft-lbs (unless otherwise indicated)

Note: *One foot-pound (ft-lb) of torque is equivalent to 12 inch-pounds (in-lbs) of torque. Torque values below approximately 15 ft-lbs are expressed in inch-pounds, since most foot-pound torque wrenches are not accurate at these smaller values.*

Automatic transaxle oil pan mounting bolts

41TE (4-speed)	165 in-lbs
62TE (6-speed)	105 in-lbs
Automatic transaxle oil filter mounting nuts 62TE (6-speed)	40 in-lbs

Drivebelt tensioner mounting bolt

3.3L and 3.8L engines	21
3.6L engine	41
4.0L engine	45
Engine oil drain plug	20
Engine oil filter cap (3.6L engine)	18

Spark plugs

3.3L and 3.8L engines	156 in-lbs
3.6L engine	168 in-lbs
4.0L engine	20
Wheel lug nuts	100

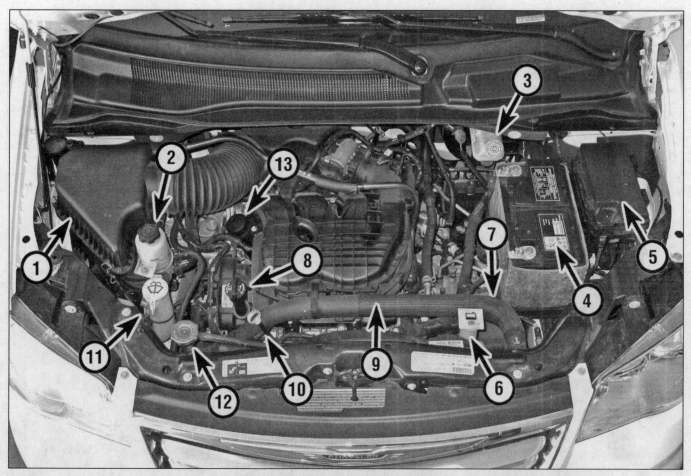

Typical engine compartment layout – 3.6L engine shown, other models similar

1	Air filter housing	6	Coolant reservoir	11	Windshield washer fluid reservoir
2	Power steering fluid reservoir	7	Transaxle fluid dipstick tube	12	Radiator cap
3	Brake fluid reservoir	8	Engine oil filler cap	13	Oil filter housing
4	Battery	9	Upper radiator hose		
5	Underhood fuse/relay block	10	Engine oil dipstick		

Typical engine compartment underside components

1	Automatic transaxle fluid pan	3	Driveaxle boots
2	Engine oil drain plug	4	Brake calipers

Typical rear underside components

1   Muffler   3   Rear shock absorbers
2   Fuel tank   4   Rear brake calipers

1 Maintenance schedule

The following maintenance intervals are based on the assumption that the vehicle owner will be doing the maintenance or service work, as opposed to having a dealer service department do the work. Although the time/mileage intervals are loosely based on factory recommendations, most have been shortened to ensure, for example, that such items as lubricants and fluids are checked/changed at intervals that promote maximum engine/driveline service life. Also, subject to the preference of the individual owner interested in keeping his or her vehicle in peak condition at all times, and with the vehicle's ultimate resale in mind, many of the maintenance procedures may be performed more often than recommended in the following schedule. We encourage such owner initiative.

When the vehicle is new it should be serviced initially by a factory authorized dealer service department to protect the factory warranty. In many cases the initial maintenance check is done at no cost to the owner (check with your dealer service department for more information).

Every 250 miles or weekly, whichever comes first

Check the engine oil level (Section 4)
Check the engine coolant level (Section 4)
Check the windshield washer fluid level (Section 4)
Check the brake fluid level (Section 4)
Check the power steering fluid level (Section 4)
Check the tires and tire pressures (Section 5)
Check the operation of all lights
Check the horn operation

Every 3,000 miles or 3 months, whichever comes first

All items listed above, plus:
Change the engine oil and filter (Section 6)

Every 6,000 miles or 6 months, whichever comes first

All items listed above, plus:
Check the wiper blade condition (Section 7)
Check and clean the battery and terminals (Section 8)
Rotate the tires (Section 9)
Check the seatbelts (Section 10)
Check the condition of all underhood hoses and connections (Section 11)
Check the cooling system hoses and connections for leaks and damage (Section 12)
Check and replace, if necessary, the air filter element (Section 13)

Every 12,000 miles or 12 months, whichever comes first

All items listed above, plus:
Check the automatic transaxle fluid level (Section 4)
Check the brake system (Section 14)
Check the suspension components and driveaxle boots (Section 15)
Check the exhaust pipes and hangers (Section 16)
Check the fuel system hoses and connections for leaks and damage (Section 17)
Replace the cabin air filter (Section 18)

Every 30,000 miles or 30 months, whichever comes first

All items listed above, plus:
Check the drivebelts (Section 19)
Replace the air filter element (Section 13)*
Replace the brake fluid (Section 20)

Every 60,000 miles or 60 months, whichever comes first

All items listed above, plus:
Check and replace, if necessary, the PCV valve (Section 23)*

Every 60 months (regardless of mileage)

Service the cooling system (drain, flush and refill) (Section 24)

Every 100,000 miles

Replace the spark plugs (Section 21)
Replace the spark plug wires (3.3L and 3.8L engines)
(Section 22)
Change the automatic transaxle fluid and filter (Section 25)*

Every 120,000 miles or 120 months, whichever comes first

Replace the timing belt (4.0L engine only) (Chapter 2B)

This item is affected by "severe" operating conditions as described below. If the vehicle in question is operated under "severe" conditions, perform all maintenance procedures marked with an asterisk (*) at the intervals specified by the mileage headings below.

Consider the conditions "severe" if most driving is done . . .
In dusty areas
Towing a trailer

Idling for extended periods and/or low-speed operation
When outside temperatures remain below freezing and most trips are less than four miles
In heavy city traffic where outside temperatures regularly reach 90-degrees F or higher

Every 3,000 miles

Check and replace, if necessary, the air filter element (Section 13)

Every 60,000 miles

Check and replace, if necessary, the PCV valve (Section 23)
Change the automatic transaxle fluid and filter (Section 25)

2   Introduction

This Chapter is designed to help the home mechanic maintain the Dodge Caravan Cargo and Grand Caravan, and Chrysler Town & Country with the goals of maximum performance, economy, safety and reliability in mind.

Included is a master maintenance schedule, followed by procedures dealing specifically with each item on the schedule. Visual checks, adjustments, component replacement and other helpful items are included. Refer to the accompanying illustrations of the engine compartment and the underside of the vehicle for the locations of various components.

Adhering to the mileage/time maintenance schedule and following the step-by-step procedures, which is simply a preventive maintenance program, will result in maximum reliability and vehicle service life. Keep in mind that it's not possible for this comprehensive program to produce the same results if you maintain some items at the specified intervals but not others.

As you service the vehicle, you'll discover that many of the procedures can - and should

- be grouped together because of the nature of the particular procedure you're performing or because of the close proximity of two otherwise unrelated components to one another.

For example, if the vehicle is raised, you should inspect the exhaust, suspension, steering and fuel systems while you're under the vehicle. When you're rotating the tires, it makes good sense to check the brakes, since the wheels are already removed. Finally, let's suppose you have to borrow or rent a torque wrench. Even if you only need it to tighten the spark plugs, you might as well check the torque of as many critical fasteners as time allows.

The first step in this maintenance program is to prepare before the actual work begins. Read through all the procedures you're planning, then gather together all the parts and tools needed. If it looks like you might run into problems during a particular job, seek advice from a mechanic or an experienced do-it-yourselfer.

Owner's Manual and VECI label information

Your vehicle owner's manual was written for your year and model and contains very

specific information on component locations, specifications, fuse ratings, part numbers, etc. The Owner's Manual is an important resource for the do-it-yourselfer to have; if one was not supplied with your vehicle, it can generally be ordered from a dealer parts department.

Among other important information, the Vehicle Emissions Control Information (VECI) label contains specifications and procedures for applicable tune-up adjustments and, in some instances, spark plugs (see Chapter 6 for more information on the VECI label). The information on this label is the exact maintenance data recommended by the manufacturer. This data often varies by intended operating altitude, local emissions regulations, month of manufacture, etc.

This Chapter contains procedural details, safety information and more ambitious maintenance intervals than you might find in manufacturer's literature. However, you may also find procedures or specifications in your Owner's Manual or VECI label that differ with what's printed here. In these cases, the Owner's Manual or VECI label can be considered correct, since it is specific to your particular vehicle.

4.2 The engine oil dipstick is located at the front of the engine and is clearly marked

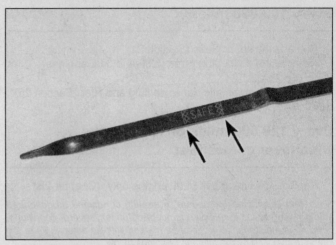

4.4 The oil level should be between the MIN and MAX marks, near the top of the cross-hatched area on the dipstick - if it isn't, add enough oil to bring the level up to or near the upper mark (do not overfill)

3   Tune-up general information

The term tune-up is used in this manual to represent a combination of individual operations rather than one specific procedure.

The engine will be kept in relatively good running condition and the need for additional work will be minimized if the routine maintenance schedule is followed closely and frequent checks are made of fluid levels and high wear items, as suggested throughout this manual from the time the vehicle is new.

More likely than not, however, there will be times when the engine is running poorly due to lack of regular maintenance. This is even more likely if a used vehicle, which hasn't received regular and frequent maintenance checks, is purchased. In such cases, an engine tune-up will be needed outside of the regular routine maintenance intervals.

The first step in any tune-up or diagnostic procedure to help correct a poor running engine is a cylinder compression check. A compression check (see Chapter 2C) will help determine the condition of internal engine components and should be used as a guide for tune-up and repair procedures. For instance, if a compression check indicates serious internal engine wear, a conventional tune-up will not improve the performance of the engine and would be a waste of time and money. Because of its importance, someone with the right equipment and the knowledge to use it properly should do the compression check.

The following procedures are those most often needed to bring a generally poor running engine back into a proper state of tune:

Minor tune-up

Check all engine related fluids (see Section 4)

Clean and inspect the battery (see Section 8)
Check all underhood hoses (see Section 11)
Check and adjust the drivebelts (see Section 19)
Check the air filter (see Section 13)
Service the cooling system (see Section 24)
Replace the spark plugs (see Section 21)
Check the PCV valve (see Section 23)

Major tune-up

All items listed under Minor tune-up plus . . .
Check the fuel system (see Section 17)
Replace the air filter (see Section 13)
Replace the spark plug wires (3.3L and 3.8L engines) (see Section 22)
Check the charging system (see Chapter 5)

4   Fluid level checks (see Maintenance Schedule for service intervals)

Note: *The following are fluid level checks to be done on a 250 mile or weekly basis. Additional fluid level checks can be found in specific maintenance procedures that follow. Regardless of the intervals, develop the habit of checking under the vehicle periodically for evidence of fluid leaks.*

1   Fluids are an essential part of the lubrication, cooling, brake and window washer systems. Because the fluids gradually become depleted and/or contaminated during normal operation of the vehicle, they must be replenished periodically. See *Recommended lubricants and fluids* in this Chapter's Specifications before adding fluid to any of the following components.

Note: *The vehicle must be on level ground when fluid levels are checked.*

Engine oil

Refer to illustrations 4.2, 4.4 and 4.5

2   Engine oil level is checked with a dipstick that is located on the side of the engine facing the front of the vehicle **(see illustration)**. The dipstick extends through a tube and into the oil pan at the bottom of the engine.

3   The oil level should be checked before the vehicle has been driven, or about 5 minutes after the engine has been shut off. If the oil is checked immediately after driving the vehicle, some of the oil will remain in the upper engine components, resulting in an inaccurate reading on the dipstick.

4   Pull the dipstick out of the tube and wipe all the oil off the end with a clean rag or paper towel. Insert the clean dipstick all the way back into the tube, then pull it out again. Note the oil level at the end of the dipstick. Add oil as necessary to bring the oil level to the top of the cross-hatched area, or MAX mark **(see illustration)**.

5   Oil is added to the engine after removing a cap located on the valve cover **(see illustration)**. Use a funnel to prevent spills as the oil is added.

6   Don't allow the level to drop below the MIN mark on the dipstick or engine damage may occur. On the other hand, don't overfill the engine by adding too much oil - it may result in oil aeration and loss of oil pressure and also could result in oil fouled spark plugs, oil leaks or seal failures.

7   Checking the oil level is an important preventive maintenance step. A consistently low oil level indicates oil leakage through damaged seals, defective gaskets or past worn rings or valve guides. If the oil looks milky in color or has water droplets in it, the block or head may be cracked and leaking coolant is entering the crankcase. The engine should be checked immediately. The condition of the oil should also be checked. Each time you check the oil level, slide your thumb and index finger

4.5 Turn the oil filler cap counterclockwise to remove it

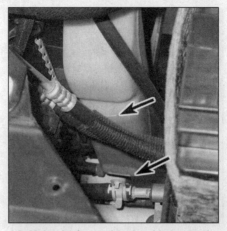

4.9 Maintain the coolant level between the MIN and MAX marks on the reservoir

4.14 The windshield washer fluid reservoir is located in the right (passenger's) side of the engine compartment

up the dipstick before wiping off the oil. If you see small dirt or metal particles clinging to the dipstick, the oil should be changed (see Section 6).

Engine coolant

Refer to illustration 4.9

Warning: *Do not allow antifreeze to come in contact with your skin or painted surfaces of the vehicle. Flush contaminated areas immediately with plenty of water. Don't store new coolant or leave old coolant lying around where it's accessible to children or pets – they're attracted by its sweet smell. Ingestion of even a small amount of coolant can be fatal! Wipe up garage floor and drip pan spills immediately. Keep antifreeze containers covered and repair cooling system leaks as soon as they're noticed.*

8   All vehicles covered by this manual are equipped with a coolant recovery system. A white plastic coolant reservoir is located at the front of the engine compartment and is connected by a hose to the radiator filler neck. If the coolant heats up sufficiently during operation, in excess of the radiator cap pressure rating, it can escape past the filler cap and into the reservoir. As the engine cools, the coolant is drawn back into the cooling system to maintain the correct level.

Warning: *Do not remove the radiator cap to check the coolant level when the engine is warm!*

9   The coolant level in the reservoir should be checked regularly. The level in the reservoir varies with the temperature of the engine. When the engine is cold, the coolant level should be mid-way between the MIN and MAX marks on the reservoir. Once the engine has warmed up, the level should be at or near the MAX mark. If it isn't, allow the engine to cool, then remove the cap from the tank and add a 50/50 mixture of ethylene glycol based antifreeze and water **(see illustration)**.

10   Drive the vehicle and recheck the coolant level. If only a small amount of coolant is required to bring the system up to the proper level, water can be used. However, repeated additions of water will dilute the antifreeze and water solution. In order to maintain the proper ratio of antifreeze and water, always top up the coolant level with the correct mixture. Don't use rust inhibitors or additives. An empty plastic milk jug or bleach bottle makes an excellent container for mixing coolant.

11   If the coolant level drops consistently, there may be a leak in the system. Inspect the radiator, hoses, filler cap, drain plugs and water pump (see Section 12). If no leaks are noted, have the pressure cap pressure tested by a service station.

12   If you have to remove the radiator cap, wait until the engine has cooled completely, then wrap a thick cloth around the cap and turn it to the first stop. If coolant or steam escapes, or if you hear a hissing noise, let the engine cool down longer, then remove the cap.

13   Check the condition of the coolant as well. It should be relatively clear. If it's brown or rust colored, the system should be drained, flushed and refilled. Even if the coolant appears to be normal, the corrosion inhibitors wear out, so it must be replaced at the specified intervals.

Windshield and rear window washer fluid

Refer to illustration 4.14

14   The fluid for the windshield and rear window washer system is stored in a plastic reservoir located at the right front corner of the engine compartment **(see illustration)**. The reservoir level should be maintained about one inch (25 mm) below the filler cap.

15   In milder climates, plain water can be used in the reservoir, but it should be kept no more than two-thirds full to allow for expansion if the water freezes. In colder climates, use windshield washer system antifreeze, available at any auto parts store, to lower the freezing point of the fluid. Mix the antifreeze with water in accordance with the manufacturer's directions on the container.

Caution: *DO NOT use cooling system antifreeze - it will damage the vehicle's paint. To help prevent icing in cold weather, warm the windshield with the defroster before using the washer.*

Brake fluid

Refer to illustration 4.17

16   The brake fluid reservoir is located on top of the brake master cylinder on the driver's side of the engine compartment near the firewall.

17   The fluid level should be maintained at the upper (FULL or MAX) mark on reservoir **(see illustration)**.

18   If additional fluid is necessary to bring the level up, use a rag to clean all dirt off the top of the reservoir to prevent contamination of the system. Also, make sure all painted surfaces around the reservoir are covered, since brake fluid will ruin paint. Carefully pour new, clean brake fluid obtained from a sealed container into the reservoir. Be sure the specified fluid is used; mixing different types of brake fluid can cause damage to the system. See

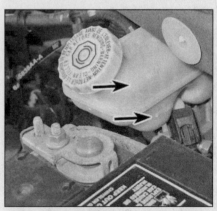

4.17 Brake fluid level, indicated on the translucent white plastic brake fluid reservoir, should be kept at the upper (FULL) mark

4.24 Location of the power steering fluid reservoir

Recommended lubricants and fluids in this Chapter's Specifications or your owner's manual.

19   At this time the fluid and the master cylinder should be inspected for contamination. Normally the brake hydraulic system won't need periodic draining and refilling, but if rust deposits, dirt particles or water droplets are observed in the fluid, the system should be dismantled, cleaned and refilled with fresh fluid. Over time brake fluid will absorb moisture from the air. Moisture in the fluid lowers the fluid boiling point; if the fluid boils, the brakes will become ineffective. Normal brake fluid is clear in color. If the brake fluid is dark brown in color, it's a good idea to replace it (see Chapter 9).

20   Reinstall the fluid reservoir cap.

21   The brake fluid in the master cylinder will drop slightly as the brake lining material at each wheel wears down during normal operation. If the master cylinder requires repeated replenishing to maintain the correct level, there is a leak in the brake system that should be corrected immediately. Check all brake lines and connections, along with the calipers and power brake booster (see Section 14 and Chapter 9 for more information).

4.31 The automatic transaxle dipstick is located at the left end of the engine – 41TE transaxles

4.26 At normal operating temperature, the power steering fluid level should be between the FILL RANGE marks

22   If you discover that the reservoir is empty or nearly empty, the system should be thoroughly inspected, refilled and then bled (see Chapter 9 for brake system bleeding).

Power steering fluid

Refer to illustrations 4.24 and 4.26

23   Check the power steering fluid level periodically to avoid steering system problems, such as damage to the pump.

Caution: *DO NOT hold the steering wheel against either stop (extreme left or right turn) for more than five seconds. If you do, the power steering pump could be damaged.*

24   The power steering reservoir is located in the right side of the engine compartment **(see illustration)**.

25   For the check, the front wheels should be pointed straight ahead and the engine should be off.

26   The reservoir has ADD and FILL RANGE fluid level marks on the side. The fluid level can be seen without removing the reservoir cap **(see illustration)**.

27   If additional fluid is required, pour the specified type directly into the reservoir, using a funnel to prevent spills.

28   If the reservoir requires frequent fluid additions, all power steering hoses, hose con-

nections, steering gear and the power steering pump should be carefully checked for leaks.

Automatic transaxle

Note: *It isn't necessary to check the transaxle fluid weekly; every 12,000 miles or 12 months will be adequate (unless a fluid leak is noticed).*

41TE (4-speed) models

Refer to illustrations 4.31 and 4.34

29   The automatic transaxle fluid level should be carefully maintained. Low fluid level can lead to slipping or loss of drive, while overfilling can cause foaming and loss of fluid.

30   With the parking brake set, start the engine, then move the shift lever through all the gear ranges, ending in Neutral. The fluid level must be checked with the vehicle level and the engine running at idle.

Note: *Incorrect fluid level readings will result if the vehicle has just been driven at high speeds for an extended period, in hot weather in city traffic, or if it has been pulling a trailer. If any of these conditions apply, wait until the fluid has cooled (about 30 minutes).*

31   With the transaxle at normal operating temperature, remove the dipstick from the filler tube. The dipstick is located on the left side of the engine compartment **(see illustration)**.

Note: *Normal operating temperature is reached after a few miles of driving.*

32   Wipe the fluid from the dipstick with a clean rag and push it back into the filler tube until the cap seats.

33   Pull the dipstick out again and note the fluid level.

34   At normal operating temperature, the fluid level should be between the two upper reference holes (HOT) **(see illustration)**. If additional fluid is required, add it directly into the tube using a funnel. Add the fluid a little at a time and keep checking the level until it's correct.

Note: *Wait at least two minutes before rechecking the fluid level to allow the fluid to fully drain into the transaxle.*

35   The condition of the fluid should also be checked along with the level. If the fluid at the end of the dipstick is a dark reddish-brown color, or if it smells burned, it should be changed. If you are in doubt about the condition of the fluid, purchase some new fluid and compare the two for color and smell.

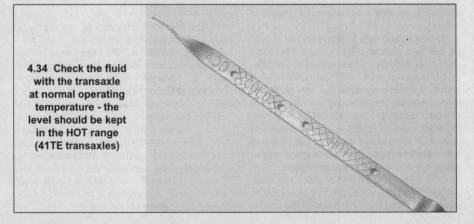

4.34 Check the fluid with the transaxle at normal operating temperature - the level should be kept in the HOT range (41TE transaxles)

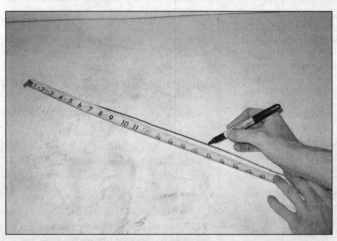

4.38a Using a standard non-painted coat hanger, straighten out the hanger then measure 16-11/16 inches from the tip . . .

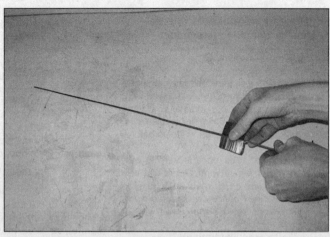

4.38b . . . and attach a piece of tape to mark the point to which the dipstick will be inserted

62TE (6-speed) models

Refer to illustrations 4.38a, 4.38b, 4.39, 4.40 and 4.43

Note: *The 62TE transaxles require the use of a scan tool to check transaxle fluid temperature and special tool #9336A (or a homemade equivalent, see Step 38) to measure the fluid level. If you do not have both tools to make the proper temperature-to-fluid level comparisons, we do not recommend attempting this procedure.*

36   Make sure the vehicle is parked on a level area.

Warning: *Make sure to set the parking brake and block the front wheels to prevent the vehicle from moving when the engine is running.*

37   Apply the parking brake, start the engine and allow it to idle for a minute, then move the shift lever through each gear position, ending in Park or Neutral.

38   Special oil dipstick tool no. 9336A will be required to check the fluid level. An alternative to this tool can be fabricated from a straightened-out coat hanger **(see illustrations)**.

39   Allow the transaxle to warm up, waiting at least two minutes, then remove the dipstick tube cap **(see illustration)**.

40   Insert the tool into the transaxle fill tube until the tip of the tool contacts the stop in the oil pan (or up to the tape if you're using a homemade dipstick) then pull it out **(see illustration)**. It may be necessary to repeat this several times to get an accurate reading.

Caution: *Do not use too much force when inserting the tool; there is a stop in the oil pan that the tool can be pushed beyond giving incorrect measurements. The approximate length that the tool should be inserted into the dipstick/fill tube is 16-11/16 inches (424 mm).*

Note: *The dipstick tool should stick out from the fill tube when it is installed.*

41   With the engine warmed up and running, check transaxle oil temperature with a scan tool.

42   Compare the reading on the dipstick tool with the transaxle fluid temperature reading on the scan tool.

43   Match the two readings with the transaxle fluid level chart **(see illustration)**, to make sure the transaxle oil level is correct

44   Add or remove transaxle fluid as neces-

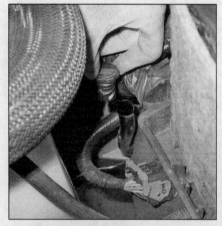

4.39 Locate the dipstick tube at the front of the transaxle (near the battery) and remove the cap

sary, then recheck the fluid level and install the dipstick tube cap.

4.40 Insert the dipstick tool into the tube, then pull it out and measure how far the fluid goes up the dipstick

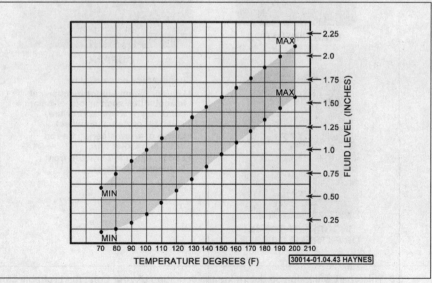

4.43 62TE transaxle fluid level-to-temperature indexing chart

5   Tire and tire pressure checks (every 250 miles or weekly)

Refer to illustrations 5.2, 5.3, 5.4a, 5.4b and 5.8

1   Periodic inspection of the tires may spare you the inconvenience of being stranded with a flat tire. It can also provide you with vital information regarding possible problems in the steering and suspension systems before major damage occurs.

2   The original tires on this vehicle are equipped with 1/2-inch wide bands that will appear when tread depth reaches 1/16-inch, at which point they can be considered worn out. Tread wear can be monitored with a simple, inexpensive device known as a tread depth indicator (see illustration).

3   Note any abnormal tread wear (see illustration). Tread pattern irregularities such as cupping, flat spots and more wear on one side than the other are indications of front end alignment and/or balance problems. If any of these conditions are noted, take the vehicle to a tire shop or service station to correct the problem.

4   Look closely for cuts, punctures and embedded nails or tacks. Sometimes a tire will hold air pressure for a short time or leak down very slowly after a nail has embedded itself in the tread. If a slow leak persists, check the valve stem core to make sure it is tight (see illustration). Examine the tread for an object that may have embedded itself in the tire or for a plug that may have begun to leak (radial tire punctures are repaired with a plug that is installed in a puncture). If a puncture is suspected, it can be easily verified by spraying a solution of soapy water onto the puncture area (see illustration). The soapy solution will bubble if there is a leak. Unless the puncture is unusually large, a tire shop or service station can usually repair the tire.

5   Carefully inspect the inner sidewall of each tire for evidence of brake fluid leakage. If you see any, inspect the brakes immediately.

6   Correct air pressure adds miles to the life span of the tires, improves mileage and enhances overall ride quality. Tire pressure cannot be accurately estimated by looking at a tire, especially if it's a radial. A tire pressure gauge is essential. Keep an accurate gauge in the glove compartment. The pressure gauges attached to the nozzles of air hoses at gas stations are often inaccurate.

7   Always check tire pressure when the tires are cold. Cold, in this case, means the vehicle has not been driven over a mile in the three hours preceding a tire pressure check. A pressure rise of four to eight pounds is not uncommon once the tires are warm.

8   Unscrew the valve cap protruding from the wheel or hubcap and push the gauge firmly onto the valve stem (see illustration).

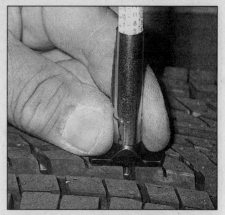

5.2 A tire tread depth indicator should be used to monitor tire wear - they are available at auto parts stores and service stations and cost very little

Note the reading on the gauge and compare the figure to the recommended tire pressure shown on the tire placard on the driver's side door. Be sure to reinstall the valve cap to keep dirt and moisture out of the valve stem mechanism. Check all four tires and, if necessary, add enough air to bring them up to the recommended pressure.

9   Don't forget to keep the spare tire inflated to the specified pressure (refer to the pressure molded into the tire sidewall).

UNDERINFLATION

INCORRECT TOE-IN OR EXTREME CAMBER

CUPPING

Cupping may be caused by:
- Underinflation and/or mechanical irregularities such as out-of-balance condition of wheel and/or tire, and bent or damaged wheel.
- Loose or worn steering tie-rod or steering idler arm.
- Loose, damaged or worn front suspension parts.

OVERINFLATION

FEATHERING DUE TO MISALIGNMENT

5.3 This chart will help you determine the condition of your tires, the probable cause(s) of abnormal wear and the corrective action necessary

5.4a If a tire loses air on a steady basis, check the valve core first to make sure it's snug (special inexpensive wrenches are commonly available at auto parts stores)

5.4b If the valve core is tight, raise the corner of the vehicle with the low tire and spray a soapy water solution onto the tread as the tire is turned slowly - slow leaks will cause small bubbles to appear

5.8 To extend the life of your tires, check the air pressure at least once a week with an accurate gauge (don't forget the spare!)

6.2 These tools are required when changing the engine oil and filter

1 *Drain pan - It should be fairly shallow in depth, but wide in order to prevent spills*
2 *Rubber gloves - When removing the drain plug and filter, it is inevitable that you will get oil on your hands (the gloves will prevent burns)*
3 *Breaker bar - Sometimes the oil drain plug is pretty tight and a long breaker bar is needed to loosen it*
4 *Socket - To be used with the breaker bar or a ratchet (must be the correct size to fit the drain plug)*
5 *Filter wrench - This is a metal band-type wrench, which requires clearance around the filter to be effective*
6 *Filter wrench - This type fits on the bottom of the filter and can be turned with a ratchet or beaker bar (different size wrenches are available for different types of filters)*

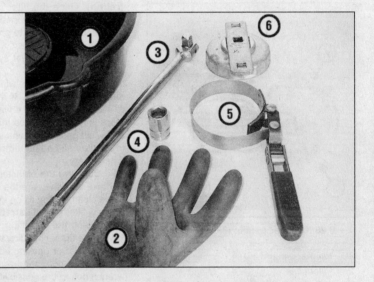

6 Engine oil and filter change (every 3000 miles or 3 months)

Refer to illustrations 6.2 and 6.7

1 Frequent oil changes are the best preventive maintenance the home mechanic can give the engine, because aging oil becomes diluted and contaminated, which leads to premature engine wear.
2 Make sure you have all the necessary tools before you begin this procedure **(see illustration)**. You should also have plenty of rags or newspapers handy for mopping up any spills.
3 Access to the underside of the vehicle is greatly improved if the vehicle can be lifted on a hoist, driven onto ramps or supported by jackstands.
Warning: *Do not work under a vehicle which is supported only by a bumper, hydraulic or scissors-type jack.*
4 If this is your first oil change, get under the vehicle and familiarize yourself with the locations of the oil drain plug and the oil filter. The engine and exhaust components will be warm during the actual work, so try to anticipate any potential problems before the engine and accessories are hot.
5 Park the vehicle on a level spot. Start the engine and allow it to reach its normal operating temperature. Warm oil and sludge will flow out more easily. Turn off the engine when it's warmed up. Remove the filler cap from the valve cover.
6 Raise the vehicle and support it securely on jackstands.
Warning: *Never get beneath the vehicle when it is supported only by a jack. The jack provided with your vehicle is designed solely for raising the vehicle to remove and replace the wheels. Always use jackstands to support the vehicle when it becomes necessary to place your body underneath the vehicle.*
7 Being careful not to touch the hot exhaust components, place the drain pan under the drain plug in the bottom of the pan and remove the plug **(see illustration)**. You may want to wear gloves while unscrewing the plug the final few turns if the engine is hot.

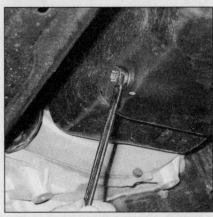

6.7 Use a proper size box-end wrench or socket to remove the oil drain plug and avoid rounding it off

6.12 Use an oil filter wrench to remove the filter (3.3L, 3.8L and 4.0L engines)

6.14 Lubricate the oil filter gasket with clean engine oil before installing the filter on the engine

6.17 Using a box end wrench or socket, turn the filter cap counterclockwise to remove it (3.6L engine)

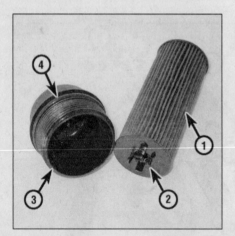

6.20 Oil filter details (3.6L engine)

1	*Filter element*	3	*Filter cap*
2	*Filter clips*	4	*O-ring*

8   Allow the old oil to drain into the pan. It may be necessary to move the pan farther under the engine as the oil flow slows to a trickle. Inspect the old oil for the presence of metal shavings and chips.

Note: *On 3.6L engines, the oil filler cap must be removed to allow all the oil to properly drain out.*

9   After all the oil has drained, wipe off the drain plug with a clean rag. Even minute metal particles clinging to the plug would immediately contaminate the new oil.

10   Clean the area around the drain plug opening, reinstall the plug and tighten it to the torque listed in this Chapter's Specifications.

11   Move the drain pan into position under the oil filter.

3.3L, 3.8L and 4.0L engines

Refer to illustrations 6.12 and 6.14

12   Loosen the oil filter by turning it counterclockwise with an oil filter wrench **(see illus-**

tration). Once the filter is loose, use your hands to unscrew it from the block. Keep the open end pointing up to prevent the oil inside the filter from spilling out.

Warning: *The exhaust system may still be hot, so be careful.*

13   With a clean rag, wipe off the mounting surface on the block. If a residue of old oil is allowed to remain, it will smoke when the block is heated up. Also make sure that none of the old gasket remains stuck to the mounting surface. It can be removed with a scraper if necessary.

14   Compare the old filter with the new one to make sure they are the same type. Smear some clean engine oil on the rubber gasket of the new filter **(see illustration)**.

15   Attach the new filter to the engine, following the tightening directions printed on the filter canister or packing box. Most filter manufacturers recommend against using a filter wrench due to the possibility of overtightening and damaging the seal.

3.6L engines

Refer to illustrations 6.17 and 6.20

16   Lift up on the outer edges of the engine cover to disengage the rubber mounts from the ballstuds, and remove the engine cover.

17   Place a rag at the base of the filter housing, then loosen the filter cap by turning it counterclockwise **(see illustration)**.

18   Remove the cap and filter from the engine, then pull the filter out of the cap.

19   Remove and discard the O-ring from the filter cap.

20   Insert a new filter into the cap, making sure the filter clips lock into the cap **(see illustration)**.

21   Install a new O-ring onto the cap and apply a light amount of engine oil to the O-ring.

22   Place the filter assembly into the filter housing and carefully thread the cap into the housing. Tighten the cap to the torque listed in this Chapter's Specifications.

All models

23   Remove all tools, rags, etc. from under the vehicle, being careful not to spill the oil in the drain pan, then lower the vehicle.

24   Add new oil to the engine through the oil filler cap in the valve cover. Use a funnel, if necessary, to prevent oil from spilling onto the top of the engine. Pour four quarts of fresh oil into the engine. Wait a few minutes to allow the oil to drain into the pan, then check the level on the oil dipstick (see Section 4). If the oil level is at or near the FULL mark on the dipstick, install the filler cap, start the engine and allow the new oil to circulate.

25   Allow the engine to run for about a minute. While the engine is running, look under the vehicle and check for leaks at the oil pan drain plug and around the oil filter. If either is leaking, stop the engine and tighten the plug or filter.

26   Wait a few minutes to allow the oil to trickle down into the pan, recheck the level on the dipstick and, if necessary, add enough oil to bring the level to the FULL mark.

27   During the first few trips after an oil change, make it a point to check frequently for leaks and proper oil level.

28   The old oil drained from the engine cannot be reused in its present state and should be disposed of. Check with your local auto parts store, disposal facility or environmental agency to see if they will accept the oil for recycling. After the oil has cooled it can be drained into a container (capped plastic jugs, topped bottles, milk cartons, etc.) for transport to one of these disposal sites. Don't dispose of the oil by pouring it on the ground or down a drain!

Oil change indicator resetting

Note: *It is possible that, driving under the best possible conditions, the oil life monitoring system may not indicate the oil needs to be changed. The manufacturer states that the oil and filter must be changed at least once every year and the oil life monitor reset.*

Note: *If the "Oil Change Required" message comes on when the vehicle is immediately restarted, the oil life monitor was not reset and the reset procedure must be done again.*
Note: *If the message is not reset, it will continue to show up each time you turn the ignition switch On or start the vehicle. It is possible to temporarily turn off the message by, pressing and releasing the "Menu" button.*
29 Turn the ignition key to the "ON" position but DO NOT start the engine.
30 Slowly depress the accelerator pedal all the way to the floor, three times within 10 seconds.
31 Turn the ignition key to the "OFF" or "LOCK" position, then start the vehicle.

7 Windshield wiper blade inspection and replacement (every 6,000 miles or 6 months)

Refer to illustrations 7.5a and 7.5b

1 The windshield wiper and blade assembly should be inspected periodically for damage, loose components and cracked or worn blade elements.
2 Road film can build up on the wiper blades and affect their efficiency, so they should be washed regularly with a mild detergent solution.
3 The action of the wiping mechanism can loosen bolts, nuts and fasteners, so they should be checked and tightened, as necessary, at the same time the wiper blades are checked.
4 If the wiper blade elements are cracked, worn or warped, or no longer clean adequately, they should be replaced with new ones.
5 Lift the arm assembly away from the glass for clearance, press the release lever, then slide the wiper blade assembly out of the hook at the end of the arm **(see illustrations)**.
6 Attach the new wiper to the arm. Connection can be confirmed by an audible click.

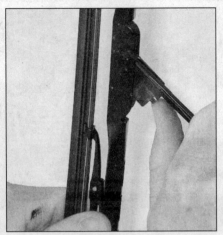

7.5a To release the blade holder, push the release lever . . .

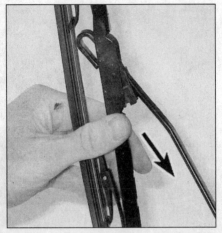

7.5b . . . and pull the wiper blade in the direction of the arrow to separate it from the arm

8 Battery check, maintenance and charging (every 6,000 miles or 6 months)

Refer to illustrations 8.1, 8.6a, 8.6b, 8.7a and 8.7b
Warning: *Certain precautions must be followed when checking and servicing the battery. Hydrogen gas, which is highly flammable, is always present in the battery cells, so keep lighted tobacco and all other open flames and sparks away from the battery. The electrolyte inside the battery is actually diluted sulfuric acid, which will cause injury if splashed on your skin or in your eyes. It will also ruin clothes and painted surfaces. When removing the battery cables, always detach the negative cable first and hook it up last!*

1 A routine preventive maintenance program for the battery in your vehicle is the only way to ensure quick and reliable starts. But before performing any battery maintenance, make sure that you have the proper equipment necessary to work safely around the battery **(see illustration)**.
2 There are also several precautions that should be taken whenever battery maintenance is performed. Before servicing the battery, always turn the engine and all accessories off and disconnect the cable from the negative terminal of the battery (see Chapter 5).
3 The battery produces hydrogen gas, which is both flammable and explosive. Never create a spark, smoke or light a match around the battery. Always charge the battery in a ventilated area.
4 Electrolyte contains poisonous and corrosive sulfuric acid. Do not allow it to get in your eyes, on your skin on your clothes. Never ingest it. Wear protective safety glasses when working near the battery. Keep children away from the battery.
5 Note the external condition of the battery. If the positive terminal and cable clamp on your vehicle's battery is equipped with a rubber protector, make sure that it's not torn or damaged. It should completely cover the

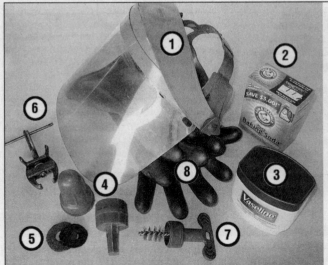

8.1 Tools and materials required for battery maintenance

1 *Face shield/safety goggles - When removing corrosion with a brush, the acidic particles can easily fly up into your eyes*
2 *Baking soda - A solution of baking soda and water can be used to neutralize corrosion*
3 *Petroleum jelly - A layer of this on the battery posts will help prevent corrosion*
4 *Battery post/cable cleaner - This wire brush cleaning tool will remove all traces of corrosion from the battery posts and cable clamps*
5 *Treated felt washers - Placing one of these on each post, directly under the cable clamps, will help prevent corrosion*
6 *Puller - Sometimes the cable clamps are very difficult to pull off the posts, even after the nut/bolt has been completely loosened. This tool pulls the clamp straight up and off the post without damage*
7 *Battery post/cable cleaner - Here is another cleaning tool which is a slightly different version of number 4 above, but it does the same thing*
8 *Rubber gloves - Another safety item to consider when servicing the battery; remember that's acid inside the battery*

8.6a Battery terminal corrosion usually appears as light, fluffy powder

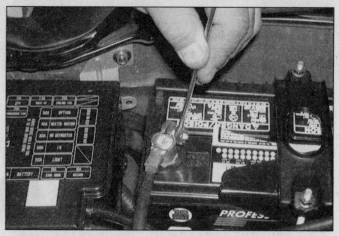

8.6b Removing a cable from the battery post with a wrench - sometimes a pair of special battery pliers are required for this procedure if corrosion has caused deterioration of the nut hex (always remove the ground (-) cable first and hook it up last!)

terminal. Look for any corroded or loose connections, cracks in the case or cover or loose hold-down clamps. Also check the entire length of each cable for cracks and frayed conductors.

6　If corrosion, which looks like white, fluffy deposits **(see illustration)** is evident, particularly around the terminals, the battery should be removed for cleaning. Loosen the cable clamp bolts with a wrench, being careful to remove the ground cable first, and slide them off the terminals **(see illustration)**. Then disconnect the hold-down clamp bolt and nut, remove the clamp and lift the battery from the engine compartment.

7　Clean the cable clamps thoroughly with a battery brush or a terminal cleaner and a solution of warm water and baking soda **(see illustration)**. Wash the terminals and the top of the battery case with the same solution but make sure that the solution doesn't get into the battery. When cleaning the cables, terminals and battery top, wear safety goggles and

rubber gloves to prevent any solution from coming in contact with your eyes or hands. Wear old clothes too - even diluted, sulfuric acid splashed onto clothes will burn holes in them. If the terminals have been extensively corroded, clean them up with a terminal cleaner **(see illustration)**. Thoroughly wash all cleaned areas with plain water.

8　Make sure that the battery tray is in good condition and the hold-down clamp fasteners are tight. If the battery is removed from the tray, make sure no parts remain in the bottom of the tray when the battery is reinstalled. When reinstalling the hold-down clamp bolts, do not overtighten them.

9　Information on removing and installing the battery can be found in Chapter 5. If you disconnected the cable(s) from the negative and/or positive battery terminals, see Chapter 5. Information on jump starting can be found at the front of this manual. For more detailed battery checking procedures, refer to the *Haynes Automotive Electrical Manual*.

Cleaning

10　Corrosion on the hold-down components, battery case and surrounding areas can be removed with a solution of water and baking soda. Thoroughly rinse all cleaned areas with plain water.

11　Any metal parts of the vehicle damaged by corrosion should be covered with a zinc-based primer, then painted.

Charging

Warning: *When batteries are being charged, hydrogen gas, which is very explosive and flammable, is produced. Do not smoke or allow open flames near a charging or a recently charged battery. Wear eye protection when near the battery during charging. Also, make sure the charger is unplugged before connecting or disconnecting the battery from the charger.*

12　Slow-rate charging is the best way to restore a battery that's discharged to the point

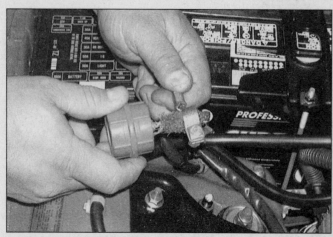

8.7a When cleaning the cable clamps, all corrosion must be removed

8.7b Regardless of the type of tool used to clean the battery posts, a clean, shiny surface should be the result

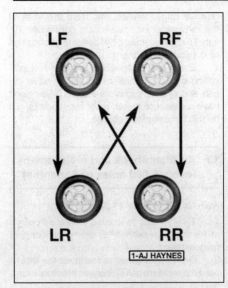

9.2 The recommended four-tire rotation pattern

where it will not start the engine. It's also a good way to maintain the battery charge in a vehicle that's only driven a few miles between starts. Maintaining the battery charge is particularly important in the winter when the battery must work harder to start the engine and electrical accessories that drain the battery are in greater use.

13   It's best to use a one or two-amp battery charger (sometimes called a trickle charger). They are the safest and put the least strain on the battery. They are also the least expensive. For a faster charge, you can use a higher amperage charger, but don't use one rated more than 1/10th the amp/hour rating of the battery. Rapid boost charges that claim to restore the power of the battery in one to two hours are hardest on the battery and can damage batteries not in good condition. This type of charging should only be used in emergency situations.

14   The average time necessary to charge a battery should be listed in the instructions that come with the charger. As a general rule, a trickle charger will charge a battery in 12 to 16 hours.

9   Tire rotation (every 6,000 miles or 6 months)

Refer to illustration 9.2

1   The tires should be rotated at the specified intervals and whenever uneven wear is noticed.

2   Refer to the **accompanying illustration** for the preferred tire rotation pattern.

3   Refer to the information in "Jacking and towing" at the front of this manual for the proper procedures to follow when raising the vehicle and changing a tire. If the brakes are to be checked, don't apply the parking brake as stated. Make sure the tires are blocked to

prevent the vehicle from rolling as it's raised.

4   Preferably, the entire vehicle should be raised at the same time. This can be done on a hoist or by jacking up each corner and then lowering the vehicle onto jackstands placed under the frame rails. Always use four jackstands and make sure the vehicle is safely supported.

5   After rotation, check and adjust the tire pressures as necessary. Tighten the lug nuts to the torque listed in this Chapter's Specifications.

10   Seat belt check (every 6,000 miles or 6 months)

1   Check seat belts, buckles, latch plates and guide loops for obvious damage and signs of wear.

2   Where the seat belt receptacle bolts to the floor of the vehicle, check that the bolts are secure.

3   See if the seat belt reminder light comes on when the key is turned to the Run or Start position.

11   Underhood hose check and replacement (every 6,000 miles or 6 months)

General

Caution: *Never remove air conditioning components or hoses until the system has been depressurized by a licensed air conditioning technician.*

1   High temperatures in the engine compartment can cause the deterioration of the rubber and plastic hoses used for engine, accessory and emission systems operation. Periodic inspection should be made for cracks, loose clamps, material hardening and leaks. Information specific to the cooling system hoses can be found in Section 12.

2   Some, but not all, hoses are secured to their fittings with clamps. Where clamps are used, check to be sure they haven't lost their tension, allowing the hose to leak. If clamps aren't used, make sure the hose has not expanded and/or hardened where it slips over the fitting, allowing it to leak.

Vacuum hoses

3   It's quite common for vacuum hoses, especially those in the emissions system, to be color-coded or identified by colored stripes molded into them. Various systems require hoses with different wall thickness, collapse resistance and temperature resistance. When replacing hoses, be sure the new ones are made of the same material.

4   Often the only effective way to check a hose is to remove it completely from the vehicle. If more than one hose is removed, be sure to label the hoses and fittings to ensure correct installation.

5   When checking vacuum hoses, be sure to include any plastic T-fittings in the check. Inspect the fittings for cracks and the hose where it fits over the fitting for distortion, which could cause leakage.

6   A small piece of vacuum hose (1/4-inch inside diameter) can be used as a stethoscope to detect vacuum leaks. Hold one end of the hose to your ear and probe around vacuum hoses and fittings, listening for the "hissing" sound characteristic of a vacuum leak.

Warning: *When probing with the vacuum hose stethoscope, be very careful not to come into contact with moving engine components such as the drivebelt, cooling fan, etc.*

Fuel hose

Warning: *There are certain precautions that must be taken when inspecting or servicing fuel system components. Work in a well-ventilated area and do not allow open flames (cigarettes, appliances, etc.) or bare light bulbs near the work area. Mop up any spills immediately and do not store fuel soaked rags where they could ignite. The fuel system is under high pressure, so if any fuel lines are to be disconnected, the pressure in the system must be relieved first (see Chapter 4 for more information).*

7   Check all rubber fuel lines for deterioration and chafing. Check especially for cracks in areas where the hose bends and just before fittings, such as where a hose attaches to the fuel filter.

8   High quality fuel line, made specifically for high-pressure fuel injection systems, must be used for fuel line replacement. Never, under any circumstances, use unreinforced vacuum line, clear plastic tubing or water hose for fuel lines.

9   Spring-type clamps are commonly used on fuel lines. These clamps often lose their tension over a period of time, and can be "sprung" during removal. Replace all spring-type clamps with screw clamps whenever a hose is replaced.

Metal lines

10   Sections of metal line are routed along the frame, between the fuel tank and the engine. Check carefully to be sure the line has not been bent or crimped and that cracks have not started in the line.

11   If a section of metal fuel line must be replaced, only seamless steel tubing should be used, since copper and aluminum tubing don't have the strength necessary to withstand normal engine vibration.

12   Check the metal brake lines where they enter the master cylinder and brake proportioning unit for cracks in the lines or loose fittings. Any sign of brake fluid leakage calls for an immediate and thorough inspection of the brake system.

Check for a chafed area that could fail prematurely.

Check for a soft area indicating the hose has deteriorated inside.

Overtightening the clamp on a hardened hose will damage the hose and cause a leak.

Check each hose for swelling and oil-soaked ends. Cracks and breaks can be located by squeezing the hose.

12.4 Hoses, like drivebelts, have a habit of failing at the worst possible time - to prevent the inconvenience of a blown radiator or heater hose, inspect them carefully as shown here

12 Cooling system check (every 6,000 miles or 6 months)

Refer to illustration 12.4

1   Many major engine failures can be attributed to a faulty cooling system. Since the vehicle is equipped with an automatic transaxle, the cooling system also cools the transaxle fluid and thus plays an important role in prolonging transaxle life.

2   The cooling system should be checked with the engine cold. Do this before the vehicle is driven for the day or after it has been shut off for at least three hours.

3   Remove the radiator pressure cap and thoroughly clean the cap, inside and out, with clean water. Also clean the filler neck on the radiator. All traces of corrosion should be removed. The coolant inside the radiator should be relatively transparent. If it is rust-colored, the system should be drained, flushed and refilled (see Section 24). If the coolant level is not up to the top, add additional antifreeze/coolant mixture (see Section 4).

4   Carefully check the large upper and lower radiator hoses along with the smaller diameter heater hoses that run from the engine to the firewall. Inspect each hose along its entire length, replacing any hose that is cracked, swollen or shows signs of deterioration. Cracks may become more apparent if the hose is squeezed **(see illustration)**. Regardless of condition, it's a good idea to replace hoses with new ones every two years.

5   Make sure all hose connections are tight. A leak in the cooling system will usually show up as white or rust-colored deposits on the areas adjoining the leak. If wire-type clamps are used at the ends of the hoses, it may be a good idea to replace them with more secure screw-type clamps.

6   Use compressed air or a soft brush to remove bugs, leaves, etc. from the front of the radiator or air conditioning condenser. Be careful not to damage the delicate cooling fins or cut yourself on them.

7   Every other inspection, or at the first indication of cooling system problems, have the cap and system pressure tested. If you don't have a pressure tester, most repair shops will do this for a minimal charge.

13 Air filter check and replacement (every 6,000 miles or 6 months)

Refer to illustrations 13.3a and 13.3b

1   The air filter is located inside a housing at the right (passenger's) side of the engine compartment.

2   On 4.0L engines, disconnect the Intake Air Temperature (IAT) sensor electrical connector.

3   To remove the air filter, release the clamps that secure the two halves of the air filter housing together, then separate the cover halves and remove the air filter element **(see illustrations)**.

Note: *On 3.6L engines, the air filter cover is held in place by three spring clips.*

4   Inspect the outer surface of the filter element. If it is dirty, replace it. If it is only moderately dusty, it can be reused by blowing it clean from the back to the front surface with compressed air. Because it is a pleated paper type filter, it cannot be washed or oiled. If it cannot be cleaned satisfactorily with compressed air, discard and replace it. While the cover is off, be careful not to drop anything down into the housing.

5   Wipe out the inside of the air filter housing.

6   Place the new filter into the air filter housing, making sure it seats properly.

7   Reinstall the cover and secure it with the clamps or latches.

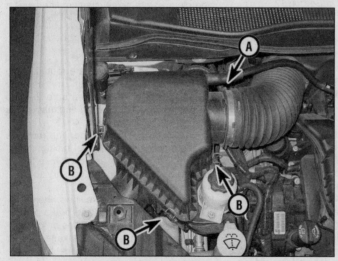

13.3a Loosen the clamp (A, only if you are removing the cover completely) and detach the intake duct, release the spring clips (B) . . .

13.3b . . . then lift the air filter housing cover and remove the air filter element – 3.6L engine shown, other models similar

14.6 With the wheel off, check the thickness of the pads through the inspection hole

15.4 Check the struts and shocks for leakage at the indicated area

14 Brake system check (every 12,000 miles or 12 months)

Refer to illustration 14.6

Warning: *The dust created by the brake system is harmful to your health. Never blow it out with compressed air and don't inhale any of it. An approved filtering mask should be worn when working on the brakes. Do not, under any circumstances, use petroleum-based solvents to clean brake parts. Use brake system cleaner only!*

Note: *For detailed photographs of the brake system, refer to Chapter 9.*

1   In addition to the specified intervals, the brakes should be inspected every time the wheels are removed or whenever a defect is suspected.

2   Any of the following symptoms could indicate a potential brake system defect: The vehicle pulls to one side when the brake pedal is depressed; the brakes make squealing or dragging noises when applied; brake pedal travel is excessive; the pedal pulsates; or brake fluid leaks, usually onto the inside of the tire or wheel.

3   Disc brakes can be visually checked without removing any parts except the wheels. Remove the hub caps (if applicable) and loosen the wheel lug nuts a quarter turn each.

4   Raise the vehicle and place it securely on jackstands.

Warning: *Never work under a vehicle that is supported only by a jack!*

5   Remove the wheels. Now visible is the disc brake caliper which contains the pads. There is an outer brake pad and an inner pad. Both must be checked for wear.

6   Measure the thickness of the pads through the inspection hole in the caliper body **(see illustrations)**. Compare the measurement with the limit given in this Chapter's Specifications; if any brake pad thickness is less than specified, then all brake pads must be replaced (see Chapter 9).

7   If you're in doubt as to the exact pad thickness or quality, remove them for measurement and further inspection (see Chapter 9).

8   Check the disc for score marks, wear and burned spots. If any of these conditions exist, the disc should be removed for servicing or replacement (see Chapter 9).

9   Before installing the wheels, check all the brake lines and hoses for damage, wear, deformation, cracks, corrosion, leakage, bends and twists, particularly in the vicinity of the rubber hoses and calipers.

10   Install the wheels, lower the vehicle and tighten the wheel lug nuts to the torque given in this Chapter's Specifications.

Brake booster check

11   Sit in the driver's seat and perform the following sequence of tests.

12   With the brake fully depressed, start the engine - the pedal should move down a little when the engine starts.

13   With the engine running, depress the brake pedal several times - the travel distance should not change.

14   Depress the brake, stop the engine and hold the pedal in for about 30 seconds - the pedal should neither sink nor rise.

15   Restart the engine, run it for about a minute and turn it off. Then firmly depress the brake several times - the pedal travel should decrease with each application.

16   If your brakes do not operate as described, the brake booster has failed. Refer to Chapter 9 for the replacement procedure.

15 Steering, suspension and driveaxle boot check (every 12,000 miles or 12 months)

Note: *For detailed illustrations of the steering and suspension components, refer to Chapter 10.*

With the wheels on the ground

Refer to illustration 15.4

1   With the vehicle stopped and the front wheels pointed straight ahead, rock the steering wheel gently back and forth. If freeplay is excessive, a front wheel bearing, steering shaft universal joint, lower arm balljoint or steering gear is worn. Refer to Chapter 10 for the appropriate repair procedure.

2   Other symptoms, such as excessive vehicle body movement over rough roads, swaying (leaning) around corners and binding as the steering wheel is turned, may indicate faulty steering and/or suspension components.

3   Check the shock absorbers by pushing down and releasing the vehicle several times at each corner. If the vehicle does not come back to a level position within one or two bounces, the shocks/struts are worn and must be replaced. When bouncing the vehicle up and down, listen for squeaks and noises from the suspension components.

4   Check the struts and shock absorbers for evidence of fluid leakage **(see illustration)**. A light film of fluid is no cause for concern. Make sure that any fluid noted is from the struts/shocks and not from some other source. If leakage is noted, replace the struts/shocks as a set.

5   Check the struts and shocks to be sure they are securely mounted and undamaged. Check the upper mounts for damage and wear. If damage or wear is noted, replace the shocks as a set (front and rear).

6   If the struts or shocks must be replaced, refer to Chapter 10 for the procedure.

Under the vehicle

Refer to illustrations 15.10 and 15.11

7   Raise the vehicle and support it securely on jackstands.

8   Check the tires for irregular wear patterns and proper inflation. See Section 5 in this Chapter for information regarding tire

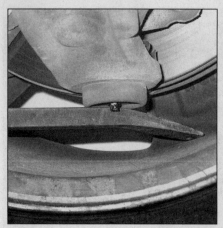

15.10 To check the balljoint for wear, try to pry the control arm up and down to make sure there is no play in the balljoint (if there is, replace it)

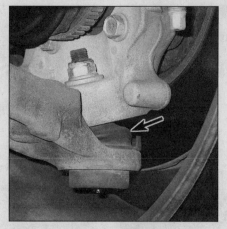

15.11 Check the balljoint boot for damage

wear and Chapter 10 for information on wheel bearing replacement.

9   Inspect the universal joint between the steering shaft and the steering gear housing. Check the steering gear housing for lubricant leakage. Make sure that the dust seals and boots are not damaged and that the boot clamps are not loose. Check the steering linkage for looseness or damage. Check the tie-rod ends for excessive play. Look for loose bolts, broken or disconnected parts and deteriorated rubber bushings on all suspension and steering components. While an assistant turns the steering wheel from side to side, check the steering components for free movement, chafing and binding. If the steering components do not seem to be reacting with the movement of the steering wheel, try to determine where the slack is located.

10   Check the balljoints for wear by trying to move each control arm up and down with a prybar **(see illustration)** to ensure that its balljoint has no play. If any balljoint does have

play, replace it. Try to turn the balljoint grease fitting with your fingers. If you can move the grease fitting, the balljoint is worn out. See Chapter 10 for the balljoint replacement procedure.

11   Inspect the balljoint boots for damage and leaking grease **(see illustration)**. Replace the balljoints with new ones if they are damaged (see Chapter 10).

12   At the rear of the vehicle, inspect the suspension arm bushings for deterioration. Additional information on suspension components can be found in Chapter 10.

Driveaxle boot check

Refer to illustration 15.14

Note: *For detailed illustrations of the driveaxles, refer to Chapter 8.*

13   The driveaxle boots are very important because they prevent dirt, water and foreign material from entering and damaging the constant velocity (CV) joints. Oil and grease can cause the boot material to deteriorate prematurely, so it's a good idea to wash the boots with soap and water. Because it constantly pivots back and forth following the steering

action of the front hub, the outer CV boot wears out sooner and should be inspected regularly.

14   Inspect the boots for tears and cracks as well as loose clamps **(see illustration)**. If there is any evidence of cracks or leaking lubricant, they must be replaced as described in Chapter 8.

16   Exhaust system check (every 12,000 miles or 12 months)

Refer to illustration 16.2

1   With the engine cold (at least three hours after the vehicle has been driven), check the complete exhaust system from the engine to the end of the tailpipe. Ideally, the inspection should be done with the vehicle on a hoist to permit unrestricted access. If a hoist isn't available, raise the vehicle and support it securely on jackstands.

2   Check the exhaust pipes and connections for evidence of leaks, severe corrosion and damage. Make sure that all brackets and hangers are in good condition and tight **(see illustration)**.

3   At the same time, inspect the underside of the body for holes, corrosion, open seams, etc. which may allow exhaust gases to enter the passenger compartment. Seal all body openings with silicone or body putty.

4   Rattles and other noises can often be traced to the exhaust system, especially the mounts and hangers. Try to move the pipes, muffler and catalytic converter. If the components can come in contact with the body or suspension parts, secure the exhaust system with new mounts.

5   Check the running condition of the engine by inspecting inside the end of the tailpipe. The exhaust deposits here are an indication of engine state-of-tune. If the pipe is black and sooty or coated with white deposits, the engine may need a tune-up, including a thorough fuel system inspection and adjustment.

15.14 Flex the driveaxle boots by hand to check for cracks and leaking grease

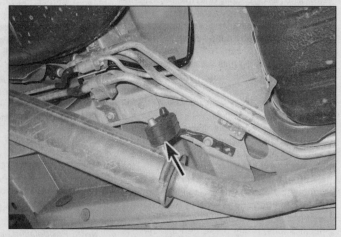

16.2 Check the exhaust system for rust, damage, or broken rubber hangers

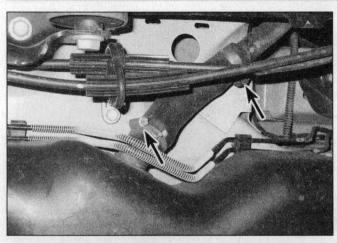

**17.6 Check the fuel system hoses and clamps for damage
and deterioration**

18.2 Press the tabs towards each other to disengage the clips

17 Fuel system check (every 12,000 miles or 12 months)

Refer to illustration 17.6

Warning: *Gasoline is flammable, so take extra precautions when you work on any part of the fuel system. Don't smoke or allow open flames or bare light bulbs near the work area, and don't work in a garage where a gas-type appliance (such as a water heater or clothes dryer) is present. Since fuel is carcinogenic, wear fuel-resistant gloves when there's a possibility of being exposed to fuel, and, if you spill any fuel on your skin, rinse it off immediately with soap and water. Mop up any spills immediately and do not store fuel-soaked rags where they could ignite. When you perform any kind of work on the fuel system, wear safety glasses and have a Class B type fire extinguisher on hand. The fuel system is under constant pressure, so, before any lines are disconnected, the fuel system pressure must be relieved (see Chapter 4).*

1   If you smell gasoline while driving or after the vehicle has been sitting in the sun, inspect the fuel system immediately.

2   Remove the fuel filler cap and inspect if for damage and corrosion. The gasket should have an unbroken sealing imprint. If the gasket is damaged or corroded, install a new cap.

3   Inspect the fuel feed line for cracks. Make sure that the connections between the fuel lines and the fuel injection system.

Warning: *Your vehicle is fuel injected, so you must relieve the fuel system pressure before servicing fuel system components. The fuel system pressure relief procedure is outlined in Chapter 4.*

4   Since some components of the fuel system - the fuel tank and the fuel lines, for example - are underneath the vehicle, they can be inspected more easily with the vehicle raised on a hoist. If that's not possible, raise the vehicle and support it on jackstands.

5   With the vehicle raised and safely supported, inspect the gas tank and filler neck for punctures, cracks and other damage. The connection between the filler neck and the tank is particularly critical. Sometimes a rubber filler neck will leak because of loose clamps or deteriorated rubber. Inspect all fuel tank

mounting brackets and straps to be sure that the tank is securely attached to the vehicle.

Warning: *Do not, under any circumstances, try to repair a fuel tank (except rubber components). A welding torch or any open flame can easily cause fuel vapors inside the tank to explode.*

6   Carefully check all hoses and lines leading away from the fuel tank. Check for loose connections, deteriorated hoses, crimped lines and other damage **(see illustration)**. Repair or replace damaged sections as necessary (see Chapter 4).

18 Cabin air filter replacement (every 12,000 miles or 12 months)

Refer to illustrations 18.2 and 18.3

Warning: *The models covered by this manual are equipped with a Supplemental Restraint System (SRS), more commonly known as airbags. Always disable the airbag system before working in the vicinity of any airbag system component to avoid the possibility of accidental deployment of the airbag, which could cause personal injury (see Chapter 12).*

1   Disengage the clips on each side of the glove box, then pull the sides inwards until the stops are clear and lower glove box (see Chapter 11).

2   Disengage the two clips at the ends of the cover **(see illustration)** and remove the cover.

3   Remove the filter from the housing **(see illustration)**.

4   Install the filter, making sure the arrow on the filter is pointing towards the floor.

Note: *The cabin air filter is labeled with an arrow and the word "Airflow" on it. The filter should be installed with the arrow pointing towards the floor.*

4   Installation is the reverse of the removal procedure.

18.3 Remove the filter from the housing, noting the position of the filter as it is removed

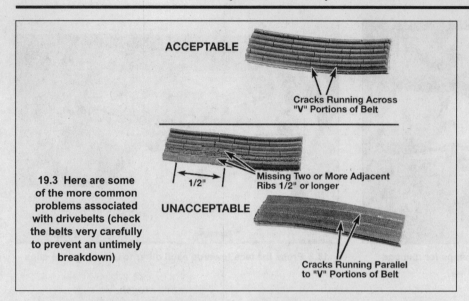

19.3 Here are some of the more common problems associated with drivebelts (check the belts very carefully to prevent an untimely breakdown)

ACCEPTABLE

Cracks Running Across "V" Portions of Belt

1/2"   Missing Two or More Adjacent Ribs 1/2" or longer

UNACCEPTABLE

Cracks Running Parallel to "V" Portions of Belt

19.5 Remove the drivebelt splash shield fasteners and shield

19 Drivebelt check, adjustment and replacement (every 30,000 miles or 30 months)

Warning: *The electric cooling fan(s) on these models can activate at any time the ignition switch is in the ON position. Make sure the ignition is OFF when working in the vicinity of the fan(s).*

1   The drivebelt is located at the front of the engine and plays an important role in the operation of the vehicle and its components. Due to its function and material makeup, the belt is prone to failure after a period of time, and should be inspected and adjusted periodically to prevent major damage.

2   All models covered in this manual use a single serpentine belt to drive all the components.

Check

Refer to illustration 19.3

3   With the engine off, open the hood and use your fingers (and a flashlight, if neces-sary), to move along the belt checking for cracks and separation of the belt plies. Also check for fraying and glazing, which gives the belt a shiny appearance. Also check the ribs on the underside of the belt. They should all be the same depth, with none of the surface uneven **(see illustration)**.

4   The serpentine belt tension is adjusted by an automatic tensioner.

Replacement

Refer to illustrations 19.5, 19.6 and 19.7

5   Apply the parking brake, loosen the right (passenger's side) front wheel lug nuts, raise the front of the vehicle and support it securely on jackstands. Remove the wheel, then remove the drivebelt splash shield **(see illustration)**.

6   The automatic tensioner must be released to allow drivebelt replacement. Place a wrench on the tensioner pulley lug and rotate it clockwise on 4.0L engines or counterclockwise on 3.3L and 3.8L engines until the belt can be removed **(see illustra-tion)**. Remove the belt and slowly release the tensioner.

7   If you're working on a 3.6L engine, insert a 3/8-inch drive ratchet into the tensioner **(see illustration)** and rotate the tensioner away (counterclockwise) from the belt until the belt can be removed, then slowly release the tensioner.

Warning: *Damage to the tensioner or pos-sible injury can occur if the tensioner snaps or springs back without the belt in place.*

8   Installation is the reverse of removal. When installing the belt, make sure the belt is centered on the pulleys.

9   Install the drivebelt splash shield, wheel and lug nuts. Lower the vehicle and tighten the lug nuts to the torque listed in this Chap-ter's Specifications.

Automatic tensioner replacement

Refer to illustration 19.12

10   Remove the wheel, then remove the drivebelt splash shield **(see illustration 19.5)**

11   Remove the drivebelt (see Steps 6 and 7).

12   Unscrew the mounting bolt from the cen-ter of the tensioner and remove the tensioner **(see illustration)**.

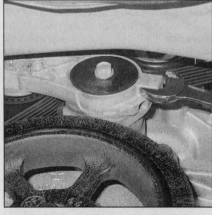

19.6 Place a wrench on the tensioner pulley lug and rotate it to relieve the belt tension (3.8L engine shown, 3.3L and 4.0L similar)

19.7 Insert a 3/8-inch drive ratchet into the square hole on the tensioner arm

19.12 The drivebelt tensioner is secured by a single bolt in the center of the tensioner – 3.8L engine shown, other models similar

13   Install the new tensioner assembly by reversing the removal procedure. Tighten the mounting bolt to the torque listed in this Chapter's Specifications.

14   Install the drivebelt as described previously in this Section.

15   Install the drivebelt splash shield, wheel and lug nuts. Lower the vehicle and tighten the lug nuts to the torque listed in this Chapter's Specifications.

20   Brake fluid change (every 30,000 miles or 30 months)

Warning: *Brake fluid can harm your eyes and damage painted surfaces, so use extreme caution when handling or pouring it. Do not use brake fluid that has been standing open or is more than one year old. Brake fluid absorbs moisture from the air. Excess moisture can cause a dangerous loss of braking effectiveness.*

1   At the specified intervals, the brake fluid should be drained and replaced. Since the brake fluid may drip or splash when pouring it, place plenty of rags around the master cylinder to protect any surrounding painted surfaces.

2   Before beginning work, purchase the specified brake fluid (see *Recommended lubricants and fluids* in this Chapter's Specifications).

3   Remove the cap from the master cylinder reservoir.

4   Using a hand suction pump or similar device, withdraw the fluid from the master cylinder reservoir.

5   Add new fluid to the master cylinder until it rises to the base of the filler neck.

6   Bleed the brake system at all four brakes until new and uncontaminated fluid is expelled from the bleeder screw (see Chapter 9). Be sure to maintain the fluid level in the master cylinder as you perform the bleeding process. If you allow the master cylinder to run dry, air will enter the system.

7   Refill the master cylinder with fluid and check the operation of the brakes. The pedal should feel solid when depressed, with no sponginess.
Warning: *Do not operate the vehicle if you are in doubt about the effectiveness of the brake system.*

21   Spark plug check and replacement (every 100,000 miles)

Refer to illustrations 21.2, 21.5, 21.7, 21.8, 21.10a, 21.10b, 21.12 and 21.13

1   On 3.3L and 3.8L engines, the spark plugs are located at the sides of the cylinder heads; on 3.6L and 4.0L engines, they are located in the center of the valve cover(s).

2   In most cases the tools necessary for spark plug replacement include a spark plug socket which fits onto a ratchet (this special socket is padded inside to protect the porcelain insulators on the new plugs and hold them in place), various extensions and a feeler gauge to check and adjust the spark plug gap (**see illustration**). Since these engines are equipped with aluminum cylinder heads, a torque wrench should be used when tightening the spark plugs.

3   The best approach when replacing the spark plugs is to purchase the new spark plugs beforehand, adjust them to the proper gap and then replace each plug one at a time. When buying the new spark plugs, be sure to obtain the correct plug for your specific engine. This information can be found in this Chapter's Specifications or in your owner's manual.

4   Allow the engine to cool completely before attempting to remove any of the plugs. During this cooling off time, each of the new spark plugs can be inspected for defects and the gaps can be checked.

5   The gap is checked by inserting the proper thickness gauge between the electrodes at the tip of the plug (**see illustration**). The gap between the electrodes should be as listed in this Chapter's Specifications or in your owner's manual. The wire should touch

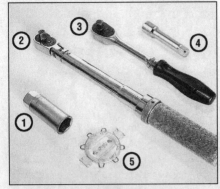

21.2 Tools required for changing spark plugs

1   *Spark plug socket - This will have special padding inside to protect the spark plug porcelain insulator*
2   *Torque wrench - Although not mandatory, use of this tool is the best way to ensure that the plugs are tightened properly*
3   *Ratchet - Standard hand tool to fit the plug socket*
4   *Extension - Depending on model and accessories, you may need special extensions and universal joints to reach one or more of the plugs*
5   *Spark plug gap gauge - This gauge for checking the gap comes in a variety of styles. Make sure the gap for your engine is included*

each of the electrodes. Also, at this time check for cracks in the spark plug body (if any are found, the plug must not be used).
Caution: *The manufacturer recommends against checking the gap on platinum-tipped spark plugs; the platinum coating could be scraped off.*

6   Cover the fender to prevent damage to the paint. Fender covers are available from auto parts stores but an old blanket will work just fine.

7   On 3.6L and 4.0L engines, remove the upper intake manifold (see Chapter 2B) to gain access to all the ignition coils (**see illustration**).

21.5 Spark plug manufacturers recommend using a wire-type gauge when checking the gap - the wire should slide between the electrodes with a slight drag

21.7 To remove an ignition coil(s), depress the tab (A), disconnect the electrical connector, remove the coil retaining bolt (B), then pull the coil straight up (3.6L and 4.0L engines)

21.8 Use a spark plug boot pulling tool to remove each end of a spark plug wire - never pull on the wire itself (3.3L and 3.8L engines)

21.10a Use a ratchet, socket and flexible extension to remove the spark plugs - 3.3L and 3.8L engines shown

21.10b Use a ratchet, socket and long extension to remove the spark plugs (3.6L engine shown, 4.0L engine similar)

8   On 3.3L and 3.8L engines, with the engine cool, remove the spark plug wire from one spark plug, using a twisting motion. Pull only on the boot at the end of the wire - do not pull on the wire **(see illustration)**.

9   If compressed air is available, use it to blow any dirt or foreign material away from the spark plug area.

Warning: *Wear eye protection!*

The idea here is to eliminate the possibility of material falling into the cylinder through the spark plug hole as the spark plug is removed.

10   Place the spark plug socket over the plug and remove it from the engine by turning it in a counterclockwise direction **(see illustrations)**.

11   Compare the spark plug with the chart on the inside back cover of this manual to get an indication of the overall running condition of the engine.

12   It's a good idea to lightly coat the threads of the spark plugs with an anti-seize compound **(see illustration)** to insure that the

spark plugs do not seize in the aluminum cylinder head.

13   It's often difficult to insert spark plugs into their holes without cross-threading them. To avoid this possibility, fit a piece of rubber hose over the end of the spark plug **(see illustration)**. The flexible hose acts as a universal joint to help align the plug with the plug hole. Should the plug begin to cross-thread, the hose will slip on the spark plug, preventing thread damage. Install the spark plug and tighten it to the torque listed in this Chapter's Specifications.

14   On 3.3L and 3.8L engines, attach the plug wire to the new spark plug, again using a twisting motion on the boot until it is firmly seated on the end of the spark plug. On 3.6L and 4.0L engines, install the ignition coils.

15   Follow the above procedure for the remaining spark plugs, replacing them one at a time to prevent mixing up the spark plug wires.

22   Spark plug wire check and replacement (3.3L and 3.8L engines) (see Maintenance schedule for intervals)

1   The spark plug wires should be replaced at the recommended intervals and/or checked when new spark plugs are installed.

2   Disconnect the spark plug wire from the ignition coil pack. Pull only on the boot at the end of the wire; don't pull on the wire itself. Use a twisting motion to free the boot/ wire from the coil. Disconnect the same spark plug wire from the spark plug, using the same twisting method while pulling on the boot.

3   Check inside the boot for corrosion, which will look like a white, crusty powder (don't mistake the white dielectric grease used on some plug wire boots for corrosion protection).

4   Push the wire and boot back onto the end of the spark plug. It should be a tight fit on the plug end. If not, remove the wire and use a pair of pliers to carefully crimp the metal connector inside the wire boot until the fit is snug.

5   Push the wire and boot back into the end of the ignition coil terminal. It should be a tight fit in the terminal. If not, remove the wire and use a pair of pliers to carefully crimp the metal connector inside the wire boot until the fit is snug.

6   Using a cloth, clean each wire along its entire length. Remove all built-up dirt and grease. As this is done, inspect for burned areas, cracks and any other form of damage. Bend the wires in several places to ensure that the conductive material inside hasn't hardened. Repeat the procedure for the remaining wires.

7   If you are replacing the spark plug wires, purchase a complete set for your particular engine. The terminals and rubber boots should already be installed on the wires. Replace the wires one at a time to avoid mixing up the firing order and make sure the terminals are securely seated on the coil pack and the spark plugs.

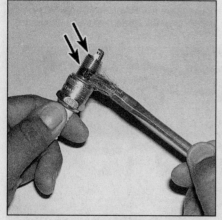

21.12 Apply a thin coat of anti-seize compound to the spark plug threads, but be careful not to get any of it near the electrodes

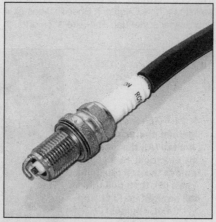

21.13 A length of snug-fitting rubber hose will save time and prevent damaged threads when installing the spark plugs

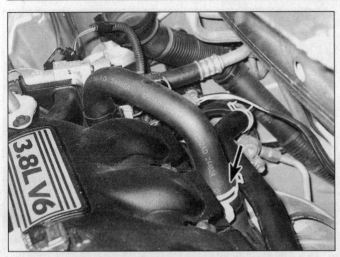

23.2a Disconnect the PCV valve hose . . .

23.2b . . . and remove the valve – 3.8L engine shown 3.3L and 4.0L engines similar

8   Attach the plug wire to the new spark plug and to the ignition coil pack using a twisting motion on the boot until it is firmly seated.

---

23   Positive Crankcase Ventilation (PCV) valve check and replacement (every 60,000 miles or 60 months)

Warning: *Do not attempt to clean the PCV valve.*
Note: *If replacing the valve, compare the old and new valves to make sure they're identical.*

3.3L, 3.8L and 4.0L engines

Refer to illustrations 23.2a and 23.2b

1   The PCV valve is located on the top of the valve cover.
2   Detach the PCV hose and remove the valve **(see illustrations)**.

3.6L engines

Refer to illustrations 23.6, 23.7a and 23.7b

3   The PCV valve is located on the end of the right valve cover.
4   Lift up on the outer edges of the engine cover to disengage the rubber mounts from the ball studs and remove the engine cover.
5   Disconnect the camshaft sensor electrical connector.
6   Use a screwdriver to pry the sensor electrical harness retainer up and off of the valve cover stud **(see illustration)**.
7   Detach the PCV hose, then remove the valve mounting screws and the valve **(see illustrations)**.

All engines

8   Shake the valve. The valve should rattle freely - if it doesn't, replace it.
9   Replace the PCV valve with the correct one for your specific vehicle and engine size and tighten the mounting screws securely.
10   Installation is the reverse of removal.

23.6 Using a long screwdriver, carefully pry the harness retainer up to release it (intake manifold removed for clarity)

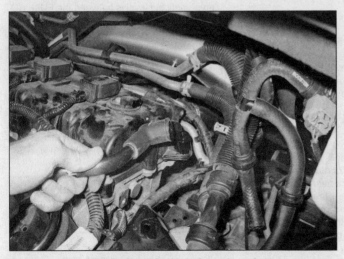

23.7a Disconnect the hose from the valve . . .

23.7b . . . then remove the screws and pull the valve out of the cover

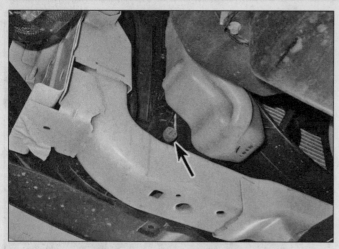

24.5 The drain fitting is located at the bottom of the radiator

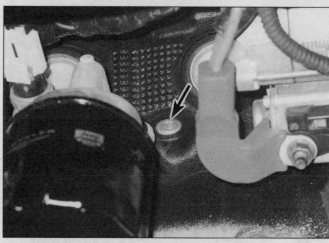

24.6 The block drain plugs are generally located about one to two inches above the oil pan - there is one on each side of the engine block

24   Cooling system servicing (draining, flushing and refilling) (every 60 months)

Warning: *Do not allow antifreeze to come in contact with your skin or painted surfaces of the vehicle. Flush contaminated areas immediately with plenty of water. Do not store new coolant or leave old coolant lying around where it's accessible to children or pets - they're attracted by its sweet smell. Ingestion of even a small amount of coolant can be fatal! Wipe up garage floor and drip pan spills immediately. Keep antifreeze containers covered and repair cooling system leaks as soon as they're noticed. Check with local authorities about the disposal of used antifreeze. Many communities have collection centers which will see that antifreeze is disposed of properly.*

Warning: *The electric cooling fan(s) on these models can activate at any time the ignition switch is in the ON position. Make sure the ignition is OFF when working in the vicinity of the fan(s). As an added precaution, disconnect the cable from the negative terminal of the battery (see Chapter 5).*

Note: *These vehicles are originally filled with Mopar 5 year/100,000 mile coolant that shouldn't be mixed with other coolants. Check the coolant reservoir under the hood to determine what type coolant you have. Always refill with the correct coolant.*

1   Periodically, the cooling system should be drained, flushed and refilled to replenish the antifreeze mixture and prevent formation of rust and corrosion, which can impair the performance of the cooling system and cause engine damage.

2   At the same time the cooling system is serviced, all hoses and the radiator (pressure) cap should be inspected, tested and replaced if faulty (see Section 12).

Draining

Refer to illustrations 24.5 and 24.6

Warning: *Wait until the engine is completely cool before beginning this procedure.*

3   With the engine cold, remove the radiator cap and set the heater control to maximum heat.

4   Move a large container, capable of holding at least 12 quarts, under the radiator drain fitting to catch the coolant mixture as it's drained.

5   Open the drain fitting located at the bottom of the radiator **(see illustration)**. Allow the coolant to completely drain out.

6   After the coolant stops flowing out of the radiator, move the container under the engine block drain plugs and allow the coolant in the block to drain **(see illustration)**.

7   While the coolant is draining, check the condition of the radiator hoses, heater hoses and clamps. Replace any damaged clamps or hoses (see Section 12).

Flushing

8   Close the radiator and engine block drain plugs. Fill the cooling system with clean water, following the *Refilling* procedure (see Step 15).

9   Start the engine and allow it to reach normal operating temperature, then rev up the engine a few times.

10   Turn the engine off and allow it to cool completely, then drain the system as described earlier.

11   Repeat Steps 9 and 10 until the water being drained is free of contaminants.

12   Severe cases of radiator contamination or clogging will require removing the radiator (see Chapter 3) and reverse flushing it. This involves inserting the hose in the bottom radiator outlet to allow the clean water to run against the normal flow, draining out through the top. A radiator repair shop should be con-

sulted if further cleaning or repair is necessary.

13   When the coolant is regularly drained and the system refilled with the correct coolant mixture, there should be no need to employ chemical cleaners or descalers.

14   Disconnect the coolant reservoir hose, remove the reservoir from the vehicle and flush it with clean water (see Chapter 3). Inspect it for damage and replace if necessary.

Refilling

15   Install the coolant reservoir, reconnect the hose and close the radiator drain fitting.

16   Remove the radiator cap. Add the correct mixture of the proper type of antifreeze/coolant and water in the ratio specified on the antifreeze container or in this Chapter's Specifications through the filler neck until it reaches the radiator cap seat.

17   Add the same coolant mixture to the reservoir until the level is between the FULL HOT and ADD marks. Install the radiator cap.

18   Run the engine until normal operating temperature is reached (the fans will cycle on, then off), then allow the engine to cool. With the engine cold, add coolant as necessary to bring it up to the correct level.

19   Keep a close watch on the coolant level and the various cooling system hoses during the first few miles of driving and check for any coolant leaks. Tighten the hose clamps and add more coolant mixture as necessary.

25   Automatic transaxle fluid and filter change (every 100,000 miles)

1   The automatic transaxle fluid and filter should be changed and the magnet cleaned at the recommended intervals.

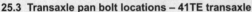

25.3 Transaxle pan bolt locations – 41TE transaxle

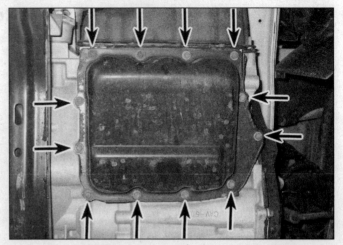

25.13 Transaxle pan bolt locations – 62TE transaxle

2   Raise the front of the vehicle, support it securely on jackstands, and apply the parking brake.

42TE transaxles

Refer to illustration 25.3

3   Place a floor jack with a block of wood under the transaxle/engine assembly and remove both engine mount-to-crossmember cradle nuts.

4   Place a container under the transaxle pan and loosen the pan bolts **(see illustration)**. Completely remove the bolts along the rear of the pan. Tap the corner of the pan to break the seal and allow the fluid to drain into the container (the remaining bolts will prevent the pan from separating from the transaxle). Remove the remaining bolts.

5   Using the floor jack, raise the transaxle/engine assembly until the pan can be detached and removed.

6   Remove the old sealant from the pan and transaxle body (don't nick or gouge the sealing surfaces) and clean the pan magnet with a clean, lint-free cloth.

7   Install a new filter and O-ring and reinstall the magnet(s).

8   Apply a 1/8-inch bead of RTV to the pan sealing surface and position it on the transaxle. Install the bolts and tighten them to the torque in this Chapter's Specifications

using a criss-cross pattern. Work up to the final torque in three or four steps.

9   Lower the engine/transaxle assembly then install the crossmember cradle nuts and tighten the nuts to the torque listed in this Chapter's Specifications.

10   Lower the vehicle and add four quarts of the specified transaxle fluid (see *Recommended lubricants and fluids* in this Chapter's Specifications). Start the engine and allow it to idle for a minute, then move the shift lever through each gear position, ending in Park or Neutral. Check for fluid leaks around the pan.

11   If necessary, add more fluid (a little at a time) until the level is between the Add and Full marks (be careful not to overfill it).

12   Make sure the dipstick is completely seated or dirt could get into the transaxle.

62TE transaxles

Refer to illustration 25.13

Note: *The 62TE transaxles require the use of a scan tool to check transaxle fluid temperature and special tool #9336A (or a homemade equivalent) to measure the fluid level. If you do not have both tools to make the proper temperature-to-fluid level comparisons, we do not recommend attempting this repair procedure.*

13   Place a container under the transaxle pan and loosen the pan bolts **(see illustra-**

tion). Completely remove the bolts along the rear of the pan. Tap the corner of the pan to break the seal and allow the fluid to drain into the container (the remaining bolts will prevent the pan from separating from the transaxle). Remove the remaining bolts and the oil pan.

14   Remove the filter retaining nuts and filter.

15   Install a new filter and tighten the fasteners to the torque listed in this Chapter's Specifications.

16   Remove the old sealant from the pan and transaxle body (don't nick or gouge the sealing surfaces) and clean the pan magnet with a clean, lint-free cloth.

17   Apply a 1/8-inch bead of RTV to the pan sealing surface and position it on the transaxle. Install the bolts and tighten them to the torque in this Chapter's Specifications using a criss-cross pattern. Work up to the final torque in three or four steps.

18   Lower the vehicle and add four quarts of the specified transaxle fluid (see *Recommended lubricants and fluids* in this Chapter's Specifications). Start the engine and allow it to idle for a minute, then move the shift lever through each gear position, ending in Park or Neutral.

19   Check the fluid level using the fluid level check procedure (see Section 4).

Notes

Chapter 2 Part A
3.3L and 3.8L V6 engines

Contents

Specifications

General

Cylinder numbers (drivebelt end-to-transmission end)
Rear bank..	1-3-5
Front bank (radiator side)...	2-4-6
Firing order	1-2-3-4-5-6

Oil pressure
At idle speed	5 psi (minimum)
At 3,000 rpm..	30 to 80 psi

Oil pump

Cover warpage limit...	0.001 inch
Outer rotor thickness (minimum)	0.301 inch
Inner rotor thickness (minimum)	0.301 inch
Rotor-to-pump cover clearance...	0.004 inch
Outer rotor-to-housing clearance..	0.015 inch
Inner rotor-to-outer rotor lobe clearance.............................	0.008 inch

Front of Vehicle

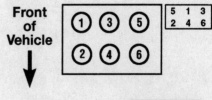

Cylinder and coil terminal locations

Torque specifications

Ft-lbs (unless otherwise indicated)

Note: *One foot-pound (ft-lb) of torque is equivalent to 12 inch-pounds (in-lbs) of torque. Torque values below approximately 15 ft-lbs are expressed in inch-pounds, since most foot-pound torque wrenches are not accurate at these smaller values.*

Camshaft sprocket bolt	40
Crankshaft pulley bolt	40
Cylinder head bolts (in sequence - **see illustration 12.18**)	
Step 1	45
Step 2	65
Step 3	65
Step 4	Tighten an additional 90-degrees (1/4 turn)
Drivebelt idler sprocket bolt	24
Driveplate-to-crankshaft bolts	70
Engine mount bracket bolts	
M8	21
M10	40
Exhaust manifold-to-cylinder head bolts	17
Exhaust manifold heat shield nut	105 in-lbs
Exhaust crossover bolts	30
Hydraulic lifter retaining bolts	105 in-lbs
Intake manifold (upper) retaining bolts*	105 in-lbs
Intake manifold (lower)-to-block bolts	17
Oil cooler fitting	20
Oil pan drain plug	20
Oil pan bolts	105 in-lbs
Oil pump pick-up tube mounting bolts	21
Oil pump cover (plate) screws	105 in-lbs
Rear main oil seal retainer bolts	105 in-lbs
Rocker arm shaft bolts	17
Timing chain cover bolts	
M8	20
M10	40
Timing chain sprocket-to-camshaft bolt	40
Valve cover-to-cylinder head bolts	105 in-lbs
Water pump bolts	See Chapter 3

Apply a non-hardening thread-locking compound to the bolt threads before installation.

1 General information

Chapter 2A is devoted to in-vehicle repair procedures for the 3.3L and 3.8L V6 engines. These engines utilize a cast-iron engine block with six cylinders arranged in a "V" shape with a 60-degree angle between the two banks. The overhead valve aluminum cylinder heads are equipped with replaceable valve guides and seats. An in-block camshaft, chain driven from the crankshaft, and hydraulic roller lifters actuate the valves through tubular pushrods.

Information concerning engine removal and installation and camshaft removal and installation can be found in Chapter 2C. The following repair procedures are based on the assumption that the engine is installed in the vehicle. If the engine has been removed from the vehicle and mounted on a stand, many of the steps outlined in Chapter 2A do not apply.

2 Repair operations possible with the engine in the vehicle

Many major repair operations can be done without removing the engine from the vehicle.

Clean the engine compartment and the exterior of the engine with degreaser before any work is done. It'll make the job easier and help keep dirt out of internal parts of the engine.

It may be helpful to remove the hood to improve engine access when repairs are performed (see Chapter 11). Cover the fenders to prevent damage to the paint. Special pads are available, but an old bedspread or blanket will also work.

If vacuum, exhaust, oil, or coolant leaks develop, indicating a need for gasket or seal replacement, the repairs can generally be done with the engine in the vehicle. The intake and exhaust manifold gaskets, timing chain cover gasket, oil pan gasket, crankshaft oil seals, and cylinder head gaskets are all accessible with the engine in the vehicle.

Exterior engine components, such as the intake and exhaust manifolds, the oil pan, the oil pump, the timing chain cover, the water pump, the starter motor, the alternator, and fuel system components can be removed for repair with the engine in the vehicle.

Cylinder heads can be removed without pulling the engine. Valve component servicing can also be done with the engine in the vehicle. Replacement of the timing chain and sprockets is also possible with the engine in the vehicle, but the camshaft cannot be removed with the engine in the vehicle. Refer to Chapter 2C for camshaft removal and installation.

Repair or replacement of piston rings, pistons, connecting rods, and rod bearings is possible with the engine in the vehicle, however, this practice is not recommended because of the cleaning and preparation work that must be done to the components.

3 Top Dead Center (TDC) for number one piston - locating

1   Top Dead Center (TDC) is the highest point in the cylinder that each piston reaches as it travels up the cylinder bore. Each piston reaches TDC on the compression stroke and again on the exhaust stroke, but TDC generally refers to piston position on the compression stroke.

2   Positioning the piston(s) at TDC is an essential part of certain procedures such as camshaft and timing chain/sprocket removal.

3   Before beginning this procedure, be sure to place the transmission in Neutral and apply the parking brake or block the rear wheels. Disable the ignition system by disconnecting the primary electrical connector at the ignition coil pack and removing the spark plugs (see Chapter 1). Also disable the fuel pump (see Chapter 4, Section 3).

4   In order to bring any piston to TDC, the crankshaft must be turned using one of the methods outlined below. When looking at the front of the engine, normal crankshaft rotation is clockwise.

a) *The preferred method is to turn the crankshaft with a socket and ratchet attached to the bolt threaded into the front of the crankshaft. Turn the bolt in a clockwise direction only. Never turn the bolt counterclockwise.*

b) *A remote starter switch, which may save some time, can also be used. Follow the instructions included with the switch. Once the piston is close to TDC, use a socket and ratchet as described in the previous paragraph.*

c) *If an assistant is available to turn the ignition switch to the Start position in short bursts, you can get the piston close to TDC without a remote starter switch. Make sure your assistant is out of the vehicle, away from the ignition switch, then use a socket and ratchet as described in Paragraph (a) to complete the procedure.*

5   Install a compression pressure gauge in the number one spark plug hole (refer to Chapter 2C). It should be a gauge with a screw-in fitting and a hose at least six inches long.

6   Rotate the crankshaft using one of the methods described above while observing for pressure on the compression gauge. The moment the gauge shows pressure, indicates that the number one cylinder has begun the compression stroke.

Note: *If a compression gauge is not available, you can simply place a blunt object over the spark plug hole and listen for compression as the engine is rotated.*

7   Once the compression stroke has begun, TDC for the compression stroke is reached by bringing the piston to the top of the cylinder.

8   If there was no compression, the piston was on the exhaust stroke. Continue rotating the crankshaft 360-degrees (1-turn).

9   These engines are not equipped with external components (crankshaft pulley, flywheel, timing hole, etc.) that are marked to identify the position of number 1 TDC. Therefore, the only method to double-check the location of TDC number 1 is to remove the timing chain cover to access the timing gears and alignment marks (see Section 10) or with the use of a degree wheel and a positive stop timing device threaded into the spark plug hole for cylinder number 1. This procedure is described in detail in the Haynes Chrysler Engine Overhaul Manual.

10   After the number one piston has been positioned at TDC on the compression stroke, TDC for any of the remaining cylinders can be located by turning the crankshaft 120-degrees and following the firing order (refer to the Specifications). For example on V6 engines, rotating the engine 120-degrees past TDC number 1 will put the engine at TDC compression for cylinder number 2.

4 Valve covers - removal and installation

Removal

1   Disconnect the cable from the negative terminal of the battery (see Chapter 5).

Front valve cover

Refer to illustration 4.4

2   Remove the spark plug wires from the spark plugs (see Chapter 1). Label each wire before removal to ensure correct reinstallation.

3   Remove the crankcase vent hose from the valve cover.

4   Remove the valve cover bolts (**see illustration**).

4.4 Front valve cover mounting bolts

4.12 Rear valve cover mounting bolts (two bolts hidden from view)

5.2 Remove the rocker arm shaft bolts from the cylinder head - be sure to start with the outer ones first

5   Remove the valve cover.
Note: *If the valve cover sticks to the cylinder head, slide a putty knife under the edge to dislodge it.*

Rear valve cover

Refer to illustration 4.12

6   Remove the spark plug wires from the spark plugs (see Chapter 1). Label each wire before removal to ensure correct reinstallation.
7   Remove the cowl cover and the wiper assembly (see Chapter 12).
8   Label and detach the vacuum lines from the throttle body.
9   Remove the ignition coil pack (see Chapter 5).
10   Remove the upper intake manifold (see Section 6).
11   Remove the breather hose from the PCV valve.
12   Remove the valve cover bolts **(see illustration).**

13   Detach the valve cover.
Note: *If the valve cover sticks to the cylinder head, slide a putty knife under the edge to dislodge it.*

Installation

14   The mating surfaces of the cylinder heads and valve covers must be perfectly clean when the valve covers are installed. If there's sealant or oil on the mating surfaces when the valve cover is installed, oil leaks may develop. Be extra careful not to nick or gouge the mating surfaces while cleaning.
15   Clean the mounting bolt threads with a die, if necessary, to remove corrosion and restore damaged threads. Use a tap to clean the threaded holes in the cylinder heads.
16   Place the valve cover and new gasket in position, then install the bolts. Tighten the bolts in several steps to the torque listed in this Chapter's Specifications.
17   Installation of the remaining components is the reverse of removal.
18   Start the engine and check carefully for oil leaks.

5   Rocker arms and pushrods - removal, inspection and installation

Removal

Refer to illustrations 5.2, 5.3 and 5.4

1   Remove the valve covers (see Section 4).
2   Loosen each rocker arm shaft bolt a little at a time, until they are all loose enough to be removed by hand **(see illustration).**
3   Remove the rocker arm and shaft assembly. If the rocker arms, washers and shaft retainer/spacers are going to be removed from the shaft, be sure to note how they are positioned **(see illustration).** To remove the bolts and retainer/spacers, use pliers to grip the edges of the retainer/spacers and pull them straight up off the shaft.
4   Remove the pushrods and store them in order to make sure they don't get mixed up during installation **(see illustration).**

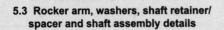

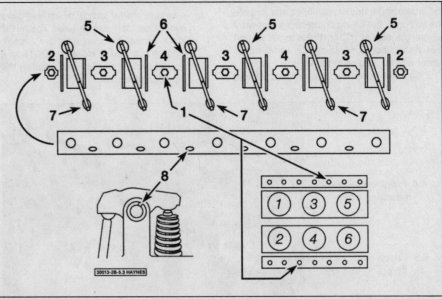

5.3 Rocker arm, washers, shaft retainer/spacer and shaft assembly details

1   *Rocker arm shaft oil feed bolt (longer length)*
2   *Shaft retainer/spacer (0.84 inch)*
3   *Shaft retainer/spacer (1.47 inches)*
4   *Shaft retainer/spacer (1.61 inches)*
5   *Rocker arm - exhaust*
6   *Washer*
7   *Rocker arm - intake (larger offset)*
8   *Rocker arm lubrication feed hole (position upward and toward the feed hole)*

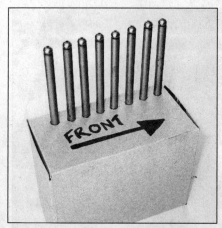

5.4 Be sure to store the pushrods in an organized manner to make sure they're reinstalled in their original locations

Inspection

Refer to illustration 5.5

5   Check each rocker arm for wear, cracks and other damage **(see illustration)**, especially where the pushrods and valve stems contact the rocker arm.

6   Check the pivot seat in each rocker arm and the pivot faces. Look for galling, stress cracks and unusual wear patterns. If the rocker arms are worn or damaged, replace them with new ones and install new pivots or shafts as well.

Note: *Keep in mind that there is no valve adjustment on these engines, so excessive wear or damage in the valve train can easily result in excessive valve clearance, which in turn will cause valve noise when the engine is running.*

7   On shaft mounted rocker arms, inspect the shafts for galling and excessive wear. Inspect the oil holes for plugging.

8   Inspect the pushrods for cracks and excessive wear at the ends. Roll each pushrod across a piece of plate glass to see if it's bent (if it wobbles, it's bent).

Installation

Caution: *Be sure that the one rocker shaft bolt that is longer than the other bolts is installed into the correct position* **(see illustration 5.3).**

Caution: *The rocker shafts should be tightened down slowly, starting with the center bolts and working toward the outer bolts. Allow at least 20 minutes bleed-down time after installing both rocker arm shafts before operating the engine.*

9   Lubricate the lower end of each pushrod with clean engine oil or moly-base grease and install them in their original locations. Make sure each pushrod seats completely in the lifter socket.

10   Apply moly-base grease to the ends of the valve stems and the upper ends of the pushrods.

11   Apply moly-base grease to the rocker arm shaft. If removed, install the rocker arms, washers, shaft retainer/spacers and bolts in the correct order. Install the rocker arm assembly onto the cylinder head. Tighten the bolts, a little at a time (working from the center out), to the torque listed in this Chapter's Specifications. As the bolts are tightened, make sure the pushrods engage properly in the rocker arms.

Caution: *Allow the engine to set for 20 minutes before starting.*

12   Install the valve covers.

---

6   Intake manifold - removal and installation

Warning: *Wait until the engine is completely cool before beginning this procedure.*

Removal

1   Relieve the fuel system pressure (see Chapter 4).

2   Disconnect the cable from the negative terminal of the battery (see Chapter 5).

3   Drain the cooling system (see Chapter 3).

Upper intake manifold

Refer to illustration 6.12

4   Remove the air filter housing and the air intake duct (see Chapter 4).

5   Disconnect the throttle cable and the cruise control cable, if equipped (see Chapter 4).

6   Disconnect the Automatic Idle Speed (AIS) motor, the Throttle Position Sensor (TPS) and Manifold Absolute Pressure (MAP) sensor connectors (see Chapter 6).

7   Disconnect the vapor purge vacuum hose (see Chapter 6).

8   Disconnect the Positive Crankcase Ventilation (PCV) hose (see Chapter 6).

9   Remove the power steering reservoir mounting bolts and loosen the side nut, then remove the power steering reservoir from the bracket. Position the assembly off to the side without disconnecting the fluid lines.

10   Disconnect the power brake booster (see Chapter 9) and Leak Detection Pump (LDP) or Natural Vacuum Leak Detection (NVLD) system vacuum hoses from the manifold (see Chapter 6).

11   Remove the EGR pipe from the manifold (see Chapter 6).

12   Remove the upper intake manifold bolts **(see illustration 6.29)**. Separate the assembly from the lower intake manifold.

Note: *Cover the intake manifold runners to prevent any objects from falling into the lower intake manifold while the upper manifold is off* **(see illustration).**

Lower intake manifold

Refer to illustrations 6.19 and 6.20

13   Remove the upper intake manifold (see Steps 1 through 12).

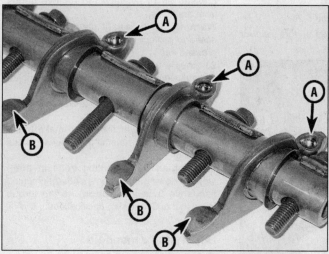

5.5 Check each rocker arm at the ball socket pivots (A) for chipping and wear and at the tips (B) for scuffing, wear and other damage

6.12 Here, shop towels have been installed in the manifold runners to prevent any objects falling into the lower intake manifold

6.19 Pry on the intake manifold only in the areas where the gasket mating surface will not get damaged

6.20 Remove the intake manifold gasket retainer screws

14   Disconnect the fuel hose fitting. Remove the fuel line (see Chapter 4).
15   Remove the ignition coil pack and bracket (see Chapter 5).
16   Disconnect the heater supply hose (see Chapter 3) and the Engine Coolant Temperature (ECT) sensor (see Chapter 6).
17   Remove the fuel rail and injector assembly (see Chapter 4).
18   Disconnect the upper radiator hose (see Chapter 3).
19   Remove the bolts and separate the lower intake manifold from the engine (see illustration 6.26). If the lower intake manifold is stuck, carefully pry on a casting protrusion (see illustration) - don't pry between the lower intake manifold and the cylinder heads, as damage to the gasket sealing surfaces may result. If you're installing a new lower intake manifold, transfer all fittings and sensors to the new manifold.
20   Remove the lower intake manifold gasket retaining screws and remove the gasket from the cylinder block (see illustration).

Installation

Lower intake manifold

Refer to illustrations 6.23 and 6.26
Note: *The mating surfaces of the cylinder heads, cylinder block, and the intake manifold must be perfectly clean when the lower intake manifold is installed. Gasket removal solvents are available at most auto parts stores and may be helpful when removing old gasket material that's stuck to the cylinder heads, cylinder block and lower intake manifold (the lower intake manifold is made of aluminum - aggressive scrapping can cause damage). Be sure to follow the instructions printed on the solvent container.*
21   Use a gasket scraper to remove all traces of sealant and old gasket material, then clean the mating surfaces with brake system cleaner. If there's old sealant or oil on the mating surfaces when the lower intake manifold is installed, oil or vacuum leaks may develop. Use a vacuum cleaner to remove gasket material that falls into the intake ports or the lifter valley.
22   Use a tap of the correct size to chase the threads in the bolt holes, then use compressed air (if available) to remove debris from the holes.
Warning: *Wear safety glasses or a face shield to protect your eyes when using compressed air!*
23   Apply a 1/4-inch bead of RTV sealant or equivalent to the cylinder heads-to-engine block junctions (see illustration).
24   Install the lower intake gasket and tighten the retainer screws.
25   Carefully lower the lower intake manifold into place and install the mounting bolts finger-tight.
26   Tighten the mounting bolts in three steps, following the recommended tightening sequence (see illustration), to the torque listed in this Chapter's Specifications.

Upper intake manifold

Refer to illustrations 6.27 and 6.29
27   Check the condition of the rubber seals that are installed into each intake runner on

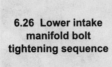

6.23 Apply RTV sealant to the corners of the cylinder head and engine block

6.26 Lower intake manifold bolt tightening sequence

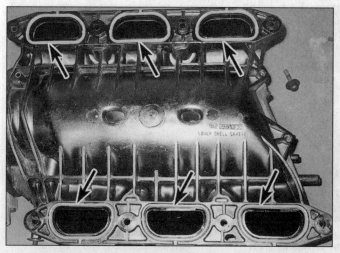

6.27 Be sure to replace the upper intake manifold seals with new ones if they are damaged

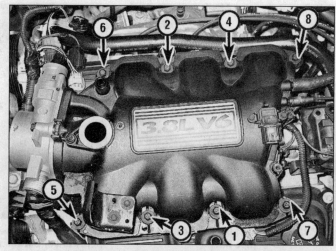

6.29 Upper intake manifold bolt tightening sequence

7.4a Exhaust crossover pipe details

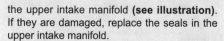

A   Exhaust crossover pipe
B   Front (left bank) exhaust manifold-to-crossover pipe flange
C   Rear (right bank) exhaust manifold-to-crossover pipe flange (behind cruise control actuator)

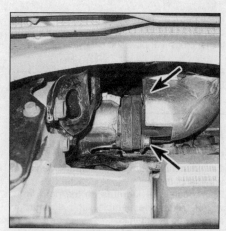

7.4b Location of the rear exhaust pipe nuts

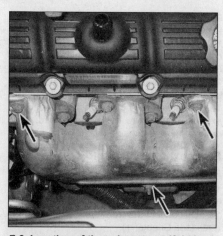

7.6 Location of the exhaust manifold heat shield mounting bolts

the upper intake manifold (see illustration). If they are damaged, replace the seals in the upper intake manifold.

28 Install the upper intake manifold onto the lower intake manifold. Install the special screws into the composite material and turn slowly to prevent damage to the upper intake manifold,

29 Tighten the mounting screws following the correct sequence (see illustration) to the torque listed in this Chapter's Specifications.

30 Installation of the remaining components is the reverse of removal.

31 Refill the cooling system (see Chapter 1), start the engine and check for leaks and proper operation.

7   Exhaust manifolds - removal and installation

1   Disconnect the cable from the negative terminal of the battery (see Chapter 5).

Removal
Rear exhaust manifold

Refer to illustrations 7.4a, 7.4b, 7.6 and 7.7

2   Remove the cowl cover (see Chapter 11) and the wiper unit (see Chapter 12).

3   Disconnect the rear bank of spark plug wires.

4   Unbolt the crossover pipe where it joins the rear exhaust manifold (see illustrations).

5   Disconnect and remove the upstream oxygen sensor connector. Remove the upstream oxygen sensor (see Chapter 6).

6   Remove the bolts and the upper heat shield (see illustration).

7   Raise the vehicle, support it securely on jackstands, and remove the engine splash

shield from the passenger's side (see illustration).

8   Loosen the power steering pump support strut lower bolt.

7.7 Right side splash shield retainers

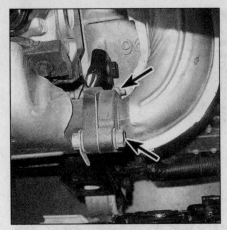

7.13 Location of the front exhaust pipe nuts

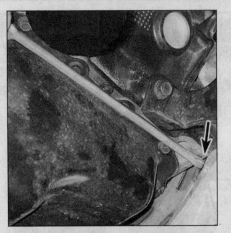

8.6a Carefully wedge a flat-bladed screwdriver between the driveplate teeth and the engine block at the transaxle bellhousing to lock the crankshaft in place

8.6b Remove the crankshaft pulley bolt with a breaker bar and a socket

9   Disconnect the downstream oxygen sensor connector.
10   Remove the bolts and disconnect the catalytic converter from the exhaust manifold (see Chapter 6).
11   Lower the vehicle and remove the power steering pump support strut upper bolt.
12   Remove the bolts attaching the rear exhaust manifold to the cylinder head, and remove the rear exhaust manifold.

Front exhaust manifold

Refer to illustration 7.13

13   Unbolt the crossover pipe where it joins the front exhaust manifold **(see illustration)**.
14   Disconnect the front bank of spark plug wires (see Chapter 1).
15   Remove the bolts and the upper heat shield.
16   Remove the bolts attaching the front exhaust manifold to the cylinder head, and remove the front exhaust manifold.

Installation

17   Clean the mating surfaces to remove all traces of old gasket material, then inspect the exhaust manifolds for distortion and cracks. Check for warpage with a precision straight-edge held against the mating surface. If a feeler gauge thicker than 0.030-inch can be inserted between the straightedge and the mating surface, take the exhaust manifold(s) to an automotive machine shop for resurfacing.
18   Place the exhaust manifold in position with a new gasket and install the mounting bolts finger tight.
Note: *Be sure to identify the exhaust manifold gasket by the correct cylinder designation and the position of the exhaust ports on the gasket.*
19   Starting in the middle and working out toward the ends, tighten the bolts to the torque listed in this Chapter's Specifications.
20   Installation of the remaining components is the reverse of removal.
21   Start the engine and check for exhaust

leaks between the exhaust manifolds and the cylinder heads and between the exhaust manifolds, crossover pipe and catalytic converter.

---

8   Crankshaft pulley - removal and installation

Removal

Refer to illustrations 8.6a, 8.6b and 8.7

1   Disconnect the cable from the negative terminal of the battery (see Chapter 5).
2   Loosen the lug nuts on the right front wheel, raise the vehicle, and support it securely on jackstands.
3   Remove the right front wheel.
4   Remove the passenger side engine splash shield (see Section 7).
5   Remove the serpentine drivebelt (see Chapter 1).
6   Remove the driveplate cover and position a large screwdriver in the ring gear teeth to keep the crankshaft from turning **(see illustration)** while a helper removes the crankshaft pulley-to-crankshaft bolt **(see illustration)**.
7   Pull the crankshaft pulley off the crankshaft with a two-jaw puller attached to the inner hub **(see illustration)**.
Caution: *Do not attach the puller to the outer edge of the pulley or damage to the pulley may result.*
Caution: *Because the pulley is recessed, an adapter may be needed between the puller bolt and the crankshaft (to prevent damage to the bore and threads in the end of the crankshaft).*

Installation

8   Install the crankshaft pulley with a special installation tool that threads to the crankshaft in place of the crankshaft pulley bolt (available at most automotive parts stores). Be sure to apply clean engine oil or multi-purpose grease to the seal contact surface of the damper hub (if it isn't lubricated, the seal

lip could be damaged and oil leakage would result). If the tool isn't available, the crankshaft pulley bolt and several washers used as spacers, may be used as long as the crankshaft pulley bolt torque is not exceeded.
9   Remove the tool and install the crankshaft pulley bolt and tighten it to the torque listed in this Chapter's Specifications.
10   Installation of the remaining components is the reverse of removal.

---

9   Crankshaft front oil seal - replacement

Refer to illustrations 9.2 and 9.3

1   Remove the crankshaft pulley (see Section 8).
2   Note how the seal is installed - the new one must be installed to the same depth and face the same way. Carefully pry the oil seal out of the cover with a seal puller or a large

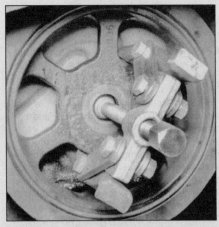

8.7 Remove the crankshaft pulley with a two-jaw puller attached to the inner hub - DO NOT pull on the outer edge of the pulley or damage may result!

9.2 Be very careful not to damage the crankshaft surface when removing the front seal

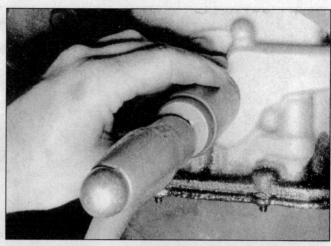

9.3 Use a seal driver or a large deep socket to gently tap the seal into place

screwdriver (see illustration). Be very careful not to distort the cover or scratch the crankshaft! Wrap tape around the tip of the screwdriver to avoid damage to the crankshaft.

3   Apply clean engine oil or multi-purpose grease to the outer edge of the new seal, then install it in the cover with the lip (spring side) facing IN. Drive the seal into place (see illustration) with a seal driver or a large socket and a hammer. Make sure the seal enters the bore squarely. Stop when the front face is at the proper depth.

4   Reinstall the crankshaft pulley (see Section 8).

10 Timing chain and sprockets - removal, inspection and installation

Warning: Wait until the engine is completely cool before beginning this procedure.

Removal

Refer to illustrations 10.11, 10.15 and 10.16

1   Disconnect the cable from the negative terminal of the battery (see Chapter 5).
2   Drain the coolant (see Chapter 1).
3   Loosen the right-front wheel lug nuts. Raise the vehicle and support it securely on jackstands. Drain the engine oil (see Chapter 1).
4   Remove the right-front wheel and engine splash shield (see Section 7).
5   Remove the oil pan (see Section 13) and the oil pump pick-up tube.
6   Remove the drivebelt (see Chapter 1).
7   Unbolt the air conditioning compressor from its bracket and set it off to one side. Use mechanics wire to tie the assembly to the fender to keep it away from the work area (see Chapter 3).
Warning: The refrigerant hoses are under pressure - don't disconnect them.

8   Remove the crankshaft pulley (see Section 8).
9   Remove the radiator lower hose (see Chapter 3). Remove the heater hose from the timing chain cover housing or, on oil cooler equipped models, the water pump inlet.
10   Remove the right side engine mount (see Section 18).
11   Unbolt and remove the idler pulley from the engine mount bracket (see illustration).
12   Remove the bolts and remove the engine mount bracket. Remove the camshaft sensor from the timing chain cover (see Chapter 6).
13   Remove the water pump (see Chapter 3).
14   Remove the bolt and remove the power steering pump support strut to the front cover.
15   Remove the timing chain cover-to engine block bolts (see illustration).
16   Temporarily install the crankshaft pulley bolt and turn the crankshaft with the bolt to align the timing marks on the crankshaft and

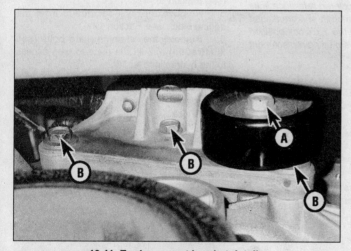

10.11 Engine mount bracket details

A   Idler pulley mounting bolt
B   Engine bracket bolts (one bolt behind idler pulley and another bolt on top of bracket not visible)

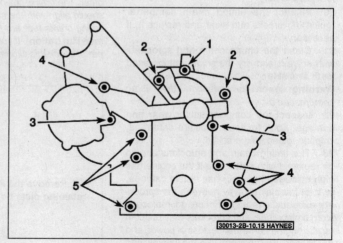

10.15 Timing chain cover bolt locations

1	M8 1.25 X 95	4	M8 1.25 X 80
2	M10 1.5 X 100	5	M8 1.25 X 45
3	M10 1.5 X 85		

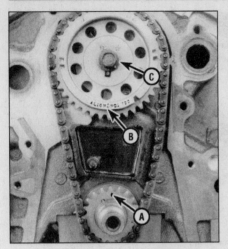

10.16 Timing chain and sprocket alignment details

A   *Crankshaft sprocket alignment mark*
B   *Camshaft sprocket alignment mark*
C   *Camshaft sprocket bolt*

camshaft sprockets. The crankshaft arrow should be at the top (12 o'clock position) and the camshaft sprocket arrow should be in the 6 o'clock position **(see illustration)**.
17   Remove the camshaft sprocket bolt. Do not turn the camshaft in the process (if you do, realign the timing marks before the sprocket is removed).
18   Use two large screwdrivers to carefully pry the camshaft sprocket off the camshaft dowel pin.
19   Timing chains and sprockets should be replaced in sets. If you intend to install a new timing chain, remove the crankshaft sprocket with a puller and install a new one. Align the key in the crankshaft with the keyway in the sprocket during installation.

Inspection

20   Inspect the timing chain dampener (guide) for cracks and wear and replace it, if necessary.
21   Clean the timing chain and sprockets with solvent and dry them with compressed air (if available).
Warning: *Wear eye protection when using compressed air.*
22   Inspect the components for wear and damage. Look for teeth that are deformed, chipped, pitted, and cracked.
23   The timing chain and sprockets should be replaced with a new one if the engine has high mileage, the chain has visible damage, or total freeplay midway between the sprockets exceeds one inch. Failure to replace a worn timing chain and sprockets may result in erratic engine performance, loss of power, and decreased fuel mileage. Loose chains can jump timing. In the worst case, chain jumping or breakage will result in severe engine damage.

10.25 Be sure the timing chain colored reference links align with marks on the sprockets

Installation

Refer to illustration 10.25

24   Use a gasket scraper to remove all traces of old gasket material and sealant from the cover and engine block. The cover is made of aluminum, so be careful not to nick or gouge it. Clean the gasket sealing surfaces with brake system cleaner.
25   Turn the camshaft to position the dowel pin at 6 o'clock **(see illustration 10.16)**. Mesh the timing chain with the camshaft sprocket, then engage it with the crankshaft sprocket. The timing marks should be aligned **(see illustration 10.16)**.
Note: *If the crankshaft has moved, turn it until the arrow stamped on the crankshaft sprocket is exactly at the top. If the camshaft was turned, install the sprocket temporarily and turn the camshaft until the sprocket timing mark is at the bottom, opposite the mark on the crankshaft sprocket. The arrows should point to each other. The timing chain colored reference links should align with the camshaft and crankshaft timing marks that are in the 3 o'clock position* **(see illustration)**. *If you are using replacement parts, check this alignment.*

26   Install the camshaft sprocket bolt and tighten it to the torque listed in this Chapter's Specifications.
27   Lubricate the chain and sprocket with clean engine oil.
28   Stick the new gasket to the cover, making sure the bottom edge of the gasket is flush with the bottom of the cover. Attach the cover to the engine block, making sure the flats of the oil pump gear are aligned with the flats on the crankshaft. Install the bolts and tighten them in a criss-cross pattern, in three steps, to the torque listed in this Chapter's Specifications.
29   Installation of the remaining components is the reverse of removal.
30   Add oil and coolant (see Chapter 1), start the engine and check for leaks.

11   Hydraulic roller lifters - removal, inspection and installation

1   A noisy valve lifter can be isolated when the engine is idling. Hold a mechanic's stethoscope or a length of hose near each valve while listening at the other end. Another method is to remove the valve cover and, with the engine idling, touch each of the valve spring retainers, one at a time. If a valve lifter is defective, it'll be evident from the shock felt at the retainer each time the valve seats.
2   The most likely causes of noisy valve lifters are dirt trapped inside the lifter and lack of oil flow, viscosity, or pressure. Before condemning the lifters, check the oil for fuel contamination, correct level, cleanliness, and correct viscosity.

Removal

Refer to illustrations 11.6, 11.7, 11.8 and 11.9

3   Remove the intake manifold (see Section 6) and valve covers (see Section 4).
4   Remove the rocker arms and pushrods (see Section 5).
5   Remove the cylinder heads from the engine block (see Section 12).
6   Remove the retaining plate bolts **(see illustration)** and lift the plate to gain access to the hydraulic roller lifters.

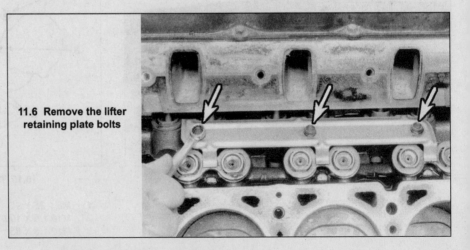

11.6 Remove the lifter retaining plate bolts

11.7 Lift off the alignment yokes

11.8 On engines with low mileage, the roller lifters can be removed by hand - if the lifters are coated with varnish, a special lifter removal tool may be required

7   Each pair of lifters is retained with an alignment yoke. Lift the yoke from the lifters **(see illustration)**.

8   There are several ways to extract the lifters from the bores. A special tool designed to grip and remove lifters is manufactured by many tool companies and is available at most automotive parts stores, but it may not be required in every case. On newer engines without a lot of varnish buildup, the lifters can often be removed with a small magnet or even with your fingers **(see illustration)**. A machinist's scribe with a bent end can be used to pull the lifters out by positioning the point under the retainer ring in the top of each lifter.

Caution: *Don't use pliers to remove the lifters unless you intend to replace them with new ones. The pliers may damage the precision machined and hardened lifters, rendering them useless.*

9   Store the lifters in a box clearly labeled to ensure they're reinstalled in their original locations **(see illustration)**.

Inspection

Refer to illustration 11.11

10   Clean the lifters with solvent and dry

them thoroughly. Do not mix them up.

11   Check each lifter wall and pushrod seat for scuffing, score marks, and uneven wear. If the lifter walls are damaged or worn, inspect the lifter bores in the engine block **(see illustration)**.

12   Check the roller of each lifter for freedom of movement, excessive looseness, flat spots, or pitting. The camshaft must also be inspected for signs of abnormal wear.

Note: *Used roller lifters can be reinstalled with a new camshaft or the original camshaft can be used if new roller lifters are installed, provided the used components are in good condition.*

Installation

13   When installing used lifters, make sure they're replaced in their original bores. Position the valve lifter with the lubrication hole facing upward toward the middle of the engine block. Soak the lifters in oil to remove trapped air. Coat the lifters with moly-based grease or engine assembly lube prior to installation.

14   Installation of the remaining components is the reverse of removal.

15   Tighten the retaining plate bolts to the

torque listed in this Chapter's Specifications.

16   Run the engine and check for oil leaks.

---

12   Cylinder heads - removal and installation

Caution: *Allow the engine to cool completely before loosening the cylinder head bolts.*

Removal

Refer to illustration 12.9

1   Disconnect the cable from the negative terminal of the battery (see Chapter 5).

2   Remove the intake manifold (see Section 6).

3   Disconnect all wires and vacuum hoses from the cylinder heads. Label them to simplify reinstallation.

4   Disconnect the ignition wires and remove the spark plugs (see Chapter 1). Label the ignition wires to simplify reinstallation.

5   Remove the exhaust manifolds (see Section 7).

11.9 Store the lifters in a box so each one will be reinstalled in its original bore

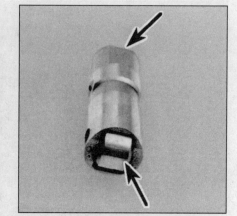

11.11 Check the roller for pitting or excessive looseness and the lifter surfaces for gouges, scoring, wear or damage

12.9 Do not pry on the cylinder head near the gasket mating surface - use the corners under the casting protrusions

12.12 Use a putty knife or gasket scraper to remove the gasket from the cylinder head

6   Remove the valve covers (see Section 4).

7   Remove the rocker arms and pushrods (see Section 5).

8   Using the new cylinder head gasket, outline the cylinders and bolt pattern on a piece of cardboard. Be sure to indicate the front (timing chain end) of the engine for reference. Punch holes at the bolt locations. Loosen each of the cylinder head mounting bolts, 1/4-turn at a time, until they can be removed by hand - work from bolt-to-bolt in the reverse of the tightening sequence **(see illustration 12.18)**. Store the bolts in a cardboard holder as they're removed - this will ensure they are reinstalled in their original locations, which is absolutely essential.

9   Lift the cylinder heads from the engine. If resistance is felt, don't pry between the cylinder head and engine block, damage to the mating surfaces will result. Recheck for cylinder head bolts that may have been overlooked, then use a hammer and wood block to tap up on the cylinder head and break the gasket seal **(see illustration)**. Be care-

ful because there are locating dowels in the engine block to position each cylinder head. As a last resort, pry each cylinder head up at the rear corner only and be careful not to damage anything. After removal, place the cylinder head on wood blocks to prevent damage to the gasket surfaces.

10   Have the cylinder head inspected and serviced by a qualified automotive machine shop.

Installation

Refer to illustrations 12.12, 12.15 and 12.18

11   The mating surfaces of each cylinder head and the engine block must be perfectly clean when the cylinder head is installed.

12   Use a gasket scraper to remove all traces of carbon and old gasket material **(see illustration)**, then clean the mating surfaces with brake system cleaner. If there's oil on the mating surfaces when the cylinder head is installed, the gasket may not seal correctly and leaks may develop. When working on the engine block, it's a good idea to cover the lifter valley with shop rags to keep debris

out of the engine. Use a shop rag or vacuum cleaner to remove any debris that falls into the cylinders.

13   Check the engine block and cylinder head mating surfaces for nicks, deep scratches, and other damage. If damage is slight, it can be removed with a file; if it's excessive, machining may be the only alternative.

14   Use a tap of the correct size to chase the threads in the cylinder head bolt holes. Dirt, corrosion, sealant, and damaged threads will affect torque readings.

15   Position the new gasket over the dowel pins in the engine block. Some gaskets are marked TOP or FRONT to ensure correct installation **(see illustration)**.

16   Carefully position the cylinder head on the engine block without disturbing the gasket.

17   With a straight-edge, check each cylinder head bolt for necking-down or stretching. If all of the threads do not contact the straight-edge, replace the bolt.

18   Install the head bolts and tighten them in the recommended sequence to the torque listed in this Chapter's Specifications (Step 1) **(see illustration)**. Next, tighten them following the recommended sequence to the Step 2 torque listed in this Chapter's Specifications. Tighten the bolts again to the same torque as a double check (Step 3). Finally, tighten each bolt an additional 90-degrees (1/4-turn) following the recommended sequence (Step 4). Do not use a torque wrench for this step; apply a paint mark to the bolt head or use a torque-angle gauge (available at most automotive parts stores) and a socket and breaker bar. **Note:** *If the bolt torque is checked with a torque wrench after the 90-degree turn and is not at least 90 ft-lbs, the bolt must be replaced.*

19   Installation of the remaining components is the reverse of removal.

20   Change the oil and filter (see Chapter 1).

21   Refill the cooling system (see Chapter 1). Start the engine and check for leaks and proper operation.

12.15 Be sure the stamped designations are facing up and forward

12.18 Cylinder head bolt TIGHTENING sequence

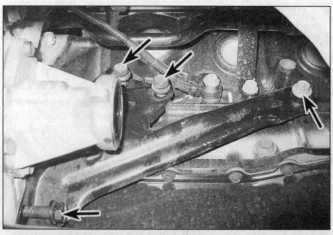

13.4 Remove the bolts from the transaxle brace

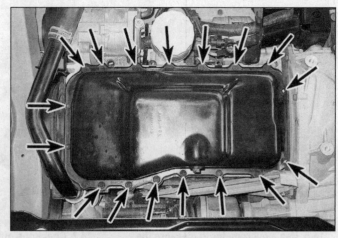

13.7a Remove the bolts from the oil pan

13.7b Use a soft faced hammer to loosen the oil pan - be careful not to dent the pan

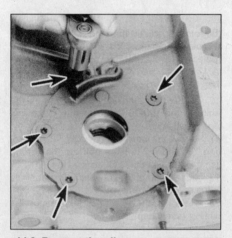

14.2 Remove the oil pump cover screws

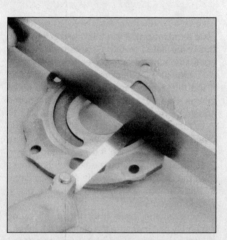

14.4 Place a straightedge across the oil pump cover and check it for warpage with a feeler gauge

13 Oil pan - removal and installation

Removal

Refer to illustrations 13.4, 13.7a and 13.7b

1 Disconnect the cable from the negative terminal of the battery (see Chapter 5).
2 Raise the front of the vehicle and support it securely on jackstands. Apply the parking brake and block the rear wheels to keep it from rolling off the stands.
3 Drain the engine oil (see Chapter 1).
4 Remove the engine/transaxle brace **(see illustration)**.
5 Remove the lower driveplate cover.
6 Remove the starter (see Chapter 5).
7 Remove the bolts and nuts, then carefully separate the oil pan from the engine block **(see illustration)**. Don't pry between the engine block and the pan or damage to the sealing surfaces could occur and oil leaks may develop. Tap the pan with a soft-face hammer to break the gasket seal **(see illustration)**. If it still sticks, slip a putty knife between the engine block and oil pan to break the bond (but be careful not to scratch the surfaces).

Installation

8 Clean the pan with solvent and remove all old sealant and gasket material from the engine block and pan mating surfaces. Clean the mating surfaces with brake system cleaner and make sure the bolt holes in the engine block are clear. Check the oil pan flange for distortion, particularly around the bolt holes. If necessary, place the pan on a wood block and use a hammer to flatten and restore the gasket surface.
9 Apply a bead of RTV sealant to the bottom surface of the timing chain cover and to the bottom of the rear main oil seal retainer. Install a new gasket on the oil pan flange.
10 Place the oil pan in position on the engine block and install the nuts/bolts.
11 Tighten the bolts to the torque listed in this Chapter's Specifications. Starting at the center, follow a criss-cross pattern and work up to the final torque in three steps.
12 Installation of the remaining components is the reverse of removal.
13 Refill the engine with oil (see Chapter 1), run it until normal operating temperature is reached, and check for leaks.

14 Oil pump - removal, inspection and installation

Removal

Refer to illustration 14.2

1 Remove the oil pan (see Section 13).
2 Remove the timing chain cover (see Section 10). Remove the oil pump cover (plate) from the timing chain cover **(see illustration)**.

Inspection

Refer to illustrations 14.4, 14.5, 14.7, 14.8 and 14.9

3 Clean all parts thoroughly in solvent and carefully inspect the rotors, pump cover, and timing chain cover for nicks, scratches, or burrs. Replace the assembly if it is damaged.
4 Use a straightedge and a feeler gauge to measure the oil pump cover for warpage **(see illustration)**. If it's warped more than the limit listed in this Chapter's Specifications, the pump should be replaced.
5 Measure the thickness of the outer rotor

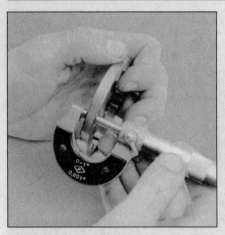

14.5 Use a micrometer to measure the thickness of the outer rotor

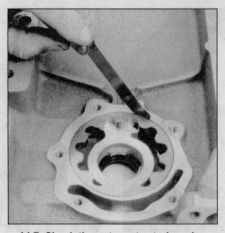

14.7 Check the outer rotor-to-housing clearance with a feeler gauge

14.8 Check the clearance between the lobes of the inner and outer rotors

(see illustration). If the thickness is less than the value listed in this Chapter's Specifications, the pump should be replaced.

6   Measure the thickness of the inner rotor. If the thickness is less than the value listed in this Chapter's Specifications, the pump should be replaced.

7   Insert the outer rotor into the timing chain cover/oil pump housing and measure the clearance between the rotor and housing (see illustration). If the measurement is more than the maximum allowable clearance listed in this Chapter's Specifications, the pump should be replaced.

8   Install the inner rotor in the oil pump assembly and measure the clearance between the lobes on the inner and outer rotors (see illustration). If the clearance is more than the value listed in this Chapter's Specifications, the pump should be replaced.

Note: Install the inner rotor with the mark facing up.

9   Place a straightedge across the face of the oil pump assembly (see illustration). If the clearance between the pump surface and

the rotors is greater than the limit listed in this Chapter's Specifications, the pump should be replaced.

Installation

10   Install the pump cover and tighten the bolts to the torque listed in this Chapter's Specifications.

11   Install the timing chain cover (see Section 10) and tighten the bolts to the torque listed in this Chapter's Specifications.

12   Installation of the remaining components is the reverse of removal.

13   Refill the engine with oil and change the oil filter (see Chapter 1).

---

15   Oil cooler - removal and installation

Removal

1   Disconnect the cable from the negative terminal of the battery (see Chapter 5).

2   Drain the coolant (see Chapter 1).

3   Raise the vehicle and support it securely on jackstands. Drain the engine oil and remove the oil filter (see Chapter 1).

4   Disconnect the coolant hoses from the inlet and outlet ports.

5   Unscrew and remove the oil cooler fitting and remove the oil cooler.

Installation

6   Lubricate the oil cooler connector on the oil filter adapter with clean engine oil.

7   Position the flat side of the oil cooler parallel to the oil pan rail and install the oil cooler onto the adapter. Install the fitting and tighten to the torque listed in this Chapter's Specifications.

8   Install the oil filter and refill the engine with oil (see Chapter 1). Also install a new oil filter.

9   Refill the cooling system (see Chapter 1). Run the engine until normal operating temperature is reached, and check for leaks.

---

16   Driveplate - removal and installation

Removal

Refer to illustration 16.4

1   Raise the vehicle and support it securely on jackstands.

2   Remove the transaxle (see Chapter 7).

3   To ensure correct alignment during reinstallation, match-mark the driveplate and backing plate to the crankshaft so they can be reassembled in the same position.

4   Remove the bolts that hold the driveplate to the crankshaft (see illustration). A special tool is available at most auto parts stores to hold the driveplate while loosening the bolts. If the tool is not available, wedge a screwdriver in the starter ring gear teeth to jam the driveplate.

5   Remove the driveplate from the crankshaft. The driveplate is fairly heavy; be sure to support it while removing the last bolt.

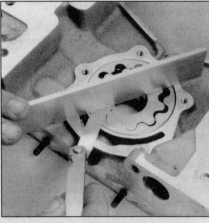

14.9 Using a straightedge and feeler gauge, check the clearance between the surface of the oil pump cover and the rotors

16.4 Mark the relative position of the driveplate to the crankshaft and, using an appropriate tool to hold the driveplate, remove the bolts

18.1a Location of the front engine mount through bolt

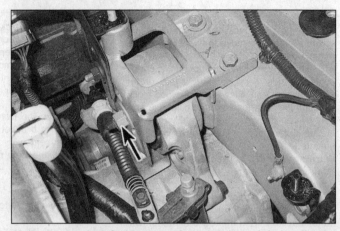

18.1b Access the left side transaxle mount through-bolt using the hole in the inner fenderwell

6   Clean the driveplate to remove grease and oil. Inspect the driveplate for damage or other defects.
7   Clean and inspect the mating surfaces of the driveplate and the crankshaft.
8   If the crankshaft rear main seal is leaking, replace it before reinstalling the driveplate (see Section 17).

Installation

9   Position the driveplate and backing plate against the crankshaft. Align the previously applied match marks. Before installing the bolts, apply thread-locking compound to the threads.
10   Hold the driveplate with the holding tool, or wedge a screwdriver in the starter ring gear teeth to keep the driveplate from turning. Tighten the bolts to the torque listed in this Chapter's Specifications.
11   The remainder of installation is the reverse of removal.

17 Rear main oil seal - replacement

1   Remove the driveplate (see Section 16).
2   Unbolt the seal retainer from the engine block and slide the retainer and seal off the end of the crankshaft.
3   Clean the engine block, oil pan and crankshaft.
4   The new seal and retainer assembly comes with a plastic installation sleeve; make sure it's in place.
5   Apply a 1/4-inch bead of RTV sealant where the lower corners of the seal retainer meet the oil pan.
6   Place the assembly over the crankshaft and push it squarely into place, making sure the dowels in the seal retainer engage the locating holes in the engine block.
7   Install, but don't tighten fully, the seal retainer bolts.
8   Remove the plastic installation sleeve, then tighten the bolts, using an alternating

pattern, to the torque listed in this Chapter's Specifications.
9   The remainder of installation is the reverse of removal.

18 Engine mounts - check and replacement

Refer to illustrations 18.1a, 18.1b, 18.1c and 18.1d

1   The engine mounting system on these models consists of four mounts (**see illustrations**). The right and left mounts support the engine/transaxle assembly while the front and rear mounts control powertrain torque. The right side engine mount is fluid-filled while the other three mounts are molded rubber.
2   Engine mounts seldom require attention, but broken or deteriorated mounts should be replaced immediately or the added strain placed on driveline components may cause damage or accelerated wear.

18.1c Remove the right side engine mount bracket and brace mounting bolts and separate the assembly from the engine mount bracket and engine compartment

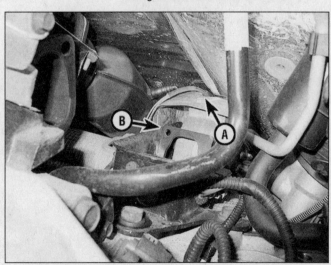

18.1d Remove the heat shield mounting bolt (A) and the heat shield to access the rear engine mount through bolt (B)

Check

3   During the check, the engine must be raised slightly to remove the weight from the mounts.

4   Raise the vehicle and support it securely on jackstands, then position a jack under the engine oil pan. Place a large wood block between the jack head and the oil pan to prevent oil pan damage, then carefully raise the engine just enough to take the weight off the mounts.

Warning: *DO NOT place any part of your body under the engine when it's supported only by a jack!*

5   Check the mounts to see if the rubber is cracked, hardened or separated from the metal backing. Sometimes the rubber will separate from the sleeve in the center of the mount.

6   Check for relative movement between the mount plates and the engine or frame (use a large screwdriver or pry bar to attempt to move the mounts). If movement is noted, lower the engine and tighten the mount fasteners.

7   Rubber preservative may be applied to the mounts to slow deterioration.

Replacement

Front mount

8   Raise the front of the vehicle and support it securely on jackstands.

9   Place a floor jack under the engine (with a wood block between the jack head and oil pan) and raise the engine slightly to relieve the weight from the mounts.

10   Remove the front engine mount through-bolt from the insulator and front crossmember-mounting bracket.

11   Remove the front engine mount bolts, the mounting bracket bolts and remove the insulator assembly.

12   Install the new mount and tighten the bolts securely.

Left mount

13   Remove the battery and battery tray (see Chapter 5).

14   Support the transaxle with a floor jack. Place a block of wood on the head of the jack to protect the transaxle.

15   Remove the mount-to-transaxle bolts and the mount-body bolts and remove the mount.

16   Installation is the reverse of removal. Tighten the bolts securely.

Right mount

17   Raise the front of the vehicle and support it securely on jackstands. Remove the air filter housing and the air intake duct from the throttle body (see Chapter 4).

18   Disconnect the PCV ventilation hose from the valve cover.

19   Place a floor jack under the engine (with a wood block between the jack head and oil pan) and raise the engine slightly to relieve the weight from the mount.

20   Remove the two right engine mount insulator vertical fasteners from the frame rail and loosen the one horizontal fastener.

21   Remove the vertical and horizontal fasteners from the engine side bracket. Remove the mount assembly.

Rear mount

22   Raise the front of the vehicle and support it securely on jackstands. Remove the left front wheel.

23   Place a floor jack under the engine (with a wood block between the jack head and oil pan) and raise the engine slightly to relieve the weight from the mount.

24   Install the new mount and tighten the bolts securely.

25   Remove the rear mount heat shield.

26   Remove the insulator through-bolt from the mount and rear mount bracket.

27   Remove the four mount fasteners and remove the mount.

Notes

Notes

Chapter 2 Part B
3.6L and 4.0L V6 engines

Contents

Specifications

General

Displacement	
3.6L	220 cubic inches
4.0L	244 cubic inches
Bore	
3.6L	3.779 inches
4.0L	3.780 inches
Stroke	
3.6L	3.268 inches
4.0L	3.583 inches
Compression ratio	10.2:1

General (continued)

Cylinder numbers (drivebelt end-to-transmission end)

    Rear bank 1-3-5

    Front bank (radiator side) 2-4-6

Firing order 1-2-3-4-5-6

Oil pressure

    At idle speed .... 5 psi (minimum)

    At 3,000 rpm

        3.6L .... 62 to 139 psi

        4.0L .... 45 to 105 psi

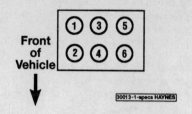

Cylinder and coil terminal locations

Camshaft

Bore diameter

    3.6L

        Cam tower 1 .... 1.2606 to 1.2615 inches

        Cam tower 2, 3, and 4 .... 0.9457 to 0.9465 inch

    4.0L .... 1.6944 to 1.6953 inches

Bearing journal diameter

    3.6L

        No. 1 .... 1.2589 to 1.2596 inches

        No. 2, 3, and 4 .... 0.9440 to 0.9447 inch

    4.0L .... 1.6905 to 1.6913 inches

Bearing clearance

    3.6L

        No. 1 .... 0.0001 to 0.0026 inch

        No. 2, 3, and 4 .... 0.0009 to 0.0025 inch

    4.0L .... 0.003 to 0.0047 inch

        Maximum .... 0.0059 inch

End play

    3.6L .... 0.003 to 0.01 inch

    4.0L .... 0.002 to 0.02 inch

Crankshaft main bearing

Main journal diameter

    3.6L .... 2.8345 ± 0.0035 inches

    4.0L .... 2.716 to 2.717 inches

Clearance

    3.6L .... 0.0009 to 0.002 (limit) inch

    4.0L .... 0.0013 to 0.0024 inch

Bearing clearance wear limit (4.0L) .... 0.0027 inch

End play

    3.6L .... 0.002 to 0.0114 (limit) inch

    4.0L .... 0.002 to 0.01 inch

End play maximum (4.0L) .... 0.013 inch

Cylinder head

Gasket thickness (compressed)

    3.6L .... 0.019 to 0.024 inch

    4.0L .... 0.059 inch

Valve seat width

    Intake

        3.6L .... 0.04 to 0.05 inch

        4.0L .... 0.031 to 0.067 inch

    Exhaust

        3.6L .... 0.055 to 0.063 inch

        4.0L .... 0.05 to 0.067 inch

Valve seat runout (maximum) .... 0.002 inch

Valves

Stem-to-guide clearance

    Intake

        3.6L .... 0.0009 to 0.0024 inch

        4.0L .... 0.0009 to 0.0026 inch

        Maximum .... 0.011 inch

    Exhaust

        3.6L .... 0.0012 to 0.0027 inch

        4.0L .... 0.002 to 0.0037 inch

        Maximum .... 0.0146 inch

Oil pump - 4.0L engines

Cover warpage limit	0.001 inch
Inner and outer rotor thickness	
Minimum	0.563 inch
Maximum	0.564 inch
Rotor-to-pump cover clearance	0.003 inch
Outer rotor-to-housing clearance	0.015 inch
Inner rotor-to-outer rotor lobe clearance	0.008 inch

Torque specifications   Ft-lbs (unless otherwise indicated)

Note: *One foot-pound (ft-lb) of torque is equivalent to 12 inch-pounds (in-lbs) of torque. Torque values below approximately 15 ft-lbs are expressed in inch-pounds, since most foot-pound torque wrenches are not accurate at these smaller values.*

Camshaft sprocket bolt - 4.0L engines	
Step 1	75
Step 2	Tighten an additional 90-degrees
Crankshaft balancer bolt	
3.6L (M6 bolt)	
Step 1	40
Step 2	Tighten an additional 105-degrees
4.0L	70
Cylinder head bolts*	
3.6L (in sequence - **see illustrations 14.43a and 14.43b**)	
Step 1	22
Step 2	33
Step 3	Tighten an additional 75-degrees
Step 4	Tighten an additional 50-degrees
Step 5	Loosen all in reverse of tightening sequence
Step 6	22
Step 7	33
Step 8	Tighten an additional 70-degrees
Step 9	Tighten an additional 70-degrees
4.0L (in sequence - **see illustration 14.43c**)	
Step 1	45
Step 2	65
Step 3	65
Step 4	Tighten an additional 90-degrees
Drivebelt idler sprocket bolt	
3.6L	18
4.0L	21
Driveplate-to-crankshaft bolts	70
Exhaust manifold-to-cylinder head (maniverter) bolts - 4.0L	21
Catalytic converter to cylinder head fasteners - 3.6L engines	27
Exhaust manifold heat shield nut - 4.0L	105 in-lbs
Exhaust crossover bolts	21
Intake manifold (upper) retaining bolts**	
3.6L	86 in-lbs
4.0L	105 in-lbs
Intake manifold (lower)-to-block bolts	
3.6L	62 in-lbs
4.0L	21
Oil cooler	
3.6L	
Bolts	35 in-lbs
Screws	106 in-lbs
4.0L	
Connector bolt	40
Oil pan drain plug	20
Oil pan	
3.6L	
Lower pan-to-upper pan nut/bolts	97 in-lbs
Upper pan-to-rear main seal housing (M6 bolts)	108 in-lbs
Upper pan-to-cylinder block (M8 bolts)	18
Upper pan-to-transaxle bolts	41
4.0L (bolts)	21
Oil pump pick-up tube mounting bolts	
3.6L	106 in-lbs
4.0L	21

* Use new bolts

**Apply a non-hardening thread-locking compound to the bolt threads before installation.

Torque specifications   Ft-lbs (unless otherwise indicated)

Note: *One foot-pound (ft-lb) of torque is equivalent to 12 inch-pounds (in-lbs) of torque. Torque values below approximately 15 ft-lbs are expressed in inch-pounds, since most foot-pound torque wrenches are not accurate at these smaller values.*

Oil pump cover (plate) screws	105 in-lbs
Oil pump-to-engine block fasteners	
3.6L	106 in-lbs
4.0L	21
Rear main oil seal retainer bolts	105 in-lbs
Rocker arm shaft bolts (in sequence - see illustration 12.15) - 4.0L	23
Timing cover bolts	
M6 bolts	
3.6L	106 in-lbs
4.0L	105 in-lbs
M8 bolts	
3.6L	18
4.0L	21
M10 bolts	
3.6L	41
4.0L	40
Timing gear splash shield bolts – 3.6L	35 in-lbs
Camshaft oil control valves - 3.6L	110
Oil pump timing chain sprocket - 3.6L (T45)	18
Valve cover-to-cylinder head bolts	
3.6L	106 in-lbs
4.0L	90 in-lbs
Water pump bolts	See Chapter 3

1 General information

Chapter 2B is devoted to in-vehicle repair procedures for the 3.6L and 4.0L V6 engines.

The 3.6 liter engine utilizes Variable Valve Timing (VVT), Dual Overhead Camshafts (DOHC), four timing chains, an aluminum cylinder block, steel cylinder sleeves or liners with six cylinders arranged in a "V"-shape, with 60-degrees between the two banks. The 3.6 liter engine has a chain driven oil pump with a multi-stage pressure regulator to increase fuel economy. The exhaust manifolds are integral with the cylinder heads to make the engine lighter.

The 4.0 liter engine also uses a "V"-shape design with 60-degrees between the two banks, a timing belt, an aluminum cylinder block with "cast-in-place" iron cylinder sleeves or liners, single overhead camshafts with hydraulic lash adjusters and four valves per cylinder.

Caution: *Neither engine is of a freewheeling design and severe engine damage will occur if the timing belt or chain breaks.*

The cylinders are numbered from front to rear on both engines. The right bank is numbered 1, 3, 5 and the left bank is numbered 2, 4, 6. The firing order is 1–2–3–4–5–6.

Information concerning engine removal and installation can be found in Chapter 2C. The following repair procedures are based on the assumption that the engine is installed in the vehicle. If the engine has been removed from the vehicle and mounted on a stand, many of the steps outlined in Chapter 2B do not apply.

2 Repair operations possible with the engine in the vehicle

Many major repair operations can be done without removing the engine from the vehicle.

Clean the engine compartment and the exterior of the engine with degreaser before any work is done. It'll make the job easier and help keep dirt out of internal parts of the engine.

It may be helpful to remove the hood to improve engine access when repairs are performed (see Chapter 11). Cover the fenders to prevent damage to the paint. Special pads are available, but an old bedspread or blanket will also work.

If vacuum, exhaust, oil, or coolant leaks develop, indicating a need for gasket

or seal replacement, the repairs can generally be done with the engine in the vehicle. The intake and exhaust manifold gaskets, timing chain cover gasket, oil pan gasket, crankshaft oil seals, and cylinder head gaskets are all accessible with the engine in the vehicle.

Exterior engine components, such as the intake and exhaust manifolds, the oil pan, the oil pump, the timing chain cover, the water pump, the starter motor, the alternator, and fuel system components can be removed for repair with the engine in the vehicle.

Cylinder heads can be removed without pulling the engine. Valve component servicing can also be done with the engine in the vehicle. Replacement of the timing chain and sprockets is also possible with the engine in the vehicle, as is camshaft and valvetrain removal and installation.

Repair or replacement of piston rings, pistons, connecting rods, and rod bearings is possible with the engine in the vehicle, however, this practice is not recommended because of the cleaning and preparation work that must be done to the components.

3 Top Dead Center (TDC) for number one piston - locating

1   Top Dead Center (TDC) is the highest point in the cylinder that each piston reaches as it travels up the cylinder bore. Each piston reaches TDC on the compression stroke and again on the exhaust stroke, but TDC generally refers to piston position on the compression stroke.

2   Positioning the piston(s) at TDC is an essential part of certain procedures such as camshaft and timing chain/sprocket removal.

3   Before beginning this procedure, be sure to place the transaxle in Neutral and apply the parking brake or block the rear wheels. Disconnect the cable from the negative terminal of the battery (see Chapter 5). Remove the ignition coils (see Chapter 5) and the spark plugs (see Chapter 1).

4   Install a compression pressure gauge in the number one spark plug hole (refer to Chapter 2C). It should be a gauge with a screw-in fitting and a hose at least six inches long.

5   Rotate the crankshaft using a socket and breaker bar on the crankshaft pulley bolt while observing for pressure on the compression gauge. The moment the gauge shows pressure, indicates that the number one cylinder

has begun the compression stroke.

6   Once the compression stroke has begun, TDC for the compression stroke is reached by bringing the piston to the top of the cylinder.

Note: *If a compression gauge is not available, you can simply place a blunt object over the spark plug hole and listen for compression as the engine is rotated. Once compression at the No.1 spark plug hole is noted, the remainder of the Step is the same.*

7   These engines are not equipped with external components (crankshaft pulley, flywheel, timing hole, etc.) that are marked to identify the position of number 1 TDC. Therefore, the only method to double-check the location of TDC number 1 is: on 3.6L engines, remove the valve cover to access the camshaft sprockets and alignment marks (see Section 10); on 4.0L engines, remove the valve cover (see Section 4) and note the rocker arm position, or use a degree wheel and a positive stop timing device threaded into the spark plug hole for cylinder number 1. This procedure is described in detail in the *Haynes Chrysler Engine Overhaul Manual.*

8   After the number one piston has been positioned at TDC on the compression stroke, TDC for any of the remaining cylinders can be located by turning the crankshaft 120-degrees and following the firing order (refer to the Specifications). For example, rotating the engine 120-degrees past TDC number 1 will put the engine at TDC compression for cylinder number 2.

4 Valve covers - removal and installation

Removal

1   Disconnect the cable from the negative terminal of the battery (see Chapter 5).

2   Remove the engine cover.

3   Remove the upper intake manifold (see Section 5).

Note: *Cover open ports on the intake to prevent debris from entering the engine.*

3.6L engines

Refer to illustrations 4.4 and 4.10

Caution: *Once the valve covers are removed, the magnetic timing wheels are exposed (see illustration 13.9). The magnetic timing wheels on the camshafts must not come in contact with any type of magnet or magnetic field. If contact is made, the timing wheels will need to be replaced.*

4.4 Lift the insulator up and off of the retaining posts then remove it from the front valve cover – 3.6L engine only

4.10 Front valve cover mounting bolts - 3.6L engine

4   Remove insulator from the front side valve cover **(see illustration)**.

5   Before removing the variable valve timing solenoid connectors from the front of each valve cover, mark them appropriately so they can be reinstalled in their original locations.

6   Disconnect the wiring harness retainers from the valve cover and move the harnesses out of the way.

7   Remove the ignition coils on both sides of the engine (see Chapter 5).

8   Mark the Camshaft Position (CMP) sensors to each valve cover so they can be reinstalled in their original locations, then remove the sensor(s) (see Chapter 6).

9   Remove the PCV valve from the rear cover (see Chapter 1).

10   Remove the valve cover fasteners **(see illustration)** and remove the cover(s).

Caution: *If the cover is stuck to the cylinder head, tap one end with a block of wood and a hammer to jar it loose. If that doesn't work, slip a flexible putty knife between the cylinder head and cover to break the gasket seal. Don't pry at the cover-to-cylinder head joint or damage to the sealing surfaces may occur*

(leading to future oil leaks).

11   Remove and discard the valve cover gasket, then remove the spark plug tube seals.

Note: *The cover gaskets can be reused if they are not damaged.*

4.0L engines

12   If you're working on the front valve cover, remove the alternator (see Chapter 5).

13   Remove the upper intake manifold brackets from both sides of the engine, and move the engine wiring harness to the side.

14   Loosen the valve cover bolts and remove both valve covers.

Note: *It may be necessary to disconnect the MVA hose from the front valve cover.*

Installation

15   The mating surfaces of each cylinder head and valve cover must be perfectly clean when the covers are installed. Use a gasket scraper to remove all traces of sealant and old gasket material, then clean the mating surfaces with brake system cleaner. If there's sealant or oil on the mating surfaces when the

cover is installed, oil leaks may develop.

16   Inspect spark plug tube seals; if damaged, carefully remove the seals using an appropriate pry tool. Position the new seal with the part number facing the valve cover, then use a socket that contacts the outer edge to drive the seal in place.

17   On 3.6L engines, apply a dab of RTV sealant at the joints where the engine front cover meets the cylinder head.

18   Install the valve cover and bolts, then tighten the bolts to the torque listed in this Chapter's specifications.

19   The remainder of installation is the reverse of removal.

5   Intake manifolds - removal and installation

Warning: *Wait until the engine is completely cool before beginning this procedure.*

Removal

1   If you will be removing the lower intake manifold, relieve the fuel system pressure (see Chapter 4).

2   Disconnect the cable from the negative terminal of the battery (see Chapter 5).

3   If equipped, remove the engine cover.

4   If you will be removing the lower intake manifold on a 4.0L engine, drain the cooling system (see Chapter 1).

Upper intake manifold

3.6L engines

Refer to illustrations 5.6, 5.7, 5.9, 5.10, 5.12 and 5.13

5   Remove the upper radiator hose retainer from the upper intake manifold (see Chapter 1).

6   Remove the intake resonator **(see illustration)**.

7   Disconnect the wiring harness from the MAP sensor and the ETC **(see illustration)**.

8   Disconnect the PCV valve hose (see

5.6 Loosen the resonator hose clamp, remove the attaching pin and remove the resonator

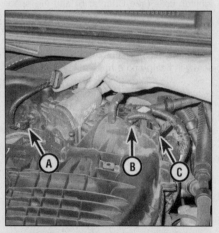

5.7 Disconnect the ETC connectors (A), the MAP sensor (B) and the electrical harness (C) retainer

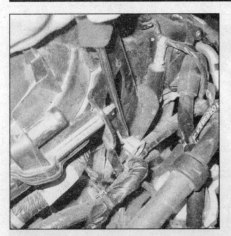

5.9 Pry the wiring harness retainer off of the bracket stud

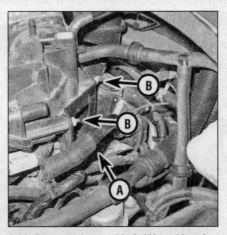

5.10 Remove the stud bolt (A) and bracket nuts (B), and remove the bracket

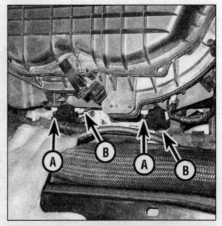

5.12 Pull the upper radiator hose back, remove the support bracket upper nuts (A), loosen the lower nuts (B) and remove the brackets from the upper intake manifold

Chapter 1), vapor purge hose and brake booster hoses.

9   Disconnect the wiring harness retainers from the upper intake support bracket and the retainer from the stud bolt **(see illustration)**.

10   Remove the nuts and stud bolt, then remove the upper intake manifold bracket **(see illustration)**.

11   Remove the nut from the bracket on the heater core return tube.

12   Remove the support bracket-to-upper manifold nuts **(see illustration)**.

13   Loosen, but do not remove, the bolts on the manifold, and remove the upper intake manifold **(see illustration)**.

14   Discard the six upper-to-lower intake manifold seals, and cover the open intake ports to prevent debris from entering the engine.

15   If required, remove the insulator from the front valve cover **(see illustration 4.4)**.

4.0L engine

16   Disconnect the electrical connectors to

the electronic throttle body (ETC), MAP sensor and the short runner valve solenoid.

17   Loosen the clamp and disconnect the air hose from the throttle body, then remove the air filter housing (see Chapter 4).

18   Disconnect the PCV valve hose, EVAP purge solenoid and the power brake booster hoses.

19   Disconnect and remove the EGR tube (see Chapter 6).

20   Disconnect the wiring harness retainers from the intake support brackets and move the harness out of the way.

21   Remove the fasteners for the power steering hose brackets and move the hose out of the way.

22   Remove the fasteners for the intake manifold support brackets at the end of the intake manifold.

23   Remove the upper intake manifold bolts and lift the upper intake manifold off of the lower manifold.

24   Cover the exposed intake ports to prevent any debris from entering the engine.

Lower intake manifold

3.6L engine

Refer to illustration 5.29

25   Remove the upper intake manifold (see Steps 5 through 16).

26   Disconnect the fuel line to the fuel rail (see Chapter 4).

27   Remove the fuel injectors and fuel rail (see Chapter 4).

Note: *The lower intake manifold can be removed with the injectors and fuel rail in place. Be careful not to damage the fuel injectors once the manifold is removed.*

28   Pry the wiring harness retainer from the end of the manifold and move the harness out of the way.

29   Remove the lower intake manifold bolts **(see illustration)**, and remove the manifold from the cylinder heads.

30   Discard the six manifold-to-cylinder head seals.

4.0L engines

31   Disconnect the upper radiator hose from

5.13 Location of the upper intake manifold bolts – 3.6L engine

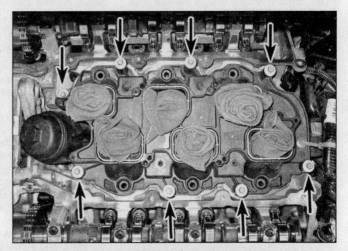

5.29 Lower intake manifold bolt locations – 3.6L engine

5.41 Install the manifold making sure the new intake seals do not fall out of the manifold

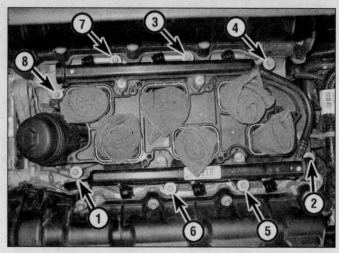

5.42 Lower intake manifold tightening sequence – 3.6L engines

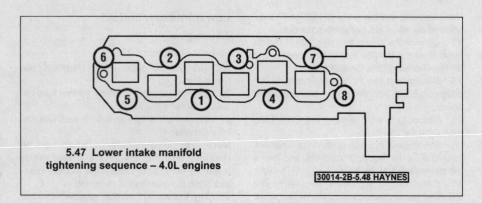

5.47 Lower intake manifold tightening sequence – 4.0L engines

30014-2B-5.48 HAYNES

the thermostat housing.

32   Remove the upper intake manifold (see Steps 17 through 25).

33   Move the power steering reservoir and bracket out of the way (see Chapter 10).

34   Disconnect the fuel injectors and coolant temperature sensor electrical connectors (see Chapter 4 and Chapter 3).

35   Disconnect the heater hose from the intake manifold and the coolant overflow hose at the thermostat housing.

36   Disconnect the fuel line, then remove the fuel rail and injectors as an assembly (see Chapter 4).

37   Remove the lower intake manifold bolts, and remove the lower intake manifold.

Installation

Lower intake manifold

Note: *The mating surfaces of the cylinder heads, cylinder block, and the intake manifold must be perfectly clean when the lower intake manifold is installed. Gasket removal solvents are available at most auto parts stores and may be helpful when removing old gasket material that's stuck to the cylinder heads, cylinder block and lower intake manifold (the lower intake manifold is made of aluminum - aggressive scrapping can cause damage). Be*

sure to follow the instructions printed on the solvent container.

38   Use a gasket scraper to remove all traces of sealant and old gasket material, then clean the mating surfaces with lacquer thinner or acetone. If there's old sealant or oil on the mating surfaces when the lower intake manifold is installed, oil or vacuum leaks may develop. Use a vacuum cleaner to remove gasket material that falls into the intake ports or the lifter valley.

3.6L engines

Refer to illustrations 5.41 and 5.42

39   If removed, install the fuel injectors and the fuel rail (see Chapter 4).

40   Install new intake manifold seals to the manifold.

Note: *Remove any rags or towels used in the manifold ports.*

41   Carefully lower the lower intake manifold into place **(see illustration)** and install the mounting bolts finger-tight.

42   Tighten the mounting bolts in steps, following the tightening sequence **(see illustration)**, to the torque listed in this Chapter's Specifications.

43   Install the upper intake manifold and the remaining steps are the reverse of the removal procedure.

4.0L engine

Refer to illustration 5.47

44   Apply a 1/4-inch bead of RTV sealant (or equivalent) to the cylinder head-to-engine block junctions.

45   Position the lower intake gaskets onto the cylinder head surface.

46   Carefully lower the lower intake manifold into place and install the mounting bolts finger-tight.

47   Tighten the mounting bolts in steps, following the tightening sequence **(see illustration)**, to the torque listed in this Chapter's Specifications.

48   Reconnect the hoses and harnesses in the reverse of removal.

49   Install the upper intake manifold; and the remaining steps are the reverse of the removal procedure.

Upper intake manifold

3.6L engine

Refer to illustration 5.53

50   Check the condition of the rubber seals that are installed into each intake runner on the upper intake manifold. If they're damaged, replace the seals in the upper intake manifold.

51   Place the insulator on the mounting pins **(see illustration 5.7)**, if removed.

52   Install the upper intake manifold onto the lower intake manifold while pulling the bolts up.

Note: *The bolts are specially made for the composite material and turn slowly to prevent damage to the upper intake manifold,*

53   Tighten the mounting bolts in sequence **(see illustration)** to the torque listed in this Chapter's Specifications.

4.0L engines

54   Install a new upper manifold gasket to the intake manifold.

55   Install the upper intake manifold onto the lower intake manifold and hand tighten the bolts.

5.53 Upper intake manifold bolt tightening sequence – 3.6L engine

56   Tighten the mounting bolts in several steps, starting in the center and working in a circular pattern to the torque listed in this Chapter's Specifications.

All models

57   Installation of the remaining components is the reverse of removal.

58   Refill the cooling system, if drained (see Chapter 1), start the engine and check for leaks and proper operation.

6   Exhaust manifolds (4.0L engine) - removal and installation

Note: *On 3.6L engines, the exhaust manifolds are integral with the cylinder head and the exhaust system bolts directly to the cylinder head.*

Removal

1   Disconnect the cable from the negative terminal of the battery (see Chapter 5).
2   Raise the vehicle, support it securely on jackstands, and remove the engine splash shield from the passenger's side.
3   If you're removing the front exhaust manifold:

  a) *Remove the engine cooling fans (see Chapter 3).*
  b) *Remove the oil dipstick tube fastener and remove the dipstick tube from the oil pan.*

4   Disconnect the upstream and downstream oxygen sensor connectors.
Note: *If the manifold is being replaced, remove both oxygen sensors (see Chapter 6).*
5   Unbolt the cross-under pipe where it joins the rear exhaust manifold/catalytic converter (maniverter).
6   Remove the exhaust manifold inlet fasteners, unhook the exhaust system hangers and lower the pipe assembly.
7   Remove the bolts and remove the upper heat shield.
8   Remove the bolts attaching the exhaust manifold (maniverter) to the cylinder head, and remove the exhaust manifold.

Installation

9   Clean the mating surfaces to remove all traces of old gasket material, then inspect the exhaust manifolds for distortion and cracks. Check for warpage with a precision straightedge held against the mating surface. If a feeler gauge thicker than 0.030-inch can be inserted between the straightedge and the mating surface, take the exhaust manifold(s) to an automotive machine shop for resurfacing.
10   Place the exhaust manifold in position with a new gasket and install the mounting bolts finger tight.
Note: *Be sure to identify the exhaust manifold gasket by the correct cylinder designation and the position of the exhaust ports on the gasket.*
11   Starting in the middle and working out toward the ends, tighten the bolts to the torque listed in this Chapter's Specifications.
12   Installation of the remaining components is the reverse of removal.
13   Start the engine and check for exhaust leaks between the exhaust manifolds and the cylinder heads and between the exhaust manifolds, crossover pipe and catalytic converter.

7.5 Using a special holding tool to prevent the crankshaft from turning, loosen, then remove the bolt

7   Crankshaft balancer - removal and installation

Removal

1   Disconnect the cable from the negative terminal of the battery (see Chapter 5).
2   Loosen the lug nuts on the right front wheel, raise the vehicle, and support it securely on jackstands.
3   Remove the right front wheel.
4   Remove the drivebelt (see Chapter 1).

3.6L engine

Refer to illustrations 7.5 and 7.6

5   The crankshaft balancer bolt is incredibly tight; using a breaker bar, socket and special tool #10198 or equivalent **(see illustration)**, hold the balancer from turning while loosening the bolt.
6   Pull the crankshaft pulley off the crankshaft **(see illustration)**.

4.0L engine

7   Remove the driveplate cover, position a large screwdriver in the ring gear teeth to keep the crankshaft from turning, while a helper removes the crankshaft pulley-to-crankshaft bolt.
8   Insert adapter #9020 or equivalent to the end of crankshaft. Install a three-jaw puller to the inner hub, pressing against the adapter on the end of the crankshaft to pull the crankshaft balancer off the crankshaft.
Caution: *Do not attach the puller to the outer edge of the pulley or damage to the pulley may result.*
Caution: *Because the pulley is recessed, adapter #9020 may be needed between the puller bolt and the crankshaft (to prevent damage to the bore and threads in the end of the crankshaft).*

Installation

3.6L engine

9   Apply clean engine oil or multi-purpose grease to the seal contact surface of the

7.6 Slide the pulley from the end of the crankshaft; a puller shouldn't be required

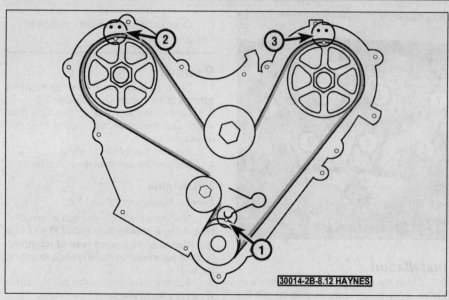

8.12 Timing belt alignment mark locations (at TDC):

1   *Crankshaft pointer aligns with the TDC mark on the oil pump*
2   *Rear camshaft timing mark aligns between the marks on the rear cover*
3   *Front camshaft timing mark aligns between the marks on the rear cover*

balancer hub (if it isn't lubricated, the seal lip could be damaged and oil leakage would result).

10   Install the crankshaft balancer, aligning the keyway on the crankshaft with the slot in the balancer. Install the bolt and tighten it by hand.

11   Prevent the engine from rotating (see Step 5) then tighten the bolt to the torque listed in this Chapter's Specifications.

12   Installation of the remaining components is the reverse of removal.

4.0L engine

13   Install the crankshaft pulley with a special installation tool that threads to the crankshaft in place of the crankshaft pulley bolt (available at most automotive parts stores). Be sure to apply clean engine oil or multi-purpose grease to the seal contact surface of the damper hub (if it isn't lubricated, the

seal lip could be damaged and oil leakage would result). If the tool isn't available, the crankshaft pulley bolt and several washers used as spacers, may be used as long as the crankshaft pulley bolt torque is not exceeded.

14   Remove the tool, install the crankshaft pulley bolt and tighten it to the torque listed in this Chapter's Specifications.

15   Installation of the remaining components is the reverse of removal.

8   Timing belt (4.0L engine) - removal, installation and adjustment

Warning: *Wait until the engine is completely cool before beginning this procedure.*
Caution: *This is not a freewheeling engine; if the belt is broken or improperly installed, the*

engine will be severely damaged.
Caution: *Do not rotate the crankshaft or cam-shafts separately during this procedure (with the timing belt removed), as damage to the valves may occur.*
Note: *Several special tools are required to complete these procedures, so read through the entire Section and obtain the special tools before beginning work.*

Removal

Refer to illustrations 8.12 and 8.16

1   Disconnect the cable from the negative terminal of the battery (see Chapter 5).

2   Loosen the lug nuts on the right front wheel, raise the front of the vehicle and support it securely on jackstands. Remove the right front wheel and the drivebelt splash shield.

3   Position the number one piston at TDC on the compression stroke (see Section 3).

4   Remove the drivebelt and drivebelt tensioner (see Chapter 1).

5   Remove the bolts from the power steering pump and set the pump and bracket aside (see Chapter 10).

6   Remove the crankshaft balancer (see Section 7).

7   Remove the lower front timing belt cover fasteners and remove the cover. Note the various type and sizes of bolts by making a diagram or taking careful notes while the timing belt cover is being removed. The bolts must be reinstalled in their original locations.

8   Place a floor jack under the engine (with a wood block between the jack head and oil pan) and raise the engine slightly to relieve the weight from the mounts.

9   Remove the air filter housing (see Chapter 4), then remove the right engine mount (see Section 20).

10   Disconnect the fuel line at the fuel rail (see Chapter 4).

11   Remove the upper front timing belt cover fasteners and remove the cover.

12   Make sure that the number one piston is still at TDC on the compression stroke by verifying that the timing marks on all three timing belt sprockets are aligned with their respective alignment marks **(see illustration)**.

13   Remove the hydraulic tensioner mounting bolts and tensioner from the side of the rear cover.

14   Loosen the bolt on the timing belt tensioner pulley and push the pulley away from the belt, then retighten the bolt.

15   Check to see that the timing belt is marked with an arrow to show which side faces out. If there isn't a mark, paint one on (only if the same belt will be reinstalled). Slide the timing belt off the sprockets and check the condition of the tensioner.

16   Inspect the timing belt **(see illustration)**. Look at the backside (the side without the teeth): If it's cracked or peeling, or it's hard, glossy and inflexible, and leaves no indentation when pressed with your fingernail, replace the belt. Look at the drive side: If teeth are missing, cracked or excessively worn, replace the belt.

8.16 When you inspect the timing belt, these are the conditions you should look for

Separation

Tooth missing

Rounded belt side

Fiber worn

9.3 Use a hook tool and pry the seal from the timing cover

9.4 Another way of removing an old oil seal is to screw a self-tapping screw partially into the seal, then use pliers as a lever to pull it from the engine

9.6 Drive the seal squarely into the cover using a socket and hammer

Installation

Caution: *Before starting the engine, carefully rotate the crankshaft by hand through at least two full revolutions (use a socket and breaker bar on the crankshaft pulley center bolt). If you feel any resistance, STOP! There is something wrong - most likely, valves are contacting the pistons. You must find the problem before proceeding. Check your work and see if any updated repair information is available.*

17   Place the hydraulic timing belt tensioner in a bench vise and slowly compress the tensioner until a 3 mm Allen wrench can be inserted through the housing to prevent the plunger from expanding.

Note: *This should take about 5 minutes to bleed down.*

18   Install the belt on the crankshaft sprocket first, and keep the belt tight on the tension side.

19   Install the belt on the front (radiator side) camshaft sprocket, the water pump pulley, and the rear camshaft sprocket and timing belt tensioner. Be careful not to nudge the camshaft sprocket(s) or crankshaft gear off the timing marks. Install the timing belt with the arrow pointing away from the engine.

20   Align the factory-made white lines on the timing belt with the punch mark on each of the camshaft sprockets and the crankshaft sprocket. Make sure all three sets of timing marks are properly aligned **(see illustration 8.12).**

Adjustment

21   Insert the tensioner into the side of the rear cover and tighten the bolts to the torque listed in this Chapter's Specifications.

22   Once the belt is in place, press the tensioner pulley toward the belt, remove the retaining pin from the tensioner and allow the plunger to extend against the pulley bracket - the tensioner will automatically apply the proper amount of tension to the belt.

23   Slowly turn the crankshaft clockwise two full revolutions, returning the number one piston to TDC on the compression stroke.

Caution: *If excessive resistance is felt while turning the crankshaft, it's an indication that the pistons are coming into contact with the valves. Go back over the procedure to correct the situation before proceeding.*

24   Make sure all the timing marks are still aligned properly **(see illustration 8.12).** Tighten the tensioner bolt to the torque listed in this Chapter's Specifications while keeping the tensioner steady with your hand.

25   Check the deflection of the timing belt by observing the force the tensioner pulley applies to the timing belt. If the belt seems loose, replace the tensioner spring.

26   Installation of the remaining components is the reverse of removal. Refer to the appropriate Sections.

9   Crankshaft front oil seal - replacement

Refer to illustrations 9.3, 9.4 and 9.6

1   Remove the crankshaft balancer (see Section 7).

2   On 4.0L engines, remove the timing belt and crankshaft sprocket (see Section 8).

3   Use a screwdriver or hook tool to carefully pry out the seal **(see illustration).**

Note: *Be careful not to damage the oil pump cover bore where the seal is seated or the nose and sealing surface of the crankshaft.*

4   Another procedure for removing the seal is to drill a small hole on each side of the seal and place a self-tapping screw in each hole **(see illustration).** Use these screws as a means of pulling the seal out without having to pry on it.

5   On 3.6L engines, if the seal is being replaced when the timing chain cover is removed, support the cover on top of two blocks of wood and drive the seal out from the backside with a hammer and punch.

Caution: *Be careful not to scratch, gouge or distort the area that the seal fits into or a leak will develop.*

6   Apply clean engine oil or multi-purpose grease to the outer edge of the new seal, then install it in the cover with the lip (spring side) facing IN. Drive the seal into place with a large socket and a hammer **(see illustration).** Make sure the seal enters the bore squarely and stop when the front face is at the proper depth.

Note: *If a large socket isn't available, a piece of pipe will also work.*

7   Check the surface on the balancer hub that the oil seal rides on. If the surface has been grooved from long-time contact with the seal, the balancer will need to be replaced.

8   Lubricate the balancer hub with clean engine oil and install the crankshaft balancer (see Section 7).

9   The remainder of installation is the reverse of the removal.

10   Timing cover, chain and sprockets (3.6L engines) - removal, inspection and installation

Warning: *Wait until the engine is completely cool before beginning this procedure.*

Caution: *The timing system is complex, and severe engine damage will occur if you make any mistakes. Do not attempt this procedure unless you are highly experienced with this type of repair. If you are at all unsure of your abilities, be sure to consult an expert. Double-check all your work and be sure everything is correct before you attempt to start the engine.*

Caution: *Do not rotate the crankshaft or camshafts separately during this procedure (with the timing chains removed), as damage to the valves may occur.*

Note: *Several special tools are required to complete these procedures, so read through the entire Section and obtain the special tools before beginning work.*

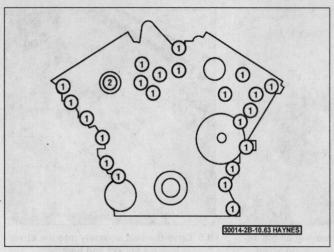

10.13 Timing chain cover bolt size and locations:

1   *M6 size bolts locations*   2   *M8 size bolt location*

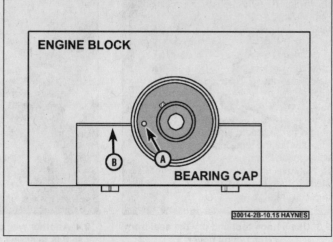

10.15 Align the dimple (A) on the crankshaft with the line (B) made where the engine block and bearing cap meets

Removal

Timing chain cover

Refer to illustration 10.13

1   Disconnect the cable from the negative terminal of the battery (see Chapter 5).

2   Drain the engine coolant (see Chapter 1).

3   Loosen the right-front wheel lug nuts. Raise the vehicle and support it securely on jackstands. Drain the engine oil (see Chapter 1).

4   Remove the right-front wheel and drivebelt splash shield (see Chapter 1).

5   Remove the drivebelt, drivebelt tensioner and idler pulley (see Chapter 1).

6   Remove the thermostat housing, upper radiator hose and disconnect the heater hose from the water pump (see Chapter 3).

7   Remove the heater core supply pipe fasteners from the rear cylinder head and move the pipe out of the way.

8   Remove the power steering pump and tie it out of the way with wire (see Chapter 10).

9   Remove the crankshaft balancer (see Section 7).

10   Remove the valve covers (see Section 4).

Caution: *Once the valve covers are removed, the magnetic timing wheels are exposed* **(see illustration 13.9)**. *The magnetic timing wheels on the camshafts must not come in contact with any type of magnet or magnetic field. If contact is made, the timing wheels will need to be replaced.*

11   Remove the upper and lower oil pans (see Section 15).

12   Once the oil pans are removed, temporarily install the engine mount crossmember and mount through-bolts. Place a floor jack under the engine (with a block of wood between the jack head and engine) and raise the engine slightly. Remove the right engine mount and bracket (see Section 20).

13   Remove the timing chain cover mounting bolts **(see illustration)**. There are seven indented prying points, one on top and three on each side; carefully pry the cover free of the engine block and cylinder heads. If it still sticks, slip a putty knife between the engine block and cover to break the bond (but be careful not to scratch the surfaces).

14   Once the cover is removed, discard the coolant housing and water pump gaskets from the back side of the timing chain cover.

Timing chain

Refer to illustrations 10.15 and 10.17

Warning: *When the timing chains are removed, do not rotate the camshafts or crankshaft; the valves and pistons can be damaged if contact is made.*

15   Temporarily install the crankshaft pulley bolt. Turn the crankshaft with the bolt to TDC number 1, on the exhaust stroke to align the timing marks on the crankshaft and camshaft sprockets. Rotate the engine clockwise only, until the mark on the crankshaft aligns with the line made where the engine block and bearing cap meets **(see illustration)**.

16   On the left (front) side camshaft phaser, the machined scribe lines should be facing away from each other, and the arrows should be pointing towards each other in a parallel line with the gasket surface of the cylinder head. On the right (rear) side camshaft phaser, the arrows should be facing away from each other and the machined scribe lines should be pointing towards each other in a parallel line with the gasket surface of the cylinder head **(see illustrations 13.10a and 13.10b)**. If, when you align the crankshaft mark with the bearing cap parting line, the camshaft marks are not in alignment as shown in **illustration 10.59**, rotate the engine one full revolution, realign the crankshaft mark, and verify that the camshaft marks are in proper alignment.

17   Verify the phaser marks are aligned with the plated links; if the plated links cannot be distinguished make sure there are 12 pins between the two marks **(see illustration)**.

Note: *Use paint or a permanent marker to mark the direction of rotation on all chains before removing them so they can be installed in the same direction.*

18   Starting with the right side chain tensioner, press the tensioner plunger in until special tool #8514 or a 3 mm Allen wrench

10.17 Verity that there are 12 pins between the mark on each phaser

can be inserted through both small holes in the top and bottom of the tensioner body, holding the plunger in the compressed position.

19   Working on the left side chain tensioner, locate the access hole on the side of the tensioner. Working through the hole, lift and hold the pawl off of the rack of the plunger in the tensioner. Press the plunger in until special tool #8514 or a 3 mm Allen wrench can be inserted through both small holes in the top and bottom of the tensioner body, holding the plunger in the compressed position.

20   Remove the timing gear splash shield fasteners, then remove the shield from the oil pump housing.

21   Remove the oil pump tensioner and sprocket (see Section 16), then remove the oil pump chain from the crankshaft gear.

Note: *The oil pump chain and sprocket do not have to be timed, but the chain should be marked to make sure it is installed in the same direction of rotation.*

22   Starting with the right side chain, slide camshaft phaser lock tool # 10202-1 from the front, between the two camshaft phasers, towards the chain (with the tool number facing up).

Note: *It may be necessary to rotate the intake camshaft a few degrees using a wrench on the camshaft flat when installing the phaser lock tool.*

23   Using a large wrench on the camshaft flats and a socket and ratchet on the oil control valves, loosen, but do not remove, the oil control valves.

24   Remove the right side camshaft phaser lock tool, then unscrew the intake camshaft oil control valve from the center of the phaser.

25   Slide the intake camshaft phaser off of the end of the camshaft, then remove the right side timing chain.

Note: *If necessary, remove the exhaust camshaft oil control valve from the center of the phaser and remove the phaser.*

26   Working on the left side chain, slide camshaft phaser lock tool # 10202-2 from the front, between the two camshaft phasers, towards the chain (with the tool number facing up).

Note: *It may be necessary to rotate the intake camshaft a few degrees using a wrench on the camshaft flat when installing the phaser lock tool.*

27   Using a large wrench on the camshaft flats and a socket and ratchet on oil control valves, loosen, but do not remove, the oil control valves

28   Remove the left side camshaft phaser lock tool, then unscrew the exhaust camshaft oil control valve from the center of the phaser.

29   Slide the exhaust camshaft phaser off of the end of the camshaft, then remove the left side timing chain.

Note: *If necessary, remove the intake camshaft oil control valve from the center of the phaser and remove the phaser.*

30   Locate the primary chain tensioner to the side of the crankshaft chain and press the tensioner plunger in until special tool #8514 or a 3 mm Allen wrench can be inserted through

the small hole in the side of the tensioner body, holding the plunger in the compressed position.

31   With the tensioner in the compressed position, remove the TORX (T30) mounting fasteners and the tensioner.

32   Remove the primary chain guide TORX (T30) mounting fasteners and the guide.

33   Remove the idler sprocket TORX (T45) mounting fastener and washer, then remove the idler sprocket, primary chain and crankshaft sprocket.

Note: *The chain should be marked to make sure it is installed in the same direction of rotation.*

34   If necessary, remove the chain tensioner (T30) fasteners and remove the tensioner(s), keeping the tensioners in the compressed position.

35   If necessary, remove the chain guide fasteners and guides for both chains.

Inspection

36   Inspect the timing chain dampener (guide) for cracks and wear and replace it, if necessary.

37   Clean the timing chain and sprockets with solvent and dry them with compressed air (if available).

Warning: *Wear eye protection when using compressed air.*

38   Inspect the components for wear and damage. Look for teeth that are deformed, chipped, pitted, and cracked.

39   The timing chain and sprockets should be replaced with new ones if the engine has high mileage, the chain has visible damage, or total freeplay midway between the sprockets exceeds one inch. Failure to replace a worn timing chain and sprockets may result in erratic engine performance, loss of power, and decreased fuel mileage. Loose chains can jump timing. In the worst case, chain jumping or breakage will result in severe engine damage.

Installation

Refer to illustrations 10.46 and 10.59

Caution: *Before starting the engine, carefully rotate the crankshaft by hand through at least two full revolutions (use a socket and breaker bar on the crankshaft pulley center bolt). If you feel any resistance, STOP! There is something wrong - most likely, valves are contacting the pistons. You must find the problem before proceeding. Check your work and see if any updated repair information is available.*

40   Use a plastic gasket scraper to remove all traces of old gasket material and sealant from the cover, engine block and cylinder heads. The cover is made of aluminum, so be careful not to nick or gouge it. Only clean the gasket sealing surfaces with rubbing alcohol (isopropyl) - do not use any oil based fluids.

41   If removed, install the chain guides and tensioners (still in the compressed position).

42   Make sure the keyway is installed on the crankshaft and the dimple on the crankshaft is aligned with the line made where the engine block and bearing cap meets (see illustra-

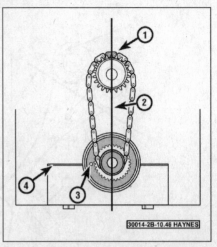

10.46 Primary chain alignment details;

1   *Primary chain plated link*
2   *12 o'clock position*
3   *Crankshaft dimple*
4   *Line formed where engine block and bearing cap meet*

tion 10.15 and 10.16).

43   Verify the camshafts are at TDC, with the alignment holes pointing up **(see illustration 13.34)**.

44   Place the primary chain on the crankshaft sprocket, with the plated link of the primary chain aligned with the arrow on the bottom of the sprocket. Insert the idler sprocket into the chain, aligning the other plated link with the machined mark of the idler sprocket.

45   Using clean engine oil, coat the sprockets and chain. Install the assembly while keeping the marks aligned, then install the idler sprocket mounting fastener finger tight.

46   Check the alignment of the marks; the plated link on the idler sprocket should be on top (12 o'clock) and the machined mark on the crankshaft should be aligned with the line made where the engine block and bearing cap meet **(see illustration)**. If the marks are all aligned, tighten the idler sprocket fastener to the torque listed in this Chapter's Specifications.

47   Install the primary chain guide and tensioner, then tighten the fasteners to the torque listed in this Chapter's Specifications. Remove the special tool from the tensioner plunger.

48   Starting with the left side chain, install the intake camshaft phaser and oil control valve, then tighten the valve finger tight, if removed.

49   Place the left side chain over the intake phaser and around the inside cogs of the idler sprocket so that the plate link of the chain is aligned with the machined arrow on the sprocket.

50   With the chain aligned at the idler sprocket, install the exhaust camshaft phaser so that the arrows are pointing towards each other and in a parallel line with the cylinder head gasket surface **(see illustration 13.10a)**, then install the oil control valve finger tight.

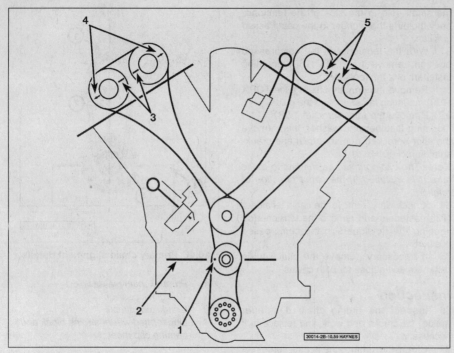

10.59 Timing mark alignment details

1   *Dimple on crankshaft*
2   *Junction of main bearing cap and cylinder block*
3   *Lines on rear bank cam phasers - must be pointing toward each other and parallel with cylinder head*

4   *Arrows on rear bank cam phasers - must be pointing away from each other*
5   *Arrows on front bank cam phasers - must be pointing toward each other*

51   Slide camshaft phaser lock tool # 10202-2 from the front, between the two camshaft phasers towards the chain with the tool number facing up.

52   Using a large wrench on the camshaft flats and a socket and ratchet on the oil control valves, tighten both valves to the torque listed in this Chapter's Specifications.

53   Working on the right side (rear bank) chain, install the exhaust camshaft phaser and oil control valve, tightening the valve finger tight, if removed.

54   Place the right side chain over the intake phaser and around the outside cogs of the idler sprocket so that the plate link of the chain is aligned with the machined circle on the sprocket.

55   With the chain aligned at the idler sprocket, install the intake camshaft phaser so that the machined lines are pointing towards each other and in a parallel line with the gasket surface of the cylinder head **(see illustration 13.10b),** then install the oil control valve finger tight.

56   Slide camshaft phaser lock tool # 10202-1 from the front, between the two camshaft phasers, towards the chain (with the tool number facing up).

57   Using a large wrench on the camshaft flats and a socket and ratchet on the oil control valves, tighten both valves to the torque listed in this Chapter's Specifications.

58   Install the oil pump timing chain, tensioner, sprocket and splash shield (see Section 16).

Note: *There are no timing or timing marks on the oil pump chain or sprocket.*

59   Verify all the marks are aligned **(see illustration),** then remove the special tool or Allen wrenches from the primary and secondary tensioners. Also remove the camshaft phaser lock tools.

60   Rotate the engine two complete turns using the machined mark on the crankshaft with the line made where the engine block and bearing caps meet as the reference. Verify all the marks are aligned and there are 12 pins between the phaser marks **(see illustration 10.17);** if the marks are off, rotate the engine two more complete turns and check again.

61   Once the timing marks are correct, install the new coolant housing and water pump housing gaskets into the grooves on the back side of the timing cover

62   Apply a 1/8-inch wide by 1/16-inch high, bead of RTV sealant to the sealing surface of the cover, then install the cover on the alignment dowels.

63   Install the cover bolts **(see illustration 10.13)** and tighten them in a criss-cross pattern, in three steps, to the torque listed in this Chapter's Specifications.

64   Installation of the remaining components is the reverse of removal.

65   Add oil and coolant (see Chapter 1), start the engine and check for leaks.

11 Camshaft oil seal (4.0L engines) - replacement

Refer to illustrations 11.8, 11.12a, 11.12b and 11.12c

1   Disconnect the cable from the negative terminal of the battery (see Chapter 5).

2   Remove the drivebelts (see Chapter 1), and the crankshaft balancer (see Section 7).

3   Rotate the engine to TDC (see Section 3) and remove the timing belt (see Section 8).

4   Remove the valve covers (see Section 4).

5   Remove the rocker arm assembly (see Section 12).

6   Place a wrench onto the flats on the timing belt sprocket, then use a ratchet and socket to remove the camshaft sprocket bolt and sprocket.

Note: *Don't mix up the camshaft sprockets. They must be installed on the same camshaft they were removed from.*

7   If you're working on the front cylinder head, drain the cooling system (see Chapter 1).

8   If you're working on the front cylinder head, remove the rear timing cover fasteners and timing cover **(see illustration).** Discard

11.8 Rear timing belt cover fastener locations; the bolts letter coded for are type and size

A   *M8 bolts (apply thread sealant)*
B   *M10 bolts*
C   *M6 bolts*
D   *M10 stud/nut*

11.12a Fabricate a seal installation tool from a piece of pipe and a large washer . . .

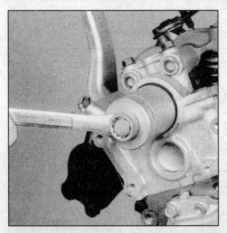

11.12b . . . and press a new seal into place with a section of pipe and a bolt of the proper size and thread pitch (don't let the camshaft turn as the bolt is tightened)

11.12c As a last resort, you can also drive a cam seal into place with a hammer and a large socket, but make sure you don't damage the sprocket positioning pin on the end of the camshaft

the O-ring seals. Note the various type and sizes of bolts by making a diagram or taking careful notes while the timing belt cover is being removed. The bolts must be reinstalled in their original locations.

9   Remove the camshaft thrust plate fasteners and remove the thrust plate from the rear of the cylinder head.

10   Carefully slide the camshaft out of the cylinder (towards the rear) about 3 to 4 inches.

11   Using a small screwdriver or punch, drive the seal out of the cylinder from the back side.

12   There are several ways to install the new seal. Fabricate a seal installation tool **(see illustrations)** or use a very large socket with an inside diameter large enough to clear the nose of the camshaft and carefully drive the seal into place **(see illustration)**. Remove the sprocket positioning pin from the nose of the cam, if necessary, to prevent damaging the pin.

13   Install the pulley onto the camshaft and hold the pulley with a large wrench, tightening the bolt to the torque in this Chapter's Specifications.

14   Installation of the remaining components is the reverse of removal.

---

12   Rocker arms and hydraulic valve lash adjusters (4.0L engines) - removal, inspection and installation

---

Note: *On 3.6L engines, the camshaft must be removed to access the rocker arms and lash adjusters; see Section 13 for removal and installation.*

1   A noisy lash adjuster can be isolated when the engine is idling. Hold a mechanic's stethoscope or a length of hose near each valve while listening at the other end.

2   The most likely causes of noisy valve lifters are dirt trapped inside the lifter and lack of oil flow, viscosity, or pressure. Before

condemning the lifters, check the oil for fuel contamination, correct level, cleanliness, and correct viscosity.

Note: *To prevent possible damage and keep air from entering the lash adjuster, keep the rocker arm assembly upright, keep the parts in order and do not allow the assembly to rest on the lash adjusters.*

Removal

3   Remove the valve covers (see Section 4) and mark the rocker arms with paint or a marker to aid installation.

4   Remove the rocker arm bolts in the reverse of the tightening sequence **(see illustration 12.15)**.

Disassembly

Refer to illustration 12.6

5   Identify the intake and exhaust rocker arms, as they are different.

6   To remove the rocker arm shafts, the dowel pins must be pulled from the shaft supports. Use a 4 mm screw with a nut threaded to the top of the screw, a washer followed by a spacer, and

thread this assembly into the pin, then loosen the nut on the screw to pull the pin out **(see illustration)**. Once the pins are removed, they must be replaced.

7   Remove the rocker shaft.

Note: *The identification notches face towards the front of the engine on the front head, and toward the back of the engine on the rear head.*

Inspection

8   Check the rocker arms for scuffing or wear on the rollers and shaft.

9   Check that the swivel pad on the lash adjuster is in place and is not broken.

10   Replace the assembly if any rocker arm shows signs of wear.

Assembly

11   Position the shafts with the notches facing up before installing the rocker arms and pedestals onto the shafts.

12   Press the new dowel pins through the pedestals until they bottom out against the rocker shaft.

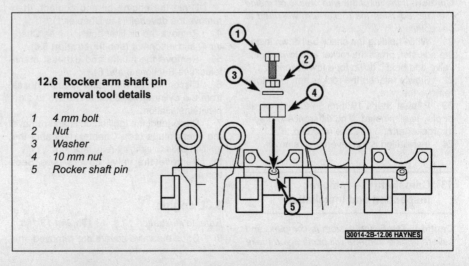

12.6 Rocker arm shaft pin removal tool details

1   4 mm bolt
2   Nut
3   Washer
4   10 mm nut
5   Rocker shaft pin

30014-2B-12.06 HAYNES

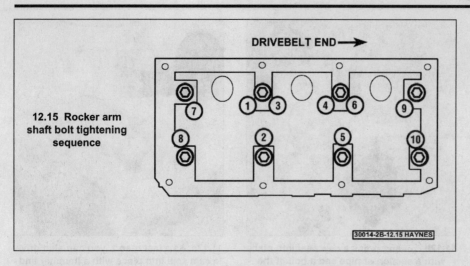

12.15 Rocker arm shaft bolt tightening sequence

DRIVEBELT END ➝

30014-2B-12.15 HAYNES

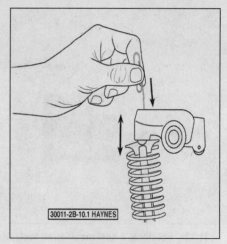

30011-2B-10.1 HAYNES

12.20 When bleeding the lash adjuster, make sure the corresponding camshaft lobe is pointing away from the rocker arm (closed valve)

Installation

Refer to illustration 12.15

13   Rotate camshaft gears clockwise until the number one cylinder intake valves start to open.

14   Install the rocker arm shaft assembly with the mark facing towards the front of the engine for the front head, and towards the back of the engine for the rear head.

15   Tighten the assembly bolts in sequence **(see illustration)** to the torque listed in this Chapter's Specifications.

16   Install the valve covers (see Section 4).

Bleeding

Refer to illustration 12.20

Note: *Use this procedure to manually bleed air from a lash adjuster.*

17   Start and run the engine until it reaches normal operating temperature.

18   Remove the valve cover (see Section 4).

19   Rotate the engine until the rocker arm in question is on the low side of the camshaft lobe.

20   Insert a small wire through the air bleed hole in the rocker arm while lightly pushing the check ball down **(see illustration)**; there will be one for the intake rockers, and two for exhaust rockers.

Caution: *If the tip of the wire breaks off inside the lash adjuster, the rocker arm will need to be replaced.*

21   While holding the check ball down inside the adjuster, press the rocker arm towards the valve and hold it down for a few seconds.

22   Slowly release the rocker arm first, then remove the wire.

23   Repeat Steps 19 through 22 until all air or play is eliminated. If no difference is made, the rocker arm(s) must be replaced.

24   Installation is the reverse of removal.

13   Camshaft(s) – removal, inspection and installation

Caution: *The timing system is complex, and severe engine damage will occur if you make*

any mistakes. Do not attempt this procedure unless you are highly experienced with this type of repair. If you are at all unsure of your abilities, be sure to consult an expert. Double-check all your work and be sure everything is correct before you attempt to start the engine.

Caution: *Once the valve covers are removed, the magnetic timing wheels are exposed. The magnetic timing wheels on the camshafts must not come in contact with any type of magnet or magnetic field. If contact is made, the timing wheels will need to be replaced.*

Note: *On 3.6L engines, the timing chain for each camshaft can be removed from the camshafts individually, without removing all the timing chains, using the tools outlined in this Section. If the tools are not available, the timing chain cover and all chains will need to be removed before the camshafts can be removed (see Section 10).*

Removal

1   Disconnect the cable from the negative terminal of the battery (see Chapter 5).

2   Loosen the lug nuts on the right front wheel, raise the front of the vehicle and support it securely on jackstands. Remove the right front wheel and the drivebelt splash shield.

3   Drain the engine oil and coolant, then remove the drivebelt (see Chapter 1).

4   Remove the air filter housing (see Chapter 4) and resonator **(see illustration 5.6)**.

5   Remove the intake and exhaust manifolds (see Sections 5 and 6).

6   Disconnect all wires and vacuum hoses from the cylinder heads. Label them to simplify reinstallation.

7   Disconnect the ignition coils and remove the spark plugs (see Chapter 1). Label the ignition coils to simplify reinstallation.

8   Remove the valve covers (see Section 4).

3.6L engine

Refer to illustration 13.9, 13.10a and 13.10b

9   Once the valve covers are removed, the

magnetic timing wheels are exposed **(see illustration)**. The magnetic timing wheels on the camshafts must not come in contact with any type of magnet or magnetic field. If contact is made, the timing wheels will need to be replaced.

10   Rotate the crankshaft clockwise and place the #1 piston at TDC on the exhaust stroke. On the left (front) side camshaft phaser the machined scribe lines should be facing away from each other, and the arrows should be pointing towards each other in a parallel line with the gasket surface of the cylinder head. On the right (rear) side camshaft phaser, the arrows should be facing away from each other, and the machined scribe lines should be pointing towards each other in a parallel line with the gaskets surface of the cylinder head **(see illustrations)**.

11   Using a permanent marker or paint, mark the camshaft phasers to the timing chains for reinstallation.

12   Working from the top of the timing chain cover, insert special tool #10200-3 down the

13.9 Location of the magnetic timing wheels – 3.6L engines

13.10a With the engine at TDC #1, the left (front) camshaft phaser scribe marks (A) should be pointing away from each other, the arrow marks (B) should be pointing towards each other in a straight line and that line should be parallel with the cylinder head surface . . .

13.10b The right (rear) phaser scribe marks should be pointing towards each other in a straight line (and that line should be parallel with the cylinder head surface)

side of the tensioner to the access hole on the side of the tensioner. Working through the small hole in the side of the tensioner, lift and hold the pawl off of the rack of the plunger in the tensioner. Slide the chain holding tool #10200-1 between the cylinder head and the back side of the chain against the chain guide forcing the rack and plunger back into the tensioner body.

Caution: *The chain holding tool must remain in place while the phasers are removed or the timing chain will fall off of into the timing cover.*

13 Slide camshaft phaser lock tool # 10202-1 (right side) or 10202-2 (left side), from the front, between the two camshaft phasers, towards the chain.

Note: *It may be necessary to rotate the intake camshaft a few degrees using a wrench on the camshaft flat when installing the phaser lock tool.*

14 Using a large wrench on the camshaft flats and a socket and ratchet on the oil control valves, loosen, then remove each of the oil control valves from the phaser end of the camshaft.

15 At the same time, carefully slide both the intake and exhaust phaser (with the phaser lock securely between them) forward until they are off the end of the camshafts.

Caution: *Do not remove the phaser lock or try to disassemble the phasers.*

16 Using the alignment holes in the camshaft as a reference point, slowly rotate both camshafts counterclockwise approximately 30-degrees Before Top-Dead-Center (BTDC). In this position the camshafts are in a neutral or no load position.

Note: *The camshaft bearing caps are marked with a number and letter code; "1I" is for the number one Intake camshaft bearing cap. The notch on the caps should always be installed towards the front.*

17 Loosen the camshaft bearing cap bolts in the reverse order of the tightening sequence **(see illustration 13.34).**

18 Remove the camshaft bearing caps and carefully lift the camshafts from the cylinder head.

19 With the camshafts removed, mark the rocker arms and so they can be installed in the same locations then remove the rockers arms.

20 Mark the hydraulic lash adjusters so they can be installed in the same locations, then remove them from the cylinder head.

4.0L engine

21 Remove the cylinder heads (see Section 14).

22 Remove the rocker arm shaft assembly (see Section 12).

23 Place a wrench onto the flats on the timing belt sprocket, then use a ratchet and socket to remove the camshaft sprocket bolt and slide the sprocket from the end of the camshaft.

Note: *Don't mix up the camshaft sprockets. They must be installed on the same camshaft they were removed from.*

24 Remove the camshaft thrust plate fasteners and remove the thrust plate from the rear of the cylinder head.

25 Carefully slide the camshaft out of the cylinder.

Inspection

Refer to illustration 13.27

26 Check the camshaft bearing surfaces for pitting, score marks, galling, and abnormal wear. If the bearing surfaces are damaged, the cylinder head will have to be replaced.

27 Compare the camshaft lobe height by measuring each lobe with a micrometer **(see illustration).** Measure each of the intake lobes and record the measurements and relative positions. Then measure each of the exhaust lobes and record the measurements and relative positions also. This will let you compare all of the intake lobes to one

another and all of the exhaust lobes to one another. If the difference between the lobes exceeds 0.005 inch, the camshaft should be replaced. Do not compare intake lobe heights to exhaust lobe heights as lobe lift may be different. Only compare intake lobes to intake lobes and exhaust lobes to exhaust lobes for this comparison.

28 Check the rocker arms and shafts for abnormal wear, pits, galling, score marks, and rough spots. Don't attempt to restore rocker arms by grinding the pad surfaces. Replace defective parts.

Installation

Caution: *Before starting the engine, carefully rotate the crankshaft by hand through at least two full revolutions (use a socket and breaker bar on the crankshaft pulley center bolt). If you feel any resistance, STOP! There is something wrong - most likely, valves are contacting the pistons. You must find the problem before proceeding. Check your work and see if any updated repair information is available.*

13.27 Use a micrometer to measure cam lobe height

13.33 Camshaft bearing cap tightening sequence 3.6L engines – left (front) side shown, right side is identical

13.34 Locate the alignment holes on the camshafts and make sure they are in the neutral position (pointing straight up) – right (rear) side shown, left side is identical

3.6L engine

Refer to illustrations 13.33 and 13.34

29   Dip the hydraulic lash adjusters in clean engine oil and install them into their original locations.

30   Apply moly-base grease or engine assembly lube to the rocker arm contact points and rollers and install them into their original locations.

31   Lubricate the camshaft bearing journals and lobes with moly-base grease or engine assembly lube, then install them carefully in the cylinder head about 30-degrees before (counterclockwise of) TDC. Don't scratch the bearing surfaces with the cam lobes!

Caution: *Do not rotate the camshafts more than a few degrees to prevent the valves from contacting the pistons.*

32   Install the camshaft bearing caps, then install the mounting bolts and finger tighten them.

33   Tighten the bearing caps in sequence **(see illustration)** to the torque listed in this Chapter's Specifications.

34   Rotate the camshafts clockwise 30-degrees, verify the alignment holes in the camshafts are at 12 o'clock (pointing straight up) or neutral position **(see illustration)**.

35   Carefully slide both the intake and exhaust phaser (with the phaser lock tool securely between them) onto the camshafts and verify the marks are aligned.

36   Install the oil control valves onto the camshaft phasers and install the bolts, then tighten the bolts to the torque listed in this Chapter's Specifications. Remove the chain holding tool and release the tensioner plunger.

Caution: *Make sure to prevent the camshafts from turning by holding the camshaft with a large wrench on the camshaft flats.*

37   Slowly rotate the engine two complete turns (360-degrees) and verify the alignment marks are correct **(see illustrations 13.10a and 13.10b)**.

38   The remainder installation is the reverse of removal

4.0L engine

39   Lubricate the camshaft bearing journals and lobes with moly-base grease or engine assembly lube, then install them carefully in the cylinder head. Don't scratch the bearing surfaces with the cam lobes!

40   Install a new thrust plate gasket and thrust plate. Install the bolts then tighten them to the torque listed in this Chapter's Specifications.

41   Make sure the mark on the crankshaft sprocket is still aligned with its mark on the oil pump. Slide the camshaft sprockets onto the camshafts and align the marks on the sprockets with their corresponding marks on the cylinder heads. Install the bolts and tighten them to the torque listed in this Chapter's Specifications.

42   Install the timing belt (see Section 8).

43   Installation of the remaining components is the reverse of removal.

14   Cylinder heads - removal and installation

Warning: *Wait until the engine is completely cool before beginning this procedure.*

Removal

1   Disconnect the cable from the negative terminal of the battery (see Chapter 5).

2   Loosen the lug nuts on the right front wheel, raise the front of the vehicle and support it securely on jackstands. Remove the right front wheel and the drivebelt splash shield.

3   Drain the engine oil and coolant, then remove the drivebelt (see Chapter 1).

4   Remove the air filter housing and resonator (see Chapter 4).

5   Remove the intake manifolds (see Section 5).

6   Disconnect all wires and vacuum hoses from the cylinder heads. Label them to simplify reinstallation.

7   Disconnect the ignition coils and remove

the spark plugs (see Chapter 1).

8   On 4.0L engines, remove the exhaust manifold, if equipped (see Section 6). On 3.6L engines, remove the catalytic converter(s) (see Chapter 6).

9   Remove the valve covers (see Section 4).

3.6L engines

10   Remove the crankshaft balancer (see Section 7).

11   Remove the oil pans (see Section 15).

12   If you're working on the front cylinder head:

   a) *Remove the alternator (see Chapter 5).*
   b) *Remove the oil dipstick tube fastener and remove the tube from the oil pan.*
   c) *Remove the a/c compressor (see Chapter 3).*
   d) *Disconnect the main engine harness connectors at the rear of the cylinder and move the harness and retainers out of the way.*

13   If you're working on the rear cylinder head;

   a) *Remove the power steering pump (see Chapter 10).*
   b) *Remove the heater core tube fasteners and move the tube away from the cylinder head.*

14   Remove the timing chain cover (see Section 10).

15   Rotate the crankshaft clockwise and place the #1 piston at TDC on the exhaust stroke. When the crankshaft is at TDC, the dimple on the crankshaft will be in line with the line made where the bearing cap meets the engine block. The front cylinder bank cam phaser arrows should be pointing toward each other and be parallel with where the cylinder head and valve cover meets. The rear side cam phaser arrows should point away from each other and the lines on the phasers should be pointing towards each other **(see illustration 10.59)**.

16   Remove the timing chain for the cylinder head or, if both cylinder heads are being

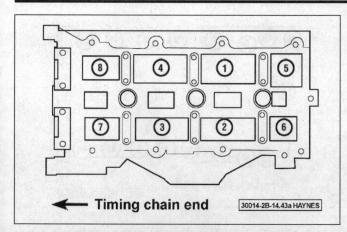

14.43a Left (front) side cylinder head bolt TIGHTENING sequence – 3.6L engines

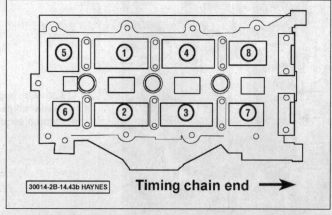

14.43b Right (rear) side cylinder head bolt TIGHTENING sequence – 3.6L engines

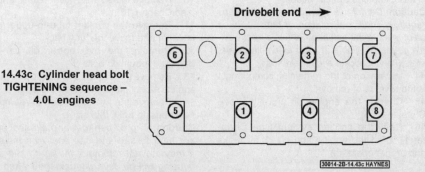

14.43c Cylinder head bolt TIGHTENING sequence – 4.0L engines

removed, remove both chains (see Section 10).

17 Remove the oil control valves from the cam phasers (sprockets) (see Section 13).

18 Remove the timing chain tensioner and chain guides (see Section 10).

19 Remove the camshafts, rocker arms and lash adjusters (see Section 13).

Caution: *Once the valve covers are removed the magnetic timing wheels are exposed. The magnetic timing wheels on the camshafts must not come in contact with any type of magnet or magnetic field. If contact is made the timing wheels will need to be replaced (see Section 13).*

Note: *Keep the rocker arms and lash adjusters in order so that they can be installed in their original locations.*

20 Loosen the cylinder head bolts in the reverse order of the tightening sequence **(see illustrations 14.43a and 14.43b)**.

21 Lift the cylinder head off the block. If resistance is felt, dislodge the cylinder head by striking it with a wood block and hammer. If prying is required, pry only on a casting protrusion - be very careful not to damage the cylinder head or block!

Caution: *Do not set the cylinder head on its gasket side; the sealing surface can be easily damaged.*

22 Have the cylinder head inspected and serviced by a qualified automotive machine shop.

4.0L engines

23 Remove the drivebelt tensioner and idler pulley (see Chapter 1).

24 Remove the power steering pump (see Chapter 10).

25 Remove the exhaust manifolds (see Section 6).

26 Place a floor jack under the engine (with a wood block between the jack head and oil pan) and raise the engine slightly to relieve the weight from the mounts.

27 Remove the right engine mount fasteners and the mount (see Section 20).

28 Remove the timing belt covers, rotate the engine to TDC and verify the timing marks are aligned **(see illustration 8.12)**, then remove

the timing belt (see Section 8).

29 Remove the EGR valve (see Chapter 12).

30 Place a wrench onto the flats on the timing belt sprocket, then use a ratchet and socket to remove the camshaft sprocket bolt and sprocket.

Note: *Don't mix up the camshaft sprockets. They must be installed in their original locations.*

31 Remove the camshaft thrust plate fasteners and remove the thrust plate from the rear of the cylinder head.

32 Carefully slide the camshaft out of the cylinder (towards the rear) about 3 to 4 inches and remove the rear timing cover-to-cylinder head bolts.

33 Loosen the cylinder head bolts in the reverse order of the tightening sequence **(see illustration 14.43c)**.

Note: *When removing the rear cylinder head, the front four cylinder head bolts can't be completely removed until after the cylinder head is removed. Loosen the bolts and raise them up, then keep them in that position using rubber bands or mechanic's wire.*

34 Lift the cylinder head off the block.

35 If resistance is felt, dislodge the cylinder head by striking it with a wood block and hammer. If prying is required, pry only on a casting protrusion - be very careful not to damage the cylinder head or block!

36 Have the cylinder head inspected and serviced by a qualified automotive machine shop.

Installation

Refer to illustrations 14.43a, 14.43b and 14.43c

37 The mating surfaces of each cylinder head and the engine block must be perfectly clean when the cylinder head is installed.

38 Carefully use a gasket scraper to remove all traces of carbon and old gasket material, then clean the mating surfaces with brake system cleaner. If there's oil on the mating surfaces when the cylinder head is installed, the gasket may not seal correctly and leaks may develop.

39 When working on the engine block, it's a good idea to cover the lifter valley with shop rags to keep debris out of the engine. Use a shop rag or vacuum cleaner to remove any debris that falls into the cylinders.

40 Check the engine block and cylinder head mating surfaces for nicks, deep scratches, and other damage. If damage is slight, it can be removed with a file; if it's excessive, machining may be the only alternative.

41 Position the new gasket over the dowel pins in the engine block. Some gaskets are marked TOP or FRONT to ensure correct installation.

42 Carefully position the cylinder head on the engine block without disturbing the gasket.

43 Install NEW cylinder head bolts and tighten them in the recommended sequence **(see illustrations)** to the torque steps listed

**15.5 Lower oil pan fastener locations –
3.6L engine**

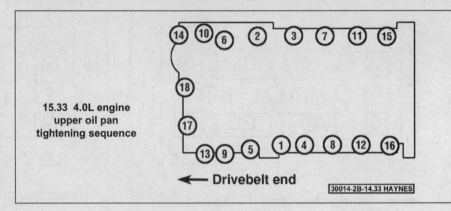

**15.33 4.0L engine
upper oil pan
tightening sequence**

← Drivebelt end

30014-2B-14.33 HAYNES

in this Chapter's Specifications.
Caution: *Do not use a torque wrench for steps requiring additional rotation or turns; apply a paint mark to the bolt head or use a torque-angle gauge (available at most automotive parts stores) and a socket and breaker bar.*
44   Installation of the remaining components is the reverse of removal.
45   Change the engine oil and filter (see Chapter 1).
46   Refill the cooling system (see Chapter 1). Start the engine and check for leaks and proper operation.

15   Oil pan - removal and installation

Removal

1   Disconnect the cable from the negative terminal of the battery (see Chapter 5).
2   Raise the front of the vehicle and support it securely on jackstands. Apply the parking brake and block the rear wheels to keep it from rolling off the stands.
3   Drain the engine oil (see Chapter 1).
4   Remove the lower splash shield fasteners and remove the splash shield.

3.6L engines

Lower oil pan

Refer to illustration 15.5

5   Remove the bolts and nuts, then carefully separate the lower oil pan from the upper oil pan **(see illustration)**. Don't pry between the upper pan and the lower pan or damage to the sealing surfaces could occur and oil leaks may develop. Tap the pan with a soft-face hammer to break the gasket seal. If it still sticks, slip a putty knife between the upper pan and lower pan to break the bond (but be careful not to scratch the surfaces).

Upper oil pan

6   Remove the dipstick tube bracket mounting bolt. Using a twisting motion, pull the dipstick tube out of the upper oil pan.
7   Remove the right side driveaxle (see Chapter 8).

8   Remove the lower oil pan (see Step 5).
9   Disconnect the exhaust crossunder pipe flange fasteners and remove the crossunder pipe.
10   Remove the engine mount crossmember (see Chapter 10).
11   Remove the coolant tube-to-upper pan fastener and move the tube back.
12   Remove the five upper oil pan-to-transaxle mounting bolts.
13   Remove the torque converter access plate, and the rubber plugs just below the plate.
14   Remove the two upper pan-to-rear main seal housing bolts (M6 size).
Caution: *The oil pan-to-rear main seal bolts are hard to see and can easily be missed. If they are not removed, the rear main seal housing will be severely damaged when the pan is lowered.*
15   Remove the nineteen upper oil pan bolts (M8 size) around the perimeter of the pan, then carefully separate the oil pan from the engine block. Use the two indented prying points on each side of the oil pan to carefully pry the pan free of the engine block. If it still sticks, slip a putty knife between the engine block and oil pan to break the bond (but be careful not to scratch the surfaces).

4.0L engines

Note: *4.0L engines use only one oil pan.*
16   Remove the dipstick tube bracket mounting bolt. Using a twisting motion, pull the dipstick tube out of the upper oil pan.
17   Disconnect the exhaust crossunder pipe flange fasteners and remove the crossunder pipe. Once the crossunder pipe is removed, remove the bracket fasteners and brackets.
18   Remove the front cylinder exhaust manifold/converter (see Section 6).
19   Remove the torque converter access plate fastener and remove the plate.
20   Remove the oil filter housing support bolt from the front of the pan then remove the oil cooler (see Section 17).
21   Remove the oil pan bolts around the perimeter of the pan, carefully separate the oil pan from the engine block and remove the gasket.

Installation

22   Clean the pan(s) with solvent and remove all old sealant and gasket material from the engine block and pan mating sur-

faces. Clean the mating surfaces with lacquer thinner or acetone and make sure the bolt holes in the engine block are clear. Check the oil pan flange(s) for distortion, particularly around the bolt holes. If necessary, place the pan(s) on a wood block and use a hammer to flatten and restore the gasket surface.

3.6L engines

Upper oil pan

23   Apply a 1/8-inch wide by 1/16-inch high bead of RTV sealant to the sealing surface of the pan. Install the upper pan and the bolts, then tighten the bolts finger-tight.
24   Tighten the upper pan-to-transaxle bolts first to the torque listed in this Chapter's Specifications.
25   Tighten the remaining bolts in a circular pattern, starting from the middle working your way outwards, to the torque listed in this Chapter's Specifications.
26   Installation of the remaining components is the reverse of removal.
27   Refill the engine with oil (see Chapter 1), Start and run the engine until normal operating temperature is reached, then check for leaks.

Lower oil pan

28   Apply a 1/8-inch wide by 1/16-inch high bead of RTV sealant to the sealing surface of the pan. Install the lower pan to the upper pan and the bolts. Then tighten the bolts in a circular pattern, starting from the middle working your way outwards, to the torque listed in this Chapter's Specifications.
29   Installation of the remaining components is the reverse of removal.
30   Refill the engine with oil (see Chapter 1). Start and run the engine until normal operating temperature is reached, then check for leaks.

4.0L engines

Refer to illustration 15.33

31   Apply a bead of RTV sealant to the line between the engine block, oil pump housing and the rear main oil seal retainer. Install a new gasket on the oil pan flange.
32   Place the oil pan in position on the engine block and install the bolts.
33   Tighten the bolts in sequence **(see illustration)** to the torque listed in this Chapter's Specifications.

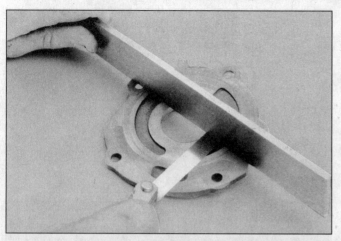

16.20 Place a straightedge across the oil pump cover and check it for warpage with a feeler gauge

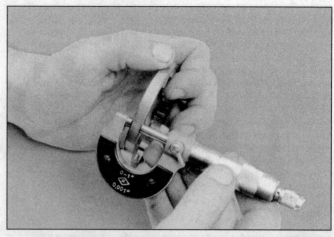

16.21 Use a micrometer to measure the thickness of the outer rotor

34   Installation of the remaining components is the reverse of removal.
35   Refill the engine with oil (see Chapter 1),. Start and run the engine until normal operating temperature is reached, then check for leaks.

16   Oil pump - removal, inspection and installation

Removal

1   Disconnect the cable from the negative terminal of the battery (see Chapter 5).
2   Raise the front of the vehicle and support it securely on jackstands. Apply the parking brake and block the rear wheels to keep it from rolling off the stands.
3   Drain the engine oil (see Chapter 1).
4   Remove the lower splash shield fasteners and remove the splash shield.

3.6L engines

5   Remove the lower and upper oil pans (see Section 15).
6   Remove the oil pump pick-up tube fastener, and remove the tube from the pump. Discard the pick-up tube O-ring.
7   Disconnect the oil pump solenoid electrical connector from the side of the engine.
8   Working from the side of the block, depress the oil pump solenoid electrical connector locking tab and push the connector into the block.
Note: *The connector will have to be maneuvered around the tensioner mounting bolt.*
9   Remove the oil pump timing gear splash shield bolts and remove the splash shield.
10   Press the oil pump chain tensioner away from the chain until a 3 mm Allen wrench can be inserted into the housing to hold the tensioner back.
11   Using a permanent marker or paint, make reference marks on the chain and oil pump gear.
12   Hold the oil pump gear from moving, then remove the T45 Torx mounting bolt and

16.23 Check the outer rotor-to-housing clearance with a feeler gauge

the oil pump gear.
13   Hold the tensioner and remove the Allen wrench, allowing the tensioner to release. Remove the spring from the dowel pin and slide the tensioner from the oil pump.
14   Remove the oil pump mounting bolts and remove the pump.

4.0L engines

15   Drain the cooling system (see Chapter 1).
16   Remove the oil pan (see Section 15).
17   Remove the timing belt and crankshaft sprocket (see Section 8).
18   Remove the pick-up tube, then remove the oil pump mounting bolts and the oil pump. Discard the pick-up tube O-ring.

Inspection

Refer to illustrations 16.20, 16.21, 16.23, 16.24 and 16.25
Note: *The oil pump on 3.6L engines is not serviceable; if there is a problem, the pump assembly must be replaced.*
19   Clean all parts thoroughly in solvent and carefully inspect the rotors, pump cover, and timing chain cover for nicks, scratches, or

16.24 Check the clearance between the lobes of the inner and outer rotors

burrs. Replace the assembly if it is damaged.
20   Use a straightedge and a feeler gauge to measure the oil pump cover for warpage **(see illustration)**. If it's warped more than the limit listed in this Chapter's Specifications, the pump should be replaced.
21   Measure the thickness of the outer rotor **(see illustration)**. If the thickness is less than the value listed in this Chapter's Specifications, the pump should be replaced.
22   Measure the thickness of the inner rotor. If the thickness is less than the value listed in this Chapter's Specifications, the pump should be replaced.
23   Insert the outer rotor into the oil pump housing and measure the clearance between the rotor and housing **(see illustration)**. If the measurement is more than the maximum allowable clearance listed in this Chapter's Specifications, the pump should be replaced.
24   Install the inner rotor in the oil pump assembly and measure the clearance between the lobes on the inner and outer rotors **(see illustration)**. If the clearance is more than the value listed in this Chapter's Specifications, the pump should be replaced.

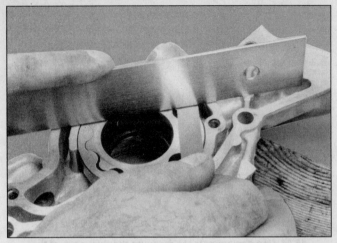

16.25 Using a straightedge and feeler gauge, check the clearance between the surface of the oil pump cover and the rotors

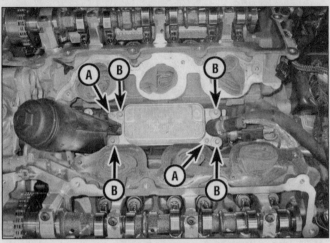

17.4 Remove the oil cooler mounting screws (A) then remove the mounting bolts (B) and cooler

25 Place a straightedge across the face of the oil pump assembly **(see illustration)**. If the clearance between the pump surface and the rotors is greater than the limit listed in this Chapter's Specifications, the pump should be replaced.

Installation

3.6L engines

26 Place the oil pump onto the engine block using the aligning dowels. Install the mounting bolts and tighten them to the torque listed in this Chapter's Specifications.
27 Slide the oil pump chain tensioner onto the pivot, then push the tensioner back against the spring. Insert a 3 mm Allen wrench into the tensioner to hold it in place.
28 Place the oil pump timing chain gear into the chain, center it onto the oil pump shaft and install the T45 mounting bolt. Tighten the bolt to the torque listed in this Chapter's Specifications.
Note: *Make sure the gear is facing the same way as when it was removed (see Step 11). There are no timing marks on the pump gear or chain, and no timing is necessary.*
29 Maneuver the oil pump solenoid into position and insert it through the block opening until it snaps in place.
30 Install the timing gear splash shield and bolts, then tighten the bolts to the torque listed in this Chapter's Specifications.
31 Installation of the remaining components is the reverse of removal.
32 Refill the engine with oil and change the oil filter (see Chapter 1).

4.0L engines

33 Install the pump cover then coat the cover bolts with thread sealer and tighten the bolts to the torque listed in this Chapter's Specifications.
Note: *Only apply thread sealer to the first 1/4-inch of cover bolt threads.*
34 Install the pump and tighten the bolts to the torque listed in this Chapter's Specifications.

35 Place a new O-ring seal onto the pick-up tube and install the tube.
36 Install the timing belt and crankshaft sprocket (see Section 8).
37 Installation of the remaining components is the reverse of removal.
38 Refill the engine with oil and change the oil filter (see Chapter 1).

17 Oil cooler - removal and installation

Warning: *Wait until the engine is completely cool before beginning this procedure.*

Removal

1 Disconnect the cable from the negative terminal of the battery (see Chapter 5).
2 Drain the coolant (see Chapter 1).

3.6L engines

Refer to illustration 17.4

3 Remove the lower intake manifold (see Section 5).
4 Remove the oil cooler mounting fasteners **(see illustration)**.
5 Remove the oil cooler and discard the seals.

4.0L engines

6 Raise the vehicle and support it securely on jackstands.
7 Drain the engine oil and remove the oil filter (see Chapter 1).
8 Disconnect the coolant hoses from the inlet and outlet ports.
9 Remove the oil cooler connector bolt from the center of the cooler and remove the oil cooler. Discard the oil cooler O-ring.

Installation

3.6L engines

10 Install new seals to the oil cooler.
11 Place the oil cooler onto the block and install the two mounting screws **(see illustration 17.4)**.

12 Install the mounting bolts and tighten the screws and bolts to the torque listed in this Chapter's Specifications.
13 Installation of the remaining components is the reverse of removal.

4.0L engines

14 Lubricate the oil cooler connector bolt and O-ring with clean engine oil.
15 Position the flat side of the oil cooler parallel to the adapter and install the oil cooler onto the adapter. Install the connector bolt and tighten it to the torque listed in this Chapter's Specifications.
16 Install new oil filter and refill the engine with oil (see Chapter 1).

All models

17 Refill the cooling system (see Chapter 1). Run the engine until normal operating temperature is reached, and check for leaks.

18 Driveplate - removal and installation

This procedure is essentially the same for all engines. Refer to Chapter 2A, Section 16 and follow the procedure outlined there, but use the torque listed in this Chapter's Specifications.

19 Rear main oil seal - replacement

This procedure is essentially the same as for the 3.3L/3.8L engines. Refer to Chapter 2A, Section 17 and follow the procedure outlined there, but use the torque value listed in this Chapter's Specifications.

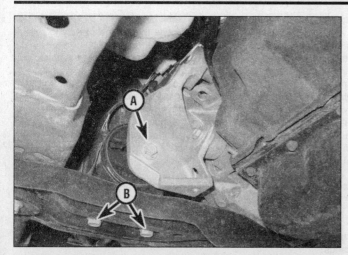

20.1a Front engine mount through bolt (A) and mount-to-subframe bolts (B)

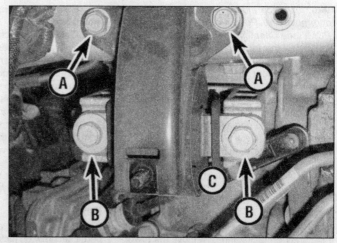

20.1b Remove the left side engine mount-to-body fasteners (A), remove the mount-to-transaxle bolts (B) and a hidden bolt at the bottom of the mount (C) then lift the mount from the engine compartment

20 Engine mounts - check and replacement

Refer to illustrations 20.1a, 20.1b, 20.1c and 20.1d

1   The engine mounting system on these models consists of four molded mounts **(see illustrations)**. The right and left mounts support the engine/transaxle assembly while the front and rear mounts control powertrain torque.

2   Engine mounts seldom require attention, but broken or deteriorated mounts should be replaced immediately, or the added strain placed on driveline components may cause damage or accelerated wear.

Check

3   During the check, the engine must be raised slightly to remove the weight from the mounts.

4   Raise the vehicle and support it securely on jackstands, then position a jack under the engine oil pan. Place a large wood block between the jack head and the oil pan to prevent oil pan damage, then carefully raise the engine just enough to take the weight off the mounts.
Warning: *DO NOT place any part of your body under the engine when it's supported only by a jack!*

5   Check the mounts to see if the rubber is cracked, hardened or separated from the metal backing. Sometimes the rubber will split right down the center.

6   Check for relative movement between the mount plates and the engine or frame (use a large screwdriver or pry bar to attempt to move the mounts). If movement is noted, lower the engine and tighten the mount fasteners.

7   Rubber preservative may be applied to the mounts to slow deterioration.

Replacement

Front mount

8   Raise the front of the vehicle and support it securely on jackstands.

9   Place a floor jack under the engine (with a wood block between the jack head and oil pan) and raise the engine slightly to relieve the weight from the mounts.

10   Remove the front engine mount through-bolt from the insulator and the engine mounting bracket.

11   Remove the front engine mount-to-crossmember bolts and remove the insulator assembly.

12   Install the new mount and tighten the bolts securely.

Left mount

13   Disconnect the cable from the negative terminal of the battery (see Chapter 5).

14   Remove the air filter and housing (see Chapter 4).

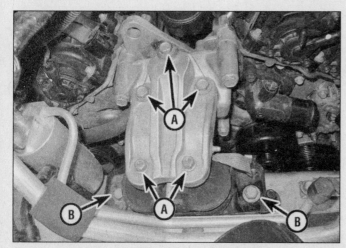

20.1c Remove the right side engine mount top bracket fasteners (A) and separate the top from the engine mount bracket then remove the mount fasteners (B) and the mount from the engine compartment

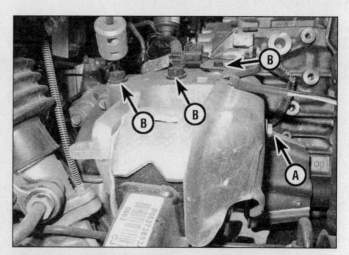

20.1d Remove the heat shield mounting bolt (A) and the heat shield to access the rear engine mount through bolt, then remove the bracket bolts (B) to access the insulator mounting bolts

Note: *On some models it may be necessary to remove the Powertrain Control Module (PCM) (see Chapter 6).*

15   Raise the front of the vehicle and support it securely on jackstands.

16   Place a floor jack under the engine (with a wood block between the jack head and oil pan) and raise the engine slightly to relieve the weight from the mounts.

17   Remove the engine mount crossmember (see Chapter 10).

18   Remove the transmission mount fasteners and remove the mount.

19   Install the new mount and tighten the bolts securely.

Right mount

20   Raise the front of the vehicle and support it securely on jackstands. Remove the lower splash shield fasteners and splash shield.

21   Remove the engine ground strap the mount bracket.

22   Place a floor jack under the engine (with a wood block between the jack head and oil pan) and raise the engine slightly to relieve the weight from the mounts.

23   Remove the two right engine mount insulator vertical fasteners from the frame rail and loosen the one horizontal fastener.

24   Remove the three bolts and two nuts from the top bracket then remove the bracket.

25   Remove the mount fasteners and remove the mount.

26   Install the new mount and tighten the bolts securely.

Rear mount

27   Raise the front of the vehicle and support it securely on jackstands.

28   Place a floor jack under the engine (with a wood block between the jack head and oil pan) and raise the engine slightly to relieve the weight from the mounts.

29   Remove the rear mount heat shield and bracket mounting bolts.

30   Remove the insulator through-bolt from the mount and the rear mount bracket.

31   Remove the four mount fasteners and remove the mount.

32   Install the new mount and tighten the bolts securely.

Chapter 2 Part C
General engine overhaul procedures

Contents

Specifications

General

Displacement	
3.3L	201 cubic inches
3.6L	220 cubic inches
3.8L	231 cubic inches
4.0L	244 cubic inches
Bore	
3.3L	3.661 inches
3.6L	3.779 inches
3.8L	3.779 inches
4.0L	3.780 inches
Stroke	
3.3L	3.188 inches
3.6L	3.268 inches
3.8L	3.425 inches
4.0L	3.583 inches
Compression ratio	
3.3L	9.35:1
3.6L	10.2:1
3.8L	9.6:1
4.0L	10.2:1
Compression pressure	100 psi minimum and no more than 25% variance between cylinders
Oil pressure	
At idle speed	5 psi (minimum)
At 3,000 rpm	
3.3L and 3.8L	30 to 80 psi
3.6L	
Warm	30 psi
Cold	128 psi
4.0L	45 to 105 psi

Camshaft - 3.3L and 3.8L engines

Camshaft bearing journal diameter

No. 1	1.9970 to 1.9990 inches
No. 2	1.9809 to 1.9828 inches
No. 3	1.9659 to 1.9679 inches
No. 4	1.9499 to 1.9520 inches

Bearing diameter

No. 1	1.9999 to 2.0009 inches
No. 2	1.9839 to 1.9849 inches
No. 3	1.9690 to 1.9699 inches
No. 4	1.9529 to 1.9540 inches
Bearing clearance	0.001 to 0.004 inch
End play	0.010 to 0.020 inch

Torque specifications

Note: *One foot-pound (ft-lb) of torque is equivalent to 12 inch-pounds (in-lbs) of torque. Torque values below approximately 15 ft-lbs are expressed in inch-pounds, since most foot-pound torque wrenches are not accurate at these smaller values.*

Ft-lbs (unless otherwise indicated)

Camshaft thrust plate bolt (3.3L and 3.8L engines)	105 in-lbs
Connecting rod bearing cap bolts*	
3.3L and 3.8L cap bolts	
Step 1	60 in-lbs
Step 2	21
Step 3	Tighten and additional 1/4 turn (90-degrees)
3.6L	
Step 1	15
Step 2	Tighten an additional 1/4 turn (90-degrees)
4.0L	
Step 1	20
Step 2	Tighten an additional 1/4 turn (90-degrees)
Crankshaft target wheel bolts (3.6L)*	89 in-lbs
Driveplate-to-crankshaft bolts	70
Driveplate-to-torque converter bolts	65
Main bearing cap bolts*	
3.3L and 3.8L **(in sequence, see illustration 11.30a)**	
Step 1	30
Step 2	Tighten an additional 1/4 turn (90-degrees)
Step 3 (side bolts)	45
3.6L **(in sequence, see illustration 11.30b, 11.30c and 11.30d)**	
Step 1 (inner bolts) M11	15
Step 2 (inner bolts)	Tighten an additional 1/4 turn (90-degrees)
Step 3 (outer bolts and windage tray) M8	16
Step 4 (outer bolts and windage tray)	Tighten an additional 1/4 turn (90-degrees)
Step 5 (side bolts)	22
4.0L **(in sequence, see illustration 11.30e, 11.30f and 11.30g)**	
Step 1 (inner bolts)	15
Step 2 (inner bolts)	Tighten an additional 1/4 turn (90-degrees)
Step 3 (outer bolts)	20
Step 4 (outer bolts)	Tighten an additional 1/4 turn (90-degrees)
Step 5 (side bolts)	21

* Use new bolts

1.1 An engine block being bored. An engine rebuilder will use special machinery to recondition the cylinder bores

1.2 If the cylinders are bored, the machine shop will normally hone the engine on a machine like this

1 General information - engine overhaul

Refer to illustrations 1.1, 1.2, 1.3, 1.4, 1.5 and 1.6

Included in this portion of Chapter 2 are general information and diagnostic testing procedures for determining the overall mechanical condition of your engine.

The information ranges from advice concerning preparation for an overhaul and the purchase of replacement parts and/or components to detailed, step-by-step procedures covering removal and installation.

The following Sections have been written to help you determine whether your engine needs to be overhauled and how to remove and install it once you've determined it needs to be rebuilt. For information concerning in-vehicle engine repair, see Chapter 2A or 2B.

The Specifications included in this Part are general in nature and include only those necessary for testing the oil pressure and checking the engine compression. Refer to Chapter 2A or 2B for additional engine Specifications.

It's not always easy to determine when, or if, an engine should be completely overhauled, because a number of factors must be considered.

High mileage is not necessarily an indication that an overhaul is needed, while low mileage doesn't preclude the need for an overhaul. Frequency of servicing is probably the most important consideration. An engine that's had regular and frequent oil and filter changes, as well as other required maintenance, will most likely give many thousands of miles of reliable service. Conversely, a neglected engine may require an overhaul very early in its service life.

Excessive oil consumption is an indication that piston rings, valve seals and/or valve guides are in need of attention. Make sure that oil leaks aren't responsible before deciding that the rings and/or guides are bad. Perform a cylinder compression check to deter-

1.3 A crankshaft having a main bearing journal ground

mine the extent of the work required (see Section 3). Also check the vacuum readings under various conditions (see Section 4).

Check the oil pressure with a gauge installed in place of the oil pressure sending unit and compare it to this Chapter's Specifications (see Section 2). If it's extremely low, the bearings and/or oil pump are probably worn out.

Loss of power, rough running, knocking or metallic engine noises, excessive valve train noise and high fuel consumption rates may also point to the need for an overhaul, especially if they're all present at the same time. If a complete tune-up doesn't remedy the situation, major mechanical work is the only solution.

An engine overhaul involves restoring the internal parts to the specifications of a new engine. During an overhaul, the piston rings are replaced and the cylinder walls are reconditioned (rebored and/or honed) **(see illustrations 1.1 and 1.2)**. If a rebore is done by an automotive machine shop, new oversize pistons will also be installed. The main bearings, connecting rod bearings and camshaft bearings are generally replaced with new ones and, if necessary, the crankshaft may be

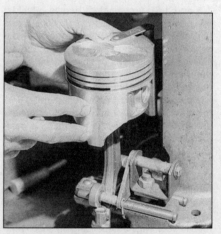

1.4 A machinist checks for a bent connecting rod, using specialized equipment

reground to restore the journals **(see illustration 1.3)**. Generally, the valves are serviced as well, since they're usually in less-than-perfect condition at this point. While the engine is being overhauled, other components, such as the starter and alternator, can be rebuilt as well. The end result should be similar to a new engine that will give many trouble free miles. **Note:** *Critical cooling system components such as the hoses, drivebelts, thermostat and water pump should be replaced with new parts when an engine is overhauled. The radiator should be checked carefully to ensure that it isn't clogged or leaking (see Chapter 3). If you purchase a rebuilt engine or short block, some rebuilders will not warranty their engines unless the radiator has been professionally flushed. Also, we don't recommend overhauling the oil pump - always install a new one when an engine is rebuilt.*

Overhauling the internal components on today's engines is a difficult and time-consuming task which requires a significant amount of specialty tools and is best left to a professional engine rebuilder **(see illustrations 1.4,**

1.5 A bore gauge being used to check the main bearing bore

1.6 Uneven piston wear like this indicates a bent connecting rod

2.2 Location of the oil pressure sending unit on 3.3L and 3.8L engines

1.5 and 1.6). A competent engine rebuilder will handle the inspection of your old parts and offer advice concerning the reconditioning or replacement of the original engine, Never purchase parts or have machine work done on other components until the block has been thoroughly inspected by a professional machine shop. As a general rule, time is the primary cost of an overhaul, especially since the vehicle may be tied up for a minimum of two weeks or more. Be aware that some engine builders only have the capability to rebuild the engine you bring them while other rebuilders have a large inventory of rebuilt exchange engines in stock. Also be aware that many machine shops could take as much as two weeks time to completely rebuild your engine depending on shop workload. Sometimes it makes more sense to simply exchange your engine for another engine that's already rebuilt to save time.

2   Oil pressure check

Refer to illustration 2.2

1   Low engine oil pressure can be a sign of an engine in need of rebuilding. A low oil pressure indicator (often called an idiot light) is not a test of the oiling system. Such indicators only come on when the oil pressure is dangerously low. Even a factory oil pressure gauge in the instrument panel is only a relative indication, although much better for driver information than a warning light. A better test is with a mechanical (not electrical) oil pressure gauge.
2   Locate the oil pressure indicator sending unit on the engine block.
  a) *On 3.3L and 3.8L engines, the oil pressure sending unit is located on the adapter directly above the oil filter (see illustration).*
  b) *On 4.0L engines, the oil pressure sending unit is located on the adapter directly above the oil filter at the front of the engine.*

  c) *On 3.6L engines, the oil pressure sending unit is located on the oil filter adapter below the intake manifolds. Refer to Chapter 2B for removal and installation of the manifolds.*
3   Unscrew and remove the oil pressure sending unit and then screw in the hose for your oil pressure gauge. If necessary, install an adapter fitting. Use Teflon tape or thread sealant on the threads of the adapter and/or the fitting on the end of your gauge's hose.
Note: *On 3.6L engines, the manifolds must be removed and installed with the hose for the pressure gauge in place to perform the test.*
4   Connect an accurate tachometer to the engine, according to the tachometer manufacturer's instructions.
5   Check the oil pressure with the engine running (normal operating temperature) at the specified engine speed, and compare it to this Chapter's Specifications. If it's extremely low, the bearings and/or oil pump are probably worn out.

3   Cylinder compression check

Refer to illustration 3.6

1   A compression check will tell you what mechanical condition the upper end of your engine (pistons, rings, valves, head gaskets) is in. Specifically, it can tell you if the compression is down due to leakage caused by worn piston rings, defective valves and seats or a blown head gasket.
Note: *The engine must be at normal operating temperature and the battery must be fully charged for this check.*
2   Begin by cleaning the area around the spark plugs before you remove them (compressed air should be used, if available). The idea is to prevent dirt from getting into the cylinders as the compression check is being done.
3   Remove all of the spark plugs from the engine (see Chapter 1).
4   Block the throttle wide open.

5   Disable the ignition and fuel systems by unplugging the wiring harness from the ignition coil pack (3.3L/3.8L engines only, see Chapter 5) and by unplugging the fuel pump module electrical connector (see Chapter 4).
6   Install a compression gauge in the spark plug hole **(see illustration)**.
7   Crank the engine over at least seven compression strokes and watch the gauge. The compression should build up quickly in a healthy engine. Low compression on the first stroke, followed by gradually increasing pressure on successive strokes, indicates worn piston rings. A low compression reading on the first stroke, which doesn't build up during successive strokes, indicates leaking valves or a blown head gasket (a cracked head could also be the cause). Deposits on the undersides of the valve heads can also cause low compression. Record the highest gauge reading obtained.
8   Repeat the procedure for the remaining cylinders and compare the results to this Chapter's Specifications.
9   Add some engine oil (about three squirts from a plunger-type oil can) to each cylinder,

3.6 A compression gauge with a threaded fitting for the spark plug hole is preferred over the type that requires hand pressure to maintain the seal

4.4 A simple vacuum gauge can be handy in diagnosing engine condition and performance

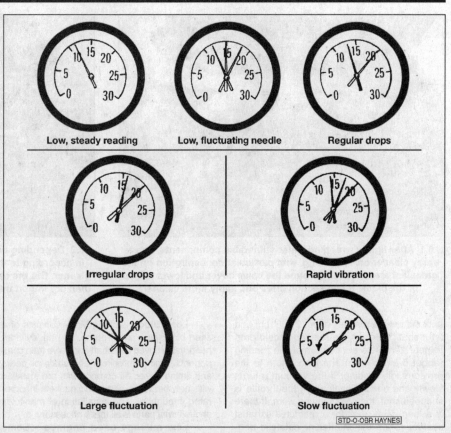

Low, steady reading   Low, fluctuating needle   Regular drops

Irregular drops   Rapid vibration

Large fluctuation   Slow fluctuation

STD-O-OBR HAYNES

4.6 Typical vacuum gauge readings

through the spark plug hole, and repeat the test.

10   If the compression increases after the oil is added, the piston rings are definitely worn. If the compression doesn't increase significantly, the leakage is occurring at the valves or head gasket. Leakage past the valves may be caused by burned valve seats and/or faces or warped, cracked or bent valves.

11   If two adjacent cylinders have equally low compression, there's a strong possibility that the head gasket between them is blown. The appearance of coolant in the combustion chambers or the crankcase would verify this condition.

12   If one cylinder is slightly lower than the others, and the engine has a slightly rough idle, a worn lobe on the camshaft could be the cause.

13   If the compression is unusually high, the combustion chambers are probably coated with carbon deposits. If that's the case, the cylinder head(s) should be removed and decarbonized.

14   If compression is way down or varies greatly between cylinders, it would be a good idea to have a leak-down test performed by an automotive repair shop. This test will pinpoint exactly where the leakage is occurring and how severe it is.

4   Vacuum gauge diagnostic checks

Refer to illustrations 4.4 and 4.6

1   A vacuum gauge provides inexpensive but valuable information about what is going on in the engine. You can check for worn rings or cylinder walls, leaking head or intake manifold gaskets, restricted exhaust, stuck or burned valves, weak valve springs, improper ignition or valve timing and ignition problems.

2   Unfortunately, vacuum gauge readings are easy to misinterpret, so they should be used in conjunction with other tests to confirm the diagnosis.

3   Both the absolute readings and the rate of needle movement are important for accurate interpretation. Most gauges measure

vacuum in inches of mercury (in-Hg). The following references to vacuum assume the diagnosis is being performed at sea level. As elevation increases (or atmospheric pressure decreases), the reading will decrease. For every 1,000 foot increase in elevation above approximately 2,000 feet, the gauge readings will decrease about one inch of mercury.

4   Connect the vacuum gauge directly to the intake manifold vacuum, not to ported (throttle body) vacuum **(see illustration)**. Be sure no hoses are left disconnected during the test or false readings will result.

5   Before you begin the test, allow the engine to warm up completely. Block the wheels and set the parking brake. With the transaxle in Park, start the engine and allow it to run at normal idle speed.

Warning: *Keep your hands and the vacuum gauge clear of the fans.*

6   Read the vacuum gauge; an average, healthy engine should normally produce about 17 to 22 in-Hg with a fairly steady needle **(see illustration)**. Refer to the following vacuum gauge readings and what they indicate about the engine's condition:

7   A low, steady reading usually indicates a leaking gasket between the intake manifold and cylinder head(s) or throttle body, a leaky vacuum hose, late ignition timing or incorrect camshaft timing. Check ignition timing with a timing light and eliminate all other possible causes, utilizing the tests provided in this Chapter before you remove the timing chain

cover to check the timing marks.

8   If the reading is three to eight inches below normal and it fluctuates at that low reading, suspect an intake manifold gasket leak at an intake port or a faulty fuel injector.

9   If the needle has regular drops of about two-to-four inches at a steady rate, the valves are probably leaking. Perform a compression check or leak-down test to confirm this.

10   An irregular drop or down-flick of the needle can be caused by a sticking valve or an ignition misfire. Perform a compression check or leak-down test and read the spark plugs.

11   A rapid vibration of about four in-Hg vibration at idle combined with exhaust smoke indicates worn valve guides. Perform a leak-down test to confirm this. If the rapid vibration occurs with an increase in engine speed, check for a leaking intake manifold gasket or head gasket, weak valve springs, burned valves or ignition misfire.

12   A slight fluctuation, say one inch up and down, may mean ignition problems. Check all the usual tune-up items and, if necessary, run the engine on an ignition analyzer.

13   If there is a large fluctuation, perform a compression or leak-down test to look for a weak or dead cylinder or a blown head gasket.

14   If the needle moves slowly through a wide range, check for a clogged PCV system, incorrect idle fuel mixture, throttle body or intake manifold gasket leaks.

15   Check for a slow return after revving the engine by quickly snapping the throttle open

6.1 After tightly wrapping water-vulnerable components, use a spray cleaner on everything, with particular concentration on the greasiest areas, usually around the valve cover and lower edges of the block. If one section dries out, apply more cleaner

6.2 Depending on how dirty the engine is, let the cleaner soak in according to the directions and then hose off the grime and cleaner. Get the rinse water down into every area you can get at; then dry important components with a hair dryer or paper towels

until the engine reaches about 2,500 rpm and let it shut. Normally the reading should drop to near zero, rise above normal idle reading (about 5 in-Hg over) and then return to the previous idle reading. If the vacuum returns slowly and doesn't peak when the throttle is snapped shut, the rings may be worn. If there is a long delay, look for a restricted exhaust system (often the muffler or catalytic converter). An easy way to check this is to temporarily disconnect the exhaust ahead of the suspected part and redo the test.

5   Engine rebuilding alternatives

The do-it-yourselfer is faced with a number of options when purchasing a rebuilt engine. The major considerations are cost, warranty, parts availability and the time required for the rebuilder to complete the project. The decision to replace the engine block, piston/connecting rod assemblies and crankshaft depends on the final inspection results of your engine. Only then can you make a cost effective decision whether to have your engine overhauled or simply purchase an exchange engine for your vehicle.

Some of the rebuilding alternatives include:

Individual parts - If the inspection procedures reveal that the engine block and most engine components are in reusable condition, purchasing individual parts and having a rebuilder rebuild your engine may be the most economical alternative. The block, crankshaft and piston/connecting rod assemblies should all be inspected carefully by a machine shop first.

Short block - A short block consists of an engine block with a crankshaft and piston/connecting rod assemblies already installed. All new bearings are incorporated and all clearances will be correct. The existing camshafts, valve train components, cylinder head and external parts can be bolted to the short block with little or no machine shop work necessary.

Long block - A long block consists of a short block plus an oil pump, oil pan, cylinder head, valve cover, camshaft and valve train components, timing sprockets and chain or gears and timing cover. All components are installed with new bearings, seals and gaskets incorporated throughout. The installation of manifolds and external parts is all that's necessary.

Low mileage used engines - Some companies now offer low mileage used engines which is a very cost effective way to get your vehicle up and running again. These engines often come from vehicles which have been in totaled in accidents or come from other countries which have a higher vehicle turnover rate. A low mileage used engine also usually has a similar warranty like the newly remanufactured engines.

Give careful thought to which alternative is best for you and discuss the situation with local automotive machine shops, auto parts dealers and experienced rebuilders before ordering or purchasing replacement parts.

6   Engine removal - methods and precautions

Refer to illustrations 6.1, 6.2, and 6.3

If you've decided that an engine must be removed for overhaul or major repair work, several preliminary steps should be taken. Read all removal and installation procedures carefully prior to committing to this job. These engines are removed by lowering the engine to the floor, along with the transaxle, and then raising the vehicle sufficiently to slide the assembly out; this will require a vehicle hoist as well as an engine hoist.

Locating a suitable place to work is extremely important. Adequate work space, along with storage space for the vehicle, will be needed. If a shop or garage isn't available, at the very least a flat, level, clean work surface made of concrete or asphalt is required.

Cleaning the engine compartment and engine before beginning the removal procedure will help keep tools clean and organized **(see illustrations 6.1 and 6.2)**.

An engine hoist will also be necessary. Make sure the hoist is rated in excess of the combined weight of the engine and transaxle. Safety is of primary importance, considering the potential hazards involved in removing the engine from the vehicle.

If you're a novice at engine removal, get at least one helper. One person cannot easily do all the things you need to do to remove a big heavy engine and transaxle assembly from the engine compartment. Also helpful is to seek advice and assistance from someone who's experienced in engine removal.

Plan the operation ahead of time. Arrange for or obtain all of the tools and equipment you'll need prior to beginning the job **(see illustration 6.3)**. Some of the equipment

6.3 Get an engine stand sturdy enough to firmly support the engine while you're working on it. Stay away from three-wheeled models: they have a tendency to tip over more easily, so get a four-wheeled unit

necessary to perform engine removal and installation safely and with relative ease are (in addition to a vehicle hoist and an engine hoist) a heavy duty floor jack (preferably fitted with a transmission jack head adapter), complete sets of wrenches and sockets as described in the front of this manual, wooden blocks, plenty of rags and cleaning solvent for mopping up spilled oil, coolant and gasoline.

Plan for the vehicle to be out of use for quite a while. A machine shop can do the work that is beyond the scope of the home mechanic. Machine shops often have a busy schedule, so before removing the engine, consult the shop for an estimate of how long it will take to rebuild or repair the components that may need work.

7 Engine - removal and installation

Refer to illustrations 7.9, 7.29, 7.31 and 7.35
Warning: *Gasoline is extremely flammable, so take extra precautions when you work on any part of the fuel system. Don't smoke or allow open flames or bare light bulbs near the work area, and don't work in a garage where a gas-type appliance (such as a water heater or clothes dryer) is present. Since gasoline is carcinogenic, wear fuel-resistant gloves when there's a possibility of being exposed to fuel, and, if you spill any fuel on your skin, rinse it off immediately with soap and water. Mop up any spills immediately and do not store fuel-soaked rags where they could ignite. The fuel system is under constant pressure, so, if any fuel lines are to be disconnected, the fuel pressure in the system must be relieved first (see Chapter 4 for more information). When you perform any kind of work on the fuel system, wear safety glasses and have a Class B type fire extinguisher on hand.*
Warning: *The engine must be completely cool before beginning this procedure.*
Warning: *The air conditioning system is under high pressure. Do not loosen any hose fittings or remove any components until after the system has been discharged. Air conditioning refrigerant must be properly discharged into an EPA-approved recovery/recycling unit at a dealer service department or an automotive air conditioning repair facility. Always wear eye protection when disconnecting air conditioning system fittings.*
Note: *Engine removal on these models is a difficult job, especially for the do-it-yourself mechanic working at home. Because of the vehicle's design, the manufacturer states that the engine and transaxle have to be removed as a unit from the bottom of the vehicle, not the top. With a floor jack and jackstands, the vehicle can't be raised high enough and supported safely enough for the engine/transaxle assembly to slide out from underneath. The manufacturer recommends that removal of the engine transaxle assembly only be performed on a frame-contact type vehicle hoist.*
Note: *Read through the entire Section before beginning this procedure. The engine and*

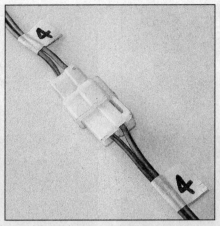
7.9 Label each wire before unplugging the connector

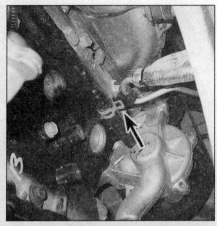
7.29 Remove the support clip attaching bolt and separate the pressure hose from the engine block

transaxle are removed as a unit from below, then separated outside the vehicle.

Removal

1   Have the air conditioning system discharged by an automotive air conditioning technician.
2   Park the vehicle on a frame-contact type vehicle hoist, then engage the arms of the hoist with the jacking points of the vehicle. Raise the hoist arms until they contact the vehicle, but not so much that the wheels come off the ground.
3   Remove the engine cover (see Chapter 1) then relieve the fuel system pressure (see Chapter 4).
4   Place protective covers on the fenders and cowl and remove the hood (see Chapter 11).
5   On 3.3L and 3.8L engines, remove the cowl cover (see Chapter 11) and the wiper unit (see Chapter 12).
6   Remove the air filter housing (see Chapter 4).
7   Remove the battery and the battery tray (see Chapter 5).
8   Remove the lower splash shield and, on 3.6L engines, disconnect then remove the vacuum pump from under the vehicle.
9   Clearly label and disconnect all vacuum lines, emissions hoses, wiring harness connectors, ground straps and fuel lines. Masking tape and/or a touch up paint applicator work well for marking items **(see illustration)**. Take instant photos or sketch the locations of components and brackets.
10   Detach the ground cable from the cylinder head.
11   Loosen the front wheel lug nuts and the driveaxle/hub nuts (see Chapter 8), then raise the vehicle on the hoist.
Note: *Keep in mind that during this procedure you'll have to adjust the height of the vehicle to perform certain operations.*
12   Drain the cooling system and engine oil and remove the drivebelt (see Chapter 1).
13   Remove the alternator and its brackets (see Chapter 5).

14   Remove the power steering fluid reservoir and set it off to the side without disconnecting the fluid lines (see Chapter 10).
15   On 3.6L engines remove the upper and lower intake manifolds (see Chapter 2B).
16   Lower the vehicle and detach the heater hoses at the firewall.
17   Detach the lower radiator hose from the engine and the upper radiator hose from the thermostat housing.
18   Remove the upper radiator support crossmember (see Chapter 11).
19   Remove the cooling fan(s), shroud(s) and radiator (see Chapter 3).
Note: *Install new transmission fluid cooler lines on reassembly (see Chapter 7).*
20   On 3.3L and 3.8L engines, remove the transaxle dipstick tube. Plug the opening with a suitable device.
21   Disconnect the shift cable from the transaxle (see Chapter 7). Also disconnect any wiring harness connectors from the transaxle.
22   Disconnect the upper air conditioning line from the condenser for additional clearance.
23   Disconnect the air conditioning lines at the compressor and the junction inside the engine compartment. Remove the air conditioning compressor (see Chapter 3).
24   Remove the power steering pump and bracket (see Chapter 10).
25   Raise the vehicle on the hoist. Remove the front wheels.
26   Remove the driveaxles (see Chapter 8).
27   Unplug the downstream oxygen sensor electrical connector.
28   Detach the exhaust pipe from the exhaust manifold and crossover pipe (see Chapter 4).
Note: *On 3.6L and 4.0L, engines, the exhaust manifold and catalytic converters are combined and are referred to as "maniverters."*
29   Remove the power steering pressure hose support clip attaching bolt **(see illustration)**. Separate the power steering hose from the engine block.
30   Remove the power steering fluid cooler, if equipped.

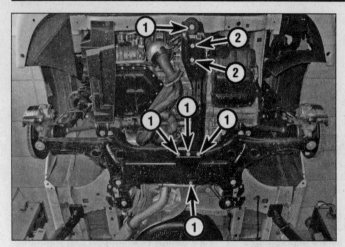

7.31 Longitudinal crossmember and transaxle front mounting bolt locations

1   *Crossmember bolts*   2   *Transaxle mount bolts*

7.35 Remember that the transaxle end of the engine will be heavier, so position the chain on the hoist so it balances the engine and the transaxle level with the vehicle

31   Remove the engine longitudinal cross-member bolts and remove the crossmember **(see illustration)**.

32   Mark the position of the driveplate and remove the torque converter bolts (see Chapter 7).

33   Lower the vehicle.

34   Support the engine with a floor jack and block of wood. Remove the right (passenger's) side engine mount, including the portion that bolts to the engine. Using one of the mount-to-engine bolts, attach one end of an engine lifting sling or chain to the mount boss. Tighten the bolt securely. Attach the other end of the sling or chain to the other side of the engine, using one of the transaxle-to-engine bolts. Be sure the positioning of the chain or sling will support the engine and transaxle in a balanced attitude.

Note: *The sling or chain must be long enough to allow the engine hoist to lower the engine/transaxle assembly to the ground, without letting the hoist arm contact the vehicle.*

35   Roll the hoist into position and attach the sling or chain to it. Take up the slack until there is slight tension on the hoist, then remove the jack from under the engine. Remember that the transaxle end of the engine will be heavier, so position the chain on the hoist so it balances the engine and the transaxle level with the vehicle **(see illustration)**.

Note: *Depending on the design of the engine hoist, it may be helpful to position the hoist from the side of the vehicle, so that when the engine/transaxle assembly is lowered, it will fit between the legs of the hoist.*

36   Recheck to be sure nothing except the remaining mount is still connecting the engine or transaxle to the vehicle. Disconnect and label anything still remaining.

37   Remove the driver's side transaxle mount (see Chapter 2A or 2B).

38   Slowly lower the engine/transaxle to the ground.

39   Once the engine/transaxle assembly is on the floor, disconnect the engine lifting hoist and

raise the vehicle until it clears the assembly.

40   Reconnect the chain or sling and raise the engine and transaxle. Support the engine with blocks of wood or another floor jack, while leaving the sling or chain attached to the right-side mounting boss. Support the transaxle with another floor jack, preferably one with a transmission jack head adapter. At this point the transaxle can be unbolted and removed from the engine. Be very careful to ensure that the components are supported securely so they won't topple off their supports during disconnection.

41   Reconnect the lifting chain to the engine, then raise the engine and attach it to an engine stand.

Installation

42   Installation is the reverse of removal, noting the following points:

a) *Check the engine/transaxle mounts. If they're worn or damaged, replace them.*

b) *Inspect the torque converter seal and bushing.*

c) *Attach the transaxle to the engine (see Chapter 7).*

d) *Add coolant, oil, power steering and transmission fluids as needed (see Chapter 1).*

e) *Run the engine and check for proper operation and leaks. Shut off the engine and recheck fluid levels.*

---

8   Engine overhaul - disassembly sequence

1   It's much easier to remove the external components if it's mounted on a portable engine stand. A stand can often be rented quite cheaply from an equipment rental yard. Before the engine is mounted on a stand, the flywheel/driveplate should be removed from the engine.

2   If a stand isn't available, it's possible to

remove the external engine components with it blocked up on the floor. Be extra careful not to tip or drop the engine when working without a stand.

3   If you're going to obtain a rebuilt engine, all external components must come off first, to be transferred to the replacement engine. These components include:

Driveplate
Ignition system components
Emissions-related components
Engine mounts and mount brackets
Engine rear cover (spacer plate between driveplate and engine block)
Intake/exhaust manifolds
Fuel injection components
Oil filter
Spark plug wires and spark plugs (3.3L/3.8L)
Thermostat and housing assembly
Water pump

Note: *When removing the external components from the engine, pay close attention to details that may be helpful or important during installation. Note the installed position of gaskets, seals, spacers, pins, brackets, washers, bolts and other small items.*

4   If you're going to obtain a short block (assembled engine block, crankshaft, pistons and connecting rods), then remove the timing belt/timing chain, cylinder head, oil pan, oil pump pick-up tube, oil pump and water pump from your engine so that you can turn in your old short block to the rebuilder as a core. See *Engine rebuilding alternatives* for additional information regarding the different possibilities to be considered.

---

9   Camshaft and bearings (3.3L and 3.8L engines only) - removal, inspection and installation

Note: *This procedure applies to the 3.3L and 3.8L engines only. Since there isn't enough room to remove the camshaft with the engine*

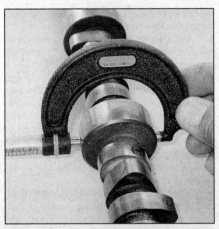

9.6 Check the diameter of each camshaft bearing journal to pinpoint excessive wear and out-of-round conditions

9.7 Measure the camshaft lobe height (greatest dimension) with a micrometer

9.8 Check the cam lobes for pitting, excessive wear and scoring. If scoring is excessive, as shown here, replace the camshaft

in the vehicle, the engine must be out of the vehicle and mounted on a stand to perform this procedure.

Removal

1   Remove the timing chain and sprockets, lifters and pushrods (see Chapter 2A).
2   Remove the bolts and the camshaft thrust plate from the engine block.
3   Use a long bolt in the camshaft sprocket bolt hole as a handle when removing the camshaft from the block.
4   Carefully pull the camshaft out. Support the cam in the block so the lobes don't nick or gouge the bearings as the cam is pulled out.

Inspection

Refer to illustrations 9.6, 9.7 and 9.8

5   After the camshaft has been removed from the engine, cleaned with solvent and dried, inspect the bearing journals for uneven wear, pitting and evidence of seizure. If the journals are damaged, the bearings in the block are probably damaged as well. Both the camshaft and bearings will have to be replaced.
Note: *Camshaft bearing replacement requires special tools and expertise that place it beyond the scope of the average home mechanic. The tools for bearing removal and installation are available at stores that carry automotive tools, possibly even found at a tool rental business. It is advisable though, if bearings are bad and the procedure is beyond your ability, remove the engine block and take it to an automotive machine shop to ensure that the job is done correctly.*
6   Measure the bearing journals with a micrometer to determine if they are excessively worn or out-of-round **(see illustration)**.
7   Measure the lobe height of each cam lobe on the intake camshaft and record your measurements **(see illustration)**. Compare the measurements for excessive variations. If the lobe heights vary more than 0.005 inch

(0.125 mm), replace the camshaft. Compare the lobe height measurements on the exhaust camshaft and follow the same procedure. Do not compare intake camshaft lobe heights with exhaust camshaft lobe heights as they are different. Only compare intake lobes with intake lobes and exhaust lobes with other exhaust lobes.
8   Check the camshaft lobes for heat discoloration, score marks, chipped areas, pitting and uneven wear **(see illustration)**. If the lobes are in good condition and if the lobe lift variation measurements recorded earlier are within the limits, the camshaft can be reused.
9   The inside diameter of each bearing can be determined with a bore gauge and outside micrometer, or an inside micrometer. Subtract the camshaft bearing journal diameters from the corresponding bearing inside diameters to determine the bearing oil clearance. If it's excessive, new bearings will be required regardless of the condition of the originals. Check this Chapter's Specifications.
10   Clean the lifters with solvent and dry them thoroughly without mixing them up.
11   Check each lifter wall, pushrod seat and foot for scuffing, score marks and uneven wear. If the lifter walls are damaged or worn (which is not very likely), inspect the lifter bores in the engine block as well. If the pushrod seats are worn, check the pushrod ends.
12   If new lifters are being installed, a new camshaft must also be installed. If a new camshaft is installed, then use new lifters as well. Never install used lifters unless the original camshaft is used and the lifters can be installed in their original locations.
13   Check the rollers carefully for wear and damage and make sure they turn freely without excessive play.

Installation

Refer to illustration 9.14

14   Lubricate the camshaft bearing journals and cam lobes with moly-base grease or engine assembly lube **(see illustration)**.

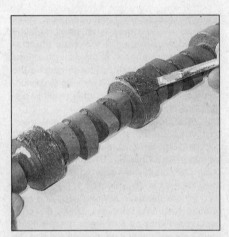

9.14 Be sure to apply camshaft assembly lube to the cam lobes and bearing journals before installing the camshaft

15   Slide the camshaft into the engine. Support the cam near the block and be careful not to scrape or nick the bearings.
16   Install the thrust plate and bolts. Tighten the bolts to the torque in this Chapter's Specifications.
17   See Chapter 2A for the timing chain installation procedure.

---

10   Pistons and connecting rods - removal and installation

Removal

Refer to illustrations 10.1, 10.3 and 10.4

Note: *Prior to removing the piston/connecting rod assemblies, remove the cylinder head, oil pan, and the timing chain cover (see Chapter 2A or 2B).*

1   Use your fingernail to feel if a ridge has formed at the upper limit of ring travel (about 1/4-inch down from the top of each cylinder).

10.1 Before you try to remove the pistons, use a ridge reamer to remove the raised material (ridge) from the top of the cylinders

10.3 Checking the connecting rod endplay (side clearance)

If carbon deposits or cylinder wear have produced ridges, they must be completely removed with a special tool **(see illustration)**. Follow the manufacturer's instructions provided with the tool. Failure to remove the ridges before attempting to remove the piston/connecting rod assemblies may result in piston breakage.

2   After the cylinder ridges have been removed, turn the engine so the crankshaft is facing up. On 3.6L engines, remove the oil pump (see Chapter 2B), then remove the outer crankshaft main bearing cap bolts and the windage tray (see Section 11).

3   Before the main bearing caps and connecting rods are removed, check the connecting rod endplay with feeler gauges. Slide them between the first connecting rod and the crankshaft throw until the play is removed **(see illustration)**. Repeat this procedure for each connecting rod. The endplay is equal to the thickness of the feeler gauge(s). Check with

an automotive machine shop for the endplay service limit (a typical end play limit should measure between 0.005 to 0.015 inch [0.127 to 0.396 mm]). If the play exceeds the service limit, new connecting rods will be required. If new rods (or a new crankshaft) are installed, the endplay may fall under the minimum allowable. If it does, the rods will have to be machined to restore it. If necessary, consult an automotive machine shop for advice.

4   Check the connecting rods and caps for identification marks. If they aren't plainly marked, use paint or marker to clearly identify each rod and cap (1, 2, 3, etc., depending on the cylinder they're associated with) **(see illustration)**.
Caution: *Do not use a punch and hammer to mark the connecting rods or they may be damaged.*

5   Loosen each of the connecting rod cap bolts 1/2-turn at a time until they can be removed by hand.
Note: *New connecting rod cap bolts must be used when reassembling the engine, but save*

the old bolts for use when checking the connecting rod bearing oil clearance.

6   Remove the number one connecting rod cap and bearing insert. Don't drop the bearing insert out of the cap.

7   Remove the bearing insert and push the connecting rod/piston assembly out through the top of the engine. Use a wooden or plastic hammer handle to push on the upper bearing surface in the connecting rod. If resistance is felt, double-check to make sure that all of the ridge was removed from the cylinder.

8   Repeat the procedure for the remaining cylinders.

9   After removal, reassemble the connecting rod caps and bearing inserts in their respective connecting rods and install the cap bolts finger tight. Leaving the old bearing inserts in place until reassembly will help prevent the connecting rod bearing surfaces from being accidentally nicked or gouged.

10   The pistons and connecting rods are now ready for inspection and overhaul at an automotive machine shop.

Piston ring installation

Refer to illustrations 10.13, 10.14, 10.15, 10.19a, 10.19b and 10.22

11   Before installing the new piston rings, the ring end gaps must be checked. It's assumed that the piston ring side clearance has been checked and verified correct.

12   Lay out the piston/connecting rod assemblies and the new ring sets so the ring sets will be matched with the same piston and cylinder during the end gap measurement and engine assembly.

13   Insert the top (number one) ring into the first cylinder and square it up with the cylinder walls by pushing it in with the top of the piston **(see illustration)**. The ring should be near the bottom of the cylinder, at the lower limit of ring travel.

14   To measure the end gap, slip feeler gauges between the ends of the ring until a

10.4 If the connecting rods or caps are not marked, use permanent ink or paint to mark the caps to the rods by cylinder number (for example, this would be number 4 cylinder connecting rod)

10.13 Install the piston ring into the cylinder then push it down into position using a piston so the ring will be square in the cylinder

10.14 With the ring square in the cylinder, measure the ring end gap with a feeler gauge

10.15 If the ring end gap is too small, clamp a file in a vise as shown and file the piston ring ends - be sure to remove all raised material

10.19a Installing the spacer/expander in the oil ring groove

gauge equal to the gap width is found **(see illustration)**. The feeler gauge should slide between the ring ends with a slight amount of drag. A typical ring gap should fall between 0.010 and 0.020 inch [0.25 to 0.50 mm] for compression rings and up to 0.030 inch [0.76 mm] for the oil ring steel rails. If the gap is larger or smaller than specified, double-check to make sure you have the correct rings before proceeding.

15   If the gap is too small, it must be enlarged or the ring ends may come in contact with each other during engine operation, which can cause serious damage to the engine. If necessary, increase the end gaps by filing the ring ends very carefully with a fine file. Mount the file in a vise equipped with soft jaws, slip the ring over the file with the ends contacting the file face and slowly move the ring to remove material from the ends. When performing this operation, file only by pushing the ring from the outside end of the file towards the vise **(see illustration)**.

16   Excess end gap isn't critical unless it's greater than 0.040 inch (1.01 mm). Again, double-check to make sure you have the correct ring type.

17   Repeat the procedure for each ring that will be installed in the first cylinder and for each ring in the remaining cylinders. Remember to keep rings, pistons and cylinders matched up.

18   Once the ring end gaps have been checked/corrected, the rings can be installed on the pistons.

19   The oil control ring (lowest one on the piston) is usually installed first. It's composed of three separate components. Slip the spacer/expander into the groove **(see illustration)**. If an anti-rotation tang is used, make sure it's inserted into the drilled hole in the ring groove. Next, install the upper side rail in the same manner **(see illustration)**. Don't use a piston ring installation tool on the oil ring side rails, as they may be damaged. Instead, place one end of the side rail into the groove between

the spacer/expander and the ring land, hold it firmly in place and slide a finger around the piston while pushing the rail into the groove. Finally, install the lower side rail.

20   After the three oil ring components have been installed, check to make sure that both the upper and lower side rails can be rotated smoothly inside the ring grooves.

21   The number two (middle) ring is installed next. It's usually stamped with a mark which must face up, toward the top of the piston. Do not mix up the top and middle rings, as they have different cross-sections.

Note: *Always follow the instructions printed on the ring package or box - different manufacturers may require different approaches.*

22   Use a piston ring installation tool and make sure the identification mark is facing the top of the piston, then slip the ring into the middle groove on the piston **(see illustration)**. Don't expand the ring any more than necessary to slide it over the piston.

23   Install the number one (top) ring in the same manner. Make sure the mark is facing up. Be careful not to confuse the number one and number two rings.

24   Repeat the procedure for the remaining pistons and rings.

10.19b DO NOT use a piston ring installation tool when installing the oil control side rails

Installation

25   Before installing the piston/connecting rod assemblies, the cylinder walls must be perfectly clean, the top edge of each cylinder bore must be chamfered, and the crankshaft must be in place.

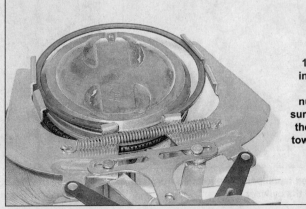

10.22 Use a piston ring installation tool to install the number 2 and the number 1 (top) rings - be sure the directional mark on the piston ring(s) is facing toward the top of the piston

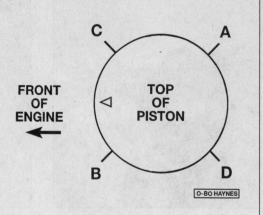

10.30 Position the piston ring end gaps as shown here before installing the piston/connecting rod assemblies into the engine

A   *Top compression ring gap*
B   *Second compression ring and oil ring spacer gap*
C   *Upper oil ring gap*
D   *Lower oil ring gap*

26   Remove the cap from the end of the number one connecting rod (refer to the marks made during removal). Remove the original bearing inserts and wipe the bearing surfaces of the connecting rod and cap with a clean, lint-free cloth. They must be kept spotlessly clean.

Connecting rod bearing oil clearance check

Refer to illustrations 10.30, 10.35, 10.37 and 10.41

27   Clean the back side of the new upper bearing insert, then lay it in place in the connecting rod.
28   Make sure the tab on the bearing fits into the recess in the rod. Don't hammer the bearing insert into place and be very careful not to nick or gouge the bearing face. Don't lubricate the bearing at this time.
29   Clean the back side of the other bearing insert and install it in the rod cap. Again, make sure the tab on the bearing fits into the recess in the cap, and don't apply any lubricant. It's critically important that the mating surfaces of the bearing and connecting rod are perfectly

clean and oil free when they're assembled.
30   Position the piston ring gaps at 90-degree intervals around the piston as shown **(see illustration)**.
31   Lubricate the piston and rings with clean engine oil and attach a piston ring compressor to the piston. Leave the skirt protruding about 1/4-inch to guide the piston into the cylinder. The rings must be compressed until they're flush with the piston.
32   Rotate the crankshaft until the number one connecting rod journal is at BDC (bottom dead center) and apply a liberal coat of engine oil to the cylinder walls.
33   With the directional stamp (arrow) on top of the piston facing the front (timing belt/timing chain end) of the engine, gently insert the piston/connecting rod assembly into the number one cylinder bore and rest the bottom edge of the ring compressor on the engine block. Install the pistons with the (arrow) mark facing toward the timing belt/ timing chain end.
34   Tap the top edge of the ring compressor to make sure it's contacting the block around its entire circumference.
35   Gently tap on the top of the piston with

the end of a wooden or plastic hammer handle **(see illustration)** while guiding the end of the connecting rod into place on the crankshaft journal. The piston rings may try to pop out of the ring compressor just before entering the cylinder bore, so keep some downward pressure on the ring compressor. Work slowly, and if any resistance is felt as the piston enters the cylinder, stop immediately. Find out what's hanging up and fix it before proceeding. Do not force the piston into the cylinder - you might break a ring and/or the piston.
36   Once the piston/connecting rod assembly is installed, the connecting rod bearing oil clearance must be checked before the rod cap is permanently installed.
37   Cut a piece of the appropriate size Plastigage slightly shorter than the width of the connecting rod bearing and lay it in place on the number one connecting rod journal, parallel with the journal axis **(see illustration)**.
38   Clean the connecting rod cap bearing face and install the rod cap. Make sure the mating mark on the cap is on the same side as the mark on the connecting rod **(see illustration 10.4)**.
39   Install the old rod bolts, at this time, and tighten them to the torque listed in this Chapter's Specifications.
Note: *Use a thin-wall socket to avoid erroneous torque readings that can result if the socket is wedged between the rod cap and the bolt. If the socket tends to wedge itself between the bolt and the cap, lift up on it slightly until it no longer contacts the cap. DO NOT rotate the crankshaft at any time during this operation.*
40   Remove the bolts and detach the rod cap, being very careful not to disturb the Plastigage. Discard the cap bolts at this time as they cannot be reused.
Note: *You MUST use new connecting rod bolts.*
41   Compare the width of the crushed Plastigage to the scale printed on the Plastigage

10.35 Use a plastic or wooden hammer handle to push the piston into the cylinder

10.37 Place Plastigage on each connecting rod bearing journal parallel to the crankshaft centerline

10.41 Use the scale on the Plastigage package to determine the bearing oil clearance - be sure to measure the widest part of the Plastigage and use the correct scale; it comes with both standard and metric scales

11.1 Checking crankshaft endplay with a dial indicator

envelope to obtain the oil clearance **(see illustration)**. The connecting rod oil clearance is usually about 0.001 to 0.002 inch. Consult an automotive machine shop for the clearance specified for the rod bearings on your engine.

42   If the clearance is not as specified, the bearing inserts may be the wrong size (which means different ones will be required). Before deciding that different inserts are needed, make sure that no dirt or oil was between the bearing inserts and the connecting rod or cap when the clearance was measured. Also, recheck the journal diameter. If the Plastigage was wider at one end than the other, the journal may be tapered. If the clearance still exceeds the limit specified, the bearing will have to be replaced with an undersize bearing.

Caution: *When installing a new crankshaft, always use a standard size bearing.*

Final installation

43   Carefully scrape all traces of the Plastigage material off the rod journal and/or bearing face. Be very careful not to scratch the bearing - use your fingernail or the edge of a plastic card.

44   Make sure the bearing faces are perfectly clean, then apply a uniform layer of clean moly-base grease or engine assembly lube to both of them. You'll have to push the piston into the cylinder to expose the face of the bearing insert in the connecting rod.

Caution: *Install new connecting rod cap bolts. Do NOT reuse old bolts - they have stretched and cannot be reused.*

45   Slide the connecting rod back into place on the journal, install the rod cap, install the new bolts and tighten them to the torque listed in this Chapter's Specifications. Again, work up to the torque in three steps.

46   Repeat the entire procedure for the remaining pistons/connecting rods.

47   The important points to remember are:

a)   *Keep the back sides of the bearing inserts and the insides of the connecting rods and caps perfectly clean when assembling them.*

b)   *Make sure you have the correct piston/rod assembly for each cylinder.*

c)   *The mark on the piston must face the front (timing belt end or timing chain of the engine.*

d)   *Lubricate the cylinder walls liberally with clean oil.*

e)   *Lubricate the bearing faces when installing the rod caps after the oil clearance has been checked.*

48   After all the piston/connecting rod assemblies have been correctly installed, rotate the crankshaft a number of times by hand to check for any obvious binding.

49   As a final step, check the connecting rod endplay again.

50   Compare the measured endplay to the tolerance listed in this Chapter's Specifications to make sure it's acceptable. If it was correct before disassembly and the original crankshaft and rods were reinstalled, it should still be correct. If new rods or a new crankshaft were installed, the endplay may be inadequate. If so, the rods will have to be removed and taken to an automotive machine shop for resizing.

11   Crankshaft - removal and installation

Removal

Refer to illustrations 11.1 and 11.3

Note: *The crankshaft can be removed only after the engine has been removed from the vehicle. It's assumed that the driveplate, crankshaft pulley, timing belt/timing chain, oil pan, oil pump body, oil filter, oil pump pick-up tube, windage tray and piston/connecting rod assemblies have already been removed. The*

rear main oil seal retainer must be unbolted and separated from the block before proceeding with crankshaft removal.

1   Before the crankshaft is removed, measure the endplay. Mount a dial indicator with the indicator in line with the crankshaft and just touching the end of the crankshaft as shown **(see illustration)**.

2   Pry the crankshaft all the way to the rear and zero the dial indicator. Next, pry the crankshaft to the front as far as possible and check the reading on the dial indicator. The distance traveled is the endplay. A typical crankshaft endplay will fall between 0.003 to 0.010 inch (0.076 to 0.254 mm). If it is greater than that, check the crankshaft thrust surfaces for wear after it's removed. If no wear is evident, new main bearings should correct the endplay.

3   If a dial indicator isn't available, feeler gauges can be used. Gently pry the crankshaft all the way to the front of the engine. Slip feeler gauges between the crankshaft and the front face of the thrust bearing or washer to determine the clearance **(see illustration)**.

11.3 Checking crankshaft endplay with feeler gauges at the thrust bearing journal

ENGINE BEARING ANALYSIS

Debris

Babbitt bearing embedded with debris from machinings

Microscopic detail of debris

Microscopic detail of gouges

Overplated copper alloy bearing gouged by cast iron debris

Aluminum bearing embedded with glass beads

Microscopic detail of glass beads

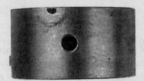

Damaged lining caused by dirt left on the bearing back

Misassembly

Result of a lower half assembled as an upper - blocking the oil flow

Excessive oil clearance is indicated by a short contact arc

Polished and oil-stained backs are a result of a poor fit in the housing bore

Result of a wrong, reversed, or shifted cap

Overloading

Damage from excessive idling which resulted in an oil film unable to support the load imposed

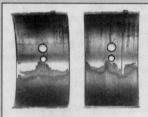

Damaged upper connecting rod bearings caused by engine lugging; the lower main bearings (not shown) were similarly affected

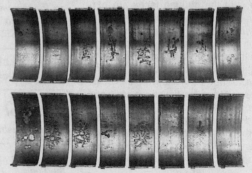

The damage shown in these upper and lower connecting rod bearings was caused by engine operation at a higher-than-rated speed under load

Misalignment

A warped crankshaft caused this pattern of severe wear in the center, diminishing toward the ends

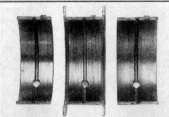

A poorly finished crankshaft caused the equally spaced scoring shown

A tapered housing bore caused the damage along one edge of this pair

A bent connecting rod led to the damage in the "V" pattern

Lubrication

Result of dry start: The bearings on the left, farthest from the oil pump, show more damage

Result of a low oil supply or oil starvation

Severe wear as a result of inadequate oil clearance

Corrosion

Microscopic detail of corrosion

Corrosion is an acid attack on the bearing lining generally caused by inadequate maintenance, extremely hot or cold operation, or inferior oils or fuels

Microscopic detail of cavitation

Example of cavitation - a surface erosion caused by pressure changes in the oil film

Damage from excessive thrust or insufficient axial clearance

Bearing affected by oil dilution caused by excessive blow-by or a rich mixture

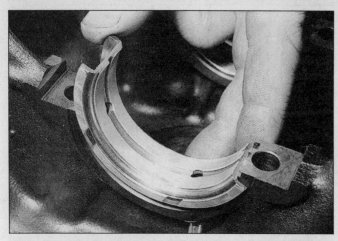

11.11 Installing a crankshaft main bearing onto the engine block main bearing saddle

11.17 Place the Plastigage onto the crankshaft bearing journal as shown

4   Loosen the main bearing cap bolts 1/4-turn at a time each, until they can be removed by hand.
Note: *New main bearing cap bolts must be used when reassembling the engine, but save the old bolts for use when checking the main bearing oil clearance.*
5   Gently tap the main bearing cap with a soft-face hammer around the perimeter of the assembly. Pull the main bearing cap straight up and off the cylinder block. Try not to drop the bearing inserts if they come out with the assembly.
6   Carefully lift the crankshaft out of the engine. It may be a good idea to have an assistant available, since the crankshaft is quite heavy and awkward to handle. With the bearing inserts in place inside the engine block and main bearing caps, reinstall the bedplate/main bearing caps onto the engine block and tighten the bolts finger tight. Make sure you install the bedplate/main bearing caps with the arrow facing the front end of the engine.

Installation

7   Crankshaft installation is the first step in engine reassembly. It's assumed at this point that the engine block and crankshaft have been cleaned, inspected and repaired or reconditioned. On 3.6L engines, install the target wheel to the crankshaft and tighten the new bolts to the torque listed in this Chapter's Specifications, if removed.
8   Position the engine block with the bottom facing up.
9   Remove the mounting bolts and lift off the main bearing caps.
10   If they're still in place, remove the original bearing inserts from the block main bearing caps. Wipe the bearing surfaces of the block and bedplate with a clean, lint-free cloth. They must be kept spotlessly clean. This is critical for determining the correct bearing oil clearance.

Main bearing oil clearance check

Refer to illustrations 11.11, 11.17 and 11.21

11   Without mixing them up, clean the back sides of the new upper main bearing inserts (with grooves and oil holes) and lay one in each main bearing saddle in the block **(see illustration)**. Each upper bearing has an oil groove and oil hole in it.
Caution: *The oil holes in the block must line up with the oil holes in the upper bearing inserts.*
The thrust washer or thrust bearing insert must be installed in the number 2 crankshaft journal. Clean the back sides of the lower main bearing inserts and lay them in the corresponding location in the main bearing caps. Make sure the tab on the bearing insert fits into the recess in the block or bedplate or main bearing caps. The upper bearings with the oil holes are installed into the engine block, while the lower bearings without the oil holes are installed in the main bearing caps.
Caution: *Do not hammer the bearing insert into place and don't nick or gouge the bearing faces. DO NOT apply any lubrication at this time.*
12   Clean the faces of the bearing inserts in the block and the crankshaft main bearing journals with a clean, lint-free cloth.
13   Check or clean the oil holes in the crankshaft, as any dirt here can go only one way - straight through the new bearings.
14   Once you're certain the crankshaft is clean, carefully lay it in position in the cylinder block.
15   Before the crankshaft can be permanently installed, the main bearing oil clearance must be checked.
16   Cut several strips of the appropriate size of Plastigage. They must be slightly shorter than the width of the main bearing journal.
17   Place one piece on each crankshaft main bearing journal, parallel with the journal axis as shown **(see illustration)**.
18   Clean the faces of the bearing inserts in the main bearing caps. Hold the bearing inserts in place and install the assembly onto the crankshaft and cylinder block. DO NOT disturb the Plastigage. Make sure you install the main bearing caps with the arrow facing the front (timing belt/timing chain end) of the engine.
Caution: *The number 2 main bearing cap must be centered over the inner bolt holes of the block. If the bearing cap is not centered the*

crankshaft counterweights can contact the main bearing cap and cause severe engine damage.
19   Apply clean engine oil to all bolt threads prior to installation, then install the old bolts finger-tight; do not install the side bolts at this time. Tighten all the bolts in the sequences shown **(see illustrations 11.30a, 11.30b and 11.30e)** progressing in steps, to the torque listed in this Chapter's Specifications. On 3.6L and 4.0L engines, only install and tighten the inner bolts. It is not necessary to install the main bearing cap outer bolts or side bolts at this time.
20   Remove the bolts in the reverse order of the tightening sequence and carefully lift the caps straight up and off the block. Do not disturb the Plastigage or rotate the crankshaft. If the cap(s) is difficult to remove, tap it gently from side-to-side with a soft-face hammer to loosen it.
21   Compare the width of the crushed Plastigage on each journal to the scale printed on the Plastigage envelope to determine the main bearing oil clearance **(see illustration)**. Check

11.21 Use the scale on the Plastigage package to determine the bearing oil clearance - be sure to measure the widest part of the Plastigage and use the correct scale; it comes with both standard and metric scales

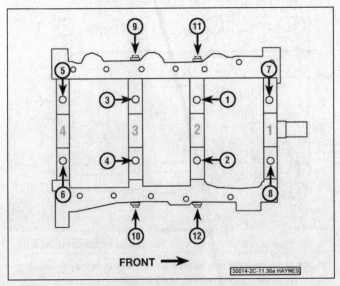

11.30a Main bearing cap bolt and side bolt tightening sequence - 3.3L and 3.8L engines

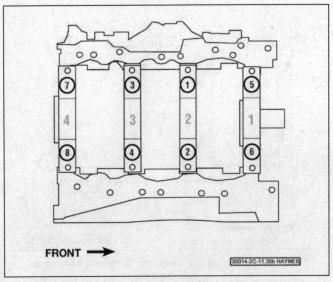

11.30b Main bearing cap inner bolt tightening sequence - 3.6L engines

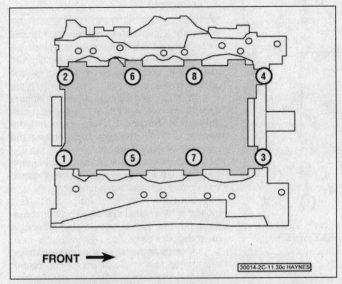

11.30c Main bearing cap outer bolt and windage tray tightening sequence - 3.6L engines

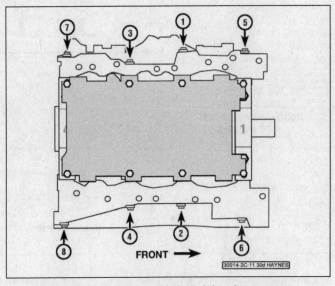

11.30d Main bearing cap side bolt tightening sequence - 3.6L engines

with an automotive machine shop for the crankshaft main bearing oil clearance limits.

22   If the clearance is not as specified, the bearing inserts may be the wrong size (which means different ones will be required). Before deciding if different inserts are needed, make sure that no dirt or oil was between the bearing inserts and the cap assembly or block when the clearance was measured. If the Plastigage was wider at one end than the other, the crankshaft journal may be tapered. If the clearance still exceeds the limit specified, the bearing insert(s) will have to be replaced with an undersize bearing insert(s).

Caution: *When installing a new crankshaft, always install a standard bearing insert set.*

23   Carefully scrape all traces of the Plastigage material off the main bearing journals and/or the bearing insert faces. Be sure to remove all residue from the oil holes. Use your fingernail or the edge of a plastic card - don't nick or scratch the bearing faces.

Final installation

Refer to illustrations 11.30a, 11.30b, 11.30c, 11.30d, 11.30e, 11.30f and 11.30g

24   Carefully lift the crankshaft out of the cylinder block.

25   Clean the bearing insert faces in the cylinder block, then apply a thin, uniform layer of moly-base grease or engine assembly lube to each of the bearing surfaces. Coat the thrust

faces as well as the journal face of the thrust bearing.

26   Make sure the crankshaft journals are clean, then lay the crankshaft back in place in the cylinder block.

27   Clean the bearing insert faces and then apply the same lubricant to them.

28   Install the main bearing caps onto the designated journals.

29   Prior to installation, apply clean engine oil to the **NEW** bolt threads, wiping off any excess, then install all bolts finger-tight.

30   Tighten the cap bolts, in sequence **(see illustrations)**, to the torque listed in this Chapter's Specifications.

31   Recheck crankshaft endplay with a feeler

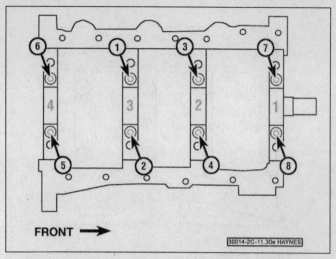

**11.30e Main bearing cap inner bolt tightening sequence -
4.0L engines**

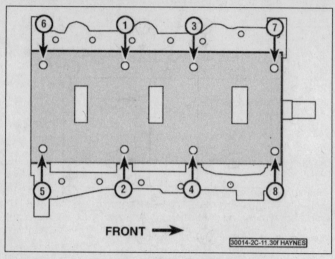

**11.30f Main bearing cap outer bolt and windage tray tightening
sequence - 4.0L engines**

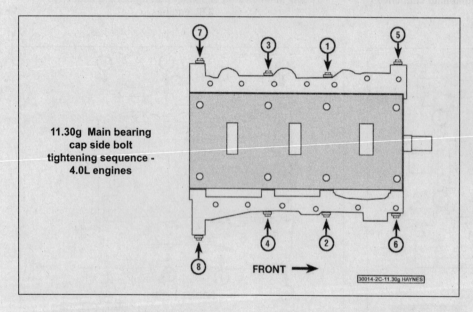

**11.30g Main bearing
cap side bolt
tightening sequence -
4.0L engines**

gauge or a dial indicator. The endplay should be correct if the crankshaft thrust faces aren't worn or damaged and if new bearings have been installed.

32   Rotate the crankshaft a number of times by hand to check for any obvious binding. It should rotate with a running torque of 50 in-lbs or less. If the running torque is too high, correct the problem at this time.

33   Install the new rear main oil seal (see Chapter 2A or 2B).

12   Engine overhaul - reassembly sequence

1   Before beginning engine reassembly, make sure you have all the necessary new parts, gaskets and seals as well as the following items on hand:

Common hand tools
A 1/2-inch drive torque wrench
New engine oil
Gasket sealant
Thread locking compound

2   If you obtained a short block it will be necessary to install the cylinder head, the oil pump and pick-up tube, the oil pan, the water pump, the timing belt/timing chain and timing cover, and the valve cover (see Chapter 2A or 2B). In order to save time and avoid problems, the external components must be installed in the following general order:

Thermostat and housing cover
Water pump
Intake and exhaust manifolds
Fuel injection components
Emission control components
Spark plug wires and spark plugs
Ignition coils
Oil filter
Engine mounts and mount brackets
Driveplate

13   Initial start-up and break-in after overhaul

Warning: *Have a fire extinguisher handy when starting the engine for the first time.*

1   Once the engine has been installed in the vehicle, double-check the engine oil and coolant levels.

2   With the spark plugs out of the engine and the ignition system and fuel pump disabled (see Section 3, Step 5), crank the engine until oil pressure registers on the gauge or the light goes out.

3   Install the spark plugs, hook up the plug wires or install the coils, and restore the ignition system and fuel pump functions.

4   Start the engine. It may take a few moments for the fuel system to build up pressure, but the engine should start without a great deal of effort.

5   After the engine starts, it should be allowed to warm up to normal operating temperature. While the engine is warming up, make a thorough check for fuel, oil and coolant leaks.

6   Shut the engine off and recheck the engine oil and coolant levels.

7   Drive the vehicle to an area with minimum traffic, accelerate from 30 to 50 mph, then allow the vehicle to slow to 30 mph with the throttle closed. Repeat the procedure 10 or 12 times. This will load the piston rings and cause them to seat properly against the cylinder walls. Check again for oil and coolant leaks.

8   Drive the vehicle gently for the first 500 miles (no sustained high speeds) and keep a constant check on the oil level. It is not unusual for an engine to use oil during the break-in period.

9   At approximately 500 to 600 miles, change the oil and filter.

10   For the next few hundred miles, drive the vehicle normally. Do not pamper it or abuse it.

11   After 2000 miles, change the oil and filter again and consider the engine broken in.

COMMON ENGINE OVERHAUL TERMS

B

Backlash - The amount of play between two parts. Usually refers to how much one gear can be moved back and forth without moving gear with which it's meshed.

Bearing Caps - The caps held in place by nuts or bolts which, in turn, hold the bearing surface. This space is for lubricating oil to enter.

Bearing clearance - The amount of space left between shaft and bearing surface. This space is for lubricating oil to enter.

Bearing crush - The additional height which is purposely manufactured into each bearing half to ensure complete contact of the bearing back with the housing bore when the engine is assembled.

Bearing knock - The noise created by movement of a part in a loose or worn bearing.

Blueprinting - Dismantling an engine and reassembling it to EXACT specifications.

Bore - An engine cylinder, or any cylindrical hole; also used to describe the process of enlarging or accurately refinishing a hole with a cutting tool, as to bore an engine cylinder. The bore size is the diameter of the hole.

Boring - Renewing the cylinders by cutting them out to a specified size. A boring bar is used to make the cut.

Bottom end - A term which refers collectively to the engine block, crankshaft, main bearings and the big ends of the connecting rods.

Break-in - The period of operation between installation of new or rebuilt parts and time in which parts are worn to the correct fit. Driving at reduced and varying speed for a specified mileage to permit parts to wear to the correct fit.

Bushing - A one-piece sleeve placed in a bore to serve as a bearing surface for shaft, piston pin, etc. Usually replaceable.

C

Camshaft - The shaft in the engine, on which a series of lobes are located for operating the valve mechanisms. The camshaft is driven by gears or sprockets and a timing chain. Usually referred to simply as the cam.

Carbon - Hard, or soft, black deposits found in combustion chamber, on plugs, under rings, on and under valve heads.

Cast iron - An alloy of iron and more than two percent carbon, used for engine blocks and heads because it's relatively inexpensive and easy to mold into complex shapes.

Chamfer - To bevel across (or a bevel on) the sharp edge of an object.

Chase - To repair damaged threads with a tap or die.

Combustion chamber - The space between the piston and the cylinder head, with the piston at top dead center, in which air-fuel mixture is burned.

Compression ratio - The relationship between cylinder volume (clearance volume) when the piston is at top dead center and cylinder volume when the piston is at bottom dead center.

Connecting rod - The rod that connects the crank on the crankshaft with the piston. Sometimes called a con rod.

Connecting rod cap - The part of the connecting rod assembly that attaches the rod to the crankpin.

Core plug - Soft metal plug used to plug the casting holes for the coolant passages in the block.

Crankcase - The lower part of the engine in which the crankshaft rotates; includes the lower section of the cylinder block and the oil pan.

Crank kit - A reground or reconditioned crankshaft and new main and connecting rod bearings.

Crankpin - The part of a crankshaft to which a connecting rod is attached.

Crankshaft - The main rotating member, or shaft, running the length of the crankcase, with offset throws to which the connecting rods are attached; changes the reciprocating motion of the pistons into rotating motion.

Cylinder sleeve - A replaceable sleeve, or liner, pressed into the cylinder block to form the cylinder bore.

D

Deburring - Removing the burrs (rough edges or areas) from a bearing.

Deglazer - A tool, rotated by an electric motor, used to remove glaze from cylinder walls so a new set of rings will seat.

E

Endplay - The amount of lengthwise movement between two parts. As applied to a crankshaft, the distance that the crankshaft can move forward and back in the cylinder block.

F

Face - A machinist's term that refers to removing metal from the end of a shaft or the face of a larger part, such as a flywheel.

Fatigue - A breakdown of material through a large number of loading and unloading cycles. The first signs are cracks followed shortly by breaks.

Feeler gauge - A thin strip of hardened steel, ground to an exact thickness, used to check clearances between parts.

Free height - The unloaded length or height of a spring.

Freeplay - The looseness in a linkage, or an assembly of parts, between the initial application of force and actual movement. Usually perceived as slop or slight delay.

Freeze plug - See Core plug.

G

Gallery - A large passage in the block that forms a reservoir for engine oil pressure.

Glaze - The very smooth, glassy finish that develops on cylinder walls while an engine is in service.

H

Heli-Coil - A rethreading device used when threads are worn or damaged. The device is installed in a retapped hole to reduce the thread size to the original size.

I

Installed height - The spring's measured length or height, as installed on the cylinder head. Installed height is measured from the spring seat to the underside of the spring retainer.

J

Journal - The surface of a rotating shaft which turns in a bearing.

K

Keeper - The split lock that holds the valve spring retainer in position on the valve stem.

Key - A small piece of metal inserted into matching grooves machined into two parts fitted together - such as a gear pressed onto a shaft - which prevents slippage between the two parts.

Knock - The heavy metallic engine sound, produced in the combustion chamber as a result of abnormal combustion - usually detonation. Knock is usually caused by a loose or worn bearing. Also referred to as detonation, pinging and spark knock. Connecting rod or main bearing knocks are created by too much oil clearance or insufficient lubrication.

L

Lands - The portions of metal between the piston ring grooves.

Lapping the valves - Grinding a valve face and its seat together with lapping compound.

Lash - The amount of free motion in a gear train, between gears, or in a mechanical assembly, that occurs before movement can begin. Usually refers to the lash in a valve train.

Lifter - The part that rides against the cam to transfer motion to the rest of the valve train.

M

Machining - The process of using a machine to remove metal from a metal part.

Main bearings - The plain, or babbit, bearings that support the crankshaft.

Main bearing caps - The cast iron caps, bolted to the bottom of the block, that support the main bearings.

O

O.D. - Outside diameter.

Oil gallery - A pipe or drilled passageway in the engine used to carry engine oil from one area to another.

Oil ring - The lower ring, or rings, of a piston; designed to prevent excessive amounts of oil from working up the cylinder walls and into the combustion chamber. Also called an oil-control ring.

Oil seal - A seal which keeps oil from leaking out of a compartment. Usually refers to a dynamic seal around a rotating shaft or other moving part.

O-ring - A type of sealing ring made of a special rubberlike material; in use, the O-ring is compressed into a groove to provide the sealing action.

Overhaul - To completely disassemble a unit, clean and inspect all parts, reassemble it with the original or new parts and make all adjustments necessary for proper operation.

P

Pilot bearing - A small bearing installed in the center of the flywheel (or the rear end of the crankshaft) to support the front end of the input shaft of the transmission.

Pip mark - A little dot or indentation which indicates the top side of a compression ring.

Piston - The cylindrical part, attached to the connecting rod, that moves up and down in the cylinder as the crankshaft rotates. When the fuel charge is fired, the piston transfers the force of the explosion to the connecting rod, then to the crankshaft.

Piston pin (or wrist pin) - The cylindrical and usually hollow steel pin that passes through the piston. The piston pin fastens the piston to the upper end of the connecting rod.

Piston ring - The split ring fitted to the groove in a piston. The ring contacts the sides of the ring groove and also rubs against the cylinder wall, thus sealing space between piston and wall. There are two types of rings: Compression rings seal the compression pressure in the combustion chamber; oil rings scrape excessive oil off the cylinder wall.

Piston ring groove - The slots or grooves cut in piston heads to hold piston rings in position.

Piston skirt - The portion of the piston below the rings and the piston pin hole.

Plastigage - A thin strip of plastic thread, available in different sizes, used for measuring clearances. For example, a strip of plastigage is laid across a bearing journal and mashed as parts are assembled. Then parts are disassembled and the width of the strip is measured to determine clearance between journal and bearing. Commonly used to measure crankshaft main-bearing and connecting rod bearing clearances.

Press-fit - A tight fit between two parts that requires pressure to force the parts together. Also referred to as drive, or force, fit.

Prussian blue - A blue pigment; in solution, useful in determining the area of contact between two surfaces. Prussian blue is commonly used to determine the width and location of the contact area between the valve face and the valve seat.

R

Race (bearing) - The inner or outer ring that provides a contact surface for balls or rollers in bearing.

Ream - To size, enlarge or smooth a hole by using a round cutting tool with fluted edges.

Ring job - The process of reconditioning the cylinders and installing new rings.

Runout - Wobble. The amount a shaft rotates out-of-true.

S

Saddle - The upper main bearing seat.

Scored - Scratched or grooved, as a cylinder wall may be scored by abrasive particles moved up and down by the piston rings.

Scuffing - A type of wear in which there's a transfer of material between parts moving against each other; shows up as pits or grooves in the mating surfaces.

Seat - The surface upon which another part rests or seats. For example, the valve seat is the matched surface upon which the valve face rests. Also used to refer to wearing into a good fit; for example, piston rings seat after a few miles of driving.

Short block - An engine block complete with crankshaft and piston and, usually, camshaft assemblies.

Static balance - The balance of an object while it's stationary.

Step - The wear on the lower portion of a ring land caused by excessive side and back-clearance. The height of the step indicates the ring's extra side clearance and the length of the step projecting from the back wall of the groove represents the ring's back clearance.

Stroke - The distance the piston moves when traveling from top dead center to bottom dead center, or from bottom dead center to top dead center.

Stud - A metal rod with threads on both ends.

T

Tang - A lip on the end of a plain bearing used to align the bearing during assembly.

Tap - To cut threads in a hole. Also refers to the fluted tool used to cut threads.

Taper - A gradual reduction in the width of a shaft or hole; in an engine cylinder, taper usually takes the form of uneven wear, more pronounced at the top than at the bottom.

Throws - The offset portions of the crankshaft to which the connecting rods are affixed.

Thrust bearing - The main bearing that has thrust faces to prevent excessive endplay, or forward and backward movement of the crankshaft.

Thrust washer - A bronze or hardened steel washer placed between two moving parts. The washer prevents longitudinal movement and provides a bearing surface for thrust surfaces of parts.

Tolerance - The amount of variation permitted from an exact size of measurement. Actual amount from smallest acceptable dimension to largest acceptable dimension.

U

Umbrella - An oil deflector placed near the valve tip to throw oil from the valve stem area.

Undercut - A machined groove below the normal surface.

Undersize bearings - Smaller diameter bearings used with re-ground crankshaft journals.

V

Valve grinding - Refacing a valve in a valve-refacing machine.

Valve train - The valve-operating mechanism of an engine; includes all components from the camshaft to the valve.

Vibration damper - A cylindrical weight attached to the front of the crankshaft to minimize torsional vibration (the twist-untwist actions of the crankshaft caused by the cylinder firing impulses). Also called a harmonic balancer.

W

Water jacket - The spaces around the cylinders, between the inner and outer shells of the cylinder block or head, through which coolant circulates.

Web - A supporting structure across a cavity.

Woodruff key - A key with a radiused backside (viewed from the side).

Chapter 3
Cooling, heating and air conditioning systems

Contents

Specifications

General

Radiator cap pressure rating	14 to 18 psi
Thermostat rating (opening temperature)...	192 degrees F
Cooling system capacity..	See Chapter 1
Refrigerant capacity*	
2010 and earlier models	
Front air conditioning only...	1.75 lbs
Front and rear air conditioning..	2.44 lbs
2011 and later models	
Front air conditioning only...	1.81 lbs
Front and rear air conditioning..	2.53 lbs

Check the refrigerant capacity listed on the underhood HVAC label; if the charge capacity listed on the label differs from that shown here, assume the label is correct.

Torque specifications   Ft-lbs (unless otherwise indicated)

Note: *One foot-pound (ft-lb) of torque is equivalent to 12 inch-pounds (in-lbs) of torque. Torque values below approximately 15 ft-lbs are expressed in inch-pounds, since most foot-pound torque wrenches are not accurate at these smaller values.*

Thermostat housing bolts	108 in-lbs
Water inlet tube bolts	
3.3L and 3.8L engines	21
3.6L engines	96 in-lbs
Water pump mounting bolts	105 in-lbs
3.3L, 3.8L and 4.0L engines	105 in-lbs
3.6L engines	96 in-lbs

1   General information

Warning: *Do not allow antifreeze to come in contact with your skin or painted surfaces of the vehicle. Rinse off spills immediately with plenty of water. Antifreeze is highly toxic if ingested. Never leave antifreeze lying around in an open container or in puddles on the floor; children and pets are attracted by it's sweet smell and may drink it. Check with local authorities about disposing of used antifreeze. Many communities have collection centers which will see that antifreeze is disposed of safely. Never dump used antifreeze on the ground or pour it into drains.*

Engine cooling system

All modern vehicles employ a pressurized engine cooling system with thermostatically controlled coolant circulation. The cooling system consists of a radiator, an expansion tank or coolant reservoir, a pressure cap (located on the expansion tank or radiator), a thermostat, a cooling fan, and a water pump.

The water pump circulates coolant through the engine. The coolant flows around each cylinder and around the intake and exhaust ports, near the spark plug areas and in close proximity to the exhaust valve guides.

A thermostat controls engine coolant temperature. During warm up, the closed thermostat prevents coolant from circulating through the radiator. As the engine nears normal operating temperature, the thermostat opens and allows hot coolant to travel through the radiator, where it's cooled before returning to the engine.

Heating system

The heating system consists of a blower fan and heater core located in a housing under the dash, the hoses connecting the heater core to the engine cooling system and the heater/air conditioning control head on the dashboard. Hot engine coolant is circulated through the heater core. When the heater mode is activated, a flap door in the housing opens to expose the heater core to the passenger compartment through air ducts. A fan switch on the control head activates the blower motor, which forces air through the core, heating the air.

Air conditioning system

The air conditioning system consists of a condenser mounted in front of the radiator, an evaporator mounted adjacent to the heater core, a compressor mounted on the engine, a receiver-drier or accumulator and the plumbing connecting all of the above components.

A blower fan forces the warmer air of the passenger compartment through the evaporator core (sort of a radiator-in-reverse), transferring the heat from the air to the refrigerant. The liquid refrigerant boils off into low pressure vapor, taking the heat with it when it leaves the evaporator.

2.2 The cooling system pressure tester is connected in place of the pressure cap, then pumped up to pressurize the system

2.5a The combustion leak detector consists of a bulb, syringe and test fluid

2   Troubleshooting

Coolant leaks

Refer to illustration 2.2

1   A coolant leak can develop anywhere in the cooling system, but the most common causes are:

a) *A loose or weak hose clamp*
b) *A defective hose*
c) *A faulty pressure cap*
d) *A damaged radiator*
e) *A bad heater core*
f) *A faulty water pump*
g) *A leaking gasket at any joint that carries coolant*

2   Coolant leaks aren't always easy to find. Sometimes they can only be detected when the cooling system is under pressure. Here's where a cooling system pressure tester comes in handy. After the engine has cooled completely, the tester is attached in place of the pressure cap, then pumped up to the pressure value equal to that of the pressure cap rating **(see illustration)**. Now, leaks that only exist when the engine is fully warmed up will become apparent. The tester can be left connected to locate a nagging slow leak.

Coolant level drops, but no external leaks

Refer to illustrations 2.5a and 2.5b

3   If you find it necessary to keep adding coolant, but there are no external leaks, the probable causes include:

a) *A blown head gasket*
b) *A leaking intake manifold gasket (only on engines that have coolant passages in the manifold)*
c) *A cracked cylinder head or cylinder block*

4   Any of the above problems will also usually result in contamination of the engine oil, which will cause it to take on a milkshake-like

2.5b Place the tester over the cooling system filler neck and use the bulb to draw a sample into the tester

appearance. A bad head gasket or cracked head or block can also result in engine oil contaminating the cooling system.

5   Combustion leak detectors (also known as block testers) are available at most auto parts stores. These work by detecting exhaust gases in the cooling system, which indicates a compression leak from a cylinder into the coolant. The tester consists of a large bulb-type syringe and bottle of test fluid **(see illustration)**. A measured amount of the fluid is added to the syringe. The syringe is placed over the cooling system filler neck and, with the engine running, the bulb is squeezed and a sample of the gases present in the cooling system are drawn up through the test fluid **(see illustration)**. If any combustion gases are present in the sample taken, the test fluid will change color.

6   If the test indicates combustion gas is present in the cooling system, you can be sure that the engine has a blown head gasket or a crack in the cylinder head or block, and will require disassembly to repair.

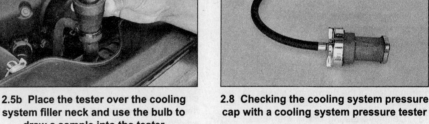

2.8 Checking the cooling system pressure cap with a cooling system pressure tester

Pressure cap

Refer to illustration 2.8

Warning: *Wait until the engine is completely cool before beginning this check.*

7   The cooling system is sealed by a spring-loaded cap, which raises the boiling point of the coolant. If the cap's seal or spring are worn out, the coolant can boil and escape past the cap. With the engine completely cool, remove the cap and check the seal; if it's cracked, hardened or deteriorated in any way, replace it with a new one.

8   Even if the seal is good, the spring might not be; this can be checked with a cooling system pressure tester **(see illustration)**. If the cap can't hold a pressure within approximately 1-1/2 lbs of its rated pressure (which is marked on the cap), replace it with a new one.

9   The cap is also equipped with a vacuum relief spring. When the engine cools off, a vacuum is created in the cooling system. The vacuum relief spring allows air back into the system, which will equalize the pressure and

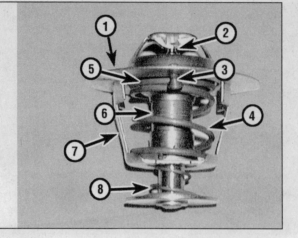

2.10 Typical thermostat

1   Flange
2   Piston
3   Jiggle valve
4   Main coil spring
5   Valve seat
6   Valve
7   Frame
8   Secondary
    coil spring

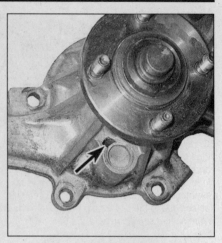

2.28 The water pump weep hole is generally located on the underside of the pump

prevent damage to the radiator (the radiator tanks could collapse if the vacuum is great enough). If, after turning the engine off and allowing it to cool down you notice any of the cooling system hoses collapsing, replace the pressure cap with a new one.

Thermostat

Refer to illustration 2.10

10   Before assuming the thermostat **(see illustration)** is responsible for a cooling system problem, check the coolant level (see Chapter 1), drivebelt tension (see Chapter 1) and temperature gauge (or light) operation.
11   If the engine takes a long time to warm up (as indicated by the temperature gauge or heater operation), the thermostat is probably stuck open. Replace the thermostat with a new one.
12   If the engine runs hot or overheats, a thorough test of the thermostat should be performed.
13   Definitive testing of the thermostat can only be made when it is removed from the vehicle. If the thermostat is stuck in the open position at room temperature, it is faulty and must be replaced.
Caution: *Do not drive the vehicle without a thermostat. The computer may stay in open loop and emissions and fuel economy will suffer.*
14   To test a thermostat, suspend the (closed) thermostat on a length of string or wire in a pot of cold water.
15   Heat the water on a stove while observing thermostat. The thermostat should fully open before the water boils.
16   If the thermostat doesn't open and close as specified, or sticks in any position, replace it.

Cooling fan

Electric cooling fan

17   If the engine is overheating and the cooling fan is not coming on when the engine temperature rises to an excessive level, unplug the fan motor electrical connector(s) and connect the motor directly to the battery with fused jumper wires. If the fan motor doesn't

come on, replace the motor.
18   If the radiator fan motor is okay, but it isn't coming on when the engine gets hot, the fan relay might be defective. A relay is used to control a circuit by turning it on and off in response to a control decision by the Powertrain Control Module (PCM). These control circuits are fairly complex, and checking them should be left to a qualified automotive technician. Sometimes, the control system can be fixed by simply identifying and replacing a bad relay.
19   Locate the fan relays in the engine compartment fuse/relay box.
20   Test the relay (see Chapter 12).
21   If the relay is okay, check all wiring and connections to the fan motor. Refer to the wiring diagrams at the end of Chapter 12. If no obvious problems are found, the problem could be the Engine Coolant Temperature (ECT) sensor or the Powertrain Control Module (PCM). Have the cooling fan system and circuit diagnosed by a dealer service department or repair shop with the proper diagnostic equipment.

Belt-driven cooling fan

22   Disconnect the cable from the negative terminal of the battery and rock the fan back and forth by hand to check for excessive bearing play.
23   With the engine cold (and not running), turn the fan blades by hand. The fan should turn freely.
24   Visually inspect for substantial fluid leakage from the clutch assembly. If problems are noted, replace the clutch assembly.
25   With the engine completely warmed up, turn off the ignition switch and disconnect the negative battery cable from the battery. Turn the fan by hand. Some drag should be evident. If the fan turns easily, replace the fan clutch.

Water pump

26   A failure in the water pump can cause serious engine damage due to overheating.

Drivebelt-driven water pump

Refer to illustration 2.28

27   There are two ways to check the opera-

tion of the water pump while it's installed on the engine. If the pump is found to be defective, it should be replaced with a new or rebuilt unit.
28   Water pumps are equipped with weep (or vent) holes **(see illustration)**. If a failure occurs in the pump seal, coolant will leak from the hole.
29   If the water pump shaft bearings fail, there may be a howling sound at the pump while it's running. Shaft wear can be felt with the drivebelt removed if the water pump pulley is rocked up and down (with the engine off). Don't mistake drivebelt slippage, which causes a squealing sound, for water pump bearing failure.

Timing chain or timing belt-driven water pump

30   Water pumps driven by the timing chain or timing belt are located underneath the timing chain or timing belt cover.
31   Checking the water pump is limited because of where it is located. However, some basic checks can be made before deciding to remove the water pump. If the pump is found to be defective, it should be replaced with a new or rebuilt unit.
32   One sign that the water pump may be failing is that the heater (climate control) may not work well. Warm the engine to normal operating temperature, confirm that the coolant level is correct, then run the heater and check for hot air coming from the ducts.
33   Check for noises coming from the water pump area. If the water pump impeller shaft or bearings are failing, there may be a howling sound at the pump while the engine is running.
Note: *Be careful not to mistake drivebelt noise (squealing) for water pump bearing or shaft failure.*
34   It you suspect water pump failure due to noise, wear can be confirmed by feeling for play at the pump shaft. This can be done by rocking the drive sprocket on the pump shaft up and down. To do this you will need to remove the tension on the timing chain or belt as well as access the water pump.

All water pumps

35   In rare cases or on high-mileage vehicles, another sign of water pump failure may be the presence of coolant in the engine oil. This condition will adversely affect the engine in varying degrees.

Note: *Finding coolant in the engine oil could indicate other serious issues besides a failed water pump, such as a blown head gasket or a cracked cylinder head or block.*

36   Even a pump that exhibits no outward signs of a problem, such as noise or leakage, can still be due for replacement. Removal for close examination is the only sure way to tell. Sometimes the fins on the back of the impeller can corrode to the point that cooling efficiency is diminished significantly.

Heater system

37   Little can go wrong with a heater. If the fan motor will run at all speeds, the electrical part of the system is okay. The three basic heater problems fall into the following general categories:

a) *Not enough heat*
b) *Heat all the time*
c) *No heat*

38   If there's not enough heat, the control valve or door is stuck in a partially open position, the coolant coming from the engine isn't hot enough, or the heater core is restricted. If the coolant isn't hot enough, the thermostat in the engine cooling system is stuck open, allowing coolant to pass through the engine so rapidly that it doesn't heat up quickly enough. If the vehicle is equipped with a temperature gauge instead of a warning light, watch to see if the engine temperature rises to the normal operating range after driving for a reasonable distance.

39   If there's heat all the time, the control valve or the door is stuck wide open.

40   If there's no heat, coolant is probably not reaching the heater core, or the heater core is plugged. The likely cause is a collapsed or plugged hose, core, or a frozen heater control valve. If the heater is the type that flows coolant all the time, the cause is a stuck door or a broken or kinked control cable.

Air conditioning system

41   If the cool air output is inadequate:

a) *Inspect the condenser coils and fins to make sure they're clear*
b) *Check the compressor clutch for slippage.*
c) *Check the blower motor for proper operation.*
d) *Inspect the blower discharge passage for obstructions.*
e) *Check the system air intake filter for clogging.*

42   If the system provides intermittent cooling air:

a) *Check the circuit breaker, blower switch and blower motor for a malfunction.*
b) *Make sure the compressor clutch isn't slipping.*

c) *Inspect the plenum door to make sure it's operating properly.*
d) *Inspect the evaporator to make sure it isn't clogged.*
e) *If the unit is icing up, it may be caused by excessive moisture in the system, incorrect super heat switch adjustment or low thermostat adjustment.*

43   If the system provides no cooling air:

a) *Inspect the compressor drivebelt. Make sure it's not loose or broken.*
b) *Make sure the compressor clutch engages. If it doesn't, check for a blown fuse.*
c) *Inspect the wire harness for broken or disconnected wires.*
d) *If the compressor clutch doesn't engage, bridge the terminals of the A/C pressure switch(es) with a jumper wire; if the clutch now engages, and the system is properly charged, the pressure switch is bad.*
e) *Make sure the blower motor is not disconnected or burned out.*
f) *Make sure the compressor isn't partially or completely seized.*
g) *Inspect the refrigerant lines for leaks.*
h) *Check the components for leaks.*
i) *Inspect the receiver-drier/accumulator or expansion valve/tube for clogged screens.*

44   If the system is noisy:

a) *Look for loose panels in the passenger compartment.*
b) *Inspect the compressor drivebelt. It may be loose or worn.*
c) *Check the compressor mounting bolts. They should be tight.*
d) *Listen carefully to the compressor. It may be worn out.*
e) *Listen to the idler pulley and bearing and the clutch. Either may be defective.*
f) *The winding in the compressor clutch coil or solenoid may be defective.*
g) *The compressor oil level may be low.*
h) *The blower motor fan bushing or the motor itself may be worn out.*
i) *If there is an excessive charge in the system, you'll hear a rumbling noise in the high pressure line, a thumping noise in the compressor, or see bubbles or cloudiness in the sight glass.*
j) *If there's a low charge in the system, you might hear hissing in the evaporator case at the expansion valve, or see bubbles or cloudiness in the sight glass.*

---

3   Air conditioning and heating system - check and maintenance

Air conditioning system

Warning: *The air conditioning system is under high pressure. Do not loosen any hose fittings or remove any components until after the system has been discharged. Air conditioning refrigerant should be properly discharged into an EPA-approved recovery/recycling unit at a*

dealer service department or an automotive air conditioning repair facility. Always wear eye protection when disconnecting air conditioning system fittings.

Caution: *All models covered by this manual use environmentally friendly R-134a. This refrigerant (and its appropriate refrigerant oils) are not compatible with R-12 refrigerant system components and must never be mixed or the components will be damaged.*

Caution: *When replacing entire components, additional refrigerant oil should be added equal to the amount that is removed with the component being replaced. Be sure to read the can before adding any oil to the system, to make sure it is compatible with the R-134a system.*

1   The following maintenance checks should be performed on a regular basis to ensure that the air conditioning continues to operate at peak efficiency.

a) *Inspect the condition of the compressor drivebelt. If it is worn or deteriorated, replace it (see Chapter 1).*
b) *Check the drivebelt tension (see Chapter 1).*
c) *Inspect the system hoses. Look for cracks, bubbles, hardening and deterioration. Inspect the hoses and all fittings for oil bubbles or seepage. If there is any evidence of wear, damage or leakage, replace the hose(s).*
d) *Inspect the condenser fins for leaves, bugs and any other foreign material that may have embedded itself in the fins. Use a fin comb or compressed air to remove debris from the condenser.*
e) *Make sure the system has the correct refrigerant charge.*
f) *If you hear water sloshing around in the dash area or have water dripping on the carpet, check the evaporator housing drain tube and insert a piece of wire into the opening to check for blockage.*

2   It's a good idea to operate the system for about ten minutes at least once a month. This is particularly important during the winter months because long term non-use can cause hardening, and subsequent failure, of the seals. Note that using the Defrost function operates the compressor.

3   If the air conditioning system is not working properly, proceed to Step 6 and perform the general checks outlined below.

4   Because of the complexity of the air conditioning system and the special equipment necessary to service it, in-depth troubleshooting and repairs beyond checking the refrigerant charge and the compressor clutch operation are not included in this manual. However, simple checks and component replacement procedures are provided in this Chapter. For more complete information on the air conditioning system, refer to the *Haynes Automotive Heating and Air Conditioning Manual.*

5   The most common cause of poor cooling is simply a low system refrigerant charge. If a noticeable drop in system cooling ability occurs, one of the following quick checks will help you determine if the refrigerant level is low.

3.9 Insert a thermometer in the center vent, turn on the air conditioning system and wait for it to cool down; depending on the humidity, the output air should be 35 to 40 degrees cooler than the ambient air temperature

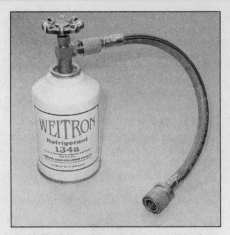

3.11 R-134a automotive air conditioning charging kit

3.13 Location of the low-side charging port

Checking the refrigerant charge

Refer to illustration 3.9

6   Warm the engine up to normal operating temperature.

7   Place the air conditioning temperature selector at the coldest setting and put the blower at the highest setting.

8   After the system reaches operating temperature, feel the larger pipe exiting the evaporator at the firewall. The outlet pipe should be cold (the tubing that leads back to the compressor). If the evaporator outlet pipe is warm, the system probably needs a charge.

9   Insert a thermometer in the center air distribution duct **(see illustration)** while operating the air conditioning system at its maximum setting - the temperature of the output air should be 35 to 40 degrees F below the ambient air temperature (down to approximately 40 degrees F). If the ambient (outside) air temperature is very high, say 110 degrees F, the duct air temperature may be as high as 60 degrees F, but generally the air conditioning is 35 to 40 degrees F cooler than the ambient air.

10   Further inspection or testing of the system requires special tools and techniques and is beyond the scope of the home mechanic.

Adding refrigerant

Refer to illustrations 3.11 and 3.13

Caution: *Make sure any refrigerant, refrigerant oil or replacement component you purchase is designated as compatible with R-134a systems.*

11   Purchase an R-134a automotive charging kit at an auto parts store **(see illustration)**. A charging kit includes a can of refrigerant, a tap valve and a short section of hose that can be attached between the tap valve and the system low side service valve.

Caution: *Never add more than one can of*

refrigerant to the system. If more refrigerant than that is required, the system should be evacuated and leak tested.

12   Back off the valve handle on the charging kit and screw the kit onto the refrigerant can, making sure first that the O-ring or rubber seal inside the threaded portion of the kit is in place.

Warning: *Wear protective eyewear when dealing with pressurized refrigerant cans.*

13   Remove the dust cap from the low-side charging port and attach the hose's quick-connect fitting to the port **(see illustration)**.

Warning: *DO NOT hook the charging kit hose to the system high side! The fittings on the charging kit are designed to fit **only** on the low side of the system.*

14   Warm up the engine and turn On the air conditioning. Keep the charging kit hose away from the fan and other moving parts.

Note: *The charging process requires the compressor to be running. If the clutch cycles off, you can put the air conditioning switch on High and leave the car doors open to keep the clutch on and compressor working. The compressor can be kept on during the charging by removing the connector from the pressure switch and bridging it with a paper clip or jumper wire during the procedure.*

15   Turn the valve handle on the kit until the stem pierces the can, then back the handle out to release the refrigerant. You should be able to hear the rush of gas. Keep the can upright at all times, but shake it occasionally. Allow stabilization time between each addition.

Note: *The charging process will go faster if you wrap the can with a hot-water-soaked rag to keep the can from freezing up.*

16   If you have an accurate thermometer, you can place it in the center air conditioning duct inside the vehicle and keep track of the output air temperature. A charged system that is working properly should cool down to

approximately 40 degrees F. If the ambient (outside) air temperature is very high, say 110 degrees F, the duct air temperature may be as high as 60 degrees F, but generally the air conditioning is 35 to 40 degrees F cooler than the ambient air.

17   When the can is empty, turn the valve handle to the closed position and release the connection from the low-side port. Reinstall the dust cap.

18   Remove the charging kit from the can and store the kit for future use with the piercing valve in the UP position, to prevent inadvertently piercing the can on the next use.

Heating systems

19   If the carpet under the heater core is damp, or if antifreeze vapor or steam is coming through the vents, the heater core is leaking. Remove it (see Section 10) and install a new unit (most radiator shops will not repair a leaking heater core).

20   If the air coming out of the heater vents isn't hot, the problem could stem from any of the following causes:

a)   *The thermostat is stuck open, preventing the engine coolant from warming up enough to carry heat to the heater core. Replace the thermostat (see Section 4).*

b)   *There is a blockage in the system, preventing the flow of coolant through the heater core. Feel both heater hoses at the firewall. They should be hot. If one of them is cold, there is an obstruction in one of the hoses or in the heater core, or the heater control valve is shut. Detach the hoses and back flush the heater core with a water hose. If the heater core is clear but circulation is impeded, remove the two hoses and flush them out with a water hose.*

c)   *If flushing fails to remove the blockage from the heater core, the core must be replaced (see Section 10).*

4.4a The thermostat housing cover and mounting bolts (3.3L and 3.8L shown, 4.0L similar)

4.4b On 3.6L engines, the thermostat is located at the right end of the engine, under the front valve cover

Eliminating air conditioning odors

21 Unpleasant odors that often develop in air conditioning systems are caused by the growth of a fungus, usually on the surface of the evaporator core. The warm, humid environment there is a perfect breeding ground for mildew to develop.

22 The evaporator core on most vehicles is difficult to access, and factory dealerships have a lengthy, expensive process for eliminating the fungus by opening up the evaporator case and using a powerful disinfectant and rinse on the core until the fungus is gone. You can service your own system at home, but it takes something much stronger than basic household germ-killers or deodorizers.

23 Aerosol disinfectants for automotive air conditioning systems are available in most auto parts stores, but remember when shopping for them that the most effective treatments are also the most expensive. The basic procedure for using these sprays is to start by running the system in the RECIRC mode for ten minutes with the blower on its highest speed. Use the highest heat mode to dry out the system and keep the compressor from engaging by disconnecting the wiring connector at the compressor.

24 The disinfectant can usually comes with a long spray hose. Insert the nozzle into an intake port inside the cabin filter housing, and spray according to the manufacturer's recommendations. Try to cover the whole surface of the evaporator core, by aiming the spray up, down and sideways. Follow the manufacturer's recommendations for the length of spray and waiting time between applications.

25 Once the evaporator has been cleaned, the best way to prevent the mildew from coming back again is to make sure your evaporator housing drain tube is clear.

Automatic heating and air conditioning systems

26 Some vehicles are equipped with an optional automatic climate control system. This system has its own computer that receives inputs from various sensors in the heating and air conditioning system. This computer, like the PCM, has self-diagnostic capabilities to help pinpoint problems or faults within the system. Vehicles equipped with automatic heating and air conditioning systems are very complex and considered beyond the scope of the home mechanic. Vehicles equipped with automatic heating and air conditioning systems should be taken to dealer service department or other qualified facility for repair.

4   Thermostat - replacement

Removal

Refer to illustrations 4.4a and 4.4b

Warning: *Do not remove the radiator cap, drain the coolant or replace the thermostat until the engine has cooled completely.*

Note: *On 3.6L engines, the thermostat is an integral part of the housing and must be replaced as an assembly.*

1   Disconnect the cable from the negative battery terminal (see Chapter 5).

2   Drain the cooling system (see Chapter 1). If the coolant is relatively new or in good condition, save it and reuse it. Read the **Warning** in Section 2.

3   On 3.6L engines, remove the air filter and intake hose assembly (see Chapter 4).

4   Follow the upper radiator hose to the engine to locate the thermostat housing cover **(see illustrations)**.

5   Loosen the hose clamp, then detach the hose from the fitting. If it's stuck, grasp it near the end with a pair of adjustable pliers and twist it to break the seal, then pull it off. If the hose is old or deteriorated, cut it off and install a new one.

Note: *If the outer surface of the large fitting that mates with the hose is deteriorated (corroded, pitted, etc.), it may be damaged further by hose removal. If it is, the thermostat housing cover will have to be replaced.*

Note: *If the hose has recently been replaced and the fitting is known to be in good condi-*

tion, the thermostat can be serviced without removing the hose from the housing cover.

6   Remove the thermostat housing cover fasteners and cover. If the cover is stuck, tap it with a soft-face hammer to jar it loose. Be prepared for some coolant to spill as the seal is broken.

Installation

7   Take note of how the thermostat and gasket or O-ring are installed.

8   Remove all traces of the old gasket from the mating surfaces and clean them thoroughly.

9   On 3.3L, 3.8L and 4.0L engines, install the new thermostat, with the jiggle pin in the 12 o'clock position, and the spring end directed into the engine.

10   Install a new gasket or O-ring, making sure that it is oriented in the same way as the original.

Note: *It is standard practice to use a thin layer of RTV sealant when installing flat replacement gaskets. However, if the gasket is designed with a raised crushable sealing surface (not flat), or if it is an O-ring, no RTV sealant is necessary.*

11   Install the thermostat housing cover, tightening the fasteners to the torque listed in this Chapter's Specifications.

12   Reattach the hose and tighten the hose clamp securely, if removed. Install all components that were previously removed.

13   On 3.6L engines reinstall the air filter and intake hose assembly.

14   Reconnect the battery (see Chapter 5).

15   Refill the cooling system (see Chapter 1).

16   Start the engine and allow it to reach normal operating temperature, then check for leaks and proper thermostat operation (as described in Section 2).

5   Engine cooling fan - replacement

Warning: *To avoid possible injury or damage, DO NOT operate the engine with a damaged fan. Do not attempt to repair fan blades - replace a damaged fan with a new one.*

Warning: *The electric fans can start at any time; keep hands, clothes and tools away from the fan until the battery is disconnected to avoid possible injury or damage.*

1   If the engine is overheating and the cooling fan is not coming on when the engine temperature rises to an excessive level, see Section 2. Check the fan relays in the underhood fuse/relay box.

2   If the relays are okay, check all wiring and connections to the fan motor. Refer to the wiring diagrams at the end of Chapter 12. If no obvious problems are found, the problem could be the Engine Coolant Temperature (ECT) sensor or the Powertrain Control Module (PCM). Have the cooling fan system and circuit diagnosed by a dealer service department or repair shop with the proper diagnostic equipment.

Replacement

Refer to illustration 5.7

3   Disconnect the cable from the negative battery terminal (see Chapter 5), then disconnect the cooling fan electrical connector(s).

4   Drain the cooling system (see Chapter 1).

5   Disconnect the upper radiator hose from the radiator.

6   Remove the coolant reservoir (see Section 6).

7   Remove the cooling fan assembly by pulling it straight up and out of the engine compartment **(see illustration)**.

8   Installation is the reverse of removal. Place the fan assembly back into the retaining clips for the side and bottom.

5.7 Lift the cooling fan upward to remove it from the engine compartment

6.2 Lift the reservoir straight up and off of the fan shroud

6   Coolant reservoir - removal and installation

Refer to illustration 6.2

Warning: *Wait until the engine is completely cool before beginning this procedure.*

1   Place a drain pan under the reservoir, then detach the reservoir hose.

2   Lift the reservoir straight up and off of the fan shroud **(see illustration)**.

3   Disconnect the hose from the reservoir.

4   Installation is the reverse of removal. While the reservoir is off the vehicle, it should be cleaned with soapy water and a brush to remove any deposits inside. Inspect it for damage and replace it if necessary. Fill the reservoir with the proper type and amount of coolant (see Chapter 1).

7   Radiator - removal and installation

Warning: *Wait until the engine is completely cool before beginning this procedure.*

Removal

Refer to illustration 7.7

1   Disconnect the cable from the negative battery terminal (see Chapter 5).

2   Set the parking brake, raise the front of the vehicle and support it securely on jackstands.

3   Drain the cooling system (see Chapter 1).

4   Remove the engine cooling fan (see Section 5).

5   Detach the coolant reservoir hose from the radiator filler neck and retainer and move it aside.

6   Disconnect the upper and lower radiator hoses from the radiator.

7   Remove the radiator support brace **(see illustration)**.

8   Carefully separate the A/C condenser from the radiator by removing the fasteners and disconnecting the condenser retaining tabs.

Note: *After separating the condenser, let it rest towards the front of the vehicle, being careful not to damage the cooling fins on it or the radiator.*

9   Lift the radiator from the vehicle.

10   Check the radiator for leaks and damage. If it needs repair, have a radiator shop or dealer service department perform the work, as special techniques are required.

11   Bugs and dirt can be removed from the radiator by spraying it from the back side with a garden hose. The radiator should be flushed out with a garden hose before reinstallation.

12   Check the radiator rubber mounts for deterioration and replace them if necessary.

Installation

13   Installation is the reverse of the removal procedure. Make sure the A/C condenser is properly attached to the radiator before seating the radiator into the lower rubber mounts.

Note: *Be sure that the flexible air seals on each side of the radiator are in the correct position while installing the radiator.*

14   After installation, fill the cooling system with the proper mixture of antifreeze and water (see Chapter 1).

15   Start the engine and check for leaks. Allow the engine to reach normal operating temperature, indicated by the upper radiator hose becoming hot. Recheck the coolant level and add more if required.

8   Water pump - replacement

Warning: *Wait until the engine is completely cool before beginning this procedure.*

1   Disconnect the cable from the negative battery terminal (see Chapter 5).

2   Set the parking brake, raise the front of the vehicle and support it securely on jackstands.

3   Drain the cooling system (see Chapter 1).

3.3L and 3.8L engines

Refer to illustrations 8.5, 8.8 and 8.9

4   Remove the engine splash shield.

7.7 Radiator support brace mounting fasteners

8.5 Water pump pulley bolts

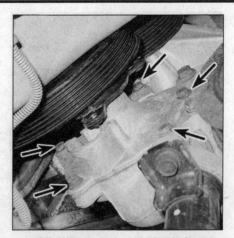

8.8 Water pump mounting bolts

8.9 Placing the water pump pulley towards the pump housing

5   Loosen the water pump pulley bolts **(see illustration)**.
6   Remove the drivebelt (see Chapter 1).
7   Remove the pulley bolts.
8   Position the pulley to allow access to the water pump mounting bolts, then remove the bolts **(see illustration)**.
9   Rotate and move the pulley inward between the pump housing and the hub, then remove the water pump and pulley together **(see illustration)**.
10   Clean the bolt threads and threaded holes in the timing case cover to remove any corrosion and sealant.
11   Remove and discard the old seal and clean the mating surfaces. Do not gouge or scratch the mating surface on the timing case cover.
12   Install a new O-ring seal in the groove that lines the water pump body, then apply a thin film of RTV sealant to hold the seal in place during installation.
Caution: *Make sure that the O-ring seal is correctly seated in the water pump groove to avoid a coolant leak.*
13   Position the water pump pulley loosely between the pump housing and drive hub.

Note: *The water pump pulley must be positioned this way to install the water pump and pulley together.*
14   Install the water pump mounting bolts and tighten them to the torque listed in this Chapter's Specifications.
Caution: *Don't overtighten the mounting bolts; doing so will damage the pump.*
15   Position the pulley onto the drive hub and install the mounting bolts finger tight.
16   Install the drivebelt (see Chapter 1).
17   Tighten the pulley bolts to the torque listed in this Chapter's Specifications.
18   The remainder of installation is the reverse of removal. Refill and bleed the cooling system (see Chapter 1). Run the engine and check for leaks and proper operation.

3.6L engines

Refer to illustrations 8.24 and 8.27

19   Remove the air filter housing (see Chapter 4).
20   Unbolt the power steering reservoir and set it to the side.
21   Remove the right side engine mount (see Chapter 2B).

22   Remove the engine mount brace from the water pump.
23   Remove the drivebelt (see Chapter 1).
24   Remove the idler pulley **(see illustration)**.
25   Raise the front of the vehicle and support it securely on jackstands, then remove the right front wheel.
26   Remove the inner fender splash shield (see Chapter 11).
27   Disconnect the bypass and lower radiator hoses **(see illustration)**.
28   Remove the water pump mounting bolts.
29   Clean the bolt threads and threaded holes in the timing case cover to remove any corrosion and sealant.
30   Remove and discard the old seal and clean the mating surfaces. Do not gouge or scratch the mating surface on the timing case cover.
31   Install a new seal, then carefully mate the pump to the engine.
32   Install the water pump mounting bolts and tighten them to the torque listed in this Chapter's Specifications.
Caution: *Don't overtighten the mounting bolts; doing so will damage the pump.*

8.24 Remove the fastener securing the idler pulley

8.27 Disconnect the bypass (A) and lower radiator (B) hoses

9.2 Pull down the insulation to release the clips securing the insulation

33   Install the drivebelt (see Chapter 1).
34   The remainder of installation is the reverse of removal. Refill and bleed the cooling system (see Chapter 1). Run the engine and check for leaks and proper operation.

4.0L engines

35   Remove the timing belt (see Chapter 2B).
36   Remove the water pump mounting bolts.
37   Clean the bolt threads and threaded holes in the timing case cover to remove any corrosion and sealant.
38   Remove and discard the old seal and clean the mating surfaces. Do not gouge or scratch the mating surface on the timing case cover.
39   Install a new O-ring seal in the groove that lines the water pump body, then apply a thin film of RTV sealant to hold the seal in place during installation.
Caution: *Make sure that the O-ring seal is correctly seated in the water pump groove to avoid a coolant leak.*
40   Carefully mate the pump to the engine.
41   Install the water pump mounting bolts and tighten them to the torque listed in this Chapter's Specifications.
Caution: *Don't overtighten the mounting bolts; doing so will damage the pump.*
42   Install the timing belt (see Chapter 2B).
43   The remainder of installation is the reverse of removal. Refill and bleed the cooling system (see Chapter 1). Run the engine and check for leaks and proper operation.

9   Blower motor resistor/power module and blower motor assembly - replacement

Warning: *The models covered by this manual are equipped with Supplemental Restraint systems (SRS), more commonly known as airbags. Always disable the airbag system before working in the vicinity of any airbag system component to avoid the possibility of*

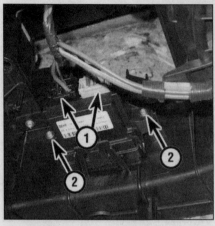

9.3 Blower motor power module details:

1   *Electrical connectors*
2   *Mounting fasteners*

accidental deployment of the airbag, which could cause personal injury (see Chapter 12).
1   Disconnect the cable from the negative battery terminal (see Chapter 5).

Front

Refer to illustration 9.2
2   Pull down the insulation under the glove box **(see illustration).**

Blower motor power module

Refer to illustration 9.3
3   Disconnect the electrical connectors for the blower motor power module **(see illustration).**
Note: *Models equipped with automatic temperature control utilize a power module instead of a blower motor resistor. They are similar in the way they are mounted and connected.*
4   Remove the mounting fasteners **(see illustration 9.3)** and withdraw the unit from the heater/air conditioning housing.
5   Installation is the reverse of removal.

Blower motor assembly

Refer to illustration 9.6
Note: *The blower motor and blower wheel are balanced to each other at the factory and replaced only as an assembly.*
6   Disconnect the electrical connector for the blower motor **(see illustration).**
7   Remove the blower motor mounting fasteners **(see illustration 9.6),** then remove the blower motor.
8   Installation is the reverse of removal.

Rear

Warning: *The air conditioning system is under high pressure. DO NOT loosen any fittings or remove any components until after the system has been discharged. Air conditioning refrigerant must be properly discharged into an EPA-approved container at a dealer service department or an automotive air conditioning repair facility. Always wear eye protection when disconnecting air conditioning system fittings.*
Warning: *Wait until the engine is completely cool before beginning this procedure.*
9   Remove the rear heating and air conditioning housing (see Section 16).

Blower motor resistor

10   With the heater/air conditioning housing on a bench, disconnect the electrical connector for the blower motor resistor.
11   Remove the mounting fasteners and withdraw the unit from the heater/air conditioning housing.
12   Installation is the reverse of removal.

Blower motor assembly

Note: *The blower motor and blower wheel are balanced to each other at the factory and replaced as an assembly only.*
13   Disconnect the electrical connector for the blower motor.
14   Remove the blower motor mounting screws on the rear of the housing.
15   Remove the blower motor from the housing.
16   Installation is the reverse of removal.

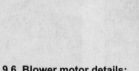

9.6 Blower motor details:

1   *Electrical connector*
2   *Mounting fasteners*

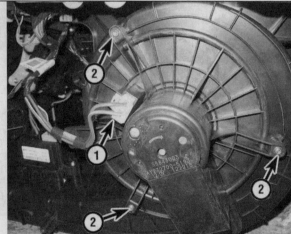

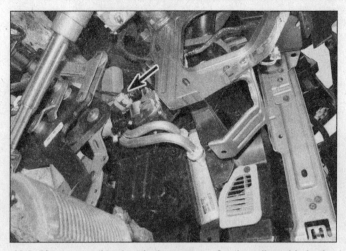

10.3 Disconnect the electrical connector for the adjustable brake pedal motor

10.4a Mounting fasteners for the heater core cover

10 Heater core - replacement

Warning: *Wait until the engine is completely cool before beginning this procedure.*

1   Disconnect the cable from the negative battery terminal (see Chapter 5). Drain the cooling system (see Chapter 1).

Front

Refer to illustrations 10.3, 10.4a, 104b and 10.5

2   Remove the center console (see Chapter 11).
3   If equipped, disconnect the electrical connector for the adjustable brake pedal motor **(see illustration)**.
4   Remove the mounting fasteners securing the heater core cover, then rotate the heater core cover to disengage the retaining tab at the firewall **(see illustrations)**.
5   Place towels underneath the heater core tube fittings and remove the retaining clamps from the tubes **(see illustration)**.
6   Pull the tubes from the heater core and carefully rotate them up and out of the way. Plug or cap the openings to minimize contamination and spilled coolant.
7   Carefully pull the heater core out of the heater/air conditioning housing.
8   Installation is the reverse of removal. Use new seals for the heater core fittings and refill the cooling system (see Chapter 1).

Rear

Warning: *The air conditioning system is under high pressure. DO NOT loosen any fittings or remove any components until after the system has been discharged. Air conditioning refrigerant must be properly discharged into an EPA-approved container at a dealer service department or an automotive air conditioning repair facility. Always wear eye protection when disconnecting air conditioning system fittings.*
Warning: *Wait until the engine is completely cool before beginning this procedure.*

10.4b Pull the cover away from the heater core tubes

9   Remove the rear heater/air conditioning housing and set it on a bench (see Section 16).
10   Remove the fastener securing the heater core tube bracket to the housing.
11   Carefully release the two plastic retainers while pulling the heater core out of the heater/air conditioning housing.
12   Remove the heater core completely from the housing.
13   Installation is the reverse of removal. Pre-fill the heater core and quickly attach the hoses. Check the cooling system level after reassembly is complete (see Chapter 1).
Note: *If the heater core was replaced and not pre-filled, thermal cycle the vehicle TWICE. This procedure ensures that the heater core is filled completely.*
To thermal cycle the vehicle, it must be operated until the thermostat opens, then turned off and allowed to cool. The coolant level in the reservoir must be maintained during this process. To verify that the rear unit is filled completely, follow this procedure:

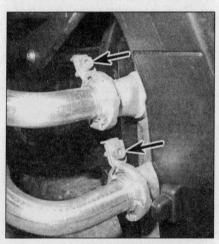

10.5 Remove the fasteners securing the clamps

a) *Begin with the vehicle at room temperature.*
b) *Start the vehicle and bring the engine to operating temperature.*
c) *Set the temperature to the full HEAT position in the front A/C control, then turn off the front system.*
d) *Start the engine and turn the rear A/C system blower on HIGH with the temperature setting in the full HEAT position.*
e) *The discharge air temperature, measured at the dual register located on the C-pillar base, should be between 135-degrees and 145-degrees F.*

11 Heater/air conditioner control assembly - removal and installation

Warning: *The models covered by this manual are equipped with Supplemental Restraint systems (SRS), more commonly known as airbags. Always disable the airbag system*

11.2 Carefully pry the heater/air conditioning control bezel assembly from the instrument panel

11.3 The heater/air conditioning electrical connectors

before working in the vicinity of any airbag system component to avoid the possibility of accidental deployment of the airbag, which could cause personal injury (see Chapter 12).

Front

Refer to illustration 11.2, 11.3 and 11.4

1   Disconnect the cable from the negative battery terminal (see Chapter 5).
2   Carefully pry the heater/air conditioning control bezel assembly from the instrument panel **(see illustration)**.
3   Disconnect the electrical connectors from the back of the heater/air conditioning control assembly **(see illustration)**.
4   Remove the mounting fasteners at each corner, then remove the control assembly from the bezel **(see illustration)**.
5   Installation is the reverse of removal.

Rear

Refer to illustrations 11.7 and 11.8

6   Disconnect the cable from the negative battery terminal (see Chapter 5).
7   Gently pry the rear heater/air conditioning control bezel assembly from the headliner **(see illustration)**.

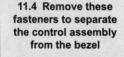

11.4 Remove these fasteners to separate the control assembly from the bezel

8   Disconnect the electrical connector from the back of the control assembly **(see illustration)**.
9   Remove the mounting fasteners and remove the control assembly from the bezel.
10   Installation is the reverse of removal. If the heater/air conditioning control assembly is being replaced, calibration/diagnostic tests will be necessary. This will require a specialized scan tool; take the vehicle to a dealer service department or other qualified repair shop to have this service performed.

12   Air conditioning compressor - removal and installation

Refer to illustration 12.5

Warning: *The air conditioning system is under high pressure. DO NOT loosen any fittings or remove any components until after the system has been discharged. Air conditioning refrigerant must be properly discharged into an EPA-approved container at a dealer service department or an automotive air conditioning repair*

11.7 Gently pry off the rear heater/air conditioning control bezel assembly

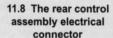

11.8 The rear control assembly electrical connector

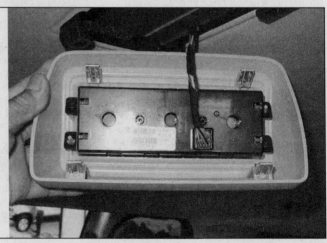

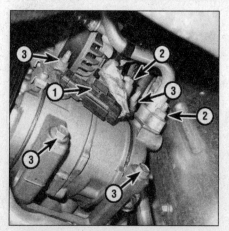

12.5 Air conditioning compressor details

1   *Electrical connector*
2   *Refrigerant line fitting nuts*
3   *Compressor mounting bolts*

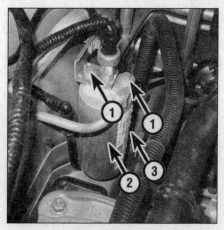

13.3 Receiver-drier details:

1   *Mounting fasteners for the A/C lines*
2   *Receiver-drier*
3   *Receiver-drier mounting fastener*

14.4 Disconnect the refrigerant lines

facility. Always wear eye protection when disconnecting air conditioning system fittings.
Caution: *When replacing entire components, additional refrigerant oil must be added equal to the amount that is removed with the component being replaced. Read the label on the oil container to verify that it is compatible with the R-134a system before adding any of it to the system.*
Note: *The receiver-drier should always be replaced when the compressor is replaced (see Section 13).*
1   Have the system discharged and the refrigerant recovered by an air conditioning technician.
2   Disconnect the cable from the negative battery terminal (see Chapter 5).
3   Raise the front of the vehicle and support it securely on jackstands.
4   Remove the drivebelt (see Chapter 1).
Note: *On V6 models, if more access is necessary for compressor removal, you can remove the alternator (see Chapter 5).*
5   Disconnect the engine wire harness connector from the compressor clutch coil **(see illustration)** and remove the bracket on top of the compressor.
6   Remove the refrigerant lines from the compressor. Plug all open fittings to prevent entry of dirt and moisture.
7   Remove the compressor mounting fasteners and lower the compressor from the vehicle.
8   If a new compressor is being installed, pour out the oil from the old compressor into a graduated container and add that amount of new refrigerant oil to the new compressor. Also follow any directions included with the new compressor.
Note: *The clutch may have to be transferred from the original compressor to the new one.*
9   Installation is the reverse of removal. Install new O-rings onto the line fittings and lightly coat them with the correct refrigerant oil.

Note: *Only use O-rings that are designed specifically for A/C system applications.*
10   Have the system evacuated, recharged and leak tested by the shop that discharged it.

13   Air conditioning receiver-drier - removal and installation

Refer to illustration 13.3
Warning: *The air conditioning system is under high pressure. DO NOT loosen any fittings or remove any components until after the system has been discharged. Air conditioning refrigerant must be properly discharged into an EPA-approved container at a dealer service department or an automotive air conditioning repair facility. Always wear eye protection when disconnecting air conditioning system fittings.*
Caution: *When replacing entire components, additional refrigerant oil must be added equal to the amount that is removed with the component being replaced. Read the label on the oil container to verify that it is compatible with the R-134a system before adding any of it to the system.*
1   Have the system discharged and the refrigerant recovered by an air conditioning technician.
2   Remove the air filter housing (see Chapter 4).
3   Remove both line fittings from the receiver-drier **(see illustration).**
Note: *Plug all openings immediately to prevent contamination.*
4   Remove the mounting fastener retaining the receiver-drier bracket to the shock tower. Note the position of the ground strap (if equipped).
5   Remove the receiver-drier.
6   Installation is the reverse of removal. Install new O-rings onto the line fittings and lightly coat them with the correct refrigerant oil.

Note: *Only use O-rings that are designed specifically for A/C system applications.*
If you are replacing the receiver-drier with a new unit, add 0.8-ounce (25 ml) of refrigerant oil to the replacement.
7   Have the system evacuated, recharged and leak tested by the shop that discharged it.

14   Air conditioning condenser - removal and installation

Refer to illustration 14.4
Warning: *The air conditioning system is under high pressure. DO NOT loosen any fittings or remove any components until after the system has been discharged. Air conditioning refrigerant must be properly discharged into an EPA-approved container at a dealer service department or an automotive air conditioning repair facility. Always wear eye protection when disconnecting air conditioning system fittings.*
Caution: *When replacing entire components, additional refrigerant oil must be added equal to the amount that is removed with the component being replaced. Read the label on the oil container to verify that it is compatible with the R-134a system before adding any of it to the system.*
Note: *If the condenser is being replaced because of damage (cracked or punctured), the receiver-drier should also be replaced (see Section 13).*
1   Have the system discharged and the refrigerant recovered by an air conditioning technician.
2   Disconnect the cable from the negative battery terminal (see Chapter 5).
3   Remove the grille assembly (see Chapter 11).
4   Disconnect the refrigerant lines from the block at the right front corner of the engine compartment **(see illustration).** Plug all open fittings to prevent entry of dirt and moisture.
5   Remove the radiator support brace (see Section 7).
6   Disconnect the automatic transaxle

fluid cooler lines from the left side of the condenser.

7   Separate the condenser from the plastic clip-type retainers.

8   Carefully pull straight up to release the condenser from the lower clips, then remove the condenser from the vehicle.

9   Installation is the reverse of removal. Make certain to fully seat the condenser into the mounting clips and retainers. Install new O-rings onto the line fittings and lightly coat them with refrigerant oil.

Note: *Only use O-rings that are designed specifically for A/C system applications.*

If you are replacing the A/C condenser with a new unit, add 1.7-ounce (50 ml) of refrigerant oil to the replacement.

10   Have the system evacuated, recharged and leak tested by the shop that discharged it.

15   Expansion valve - removal and installation

Warning: *The air conditioning system is under high pressure. DO NOT loosen any fittings or remove any components until after the system has been discharged. Air conditioning refrigerant must be properly discharged into an EPA-approved container at a dealer service department or an automotive air conditioning repair facility. Always wear eye protection when disconnecting air conditioning system fittings.*

1   Have the air conditioning system refrigerant discharged and recovered by an air conditioning technician.

2   Disconnect the cable from the negative battery terminal (see Chapter 5).

Front

Refer to illustration 15.3

3   Remove the nut securing both line fittings to the valve and remove the lines while discarding the seals. Plug all openings quickly to minimize contamination **(see illustration)**.

4   Remove the mounting fasteners for the valve, then remove the valve while discarding any other seals. Again, plug all openings.

5   Installation is the reverse of removal. Install new O-rings onto the line fittings and lightly coat them with the correct refrigerant oil.

Note: *Only use O-rings that are designed specifically for A/C system applications.*

6   Have the system evacuated, recharged and leak tested by the shop that discharged it.

Rear

7   Raise the vehicle and support it securely on jackstands.

8   Working behind the rear wheel housing, remove the nut securing both line fittings to the valve and remove the lines while dis-

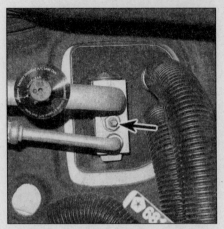

15.3 Refrigerant line fitting nut at the expansion valve

carding the seals. Plug all openings quickly to minimize contamination.

9   Remove the mounting fasteners for the valve, then remove the valve while discarding any other seals. Again, plug all openings.

10   Installation is the reverse of removal. Install new O-rings onto the line fittings and lightly coat them with the correct refrigerant oil.

Note: *Only use O-rings that are designed specifically for A/C system applications.*

11   Have the system evacuated, recharged and leak tested by the shop that discharged it.

16   Rear heating and air conditioning housing - removal and installation

Refer to illustration 16.4

Warning: *The air conditioning system is under high pressure. DO NOT loosen any fittings or remove any components until after the system has been discharged. Air conditioning refrigerant must be properly discharged into an EPA-approved container at a dealer service department or an automotive air conditioning repair facility. Always wear eye protection when disconnecting air conditioning system fittings.*

Warning: *Wait until the engine is completely cool before beginning this procedure.*

1   Have the air conditioning system refrigerant discharged and recovered by an air conditioning technician.

2   Disconnect the cable from the negative battery terminal (see Chapter 5).

3   Remove the refrigerant lines and expansion valve from the heater/air conditioning housing under the vehicle (see Section 15) and plug or cap all open ends.

Note: *Discard the old refrigerant line seals; new seals will be required when the lines are reconnected.*

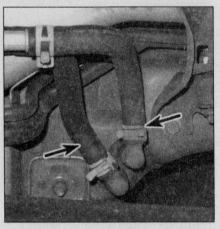

16.4 Heater hoses at the rear heater core pipes

4   Raise the rear of the vehicle and support it securely on jackstands. Working under the vehicle, pinch off the heater hoses at the rear heater core with locking pliers, or equivalent, then detach them from the core **(see illustration)**.

Caution: *Line the jaws of the pliers with a rag to prevent damage to the hose.*

Plug or cap the hose and core ends to minimize coolant loss.

Note: *Be prepared for some coolant to spill when disconnecting the hoses from the heater core.*

5   Lower the vehicle, then remove the right rear trim panels (see Chapter 11).

6   Remove the lower air duct from above the rear wheel housing.

7   Remove the strap from the rear quarter panel and the floor.

8   Remove the upper air ducts from the heater/air conditioning housing.

9   Remove the fasteners securing the heater core tubes to the floor and right quarter panel.

10   Disconnect the wiring harness from the heater/air conditioning harness connector.

11   Remove the mounting fasteners that secure the housing to the metal brackets.

12   Carefully lift the heater/air conditioning housing high enough to clear the floor and remove it from the vehicle. Be sure that no wires or brackets are still connected to the housing as it is being removed.

13   Installation is the reverse of removal. Install new seals (coated with clean refrigerant oil) at the refrigerant lines. Top off the cooling system and have the air conditioning system evacuated, recharged and leak tested.

Note: *If the heater core was emptied and not pre-filled, thermal cycle the vehicle TWICE. This procedure ensures that the heater core is filled completely.*

To thermal cycle the vehicle, refer to the procedure at the end of Section 10.

Chapter 4
Fuel and exhaust systems

Contents

Specifications

Fuel system

Fuel system pressure (all models) .... 53 to 63 psi

Torque specifications

Ft-lbs (unless otherwise indicated)

Note: *One foot-pound (ft-lb) of torque is equivalent to 12 inch-pounds (in-lbs) of torque. Torque values below approximately 15 ft-lbs are expressed in inch-pounds, since most foot-pound torque wrenches are not accurate at these smaller values.*

Fuel rail bolts
    3.3L and 3.8L engines .... 106 in-lbs
    3.6L engines .... 45 in-lbs
    4.0L engines 20.5
Throttle body mounting bolts
    3.3L and 3.8L engines .... 65 in-lbs
    3.6L engines .... 80 in-lbs
    4.0L engines .... 50 in-lbs

2.2 Fuel pump relay fuse location on a 2012 3.6L model (be sure to check the underside of the fuse relay box for the exact location on your vehicle)

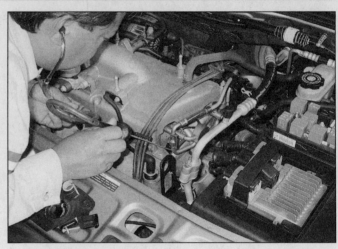

2.9 An automotive stethoscope is used to listen to the fuel injectors in operation

1   General information

Fuel system warnings

Gasoline is extremely flammable and repairing fuel system components can be dangerous. Consider your automotive repair knowledge and experience before attempting repairs which may be better suited for a professional mechanic.

- Don't smoke or allow open flames or bare light bulbs near the work area
- Don't work in a garage with a gas-type appliance (water heater, clothes dryer)
- Use fuel-resistant gloves. If any fuel spills on your skin, wash it off immediately with soap and water
- Clean up spills immediately
- Do not store fuel-soaked rags where they could ignite
- Prior to disconnecting any fuel line, you must relieve the fuel pressure (see Section 3)
- Wear safety glasses
- Have a proper fire extinguisher on hand

Fuel system

The fuel system consists of the fuel tank, electric fuel pump/fuel level sending unit (located in the fuel tank), fuel rail and fuel injectors. The fuel injection system is a multi-port system; multi-port fuel injection uses timed impulses to inject the fuel directly into the intake port of each cylinder. The Powertrain Control Module (PCM) controls the injectors. The PCM monitors various engine parameters and delivers the exact amount of fuel required into the intake ports.

Fuel is circulated from the fuel pump to the fuel rail through fuel lines running along the underside of the vehicle. Various sections of the fuel line are either rigid metal or nylon, or flexible fuel hose. The various sections of the fuel hose are connected either by quick-connect fittings or threaded metal fittings.

Exhaust system

The exhaust system consists of the exhaust manifold(s), catalytic converter(s), muffler(s), tailpipe and all connecting pipes, flanges and clamps. The catalytic converters are an emission control device added to the exhaust system to reduce pollutants.

2   Troubleshooting

Fuel pump

Refer to illustration 2.2

1   The fuel pump is located inside the fuel tank. Sit inside the vehicle with the windows closed, turn the ignition key to ON (not START) and listen for the sound of the fuel pump as it's briefly activated. You will only hear the sound for a second or two, but that sound tells you that the pump is working. Alternatively, have an assistant listen at the fuel filler cap.

2   If the pump does not come on, check the fuel pump relay fuse **(see illustration)**.

Note: *The fuel pump "relay" is actually just a circuit incorporated into the Totally Integrated Power Module, which is part of the underhood fuse/relay block; there is no replaceable fuel pump relay.*

If the fuse is okay, check the wiring back to the fuel pump. If the fuse and wiring are okay, the fuel pump module is probably defective. If the pump runs continuously with the ignition key in the ON position, the Totally Integrated Power Module or Powertrain Control Module (PCM) is probably defective. Have the circuit checked by a professional mechanic.

Fuel injection system

Refer to illustration 2.9

Note: *The following procedure is based on the assumption that the fuel pump is working and the fuel pressure is adequate (see Section 4).*

3   Check all electrical connectors that are related to the system. Check the ground wire connections for tightness.

4   Verify that the battery is fully charged (see Chapter 5).

5   Inspect the air filter element (see Chapter 1).

6   Check all fuses related to the fuel system (see Chapter 12).

7   Check the air induction system between the throttle body and the intake manifold for air leaks. Also inspect the condition of all vacuum hoses connected to the intake manifold and to the throttle body.

8   Remove the air intake duct from the throttle body and look for dirt, carbon, varnish, or other residue in the throttle body, particularly around the throttle plate. If it's dirty, clean it with carb cleaner, a toothbrush and a clean shop towel.

9   With the engine running, place an automotive stethoscope against each injector, one at a time, and listen for a clicking sound that indicates operation **(see illustration)**.

Warning: *Stay clear of the drivebelt and any rotating or hot components.*

Note: *This check will not be possible on some models, as the upper intake manifold (plenum) is in the way.*

10   If you can hear the injectors operating, but the engine is misfiring, the electrical circuits are functioning correctly, but the injectors might be dirty or clogged. Try a commercial injector cleaning product (available at auto parts stores). If cleaning the injectors doesn't help, replace the injectors.

11   If an injector is not operating (it makes no sound), disconnect the injector electrical connector and measure the resistance

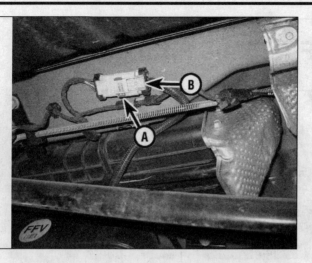

3.2 To relieve the pressure in the fuel system, disable the electric fuel pump by unplugging the electrical connector in the fuel pump module harness; slide out the connector lock (A), then depress the tab (B) and pull the two halves apart

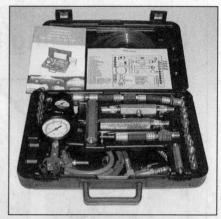

4.2 This typical fuel pressure testing kit contains all the necessary fittings and adapters, along with the fuel pressure gauge, to test most automotive fuel systems

across the injector terminals with an ohmmeter. Compare this measurement to the other injectors. If the resistance of the non-operational injector is quite different from the other injectors, replace it.

12   If the injector is not operating, but the resistance reading is within the range of resistance of the other injectors, the PCM or the circuit between the PCM and the injector might be faulty.

3   Fuel pressure relief procedure

Refer to illustration 3.2
Warning: *Gasoline is extremely flammable. See* **Fuel system warnings** *in Section 1.*
1   Remove the fuel filler cap to relieve any pressure built-up in the fuel tank.
2   Unplug the electrical connector in the fuel pump module harness, at the rear of the fuel tank **(see illustration)**.
3   Start the engine; it should run momentarily then stall. Crank the engine several more times to ensure the fuel system has

been completely relieved. Disconnect the cable from the negative terminal of the battery before working on the fuel system.
4   It's a good idea to cover any fuel connection to be disassembled with rags to absorb the residual fuel that may leak out. Properly dispose of the rags.

4   Fuel pressure - check

Refer to illustrations 4.2, 4.4a and 4.4b
Warning: *Gasoline is extremely flammable. See* **Fuel system warnings** *in Section 1.*
Note: *The following procedure assumes that the fuel pump is receiving voltage and runs.*
1   Relieve the fuel system pressure (see Section 3).
2   In addition to a fuel pressure gauge capable of reading fuel pressure up to 70 psi, you'll need a hose and an adapter suitable for tee-ing into the fuel system at the quick-connect fitting between the fuel delivery hose and the fuel rail **(see illustration)**.

3   Disconnect the quick-connect fitting at the connection between the fuel delivery hose and the fuel rail (if you're unfamiliar with quick-connect fittings, refer to Section 5).
4   Tee-in the fuel pressure gauge between the fuel delivery hose and the fuel rail **(see illustrations)**.
5   Start the engine and allow it to idle. Note the gauge reading as soon as the pressure stabilizes, and compare it with the pressure listed in this Chapter's Specifications.
6   If the fuel pressure is not within specifications, check the following:
 a) *If the pressure is lower than specified, check for a restriction in the fuel system (kinked fuel line, plugged fuel pump inlet strainer or clogged fuel filter). If no restrictions are found, replace the fuel pump module (see Section 8).*
 b) *If the fuel pressure is higher than specified, replace the fuel pump module (see Section 8).*

4.4a Connect the fuel pressure gauge hoses to the fuel delivery hose and the fuel rail (3.8L engine)

4.4b The fuel pressure gauge is installed between the fuel feed line (A) and fuel rail (B) (3.6L engine)

Disconnecting Fuel Line Fittings

Two-tab type fitting; depress both tabs with your fingers, then pull the fuel line and the fitting apart

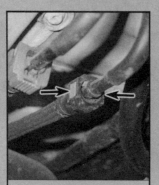

On this type of fitting, depress the two buttons on opposite sides of the fitting, then pull it off the fuel line

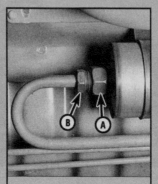

Threaded fuel line fitting; hold the stationary portion of the line or component (A) while loosening the tube nut (B) with a flare-nut wrench

Plastic collar-type fitting; rotate the outer part of the fitting

Metal collar quick-connect fitting; pull the end of the retainer off the fuel line and disengage the other end from the female side of the fitting . . .

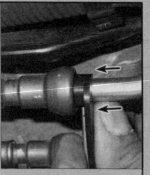

. . . insert a fuel line separator tool into the female side of the fitting, push it into the fitting and pull the fuel line off the pipe

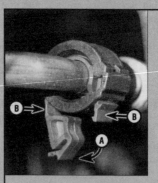

Some fittings are secured by lock tabs. Release the lock tab (A) and rotate it to the fully-opened position, squeeze the two smaller lock tabs (B) . . .

. . . then push the retainer out and pull the fuel line off the pipe

Spring-lock coupling; remove the safety cover, install a coupling release tool and close the tool around the coupling . . .

. . . push the tool into the fitting, then pull the two lines apart

Hairpin clip type fitting: push the legs of the retainer clip together, then push the clip down all the way until it stops and pull the fuel line off the pipe

6.1 Here's a typical exhaust system hanger. Inspect them regularly and replace at the first sign of damage or deterioration

7   Turn off the engine. Fuel pressure should not fall more than 8 psi over five minutes. If it does, the problem could be a leaky fuel injector, fuel line leak, or faulty fuel pump module.

8   Relieve the fuel system pressure, then disconnect the fuel pressure gauge. Reconnect the fuel line and wipe up any spilled gasoline.

5   Fuel lines and fittings - general information and disconnection

Warning: *Gasoline is extremely flammable. See **Fuel system warnings** in Section 1.*

1   Relieve the fuel pressure before servicing fuel lines or fittings (see Section 3), then disconnect the cable from the negative battery terminal (see Chapter 5) before proceeding.

2   The fuel supply line connects the fuel pump in the fuel tank to the fuel rail on the engine. The Evaporative Emission (EVAP) system lines connect the fuel tank to the EVAP canister and connect the canister to the intake manifold.

3   Whenever you're working under the vehicle, be sure to inspect all fuel and evaporative emission lines for leaks, kinks, dents and other damage. Always replace a damaged fuel or EVAP line immediately.

4   If you find signs of dirt in the lines during disassembly, disconnect all lines and blow them out with compressed air. Inspect the fuel strainer on the fuel pump pick-up unit for damage and deterioration.

Steel tubing

5   It is critical that the fuel lines be replaced with lines of equivalent type and specification.

6   Some steel fuel lines have threaded fittings. When loosening these fittings, hold the stationary fitting with a wrench while turning the tube nut.

Plastic tubing

7   When replacing fuel system plastic tubing, use only original equipment replacement plastic tubing.

Caution: *When removing or installing plastic fuel line tubing, be careful not to bend or twist it too much, which can damage it. Also,* plastic fuel tubing is NOT heat resistant, so keep it away from excessive heat.

Flexible hoses

8   When replacing fuel system flexible hoses, use only original equipment replacements.

9   Don't route fuel hoses (or metal lines) within four inches of the exhaust system or within ten inches of the catalytic converter. Make sure that no rubber hoses are installed directly against the vehicle, particularly in places where there is any vibration. If allowed to touch some vibrating part of the vehicle, a hose can easily become chafed and it might start leaking. A good rule of thumb is to maintain a minimum of 1/4-inch clearance around a hose (or metal line) to prevent contact with the vehicle underbody.

6   Exhaust system servicing - general information

Refer to illustration 6.1

Warning: *Allow exhaust system components to cool before inspection or repair. Also, when working under the vehicle, make sure it is securely supported on jackstands.*

1   The exhaust system consists of the exhaust manifolds, catalytic converter, muffler, tailpipe and all connecting pipes, flanges and clamps. The exhaust system is isolated from the vehicle body and from chassis components by a series of rubber hangers **(see illustration)**. Periodically inspect these hangers for cracks or other signs of deterioration, replacing them as necessary.

2   Conduct regular inspections of the exhaust system to keep it safe and quiet. Look for any damaged or bent parts, open seams, holes, loose connections, excessive corrosion or other defects which could allow exhaust fumes to enter the vehicle. Do not repair deteriorated exhaust system components; replace them with new parts.

3   If the exhaust system components are extremely corroded, or rusted together, a cutting torch is the most convenient tool for removal. Consult a properly-equipped repair shop. If a cutting torch is not available, you can use a hacksaw, or if you have compressed air, there are special pneumatic cutting chisels that can also be used. Wear safety goggles to protect your eyes from metal chips and wear work gloves to protect your hands.

4   Here are some simple guidelines to follow when repairing the exhaust system:
a) *Work from the back to the front when removing exhaust system components.*
b) *Apply penetrating oil to the exhaust system component fasteners to make them easier to remove.*
c) *Use new gaskets, hangers and clamps.*
d) *Apply anti-seize compound to the threads of all exhaust system fasteners during reassembly.*
e) *Be sure to allow sufficient clearance between newly installed parts and all points on the underbody to avoid overheating the floor pan and possibly damaging the interior carpet and insulation. Pay particularly close attention to the catalytic converter and heat shield.*

7   Fuel tank - removal and installation

Refer to illustrations 7.5, 7.7 and 7.8

Warning: *Gasoline is extremely flammable. See **Fuel system warnings** in Section 1.*

Note: *The following procedure is much easier to perform if the fuel tank is empty. If the fuel tank isn't empty or nearly empty, you can siphon fuel from the tank with a siphon kit, available at most auto parts stores. NEVER start the siphoning action with your mouth!*

1   Remove the fuel filler cap to relieve fuel tank pressure.

2   Relieve the fuel system pressure (see Section 3).

3   Disconnect the cable from the negative terminal of the battery (see Chapter 5).

4   Raise the rear of the vehicle and support it securely on jackstands.

5   Loosen the hose clamp and disconnect the fuel filler hose from the fuel tank **(see illustration)**.

7.5 Loosen the clamp and detach the filler hose from the fuel tank

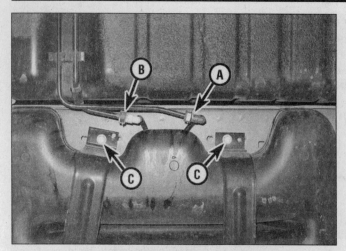

7.7 Disconnect the fuel delivery line (A) and EVAP line (B). (C) are the front fuel tank strap bolts

7.8 EVAP system integrity monitor switch electrical connector (A) and fuel fill vapor hose (B)

6   Unplug the electrical connector in the fuel pump module harness **(see illustration 3.2)**.

7   Disconnect the fuel line and EVAP line quick-connect fittings, both of which are located at the front of the fuel tank **(see illustration)**. If you're unfamiliar with fuel line quick-connect fittings, refer to Section 5.

8   Disconnect the fuel fill vapor hose and the electrical connector from the EVAP system integrity monitor switch **(see illustration)**.

9   Support the fuel tank with a transmission jack or with a floor jack. If you're using a floor jack, put a piece of plywood between the jack head and the tank to protect the tank.

10   Remove the fuel tank strap bolts **(see illustration 7.7)**.

11   Carefully lower the fuel tank from the vehicle, making sure no hoses or wiring harness are still attached.

12   Installation is the reverse of removal.

Tighten the fuel tank strap bolts securely.

13   Start the engine and check for leaks at any fuel line connectors that were disconnected.

8   Fuel pump/fuel pressure regulator/fuel level sending unit assembly - removal and installation

Refer to illustrations 8.6, 8.7 and 8.8

Warning: *Gasoline is extremely flammable. See* **Fuel system warnings** *in Section 1.*

1   Relieve the fuel system pressure (see Section 3).

2   Disconnect the cable from the negative battery terminal (see Chapter 5).

3   Remove the fuel tank (see Section 7).

4   Disconnect the fuel delivery line quick-

connect fitting from the fuel pump/fuel pressure regulator/fuel level sending unit assembly (see Section 5).

5   Disconnect the electrical connector from the fuel pump/fuel pressure regulator/fuel level sending unit assembly.

6   Before removing the fuel pump/fuel pressure regulator/fuel level sending unit assembly, make alignment marks on the assembly and the fuel tank **(see illustration)**, if marks don't already exist, to ensure the assembly will be correctly realigned when it's installed again.

7   Using a brass punch and hammer, loosen the locknut that secures the fuel pump/fuel pressure regulator/fuel level sending unit assembly **(see illustration)**.

8   Carefully lift the fuel pump/fuel pressure regulator/fuel level sending unit assembly from the fuel tank **(see illustration)**. Angle the module so that you don't bend the float arm of

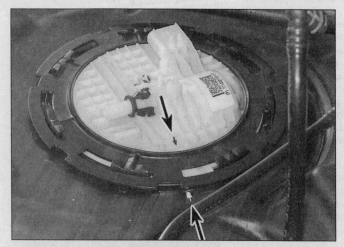

8.6 Before removing the fuel pump module, make alignment marks (if none exist) on the mounting flange for the fuel pump/ pressure regulator/sending unit assembly and on the fuel tank. These marks will help you reinstall the assembly so it's correctly oriented

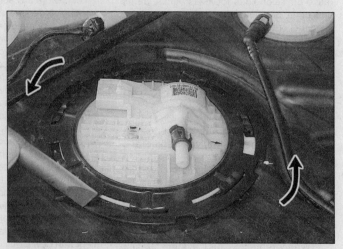

8.7 Using a brass punch and hammer, loosen the locknut that secures the fuel pump/fuel pressure regulator/fuel level sending unit assembly

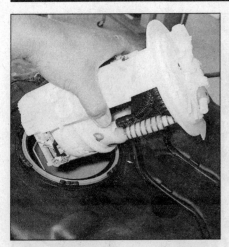

8.8 Carefully remove the fuel pump/fuel pressure regulator/fuel level sending unit from the fuel tank. Angle the assembly so that you don't bend the fuel level sending unit float arm or damage the fuel pump inlet strainer

the fuel level sending unit or damage the fuel pump inlet strainer.

9   While the pump is removed, inspect the pump inlet strainer. Make sure that it's not clogged or damaged. If the inlet strainer is dirty, try washing it in clean solvent. If it's still clogged, replace it.

10   Installation is the reverse of removal. Be sure to line up the marks, and tighten the fuel pump module locknut securely.

9   Fuel level sending unit - replacement

1   Remove the fuel pump/fuel pressure regulator/fuel level sending unit assembly (see Section 8).

2   Mark the position of the sending unit to the module, also note the positions of the two wires on the sending unit - they must be returned to their same terminals.

3   Using a special terminal removal tool or a suitable substitute, disengage each terminal from the sending unit.

4   Disengage the retaining lugs, then slide the sending unit off the fuel pump module housing.

5   Installation is the reverse of removal.

10   Air filter housing - removal and installation

Air intake duct

1   Loosen the hose clamps that secure the air intake duct to the air filter housing cover and to the throttle body, then remove the air intake duct.

2   Installation is the reverse of removal.

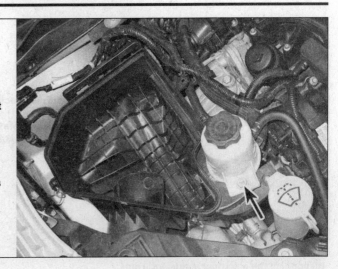

10.5 Remove the power steering fluid reservoir nut, and set the reservoir aside. Detach all wiring harness retainers, then pull up on the air filter housing to detach the grommets from the ballstuds

Air filter housing

Refer to illustration 10.5

3   Loosen the hose clamp and detach the air intake duct from the housing.

4   Detach the cover from the air filter housing.

5   Remove the nut securing the power steering fluid reservoir to the filter housing **(see illustration)**, then move the reservoir aside.

6   To detach the air filter housing assembly, simply pull it straight up and disengage the two grommets on the underside of the housing from their corresponding locator pins on the vehicle **(see illustration 10.5)**.

7   Inspect the rubber mounting grommets on the underside of the air filter housing. If the grommets are cracked, dried out, torn or otherwise damaged, replace them.

8   Installation is the reverse of removal.

11   Throttle body - removal and installation

Refer to illustration 11.5

Warning: *Wait until the engine is completely cool before beginning this procedure.*

1   Disconnect the cable from the negative battery terminal (see Chapter 5). Remove the engine covers

2   Detach the air intake duct or resonator, as applicable, from the throttle body.

3   If the throttle body has coolant lines attached to it, clamp off and disconnect the lines.

4   Disconnect the throttle body electrical connector.

5   Remove the throttle body mounting fasteners and detach the throttle body from the upper intake manifold **(see illustration)**.

6   Remove the throttle body gasket and inspect it for cracks, tears and deterioration. If it isn't in perfect condition, replace it.

7   Make sure that the gasket mating surfaces of the throttle body and the intake manifold are clean.

8   Installation is the reverse of removal. Tighten the throttle body bolts to the torque listed in this Chapter's Specifications.

12   Fuel rail and injectors - removal and installation

Refer to illustrations 12.5, 12.6a, 12.6b, 12.8, 12.9, 12.10a and 12.10b

Warning: *Gasoline is extremely flammable. See* **Fuel system warnings** *in Section 2.*

Warning: *Wait until the engine is completely cool before beginning this procedure.*

1   Relieve the fuel system pressure (see Section 3).

2   Disconnect the cable from the negative terminal of the battery (see Chapter 5).

3   Remove the upper intake manifold (see Chapter 2A or 2B).

4   Disconnect the fuel delivery line quick-connect fitting and disconnect the fuel delivery line from the fuel rail (if you're unfamiliar with quick-connect fittings, see Section 5).

5   Disconnect the fuel injector electrical connectors **(see illustration)**. Detach the

11.5 Throttle body mounting bolts (upper intake manifold removed for clarity) - 3.6L engine shown, others similar

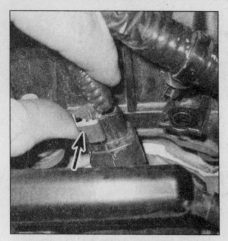

12.5 Slide the connector lock up and disconnect the electrical connector from the fuel injector

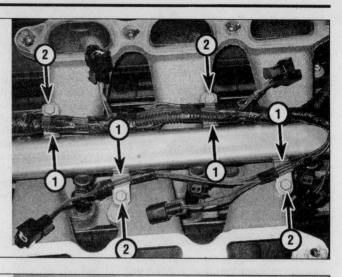

12.6a Fuel injector harness clips (1) and fuel rail mounting bolts (2) - 3.3L/3.8L engines

12.6b Fuel rail mounting bolts - 3.6L engine shown, 4.0L engine similar

injector wiring harness mounting clips from the fuel rail (if equipped) and set the harness aside.

6   Remove the fuel rail mounting bolts **(see illustrations)**.

7   Carefully pull up on the fuel rail to disengage the injectors from their respective bores in the intake manifold, then remove the fuel rail and injectors as a single assembly. The injectors might initially stick in their bores, but they'll pull free when sufficient force is applied.

8   **3.3L/3.8L engines** - Rotate each injector to disengage the retainer clip from the flange on the injector mounting pipe and pull it out of the fuel rail **(see illustration)** (the retainer clip stays on the injector).

     3.6L/4.0L engines - Pull the injectors straight out of the fuel rail (there are no retaining clips).

9   Remove the O-rings from each injector **(see illustration)** and discard them. Install new O-rings and coat them with some clean

engine oil to facilitate installation of the injectors.

10   **3.3L/3.8L engines** - Before installing each injector into the fuel rail, install the injector retainer clip by sliding the open end into its slot in the injector **(see illustration)**. When

installing each injector, make sure that the flat side of the retainer clip is aligned with the flat side of the flange on the injector mounting pipe, and that the slots in the other two sides of the retainer clip are aligned with the curved parts of the flange **(see illustration)**.

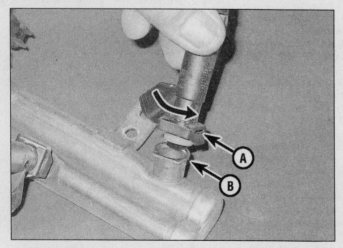

12.8 3.3L/3.8L engines - Rotate each injector to disengage the retainer (A) from the flange (B), then pull the injector out of the fuel rail

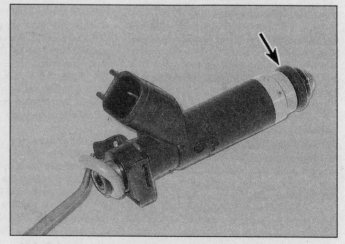

12.9 Remove the O-rings from each injector. Discard them and install new O-rings

All models - Make sure that the injector is square to the bore of the mounting pipe and push it down into the mounting pipe until it's fully seated.

11   Installation is otherwise the reverse of removal. Tighten the fuel rail retaining bolts to the torque listed in this Chapter's Specifications.

12   Start the engine and check for leaks at the quick-connect fitting that connects the fuel supply hose to the fuel rail. Also look for leaks at the upper end of each injector, where it's installed into the fuel rail.

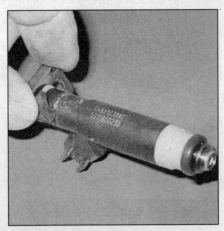

12.10a Before installing each injector into the fuel rail, install the injector clip by sliding the open end into the top slot of the injector (3.3L/3.8L engines)

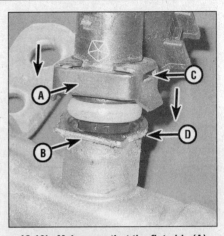

12.10b Make sure that the flat side (A) of the retainer clip is aligned with the flat side (B) of the flange on the injector mounting pipe and that the slots (C) in each side of the retainer clip are aligned with the curved parts (D) of the flange. With the injector square to the bore of the mounting pipe, push it into the pipe until it seats (3.3L/3.8L engines)

Notes

Chapter 5
Engine electrical systems

Contents

Specifications

Charging system
Charging voltage	13.5 to 14.5 volts

Torque specifications
	Ft-lbs
Alternator bracket nut/bolt (3.3L and 3.8L engines)	21
Alternator mounting bolts	
3.3L, 3.8L and 4.0L engines	40
3.6L engines	18
Starter mounting bolts	
3.3L and 3.8L engines	35
3.6L and 4.0L engines	41

1 General information and precautions

General information

Ignition system

The electronic ignition system consists of the Crankshaft Position (CKP) sensor, the Camshaft Position (CMP) sensor, the Knock Sensor (KS), the Powertrain Control Module (PCM), the ignition switch, the battery, the individual ignition coils or a coil pack, and the spark plugs. For more information on the CKP, CMP and KS sensors, as well as the PCM, refer to Chapter 6.

Charging system

The charging system includes the alternator (with an integral voltage regulator), the Powertrain Control Module (PCM), the Body Control Module (BCM), a charge indicator light on the dash, the battery, a fuse or fusible link and the wiring connecting all of these components. The charging system supplies electrical power for the ignition system, the lights, the radio, etc. The alternator is driven by the drivebelt.

Starting system

The starting system consists of the battery, the ignition switch, the starter relay, the Powertrain Control Module (PCM), the Body Control Module (BCM), the Transmission Range (TR) switch, the starter motor and solenoid assembly, and the wiring connecting all of the components.

Precautions

Always observe the following precautions when working on the electrical system:

a) *Be extremely careful when servicing engine electrical components. They are easily damaged if checked, connected or handled improperly.*

b) *Never leave the ignition switched on for long periods of time when the engine is not running.*

c) *Never disconnect the battery cables while the engine is running.*

d) *Maintain correct polarity when connecting battery cables from another vehicle during jump starting - see the "Booster battery (jump) starting" Section at the front of this manual.*

e) *Always disconnect the cable from the negative battery terminal before working on the electrical system, but read the battery disconnection procedure first (see Section 3).*

It's also a good idea to review the safety-related information regarding the engine electrical systems located in the *Safety first!* Section at the front of this manual before beginning any operation included in this Chapter.

2 Troubleshooting

Ignition system

1   If a malfunction occurs in the ignition system, do not immediately assume that any particular part is causing the problem. First, check the following items:

a) *Make sure that the cable clamps at the battery terminals are clean and tight.*

b) *Test the condition of the battery (see Steps 21 through 24). If it doesn't pass all the tests, replace it.*

c) *Check the ignition coil or coil pack connections.*

d) *Check any relevant fuses in the engine compartment fuse and relay box (see Chapter 12). If they're burned, determine the cause and repair the circuit.*

Check

Refer to illustration 2.3

Warning: *Because of the high voltage generated by the ignition system, use extreme care when performing a procedure involving ignition components.*

Warning: *If you're working on a model with a 3.6L or 4.0L engine, relieve the fuel system pressure by disconnecting the fuel pump module electrical connector (see Chapter 4, Section 3).*

Note: *The ignition system components on these vehicles are difficult to diagnose. In the event of ignition system failure that you can't diagnose, have the vehicle tested at a dealer service department or other qualified auto repair facility.*

Note: *You'll need a spark tester for the following test. Spark testers are available at most auto supply stores.*

2   If the engine turns over but won't start, verify that there is sufficient ignition voltage to fire the spark plugs as follows.

3   On models with a coil-over-plug type ignition system, remove a coil and install the tester between the boot at the lower end of the coil and the spark plug **(see illustration)**. On models with spark plug wires, disconnect a spark plug wire from a spark plug and install the tester between the spark plug wire boot and the spark plug.

4   Crank the engine and note whether or not the tester flashes.

Caution: *Do NOT crank the engine or allow it to run for more than five seconds; running the engine for more than five seconds may set a Diagnostic Trouble Code (DTC) for a cylinder misfire.*

Models with a coil-over-plug type ignition system

5   If the tester flashes during cranking, the coil is delivering sufficient voltage to the spark plug to fire it. Repeat this test for each cylinder to verify that the other coils are OK.

6   If the tester doesn't flash, remove a coil from another cylinder and swap it for the one being tested. If the tester now flashes, you know that the original coil is bad. If the tester still doesn't flash, the PCM or wiring harness is probably defective. Have the PCM checked out by a dealer service department or other qualified repair shop (testing the PCM is beyond the scope of the do-it-yourselfer because it requires expensive special tools).

7   If the tester flashes during cranking but a misfire code (related to the cylinder being tested) has been stored, the spark plug could be fouled or defective.

Models with spark plug wires

8   If the tester flashes during cranking, sufficient voltage is reaching the spark plug to fire it.

9   Repeat this test on the remaining cylinders.

10   Proceed on this basis until you have verified that there's a good spark from each spark plug wire. If there is, then you have verified that the coils in the coil pack are functioning correctly and that the spark plug wires are OK.

11   If there is no spark from a spark plug wire, then either the coil is bad, the plug wire is bad or a connection at one end of the plug wire is loose. Assuming that you're using new plug wires or known good wires, then the coil is probably defective. Also inspect the coil pack electrical connector. Make sure that it's clean, tight and in good condition.

12   If all the coils are firing correctly, but the engine misfires, then one or more of the plugs might be fouled. Remove and check the spark plugs or install new ones (see Chapter 1).

13   No further testing of the ignition system is possible without special tools. If the problem persists, have the ignition system tested by a dealer service department or other qualified repair shop.

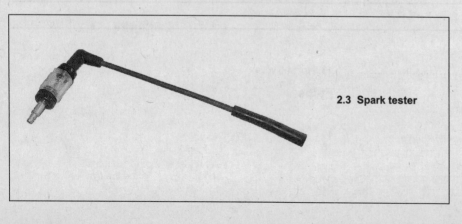

2.3 Spark tester

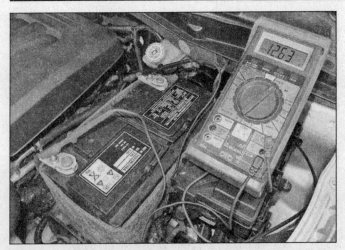

2.21 To test the open circuit voltage of the battery, connect the black probe of the voltmeter to the negative terminal and the red probe to the positive terminal of the battery; a fully charged battery should be at least 12.6 volts

2.23 Connect a battery load tester to the battery and check the battery condition under load following the tool manufacturer's instructions

Charging system

14   If a malfunction occurs in the charging system, do not automatically assume the alternator is causing the problem. First check the following items:

a) *Check the drivebelt tension and condition, as described in Chapter 1. Replace it if it's worn or deteriorated.*

b) *Make sure the alternator mounting bolts are tight.*

c) *Inspect the alternator wiring harness and the connectors at the alternator and voltage regulator. They must be in good condition, tight and have no corrosion.*

d) *Check the fusible link (if equipped) or main fuse in the underhood fuse/relay box. If it is burned, determine the cause, repair the circuit and replace the link or fuse (the vehicle will not start and/or the accessories will not work if the fusible link or main fuse is blown).*

e) *Start the engine and check the alternator for abnormal noises (a shrieking or squealing sound indicates a bad bearing).*

f) *Check the battery. Make sure it's fully charged and in good condition (one bad cell in a battery can cause overcharging by the alternator).*

g) *Disconnect the battery cables (negative first, then positive). Inspect the battery posts and the cable clamps for corrosion. Clean them thoroughly if necessary (see Chapter 1). Reconnect the cables (positive first, negative last).*

Alternator - check

15   Use a voltmeter to check the battery voltage with the engine off. It should be at least 12.6 volts **(see illustration 2.21)**.
16   Start the engine and check the battery voltage again. It should now be approximately 13.5 to 15 volts.

17   If the voltage reading is more or less than the specified charging voltage, the voltage regulator is probably defective, which will require replacement of the alternator (the voltage regulator is not replaceable separately). Remove the alternator and have it bench tested (most auto parts stores will do this for you).
18   The charging system (battery) light on the instrument cluster lights up when the ignition key is turned to ON, but it should go out when the engine starts.
19   If the charging system light stays on after the engine has been started, there is a problem with the charging system. Before replacing the alternator, check the battery condition, alternator belt tension and electrical cable connections.
20   If replacing the alternator doesn't restore voltage to the specified range, have the charging system tested by a dealer service department or other qualified repair shop.

Battery - check

Refer to illustrations 2.21 and 2.23

21   Check the battery state of charge. Visually inspect the indicator eye on the top of the battery (if equipped with one); if the indicator eye is black in color, charge the battery as described in Chapter 1. Next perform an open circuit voltage test using a digital voltmeter.
Note: *The battery's surface charge must be removed before accurate voltage measurements can be made. Turn on the high beams for ten seconds, then turn them off and let the vehicle stand for two minutes.*
With the engine and all accessories Off, touch the negative probe of the voltmeter to the negative terminal of the battery and the positive probe to the positive terminal of the battery **(see illustration)**. The battery voltage should be 12.6 volts or slightly above. If the battery

is less than the specified voltage, charge the battery before proceeding to the next test. Do not proceed with the battery load test unless the battery charge is correct.
22   Disconnect the negative battery cable, then the positive cable from the battery.
23   Perform a battery load test. An accurate check of the battery condition can only be performed with a load tester **(see illustration)**. This test evaluates the ability of the battery to operate the starter and other accessories during periods of high current draw. Connect the load tester to the battery terminals. Load test the battery according to the tool manufacturer's instructions. This tool increases the load demand (current draw) on the battery.
24   Maintain the load on the battery for 15 seconds and observe that the battery voltage does not drop below 9.6 volts. If the battery condition is weak or defective, the tool will indicate this condition immediately.
Note: *Cold temperatures will cause the minimum voltage reading to drop slightly. Follow the chart given in the manufacturer's instructions to compensate for cold climates. Minimum load voltage for freezing temperatures (32 degrees F) should be approximately 9.1 volts.*

Starting system

The starter rotates, but the engine doesn't

25   Remove the starter (see Section 8). Check the overrunning clutch and bench test the starter to make sure the drive mechanism extends fully for proper engagement with the flywheel ring gear. If it doesn't, replace the starter.
26   Check the flywheel ring gear for missing teeth and other damage. With the ignition turned off, rotate the flywheel so you can check the entire ring gear.

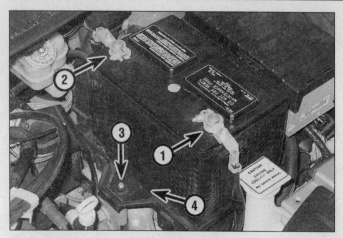

4.1 Battery details:

1	Negative cable	3	Battery hold down clamp nut
2	Positive cable	4	Battery hold down clamp

4.3 Remove the thermo-wrap from the battery

The starter is noisy

27   If the solenoid is making a chattering noise, first check the battery (see Steps 21 through 24). If the battery is okay, check the cables and connections.

28   If you hear a grinding, crashing metallic sound when you turn the key to Start, check for loose starter mounting bolts. If they're tight, remove the starter and inspect the teeth on the starter pinion gear and flywheel ring gear. Look for missing or damaged teeth.

29   If the starter sounds fine when you first turn the key to Start, but then stops rotating the engine and emits a zinging sound, the problem is probably a defective starter drive that's not staying engaged with the ring gear. Replace the starter.

The starter rotates slowly

30   Check the battery (see Steps 21 through 24).

31   If the battery is okay, verify all connections (at the battery, the starter solenoid and motor) are clean, corrosion-free and tight. Make sure the cables aren't frayed or damaged.

32   Check that the starter mounting bolts are tight so it grounds properly. Also check the pinion gear and flywheel ring gear for evidence of a mechanical bind (galling, deformed gear teeth or other damage).

The starter does not rotate at all

33   Check the battery (see Steps 21 through 24).

34   If the battery is okay, verify all connections (at the battery, the starter solenoid and motor) are clean, corrosion-free and tight. Make sure the cables aren't frayed or damaged.

35   Check all of the fuses in the underhood fuse/relay box.

36   Check that the starter mounting bolts are tight so it grounds properly.

37   Check for voltage at the starter solenoid "S" terminal when the ignition key is turned to the start position. If voltage is present, replace the starter/solenoid assembly. If no voltage is present, the problem could be the starter relay, the Transmission Range (TR) switch (see Chapter 6), or with an electrical connector somewhere in the circuit (see the wiring diagrams at the end of Chapter 12). Also, on many modern vehicles, the Powertrain Control Module (PCM) and the Body Control Module (BCM) control the voltage signal to the starter solenoid; on such vehicles a special scan tool is required for diagnosis.

3   Battery - disconnection

Warning: *Always disconnect the cable from the negative battery terminal FIRST and hook it up LAST or the battery may be shorted by the tool being used to loosen the cable clamps.*

Warning: *Hydrogen gas is produced by the battery, so keep open flames and lighted cigarettes away from it at all times. Always wear eye protection when working around the battery. Rinse off spilled electrolyte immediately with large amounts of water.*

Some systems on the vehicle require battery power to be available at all times, either to maintain continuous operation (alarm system, power door locks, etc.), or to maintain control unit memory (radio station presets, Powertrain Control Module and other control units). When the battery is disconnected, the power that maintains these systems is cut. So, before you disconnect the battery, please note that on a vehicle with power door locks, it's a wise precaution to remove the key from the ignition and to keep it with you, so that it does not get locked inside if the power door locks should engage accidentally when the battery is reconnected!

Devices known as "memory-savers" can be used to avoid some of these problems. Precise details vary according to the device used. The typical memory saver is plugged into the cigarette lighter and is connected to a spare battery. Then the vehicle battery can be disconnected from the electrical system. The memory saver will provide sufficient current to maintain audio unit security codes, PCM memory, etc. and will provide power to always hot circuits such as the clock and radio memory circuits.

Warning: *Some memory savers deliver a considerable amount of current in order to keep vehicle systems operational after the main battery is disconnected. If you're using a memory saver, make sure that the circuit concerned is actually open before servicing it.*

Warning: *If you're going to work near any of the airbag system components, the battery MUST be disconnected and a memory saver must NOT be used. If a memory saver is used, power will be supplied to the airbag, which means that it could accidentally deploy and cause serious personal injury.*

To disconnect the battery for service procedures requiring power to be cut from the vehicle, loosen the cable end nut and disconnect the cable from the negative battery terminal. Isolate the cable end to prevent it from coming into accidental contact with the battery terminal.

4   Battery - removal and installation

Refer to illustrations 4.1 and 4.3

1   Disconnect the cable from the negative battery terminal first, then disconnect the cable from the positive battery terminal **(see illustration)**.

2   Remove the battery hold-down clamp.

3   Remove the battery thermo-wrap **(see illustration)**.

4   Lift out the battery. Be careful - it's heavy.

Note: *Battery straps and handlers are available at most auto parts stores for reasonable prices. They make it easier to remove and carry the battery.*

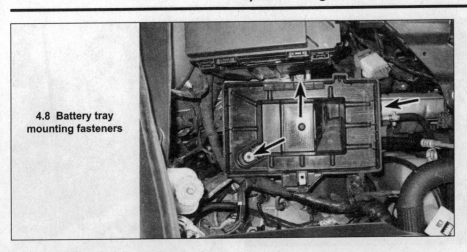

4.8 Battery tray mounting fasteners

6.2 Remove the two power steering fluid reservoir-to-intake manifold mounting bolts (A)

5   If you are replacing the battery, make sure you get one that's identical, with the same dimensions, amperage rating, cold cranking rating, etc.
6   Installation is the reverse of removal. Be sure to connect the positive cable first and the negative cable last.

Battery tray

Refer to illustration 4.8
7   Remove the battery (see Steps 1 through 4).
8   Remove the battery tray mounting bolt and nuts **(see illustration)**.
9   Lift the battery tray out of the engine compartment.
10   Thoroughly wash the battery tray in clean water, then dry it with compressed air.
11   Installation is the reverse of removal.

5   Battery cables - replacement

1   When removing the cables, always disconnect the cable from the negative battery terminal first and hook it up last, or you might accidentally short out the battery with the tool you're using to loosen the cable clamps. Even if you're only replacing the cable for the positive terminal, be sure to disconnect the negative cable from the battery first.
2   Disconnect the old cables from the battery, then trace each of them to their opposite ends and disconnect them. Be sure to note the routing of each cable before disconnecting it to ensure correct installation.
3   If you are replacing any of the old cables, take them with you when buying new cables. It is vitally important that you replace the cables with identical parts.
4   Clean the threads of the solenoid or ground connection with a wire brush to remove rust and corrosion. Apply a light coat of battery terminal corrosion inhibitor or petroleum jelly to the threads to prevent future corrosion.
5   Attach the cable to the solenoid or ground connection and tighten the mounting nut/bolt securely.
6   Before connecting a new cable to the battery, make sure that it reaches the battery post without having to be stretched.
7   Connect the cable to the positive battery terminal first, *then* connect the ground cable to the negative battery terminal.

6   Ignition coil pack or coils - replacement

3.3L/3.8L models

Refer to illustrations 6.2, 6.4 and 6.5
1   Disconnect the cable from the negative terminal of the battery (see Section 3).
2   Remove the two power steering reservoir-to-intake manifold mounting bolts **(see illustration)**. Loosen the lower power steering reservoir mounting nut from the stud on the ignition coil mounting bracket, then lift up the power steering reservoir and set it aside.
3   Disconnect the spark plug wires from the ignition coil pack.
4   Remove the two ignition coil mounting nuts **(see illustration)**.
5   Remove the ignition coil pack and disconnect the electrical connector from the coil **(see illustration)**.
6   Installation is the reverse of removal.

6.4 Remove the two mounting nuts and remove the coil pack from the engine

6.5 To disconnect the electrical connector from the ignition coil pack, slide the lock out (1), then depress the release tab (2) and pull off the connector

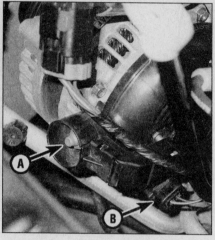

6.11 Ignition coil electrical connectors (A) and mounting fasteners (B) - 3.6L engine (front cylinder bank) shown, 4.0L similar

7.2 Remove the nut from the B+ stud terminal (A) and disconnect the battery cable from the stud, then disconnect the field wire electrical connector (B) from the alternator (3.3L and 3.8L engines)

4.0L and 3.6L models

Refer to illustration 6.11

7   Disconnect the cable from the negative terminal of the battery (see Section 3).
8   Remove the engine cover (see Chapter 1).
9   On 3.6L engines, disconnect and remove the resonator (see Chapter 4).
10   Remove the upper intake manifold (see Chapter 2B).
Note: *The ignition coils for cylinders 1 and 3 can be removed without having to remove the upper intake manifold.*
11   Disconnect the electrical connector to the ignition coil **(see illustration)**.
12   Remove the ignition coil mounting bolt.
13   Grasp the coil firmly and pull it off the spark plug using a twisting motion.
14   Installation is the reverse of removal. Tighten the ignition coil bolts securely.

7   Alternator - removal and installation

1   Disconnect the cable from the negative terminal of the battery (see Section 3).

3.3L/3.8L models

Refer to illustrations 7.2, 7.6 and 7.7

2   Open the protective cover, then remove the nut that secures the B+ wire terminal to the stud on the back of the alternator, and disconnect the field wire from the stud **(see illustration)**.
3   Disconnect the field wire electrical connector from the alternator.
4   Remove the drivebelt (see Chapter 1).
5   Remove the alternator bracket fasteners and bracket from the rear of the alternator.
6   Remove the two mounting bolts from the drivebelt side of the alternator **(see illustration)**.
7   Remove the alternator **(see illustration)**.
8   Installation is the reverse of removal. Tighten the alternator bolts to the torque listed in this Chapter's Specifications.

3.6L models

Refer to illustrations 7.13, 7.16a and 7.16b

Warning: *The engine must be completely cool before beginning this procedure.*
9   Remove the engine cover (see Chapter 1).

10   Remove the air filter housing (see Chapter 4).
11   Drain some of the coolant (see Chapter 1) and remove the upper radiator hose.
12   Remove the radiator cooling fan and shroud (see Chapter 3).
13   Open the protective cover, remove the nut that secures the B+ wire terminal to the stud on the back of the alternator, and disconnect the field wire from the stud **(see illustration)**.
14   Disconnect the field wire electrical connector from the alternator.
15   Remove the drivebelt (see Chapter 1).
16   Remove the alternator mounting fasteners **(see illustrations)**.
17   Remove the alternator.
18   Installation is the reverse of removal. Tighten the alternator bolts to the torque listed in this Chapter's Specifications. Refill the cooling system.

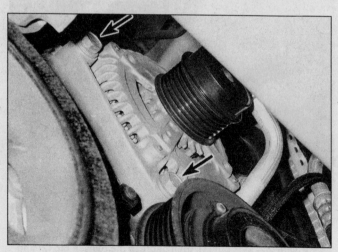

7.6 To detach the alternator, remove these two bolts

7.7 Carefully remove the alternator from the top

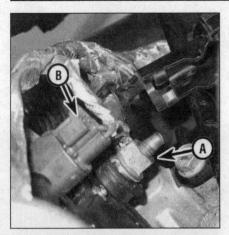

7.13 Remove the nut from the B+ stud terminal (A) and disconnect the battery cable from the stud, then disconnect the field wire electrical connector (B) from the alternator (3.6L engine)

7.16a Alternator lower mounting nut/bolt

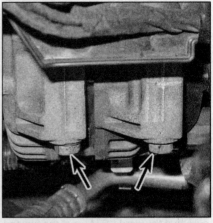

7.16b Alternator upper mounting bolts

4.0L models

19   Remove the engine cover (see Chapter 1).
20   Open the protective cover, remove the nut that secures the B+ wire terminal to the stud on the back of the alternator, and disconnect the field wire from the stud
21   Disconnect the field wire electrical connector from the alternator.
22   Remove the drivebelt (see Chapter 1).
23   Remove the alternator mounting bolt and through bolt and nut.
24   Remove the alternator.
25   Installation is the reverse of removal. Tighten the alternator bolts to the torque listed in this Chapter's Specifications.
26   Refill the cooling system (see Chapter 1).

---

8   Starter motor - removal and installation

---

1   Disconnect the cable from the negative terminal of the battery (see Section 3).

2   Raise the front of the vehicle and place it securely on jackstands.
3   Support the engine with an engine support fixture across the top of the motor or a floor jack with a block of wood placed under the transaxle.

3.3L, 3.8L and 4.0L models

Refer to illustrations 8.4, 8.6, 8.7 and 8.8

4   Remove the nut that secures the battery (B+) cable to the stud terminal on the solenoid, disconnect the B+ cable, then disconnect the solenoid electrical connector from the solenoid **(see illustration)**.
5   Remove the starter top mounting bolt/stud.
6   Remove the two front transaxle mount-to-starter motor mounting bolts **(see illustration)**, then remove the starter assembly.
7   Remove the starter spacer **(see illustration)**.
8   When installing the starter, don't forget to install the spacer. Make sure that the word UP on the spacer is facing toward the starter motor **(see illustration)** and that the lip on the

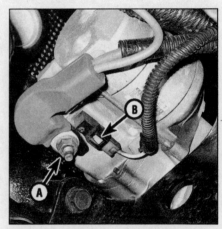

8.4 Remove the nut that secures the battery cable to the stud terminal on the solenoid (A), disconnect the B+ cable, then depress this release tab (B) and disconnect the electrical connector from the solenoid

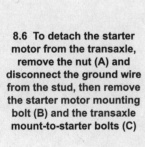

8.6 To detach the starter motor from the transaxle, remove the nut (A) and disconnect the ground wire from the stud, then remove the starter motor mounting bolt (B) and the transaxle mount-to-starter bolts (C)

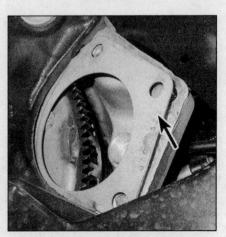

8.7 Remove the starter spacer and put it in a safe place so that you don't lose it. The spacer MUST be installed along with the starter

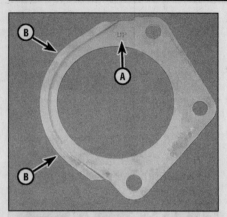

8.8 When installing the spacer, make sure that the word UP (A) is at the top and facing toward the starter motor. Also make sure that the lip (B) on the left side of the spacer is inserted between the engine block and the transaxle bellhousing

spacer is inserted between the block and the transaxle bellhousing **(see illustration 8.7)**.

9   Installation is otherwise the reverse of removal. Don't forget to install the spacer, and tighten the starter mounting bolts to the torque listed in this Chapter's Specifications.

3.6L models

10   Remove the catalytic converter (see Chapter 4).

11   Remove the front engine mount through-bolt, then remove the mount bracket-to-engine bolts and bracket.

12   Remove the nut that secures the battery (B+) cable to the stud terminal on the solenoid, disconnect the B+ cable, then disconnect the solenoid electrical connector from the solenoid.

13   Remove the starter mounting bolts, then remove the starter assembly.

14   Installation is the reverse of removal. Tighten the starter mounting bolts to the torque listed in this Chapter's Specifications.

Chapter 6
Emissions and engine control systems

Contents

Specifications

Torque specifications   Ft-lbs (unless otherwise indicated)

Note: *One foot-pound (ft-lb) of torque is equivalent to 12 inch-pounds (in-lbs) of torque. Torque values below approximately 15 ft-lbs are expressed in inch-pounds, since most foot-pound torque wrenches are not accurate at these smaller values.*

Camshaft Position (CMP) sensor mounting bolt
    3.3L/3.8L engines.. 125 in-lbs
    3.6L engines... 80 in-lbs
    4.0L engines... 106 in-lbs
Engine Coolant Temperature (ECT) sensor
    3.3L, 3.8L and 4.0L engines............................... 60 in-lbs
    3.6L engines... 96 in-lbs
Exhaust Gas Recirculation (EGR) valve-to-cylinder head bolts
    3.3L/3.8L engines.. 22
    4.0L engine .... 132 in-lbs
EGR tube flange-to-EGR valve bolts
    3.3L/3.8L engines.. 132 in-lbs
    4.0L engine 22
EGR airflow control valve bolts (4.0L engine) .... 115 in-lbs
Knock sensor(s)
    3.3L, 3.8L and 4.0L engines............................... 15
    3.6L engines... 16
Oxygen sensors... 30
Transaxle speed sensors
    42TE transaxle (input and output)....................... 20
    62TE transaxle (input, output and transfer shaft).............. 105 in-lbs

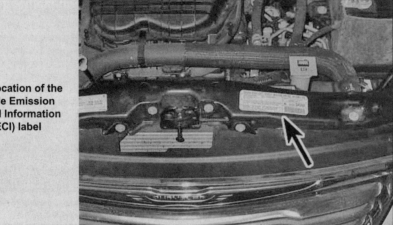

1.13 Location of the Vehicle Emission Control Information (VECI) label

1　General information

To prevent pollution of the atmosphere from incompletely burned and evaporating gases, and to maintain good driveability and fuel economy, a number of emission control systems are incorporated. They include the:

Catalytic converter

A catalytic converter is an emission control device in the exhaust system that reduces certain pollutants in the exhaust gas stream. There are two types of converters: oxidation converters and reduction converters.

Oxidation converters contain a monolithic substrate (a ceramic honeycomb) coated with the semi-precious metals platinum and palladium. An oxidation catalyst reduces unburned hydrocarbons (HC) and carbon monoxide (CO) by adding oxygen to the exhaust stream as it passes through the substrate, which, in the presence of high temperature and the catalyst materials, converts the HC and CO to water vapor (H_2O) and carbon dioxide (CO_2).

Reduction converters contain a monolithic substrate coated with platinum and rhodium. A reduction catalyst reduces oxides of nitrogen (NOx) by removing oxygen, which in the presence of high temperature and the catalyst material produces nitrogen (N) and carbon dioxide (CO_2).

Catalytic converters that combine both types of catalysts in one assembly are known as "three-way catalysts" or TWCs. A TWC can reduce all three pollutants.

Evaporative Emissions Control (EVAP) system

The Evaporative Emissions Control (EVAP) system prevents fuel system vapors (which contain unburned hydrocarbons) from escaping into the atmosphere. On warm days, vapors trapped inside the fuel tank expand until the pressure reaches a certain threshold. Then the fuel vapors are routed from the fuel tank through the fuel vapor vent valve and the fuel vapor control valve to the EVAP canister, where they're stored temporarily until the next time the vehicle is operated. When the conditions are right (engine warmed up, vehicle up to speed, moderate or heavy load on the engine, etc.) the PCM opens the canister purge valve, which allows fuel vapors to be drawn from the canister into the intake manifold. Once in the intake manifold, the fuel vapors mix with incoming air before being drawn through the intake ports into the combustion chambers where they're burned up with the rest of the air/fuel mixture. The EVAP system is complex and virtually impossible to troubleshoot without the right tools and training.

Exhaust Gas Recirculation (EGR) system

The EGR system reduces oxides of nitrogen by recirculating exhaust gases from the exhaust manifold, through the EGR valve and intake manifold, then back to the combustion chambers, where it mixes with the incoming air/fuel mixture before being consumed. These recirculated exhaust gases dilute the incoming air/fuel mixture, which cools the combustion chambers, thereby reducing NOx emissions.

The EGR system consists of the Powertrain Control Module (PCM), the EGR valve, the EGR valve position sensor and various other information sensors that the PCM uses to determine when to open the EGR valve. The degree to which the EGR valve is opened is referred to as "EGR valve lift." The PCM is programmed to produce the ideal EGR valve lift for varying operating conditions. The EGR valve position sensor, which is an integral part of the EGR valve, detects the amount of EGR valve lift and sends this information to the PCM. The PCM then compares it with the appropriate EGR valve lift for the operating conditions. The PCM increases current flow to the EGR valve to increase valve lift and reduces the current to reduce the amount of lift. If EGR flow is inappropriate to the operating conditions (idle, cold engine, etc.) the PCM simply cuts the current to the EGR valve and the valve closes.

Secondary Air Injection (AIR) system

Some models are equipped with a secondary air injection (AIR) system. The secondary air injection system is used to reduce tailpipe emissions on initial engine start-up. The system uses an electric motor/pump assembly, relay, vacuum valve/solenoid, air shut-off valve, check valves and tubing to inject fresh air directly into the exhaust manifolds. The fresh air (oxygen) reacts with the exhaust gas in the catalytic converter to reduce HC and CO levels. The air pump and solenoid are controlled by the PCM through the AIR relay. During initial start-up, the PCM energizes the AIR relay, the relay supplies battery voltage to the air pump and the vacuum valve/solenoid, engine vacuum is applied to the air shut-off valve which opens and allows air to flow through the tubing into the exhaust manifolds. The PCM will operate the air pump until closed loop operation is reached (approximately four minutes). During normal operation, the check valves prevent exhaust backflow into the system.

Powertrain Control Module (PCM)

The Powertrain Control Module (PCM) is the brain of the engine management system. It also controls a wide variety of other vehicle systems. In order to program the new PCM, the dealer needs the vehicle as well as the new PCM. If you're planning to replace the PCM with a new one, there is no point in trying to do so at home because you won't be able to program it yourself.

Positive Crankcase Ventilation (PCV) system

The Positive Crankcase Ventilation (PCV) system reduces hydrocarbon emissions by scavenging crankcase vapors, which are rich in unburned hydrocarbons. A PCV valve or orifice regulates the flow of gases into the intake manifold in proportion to the amount of intake vacuum available.

The PCV system generally consists of the fresh air inlet hose, the PCV valve or orifice and the crankcase ventilation hose (or PCV hose). The fresh air inlet hose connects the air intake duct to a pipe on the valve cover. The crankcase ventilation hose (or PCV hose) connects the PCV valve or orifice in the valve cover to the intake manifold.

Vehicle Emission Control Information (VECI) label

Refer to illustration 1.13

This label (**see illustration**), located under the hood on the radiator support, indicates what emission control systems the vehicle is equipped with and for what market the vehicle is certified (California, Federal, etc.), as well as any tune-up specifications and adjustments that may be needed.

Information Sensors

Accelerator Pedal Position (APP) sensor - as you press the accelerator pedal, the APP sensor alters its voltage signal to the PCM in proportion to the angle of the pedal, and the PCM commands a motor inside the throttle body to open or close the throttle plate accordingly

Camshaft Position (CMP) sensor - produces a signal that the PCM uses to identify the number 1 cylinder and to time the firing sequence of the fuel injectors

Crankshaft Position (CKP) sensor - produces a signal that the PCM uses to calculate engine speed and crankshaft position, which enables it to synchronize ignition timing with fuel injector timing, and to detect misfires

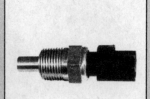

Engine Coolant Temperature (ECT) sensor - a thermistor (temperature-sensitive variable resistor) that sends a voltage signal to the PCM, which uses this data to determine the temperature of the engine coolant

Fuel tank pressure sensor - measures the fuel tank pressure and controls fuel tank pressure by signaling the EVAP system to purge the fuel tank vapors when the pressure becomes excessive

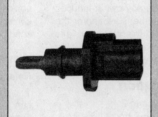

Intake Air Temperature (IAT) sensor - monitors the temperature of the air entering the engine and sends a signal to the PCM to determine injector pulse-width (the duration of each injector's on-time) and to adjust spark timing (to prevent spark knock)

Knock sensor - a piezoelectric crystal that oscillates in proportion to engine vibration which produces a voltage output that is monitored by the PCM. This retards the ignition timing when the oscillation exceeds a certain threshold

Manifold Absolute Pressure (MAP) sensor - monitors the pressure or vacuum inside the intake manifold. The PCM uses this data to determine engine load so that it can alter the ignition advance and fuel enrichment

Mass Air Flow (MAF) sensor - measures the amount of intake air drawn into the engine. It uses a hot-wire sensing element to measure the amount of air entering the engine

Oxygen sensors - generates a small variable voltage signal in proportion to the difference between the oxygen content in the exhaust stream and the oxygen content in the ambient air. The PCM uses this information to maintain the proper air/fuel ratio. A second oxygen sensor monitors the efficiency of the catalytic converter

Throttle Position (TP) sensor - a potentiometer that generates a voltage signal that varies in relation to the opening angle of the throttle plate inside the throttle body. Works with the PCM and other sensors to calculate injector pulse width (the duration of each injector's on-time)

Photos courtesy of Wells Manufacturing, except APP and MAF sensors.

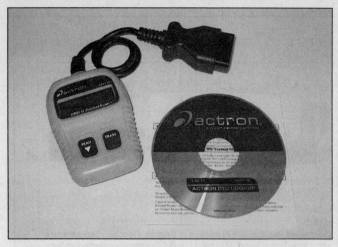

2.4a Simple code readers are an economical way to extract trouble codes when the CHECK ENGINE light comes on

2.4b Hand-held scan tools like these can extract trouble codes and also perform diagnostics

2   On Board Diagnosis (OBD) system

General description

1   All models are equipped with the second generation OBD-II system. This system consists of an on-board computer known as the Powertrain Control Module (PCM), and information sensors, which monitor various functions of the engine and send data to the PCM. This system incorporates a series of diagnostic monitors that detect and identify fuel injection and emissions control system faults and store the information in the computer memory. This system also tests sensors and output actuators, diagnoses drive cycles, freezes data and clears codes.

2   The PCM is the brain of the electronically controlled fuel and emissions system. It receives data from a number of sensors and other electronic components (switches, relays, etc.). Based on the information it receives, the PCM generates output signals to control various relays, solenoids (fuel injectors) and other actuators. The PCM is specifically calibrated to optimize the emissions, fuel economy and driveability of the vehicle.

3.1 The 16-pin Data Link Connector (DLC) is located under the left side of the dash

3   It isn't a good idea to attempt diagnosis or replacement of the PCM or emission control components at home while the vehicle is under warranty. Because of a federally-mandated warranty which covers the emissions system components and because any owner-induced damage to the PCM, the sensors and/or the control devices may void this warranty, take the vehicle to a dealer service department if the PCM or a system component malfunctions.

Scan tool information

Refer to illustrations 2.4a and 2.4b

4   Because extracting the Diagnostic Trouble Codes (DTCs) from an engine management system is now the first step in troubleshooting many computer-controlled systems and components, a code reader, at the very least, will be required **(see illustration)**. More powerful scan tools can also perform many of the diagnostics once associated with expensive factory scan tools **(see illustration)**. If you're planning to obtain a generic scan tool for your vehicle, make sure that it's compatible with OBD-II systems. If you don't plan to purchase a code reader or scan tool and don't have access to one, you can have the codes extracted by a dealer service department or an independent repair shop.
Note: *Some auto parts stores even provide this service.*

3   Obtaining and clearing Diagnostic Trouble Codes (DTCs)

All models covered by this manual are equipped with on-board diagnostics. When the PCM recognizes a malfunction in a monitored emission or engine control system, component or circuit, it turns on the Malfunction Indicator Light (MIL) on the dash. The PCM will continue to display the MIL until the problem is fixed and the Diagnostic Trouble Code (DTC) is cleared from the PCM's memory. You'll need a scan tool to access any DTCs

stored in the PCM.
Before outputting any DTCs stored in the PCM, thoroughly inspect ALL electrical connectors and hoses. Make sure that all electrical connections are tight, clean and free of corrosion. And make sure that all hoses are correctly connected, fit tightly and are in good condition (no cracks or tears).

Accessing the DTCs

Refer to illustration 3.1

1   The Diagnostic Trouble Codes (DTCs) can only be accessed with a code reader or scan tool. Professional scan tools are expensive, but relatively inexpensive generic code readers or scan tools **(see illustrations 2.4a and 2.4b)** are available at most auto parts stores. Simply plug the connector of the scan tool into the diagnostic connector **(see illustration)**. Then follow the instructions included with the scan tool to extract the DTCs.

2   Once you have outputted all of the stored DTCs, look them up on the accompanying DTC chart.

3   After troubleshooting the source of each DTC, make any necessary repairs or replace the defective component(s).

Clearing the DTCs

4   Clear the DTCs with the code reader or scan tool in accordance with the instructions provided by the tool's manufacturer.

Diagnostic Trouble Codes

5   The accompanying tables are a list of the Diagnostic Trouble Codes (DTCs) that can be accessed by a do-it-yourselfer working at home (there are many, many more DTCs available to professional mechanics with proprietary scan tools and software, but those codes cannot be accessed by a generic scan tool). If, after you have checked and repaired the connectors, wire harness and vacuum hoses (if applicable) for an emission-related system, component or circuit, the problem persists, have the vehicle checked by a dealer service department or other qualified repair shop.

OBD-II trouble codes

Code	Probable cause
P0016	Crankshaft/camshaft timing misalignment
P0031	Upstream oxygen sensor (cylinder bank no. 1), heater circuit low voltage
P0032	Upstream oxygen sensor heater (cylinder bank no. 1), heater circuit high voltage
P0037	Downstream oxygen sensor (cylinder bank no. 1), heater circuit low voltage
P0038	Downstream oxygen sensor (cylinder bank no. 1), heater circuit high voltage
P0068	Manifold pressure/throttle position correlation - high-flow/vacuum leak
P0070	Ambient temperature sensor stuck
P0071	Ambient temperature sensor performance
P0072	Ambient temperature sensor, low voltage
P0073	Ambient temperature sensor, high voltage
P0107	Manifold Absolute Pressure (MAP) sensor, low voltage
P0108	Manifold Absolute Pressure (MAP) sensor, high voltage
P0110	Intake Air Temperature (IAT) sensor, stuck
P0111	Intake Air Temperature (IAT) sensor performance
P0112	Intake Air Temperature (IAT) sensor, low voltage
P0113	Intake Air Temperature (IAT) sensor, high voltage
P0116	Engine Coolant Temperature (ECT) sensor performance
P0117	Engine Coolant Temperature (ECT) sensor, low voltage
P0118	Engine Coolant Temperature (ECT) sensor, high voltage
P0121	Throttle Position (TP) sensor performance
P0122	Throttle Position (TP) sensor, low voltage
P0123	Throttle Position (TP) sensor, high voltage
P0125	Insufficient coolant temperature for closed-loop control; closed-loop temperature not reached
P0128	Thermostat rationality
P0129	Barometric pressure out-of-range (low)
P0131	Upstream oxygen sensor (cylinder bank no. 1), low voltage or shorted to ground
P0132	Upstream oxygen sensor (cylinder bank no. 1), high voltage or shorted to voltage

OBD-II trouble codes (continued)

Code	Probable cause
P0133	Upstream oxygen sensor (cylinder bank no. 1), slow response
P0134	Upstream oxygen sensor (cylinder bank no. 1), sensor remains at center (not switching)
P0135	Upstream oxygen sensor (cylinder bank no. 1), heater failure
P0137	Downstream oxygen sensor (cylinder bank no. 1), low voltage or shorted to ground
P0138	Downstream oxygen sensor (cylinder bank no. 1), high voltage or shorted to voltage
P0139	Downstream oxygen sensor (cylinder bank no. 1), slow response
P0140	Downstream oxygen sensor (cylinder bank no. 1), sensor remains at center (not switching)
P0141	Downstream oxygen sensor (cylinder bank no. 1), heater failure
P0171	Fuel control system too lean (cylinder bank no. 1)
P0172	Fuel control system too rich (cylinder bank no. 1)
P0201	Injector circuit malfunction - cylinder no. 1
P0202	Injector circuit malfunction - cylinder no. 2
P0203	Injector circuit malfunction - cylinder no. 3
P0204	Injector circuit malfunction - cylinder no. 4
P0205	Injector circuit malfunction - cylinder no. 5
P0206	Injector circuit malfunction - cylinder no. 6
P0300	Multiple cylinder misfire detected
P0301	Cylinder no. 1 misfire detected
P0302	Cylinder no. 2 misfire detected
P0303	Cylinder no. 3 misfire detected
P0304	Cylinder no. 4 misfire detected
P0305	Cylinder no. 5 misfire detected
P0306	Cylinder no. 6 misfire detected
P0315	No crank sensor learned
P0320	No crankshaft reference signal at Powertrain Control Module (PCM)
P0325	Knock sensor circuit malfunction
P0335	Crankshaft Position (CKP) sensor circuit
P0339	Crankshaft Position (CKP) sensor intermittent
P0340	Camshaft Position (CMP) sensor circuit

Code	Probable cause
P0344	Camshaft Position (CMP) sensor intermittent
P0351	Ignition coil no. 1, primary circuit
P0352	Ignition coil no. 2, primary circuit
P0353	Ignition coil no. 3, primary circuit
P0401	Exhaust Gas Recirculation (EGR) system failure
P0403	Exhaust Gas Recirculation (EGR) solenoid circuit
P0404	Exhaust Gas Recirculation (EGR) sensor performance
P0405	Exhaust Gas Recirculation (EGR) sensor low voltage
P0406	Exhaust Gas Recirculation (EGR) sensor high voltage
P0420	Catalytic converter efficiency below threshold (upstream catalyst, cylinder bank no. 1)
P0432	Catalyst system efficiency below threshold (cylinder bank no. 2)
P0440	General Evaporative Emission Control (EVAP) system failure
P0441	Evaporative Emission Control (EVAP) system, incorrect purge flow
P0442	Evaporative Emission Control (EVAP) system, medium leak (0.040-inch) detected
P0443	Evaporative Emission Control (EVAP) system, purge solenoid circuit malfunction
P0452	Natural Vacuum Leak Detector (NVLD) pressure sensor circuit, low voltage
P0453	Natural Vacuum Leak Detector (NVLD) pressure sensor circuit, high input
P0455	Evaporative Emission Control (EVAP) system, large leak detected
P0456	Evaporative Emission Control (EVAP) system, small leak (0.020-inch) detected
P0460	Fuel level sending unit, no change as vehicle is operated
P0461	Fuel level sensor circuit, range or performance problem
P0462	Fuel level sending unit or sensor circuit, low voltage
P0463	Fuel level sending unit or sensor circuit, high voltage
P0480	Low-speed fan control relay circuit malfunction
P0498	Natural Vacuum Leak Detector (NVLD) canister vent valve solenoid circuit, low voltage
P0499	Natural Vacuum Leak Detector (NVLD) canister vent valve solenoid circuit, high voltage
P0500	No vehicle speed signal (four-speed automatic transaxles)
P0501	Vehicle speed sensor, range or performance problem
P0506	Idle speed control system, rpm lower than expected
P0507	Idle speed control system, rpm higher than expected

OBD-II trouble codes (continued)

Code	Probable cause
P0508	Idle Air Control (IAC) valve circuit, low voltage
P0509	Idle Air Control (IAC) valve circuit, high voltage
P0513	Invalid SKIM key (engine immobilizer problem)
P0516	Battery temperature sensor, low voltage
P0517	Battery temperature sensor, high voltage
P0519	Idle speed performance
P0522	Engine oil pressure sensor/switch circuit, low voltage
P0532	Air conditioning refrigerant pressure sensor, low voltage
P0533	Air conditioning refrigerant pressure sensor, high voltage
P0551	Power Steering Pressure (PSP) switch circuit, range or performance problem
P0562	Battery voltage low
P0563	Battery voltage high
P0579	Speed control switch circuit, range or performance problem
P0580	Speed control switch circuit, low voltage
P0581	Speed control switch circuit, high voltage
P0582	Speed control vacuum solenoid circuit
P0586	Speed control vent solenoid circuit
P0594	Speed control servo power circuit
P0600	Serial communication link malfunction
P0601	Powertrain Control Module (PCM), internal controller failure
P0622	Alternator field control circuit malfunction or field not switching correctly
P0627	Fuel pump relay circuit
P0630	Vehicle Identification Number (VIN) not programmed in Powertrain Control Module (PCM)
P0632	Odometer not programmed in Powertrain Control Module (PCM)
P0633	SKIM key not programmed in Powertrain Control Module (PCM)
P0645	Air conditioning clutch relay circuit
P0685	Automatic Shutdown (ASD) relay control circuit
P0688	Automatic Shutdown (ASD) relay sense circuit, low voltage
P0700	Electronic Automatic Transaxle (EATX) control system malfunction or DTC present
P0703	Brake switch circuit malfunction

Code	Probable cause
P0833	Clutch released switch circuit
P0850	Park/Neutral switch malfunction
P0856	Traction control torque request circuit

4   Accelerator Pedal Position (APP) sensor - replacement

Refer to illustration 4.2

1   Remove the knee bolster trim panel and the knee bolster (see *Dashboard trim panels - removal and installation* in Chapter 11).

2   Disconnect the electrical connector from the upper end of the APP sensor assembly **(see illustration)**.

3   Remove the accelerator pedal/APP sensor assembly mounting nuts and remove the assembly.

4   Installation is the reverse of removal.

5   Camshaft Position (CMP) sensor - replacement

3.3L/3.8L models

Refer to illustrations 5.3, 5.4a, 5.4b, 5.6a and 5.6b

Note: *The CMP sensor is located at the right end of the engine, on the timing chain cover.*

1   Disconnect the cable from the negative terminal of the battery (see Chapter 5).

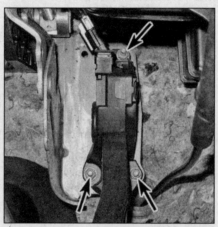

4.2   APP sensor fasteners

2   Remove the air intake duct and the air filter housing (see Chapter 4).

3   Disconnect the CMP sensor electrical connector **(see illustration)**.

4   Remove the CMP sensor mounting bolt and pull it up and out of the timing chain cover **(see illustrations)**.

5   If you're going to reinstall the same sen-

5.3   To disconnect the electrical connector from the CMP sensor on a 3.3L/3.8L V6, slide the red lock (A) to the left, then depress the release tab (B) and pull off the connector

sor, remove the old O-ring from the CMP sensor and install a new one.

6   If you're installing the old CMP sensor, thoroughly clean off the sensor face and install a new paper spacer on the face before

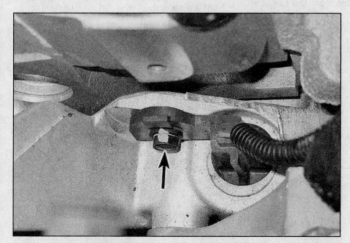

5.4a   To detach the CMP sensor from the timing chain cover on a 3.3L/3.8L V6, remove the sensor mounting bolt

5.4b   Before pulling the CMP sensor out of the timing chain cover on a 3.3L/3.8L V6, rotate the sensor away from the engine as shown

5.6a This is what the paper spacer looks like when you buy it at the parts department. Pop the pre-cut spacer out, peel off the adhesive backing . . .

installing the sensor **(see illustrations)**.
Note: *If you're installing a new CMP sensor, the paper spacer should already be installed. If not, make sure that you install one before installing the sensor.*

7   Apply clean engine oil to the O-ring, then carefully install the CMP sensor in the timing chain cover and rotate it into position.

8   Tighten the CMP sensor mounting bolt to the torque listed in this Chapter's Specifications. The remainder of installation is the reverse of removal.

3.6L models

Refer to illustrations 5.13a and 5.13b

Caution: *After the sensor has been removed, do not insert any magnetic tools into the hole in the valve cover. Doing so could damage the magnetic timing wheels on the ends of the camshafts.*

Note: *There are two CMP sensors on this engine; one at the right end of each valve cover. The sensor on the rear cylinder bank is the bank 1 CMP sensor and the sensor on the front cylinder bank is the bank 2 CMP sensor.*

5.6b . . . and install the spacer on the end of the CMP sensor

9   Disconnect the cable from the negative terminal of the battery (see Chapter 5).

10   Remove the air filter housing (see Chapter 4).

11   If you're removing the sensor from the front cylinder bank (bank 2), remove the upper intake manifold (see Chapter 2B).

12   Disconnect the electrical connector from the sensor.

13   Unscrew the sensor mounting bolt and pull the sensor from the valve cover **(see illustrations)**.

14   If you're going to reinstall the same sensor, check the O-ring for damage. If it's OK, it can be reused.

15   Apply a film of clean engine oil to the O-ring, then insert the sensor into the valve cover and install the mounting bolt, tightening it securely.

16   The remainder of installation is the reverse of removal.

4.0L models

Note: *The CMP sensor is located at the front (right end) of the engine, underneath the alternator.*

17   Disconnect the cable from the negative

terminal of the battery (see Chapter 5).

18   Remove the mounting bolts and reposition the alternator (see Chapter 5).

19   Disconnect the electrical connector from the sensor.

20   Unscrew the sensor mounting bolt and remove the sensor.

21   Apply a film of clean engine oil to the O-ring, then install the sensor and mounting bolt, tightening the bolt securely.

22   The remainder of installation is the reverse of removal.

6   Crankshaft Position (CKP) sensor - replacement

3.3L/3.8L V6 models

Refer to illustrations 5.3a and 5.3b

Note: *The CKP sensor is located on the upper part of the transaxle bellhousing, above the differential.*

1   Disconnect the cable from the negative terminal of the battery (see Chapter 5).

2   Raise the vehicle and place it securely on jackstands.

3   Disconnect the electrical connector from the CKP sensor **(see illustrations)**.

4   Remove the CKP sensor mounting bolt and remove the CKP sensor. If you're going to reinstall the same sensor, check the O-ring for damage. If it's OK, it can be reused.

5   Apply a film of clean engine oil to the O-ring, then insert the sensor into the bellhousing. Tighten the bolt securely.

3.6L models

Refer to illustration 6.9

Note: *The CKP sensor is located at the left rear side of the cylinder block and is accessed from underneath.*

6   Disconnect the cable from the negative terminal of the battery (see Chapter 5).

7   Raise the vehicle and support it securely on jackstands.

8   Pull back the heat shield (if equipped) from the sensor.

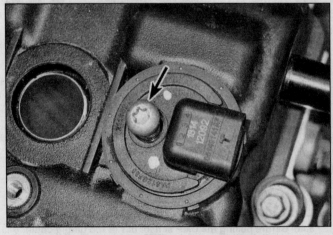

5.13a Remove the CMP sensor mounting bolt . . .

5.13b . . . then pull the sensor straight up and out of the valve cover (3.6L models)

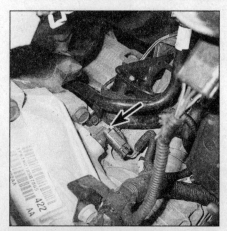

6.3a On 3.3L/3.8L V6 models, the CKP sensor is located on the upper backside of the transaxle bellhousing

9   Disconnect the electrical connector from the sensor **(see illustration)**.
10   Unscrew the mounting bolt and remove the sensor from the engine block.
11   If you're going to reinstall the same sensor, check the O-ring for damage. If it's OK, it can be reused.
12   Apply a film of clean engine oil to the O-ring, then insert the sensor into the bellhousing. Tighten the bolt securely.

4.0L models

Note: *The CKP sensor is located on the driver's side of the vehicle, above the differential housing.*
13   Disconnect the cable from the negative terminal of the battery (see Chapter 5).
14   Disconnect the electrical connector from the sensor.
15   Unscrew the mounting bolt and remove the sensor.
16   If you're going to reinstall the same sensor, check the O-ring for damage. If it's OK, it can be reused.
17   Apply a film of clean engine oil to the O-ring, then install the sensor and tighten the bolt securely.

7.4 Mark the positions of the variable valve timing solenoids

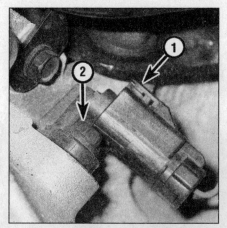

6.3b To detach the CKP sensor from the transaxle bellhousing on a 3.3L/3.8L V6, depress this release tab (1) and disconnect the sensor electrical connector, then remove the CKP sensor mounting bolt (2) and remove the sensor

---

7   Variable valve timing solenoid(s) (3.6L models) - replacement

---

Refer to illustrations 7.4 and 7.5
Warning: *Wait until the engine has cooled completely before beginning this procedure.*
Note: *The variable valve timing solenoids are located at the right end of the valve covers.*
Note: *The manufacturer states that if you're going to replace either of the right (rear, or bank 1) cylinder bank sensors, you'll have to have the air conditioning system discharged by a licensed automotive air conditioning technician, then you'll have to remove the refrigerant lines from between the firewall and the condenser for access to the solenoids. We found that there was plenty of room to remove the solenoids on our 2012 Grand Caravan without removing or repositioning the refrigerant lines.*
1   Disconnect the cable from the negative battery terminal (see Chapter 5).

7.5 Remove the Torx screws and twist the solenoid out of the valve cover

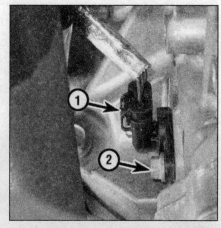

6.9 CKP sensor details (3.6L engine)

1   Electrical connector retaining tab
2   CKP sensor mounting bolt

2   Remove the air filter housing (see Chapter 4).
3   Disconnect the solenoid valve electrical connector.
4   If you're removing more than one solenoid, mark their positions (LI for left intake, LE for left exhaust. etc) **(see illustration)**.
5   Unscrew the solenoid valve mounting Torx screws and remove the camshaft position actuator solenoid **(see illustration)**.
6   Remove the solenoid valve O-ring and inspect its condition. If it's cracked, torn or otherwise deteriorated, replace it.
7   Lubricate the sensor O-ring with clean engine oil. Installation is otherwise the reverse of removal.

---

8   Engine Coolant Temperature (ECT) sensor - replacement

Warning: *Wait until the engine has cooled completely before beginning this procedure.*
Caution: *Handle the Engine Coolant Temperature (ECT) sensor with care. Damage to the ECT sensor will affect the operation of the entire fuel injection system.*

3.3L, 3.8L and 4.0L models

Refer to illustrations 8.5, 8.6 and 8.7
Note: *The ECT sensor is located at the left end of the engine, on the lower intake manifold.*
1   Disconnect the cable from the negative terminal of the battery (see Chapter 5).
2   Drain the engine coolant to a point lower than that of the sensor (see Chapter 1).
3   Detach the power steering fluid reservoir (see Chapter 10) and set it aside (don't disconnect the power steering fluid hoses).
4   Remove the ignition coil (see Chapter 5), then remove the ignition coil mounting bracket.
5   Disconnect the electrical connector from

8.5 To disconnect the electrical connector from the ECT sensor on a 3.3L/3.8L V6, push the red lock (1) away from the sensor (toward the harness), then depress the release tab (2) and pull off the connector

8.6 Unscrew the ECT from the lower intake manifold with a wrench

the ECT sensor **(see illustration)**.

6   Unscrew the ECT sensor from the lower intake manifold **(see illustration)**.

7   Before installing the new ECT sensor, wrap the threads of the sensor with Teflon tape to prevent coolant leakage **(see illustration)**.

8   Installation is otherwise the reverse of removal. Tighten the ECT sensor to the torque listed in this Chapter's Specifications.

9   Refill the cooling system (see Chapter 1).

3.6L models

Refer to illustration 8.12

Note: *The ECT sensor is threaded into the left front end of the front cylinder head.*

10   Disconnect the cable from the negative terminal of the battery (see Chapter 5).

11   Drain the engine coolant to a point lower than that of the sensor (see Chapter 1).

12   Disconnect the electrical connector from the sensor, then unscrew the sensor from the cylinder head **(see illustration)**.

13   Before installing the new ECT sensor, wrap the threads of the sensor with Teflon tape to prevent coolant leakage **(see illustration 8.7)**.

14   Installation is otherwise the reverse of removal. Tighten the ECT sensor to the torque listed in this Chapter's Specifications.

15   Refill the cooling system (see Chapter 1).

9   Intake Air Temperature (IAT) sensor - replacement

Refer to illustration 9.2

Note: *The IAT sensor is located on the air filter housing on 3.3L, 3.8L and 4.0L mod-*

els. On 3.6L models, it's located on the air intake resonator connected to the throttle body

1   Disconnect the cable from the negative terminal of the battery (see Chapter 5).

2   Disconnect the electrical connector from the IAT sensor **(see illustration)**.

3   Remove the sensor by turning it 1/4-turn counterclockwise and pulling it out of the air filter housing or air intake resonator.

4   Inspect the condition of the sensor O-ring. If it is cracked, torn or otherwise deteriorated, replace it.

5   Installation is the reverse of removal.

10   Knock sensor - replacement

Warning: *Wait for the engine to cool completely before performing this procedure.*

8.7 Wrap the threads of the ECT sensor with Teflon tape to prevent coolant from leaking past the threads

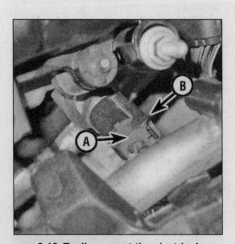

8.12 To disconnect the electrical connector from the ECT sensor, slide the red lock (A) up, then depress the retaining tab (B) and pull the connector off

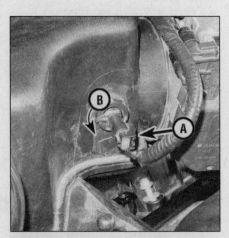

9.2 Depress the tab (A) and disconnect the electrical connector, then twist the IAT sensor 1/4-turn counterclockwise (B) and pull it from the resonator or air filter housing (3.6L engine shown)

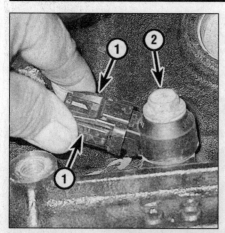

10.3 To disconnect the electrical connector from the knock sensor, depress the release tabs (1), then remove the sensor mounting bolt (2) (3.3L/3.8L engines)

3.3L/3.8L models

Refer to illustration 10.3
Note: *The knock sensor is located on the rear side of the engine block.*
1   Disconnect the cable from the negative terminal of the battery (see Chapter 5).
2   Raise the front of the vehicle and place it securely on jackstands.
3   Disconnect the electrical connector from the knock sensor **(see illustration)**.
4   Remove the sensor mounting bolt and detach the sensor from the engine block.
5   Installation is the reverse of removal. Tighten the knock sensor to the torque listed in this Chapter's Specifications.

3.6L and 4.0L models

Refer to illustration 10.9

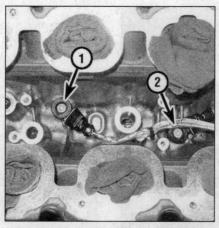

10.9 Knock sensor details - 3.6L engine (4.0L engine similar, but only has one knock sensor)

1   *Sensor one*   2   *Sensor two*

Note: *The knock sensor(s) are located in the valley between the cylinder heads. 4.0L engines have one sensor, 3.6L engines have two.*
Note: *Due to the work involved, if you are replacing a knock sensor on a 3.6L engine, it's a good idea to replace both of them.*
6   If you're working on a 3.6L engine, relieve the fuel system pressure (see Chapter 4) and drain the cooling system (see Chapter 1).
7   Disconnect the cable from the negative terminal of the battery (see Chapter 5).
8   If you're working on a 4.0L engine, remove the upper intake manifold. If you're working on a 3.6L engine, remove the lower intake manifold and the engine oil cooler (see Chapter 2B).
9   Disconnect the electrical connector(s) from the knock sensor(s) **(see illustration)**.

10   Remove the mounting bolt(s) and detach the sensor(s) from the engine block.
11   Installation is the reverse of removal. Tighten the knock sensor to the torque listed in this Chapter's Specifications.
12   On 3.6L engines, refill the cooling system.

11 Manifold Absolute Pressure (MAP) sensor - replacement

Refer to illustrations 11.2a and 11.2b
Note: *The MAP sensor is located on the upper intake manifold on all engines.*
1   Disconnect the cable from the negative terminal of the battery (see Chapter 5). On 3.6L engines, remove the engine cover by pulling it up off the ballstuds.
2   Disconnect the electrical connector from the MAP sensor **(see illustrations)**.
3   Remove the MAP sensor retaining screws and remove the sensor.
4   Installation is the reverse of removal.

12 Oxygen sensors - general information and replacement

1   Be particularly careful when servicing an oxygen sensor:
 a) *Oxygen sensors have a permanently attached pigtail and an electrical connector that cannot be removed. Damaging or removing the pigtail or electrical connector will render the sensor useless.*
 b) *Keep grease, dirt and other contaminants away from the electrical connector and the louvered end of the sensor.*
 c) *Do not use cleaning solvents of any kind on an oxygen sensor.*

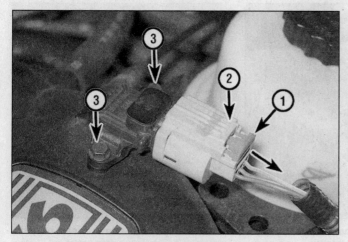

11.2a MAP sensor details - 3.3L/3.8L engines

1   *Connector lock (slide out)*
2   *Connector retaining tab (depress)*
3   *Sensor retaining screws*

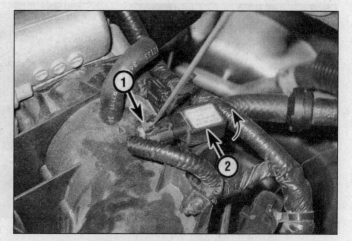

11.2b MAP sensor details - 3.6L and 4.0L engines

1   *Connector lock (slide out, then depress and unplug connector)*
2   *MAP sensor (rotate 1/4-turn counterclockwise, then pull out)*

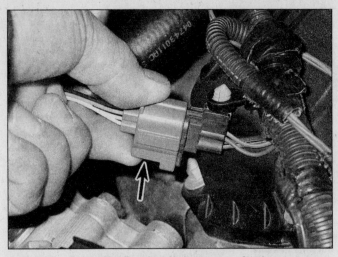

12.4a To disconnect the electrical connector for the upstream oxygen sensor, depress the release tab and pull off the connector (3.3L/3.8L engine shown)

12.4b Disconnect the electrical connector for the downstream oxygen sensor (3.3L/3.8L engine shown)

d) Oxygen sensors are extremely delicate. Do not drop a sensor or handle it roughly.

e) Make sure that the silicone boot on the sensor is installed in the correct position. Otherwise, the boot might melt and it might prevent the sensor from operating correctly.

Replacement

Refer to illustrations 12.4a, 12.4b, 12.5a, 12.5b and 12.5c

Note: *Because it is installed in the exhaust manifold, catalytic converter or pipe, all of which contract when cool, an oxygen sensor might be very difficult to loosen when the engine is cold. Rather than risk damage to the sensor, start and run the engine for a minute*

or two, then shut it off. Be careful not to burn yourself during the following procedure.

Note: *On 3.3L/3.8L V6 engines, the upstream sensor is located on top of the rear exhaust manifold, above the flange. On 3.6L and 4.0L engines, the upstream sensors are located at the top of the catalytic converters.*

Note: *The downstream oxygen sensor is located on the side of the rear catalytic converter on all 3.3L/3.8L models, and on the side of each catalytic converter on 3.6L and 4.0L models.*

Note: *This procedure applies to upstream and downstream sensors.*

2   Disconnect the cable from the negative terminal of the battery (see Chapter 5).

3   Raise the vehicle and place it securely on jackstands.

4   Trace the electrical lead from the oxygen sensor to the electrical connector **(see illus-**

trations) and disconnect it.

5   Using a special oxygen sensor socket, unscrew the sensor **(see illustrations)**.

6   After removing the old sensor, clean the threads of the sensor bore in the exhaust manifold (upstream sensor), or catalytic converter (downstream sensor).

7   If you're going to install the old sensor, apply anti-seize compound to the threads of the sensor to facilitate future removal. If you're going to install a new oxygen sensor, it's not necessary to apply anti-seize compound to the threads. The threads on new sensors already have anti-seize compound on them.

8   Install the oxygen sensor and tighten it securely.

9   Installation is otherwise the reverse of removal.

12.5a Unscrew the upstream oxygen sensor with a special oxygen sensor socket (3.3L/3.8L engine shown)

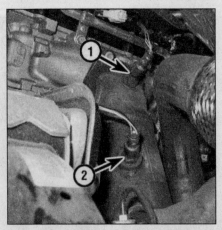

12.5b Front cylinder bank (bank 2) oxygen sensor details

1   Upstream O2 sensor
2   Downstream O2 sensor

12.5c Unscrew the downstream oxygen sensor. An oxygen sensor socket is being used to unscrew the downstream sensor, but there's plenty of room to work here so you could also use a wrench on this sensor (3.3L/3.8L engine shown)

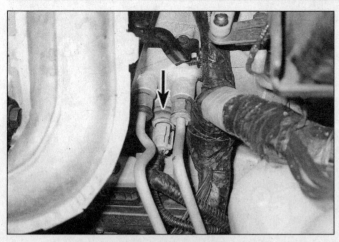

15.2 Location of the transaxle input speed sensor (42TE transaxle)

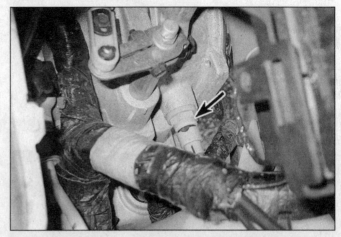

15.6 Location of the transaxle output speed sensor (42TE transaxle)

13 Throttle Position (TP) sensor - replacement

The TP sensor is an integral component of the electronic throttle body, and is not separately serviceable. If you need to replace the TP sensor, you must replace the throttle body (see Chapter 4).

14 Transmission Range (TR) and transmission temperature sensors - replacement

The TR sensor and transmission temperature sensor (which is an integral part of the TR sensor) are located on the automatic transaxle valve body. In order to replace the TR sensor/transmission temperature sensor, you must remove the valve body, which is beyond the scope of the home mechanic.

15 Transaxle speed sensors - replacement

42TE transaxle

Note: *The transaxle speed sensors are located on the front side of the transaxle. The sensor closest to the engine is the input speed sensor, and the sensor on the far left end (driver's side) is the output speed sensor.*

1   Disconnect the cable from the negative battery terminal (see Chapter 5).

Input speed sensor

Refer to illustration 15.2

2   Disconnect the electrical connector from the sensor **(see illustration)**.
3   Unscrew the sensor from the case.
4   If you're going to install the same sensor, remove the old O-ring from the sensor and install a new one.
5   Installation is the reverse of removal.

15.12 Location of the transaxle input speed sensor (62TE transaxle)

Tighten the sensor to the torque listed in this Chapter's Specifications.

Output speed sensor

Refer to illustration 15.6

6   Disconnect the electrical connector from the sensor **(see illustration)**.
7   Unscrew the sensor from the case.
8   If you're going to install the same sensor, remove the old O-ring from the sensor and install a new one.
9   Installation is the reverse of removal. Tighten the sensor to the torque listed in this Chapter's Specifications.

62TE transaxle

10   Disconnect the cable from the negative battery terminal (see Chapter 5).

Input speed sensor

Refer to illustration 15.12

Note: *This sensor is located on the top of the transaxle.*

11   Remove the battery and the battery tray (see Chapter 5).

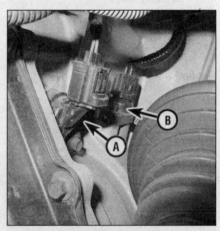

15.17 Location of the transaxle output speed sensor (A) and transfer shaft speed sensor (B) (62TE transaxle)

12   Disconnect the electrical connector from the input speed sensor **(see illustration)**.
13   Remove the retaining bolt and remove the sensor from the case.
14   If you're going to install the same sensor, remove the old O-ring from the sensor and install a new one.
15   Installation is the reverse of removal. Tighten the sensor to the torque listed in this Chapter's Specifications.

Output speed sensor/transfer shaft speed sensor

Refer to illustration 15.17

Note: *These sensors are located on the left rear side of the transaxle.*

16   Loosen the left front wheel lug nuts, raise the vehicle and support it securely on jackstands. Remove the wheel and the inner fender splash shield (see Chapter 11).
17   Disconnect the electrical connector from the sensor **(see illustration)**.
18   Remove the retaining bolt and remove the sensor from the case.

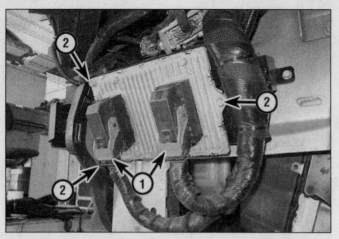

16.4 PCM mounting details

1   *Connector latches (flip up to release connectors)*
2   *Mounting bolts*

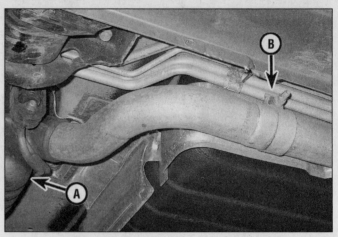

**17.4a To disconnect the rear end of the catalytic converter
(A) from the exhaust pipe, loosen this clamp bolt (B)
(3.3L/3.8L models)**

**17.4b To disconnect the forward end of
the catalytic converter from the exhaust
manifold, remove these four bolts (upper
right bolt not visible in this photo) . . .**

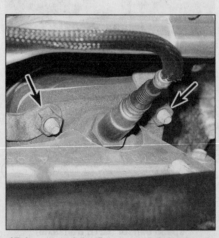

**17.4c . . . and the flag nuts at the exhaust
manifold flange (3.3L/3.8L models)**

19   If you're going to install the same sensor, remove the old O-ring from the sensor and install a new one.
20   Installation is the reverse of removal. Tighten the sensor to the torque listed in this Chapter's Specifications. Tighten the wheel lug nuts to the torque listed in the Chapter 1 Specifications.

16 Powertrain Control Module (PCM) - replacement

Refer to illustration 16.4
Caution: *To avoid electrostatic discharge damage to the PCM, handle the PCM only by its case. Do not touch the electrical terminals during removal and installation. If available, ground yourself to the vehicle with an anti-static ground strap, available at computer supply stores.*

Note: *If you're replacing the PCM, you must input the mileage and the Vehicle Identification Number (VIN) in the new PCM. This will have to be performed at a dealer service department or other qualified repair facility.*
1   Disconnect the cable from the negative terminal of the battery (see Chapter 5).
2   Loosen the left front wheel lug nuts. Raise the front of the vehicle and place it securely on jackstands. Remove the left front wheel.
3   Remove the left front inner fender splash shield (see Chapter 11).
4   Unlock the electrical connectors and disconnect them from the PCM **(see illustration)**.
5   Remove the PCM mounting bolts and remove the PCM.
6   Installation is the reverse of removal. Tighten the wheel lug nuts to the torque listed in the Chapter 1 Specifications.

17 Catalytic converter - replacement

Warning: *Wait until the engine has cooled completely before beginning this procedure.*
Note: *On 4.0L engines, the catalytic converters are integral with the exhaust manifolds - refer to Chapter 2B for the removal and installation procedure.*
1   Raise the vehicle and place it securely on jackstands.
2   Remove the oxygen sensor(s) from the converter (see Section 12).
3   Before trying to loosen the nuts and bolts at the flange(s) and the clamp bolt and nut behind the converter (on models so equipped), spray them with penetrating oil and wait the specified amount of time (see the instructions on the can) for the penetrant to loosen things up.

3.3L/3.8L models

Refer to illustrations 17.4a, 17.4b and 17.4c
4   Loosen the clamp behind the catalytic converter and slide it back, or remove the exhaust pipe flange fasteners, as applicable, then remove the nuts and bolts that attach the converter to the exhaust manifold **(see illustrations)**. Notice the odd nuts used with the bolts that secure the catalyst mounting flange to the exhaust manifold flange **(see illustration)**. They're referred to as "flag nuts" because the small flags attached to the nuts mean that you can loosen or tighten the bolts without having to hold the nuts. If you have to replace these flag nuts, use original equipment flag nuts, or you might have a hard time tightening the new bolts. And you will most certainly have a hard time loosening the same bolts the next time that you have to separate the catalyst from the exhaust manifold.
5   Separate the catalytic converter from the exhaust system.
6   If you're replacing the old catalytic converter, take it with you when you purchase a

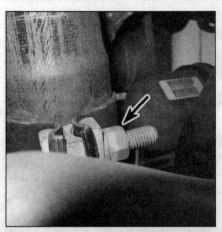

17.12 Exhaust under-pipe-to-rear exhaust pipe clamp (3.6L models)

17.13 Exhaust under-pipe-to-catalytic converter fasteners (3.6L models)

17.14 Catalytic converter-to-cylinder head bolts (one not visible here)

new unit. Make sure that the new unit is identical to the old unit.

7   Before installing the converter, coat the threads of the exhaust manifold flange nuts and bolts and the clamp bolt with anti-seize compound. Tighten the fasteners securely.

8   Installation is otherwise the reverse of removal.

3.6L models

Refer to illustrations 17.12, 17.13 and 17.14

9   If you're removing the rear catalytic converter, loosen the right front wheel lug nuts and the right driveaxle/hub nut (see Chapter 8).

10   Raise the front of the vehicle and support it securely on jackstands.

11   If you're removing the rear catalytic converter, remove the right front wheel and the right driveaxle and intermediate shaft (see Chapter 8).

12   If you're removing the rear catalytic converter, loosen the exhaust under-pipe-to-rear exhaust pipe clamp **(see illustration)**, then separate the exhaust pipe from the under-pipe. Support the rear portion of the exhaust system with a floor jack.

13   Remove the exhaust under-pipe-to-catalytic converter fasteners **(see illustration)**. If you're removing the rear converter, remove the under-pipe fasteners from both converters and remove the under-pipe completely.

14   Remove the converter-to-cylinder head bolts **(see illustration)** and guide the converter out from the bottom of the vehicle.

15   Before installing the converter, coat the threads of the exhaust manifold flange nuts and bolts and the clamp bolt with anti-seize compound. Tighten the fasteners securely.

16   Installation is otherwise the reverse of removal.

---

18   Evaporative emissions control (EVAP) system - component replacement

---

EVAP canister purge solenoid

Refer to illustration 18.2

Note: *The EVAP canister purge solenoid is located in the right rear corner of the engine compartment.*

1   Remove the air filter housing (see Chapter 4).

2   Clearly label the EVAP hoses to ensure correct reassembly **(see illustration)**, then disconnect them from the solenoid.

3   Slide out the red lock, depress the tab and disconnect the electrical connector from the EVAP canister purge solenoid.

4   Remove the mounting bracket nut and detach the purge solenoid from the inner fender panel.

5   Installation is the reverse of removal.

Evaporative System Integrity Monitor (ESIM)

Refer to illustration 18.7

Note: *The ESIM is also known as the leak detector. It's located at the rear of the fuel tank.*

6   Raise the vehicle and place it securely on jackstands.

7   Disconnect the electrical connector from the ESIM **(see illustration)**.

8   Detach the canister filter hose from the ESIM **(see illustration 18.7)**.

9   Push the lock tab toward the ESIM, rotate the ESIM 1/4-turn counterclockwise, then detach it from the EVAP canister.

10   Installation is the reverse of removal.

EVAP canister

Note: *The EVAP canister is located above the rear of the fuel tank.*

11   Raise the vehicle and place it securely on jackstands.

12   Remove the fuel tank (see Chapter 4).

13   Clearly label the EVAP hoses to ensure correct reassembly, then disconnect them from the canister.

14   Installation is the reverse of removal.

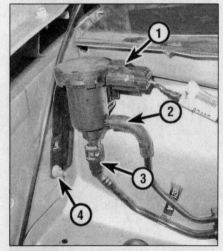

18.2 Canister purge solenoid details

1   *Electrical connector*
2   *Purge hose*
3   *Fuel tank vapor hose*
4   *Solenoid mounting bracket nut*

18.7   Evaporative System Integrity Monitor (ESIM) details

1   EVAP canister   4   Canister filter hose
2   Lock tab   5   Electrical connector
3   ESIM

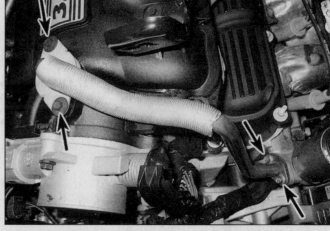

19.1   To detach the EGR tube from the EGR valve and from the intake manifold, remove these four bolts

19   Exhaust Gas Recirculation (EGR) system - component replacement

Warning: *Make sure that the engine is cool before removing any EGR component.*
Note: *3.6L models are not equipped with an EGR system.*

3.3L/3.8L V6 models
EGR tube

Refer to illustration 19.1
Note: *The EGR tube connects the EGR valve (which is located at the right front corner of the front cylinder head) to the top of the intake manifold.*
1   Remove the bolts that attach the EGR tube to the intake manifold **(see illustration)**.
2   Remove the bolts that attach the EGR tube to the EGR valve **(see illustration 19.1)**.

3   Remove the EGR tube.
4   Installation is the reverse of removal. Use new gaskets and tighten the EGR tube bolts to the torque listed in this Chapter's Specifications.

EGR valve/transducer assembly

Refer to illustrations 19.5, 19.7 and 19.8
Note: *The EGR valve/transducer assembly is located at the right front corner of the front cylinder head.*
5   Disconnect the electrical connector from the transducer **(see illustration)**.
6   Remove the bolts that attach the EGR tube to the EGR valve **(see illustration 19.1)**.
7   Remove the two EGR valve mounting bolts **(see illustration)** and remove the EGR valve and transducer assembly. Remove the alternator if necessary (see Chapter 5).
8   Remove the old EGR valve gasket **(see illustration)** and discard it. Clean off all old

gasket material from the gasket mating surfaces of the EGR valve and the cylinder head.
9   Installation is the reverse of removal. Use a new gasket and tighten the EGR valve bolts and the EGR tube bolts to the torque listed in this Chapter's Specifications.

4.0L models

EGR valve

Note: *The EGR valve is located at the left rear end of the engine, on the rear cylinder bank.*
10   Disconnect the cable from the negative terminal of the battery (see Chapter 5).
11   Remove the bolts that attach the EGR valve tube to the EGR valve. Detach the tube and remove the old gasket.
12   Disconnect the EGR valve electrical connector.
13   Unscrew the mounting bolts and detach

19.5   To disconnect the electrical connector from the EGR valve transducer, slide the red lock (1) up, then depress the release tab (2) and pull off the connector

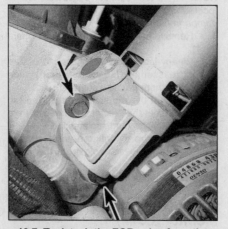

19.7   To detach the EGR valve from the cylinder head, remove these two bolts

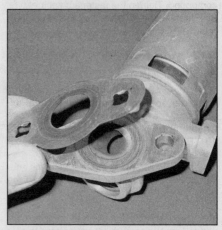

19.8   Remove and discard the old EGR valve gasket

the EGR valve from the cylinder head.

14   Remove the old gasket and clean all gasket mating surfaces.

15   Installation is the reverse of removal. Use new gaskets and tighten all fasteners to the torque listed in this Chapter's Specifications.

EGR airflow control valve

Note: *The EGR air control valve is located above the intake manifold.*

16   Disconnect the cable from the negative terminal of the battery (see Chapter 5).

17   Remove the engine cover by pulling it off its ballstuds.

18   Loosen the hose clamp and remove the intake tube from the valve.

19   Unplug the electrical connector from the valve.

20   Unscrew the bolts and detach the airflow control valve.

21   Remove the old gasket and clean all gasket mating surfaces.

22   Installation is the reverse of removal. Use a new gasket and tighten the fasteners to the torque listed in this Chapter's Specifications.

20   Positive Crankcase Ventilation (PCV) system

1   The Positive Crankcase Ventilation (PCV) system reduces hydrocarbon emissions by scavenging crankcase vapors. It does this by circulating fresh air from the air filter housing through the crankcase, where it mixes with blow-by gases, before being drawn through a PCV valve into the intake manifold.

2   The PCV system consists of the PCV valve and two hoses. The fresh air inlet hose connects the air filter housing to the valve cover. The crankcase ventilation hose (or PCV hose) connects the rear valve cover to the intake manifold. The PCV valve is located at the valve cover end of the crankcase ventilation hose that connects to the intake manifold.

3   To maintain idle quality, the PCV valve restricts the flow when the intake manifold vacuum is high. If abnormal operating conditions (such as piston ring problems) arise, the system is designed to allow excessive amounts of blow-by gases to flow back through the crankcase vent tube into the air cleaner to be consumed by normal combustion.

4   Checking and replacement of the PCV valve is covered in Chapter 1.

Notes

Chapter 7
Automatic transaxle

Contents

Specifications

General
Lubricant type and capacity.. See Chapter 1

Torque specifications
Ft-lbs (unless otherwise indicated)

Note: *One foot-pound (ft-lb) of torque is equivalent to 12 inch-pounds (in-lbs) of torque. Torque values below approximately 15 ft-lbs are expressed in inch-pounds, since most foot-pound torque wrenches are not accurate at these smaller values.*

Shift cable adjustment screw	70 in-lbs
Torque converter-to-driveplate bolts	65
Transaxle seal housing bolts (right side only)	105 in-lbs
Transaxle-to-engine bolts	
3.3L (42TE transaxles)	70
3.6L, 3.8L and 4.0L (62TE transaxles)	
Upper bolts (6)	70
Lower bolts (4)	44
Transaxle brace	70

1   General information

These models are equipped with the 42TE (4-speed) or the 62TE (6-speed) automatic transaxle. The automatic transaxle and the differential are housed in a compact, lightweight, two-piece aluminum alloy housing.

These models are equipped with a Transmission Control Module (TCM) which is the brain of the transaxle. The TCM monitors engine and transaxle operating parameters through numerous sensors, then generates output signals to various relays and solenoids to regulate hydraulic pressures, optimize drivability, provide efficient torque management and maintain maximum fuel economy. All models incorporate the TCM into the PCM. The TCM is part of the On-Board Diagnostic system OBD-II. For more information, see Chapter 6.

Because of the complexity of the automatic transaxles and the specialized equipment necessary to perform most service operations, this Chapter contains only those procedures related to general diagnosis, adjustment and removal and installation procedures.

If the transaxle requires major repair work, it should be left to a dealer service department or an automotive or transmission repair shop. Once properly diagnosed you can, however, remove and install the transaxle yourself and save the expense, even if the repair work is done by a transmission shop.

2   Diagnosis - general

1   Automatic transaxle malfunctions may be caused by five general conditions:

a) *Poor engine performance*
b) *Improper adjustments*
c) *Hydraulic malfunctions*
d) *Mechanical malfunctions*
e) *Malfunctions in the computer or its signal network*

2   Diagnosis of these problems should always begin with a check of the easily repaired items: fluid level and condition (see Chapter 1), shift cable adjustment and shift lever installation. Next, perform a road test to determine if the problem has been corrected or if more diagnosis is necessary. If the problem persists after the preliminary tests and corrections are completed, additional diagnosis should be performed by a dealer service department or other qualified transmission repair shop. Refer to the "Troubleshooting" Section at the front of this manual for information on symptoms of transaxle problems.

Preliminary checks

3   Drive the vehicle to warm the transaxle to normal operating temperature.
4   Check the fluid level as described in Chapter 1:

a) *If the fluid level is unusually low, add enough fluid to bring the level within the*

designated area of the dipstick, then check for external leaks (see following).
b) *If the fluid level is abnormally high, drain off the excess, then check the drained fluid for contamination by coolant. The presence of engine coolant in the automatic transaxle fluid indicates that a failure has occurred in the internal radiator oil cooler walls that separate the coolant from the transaxle fluid (see Chapter 3).*
c) *If the fluid is foaming, drain it and refill the transaxle, then check for coolant in the fluid, or a high fluid level.*

5   Check the engine idle speed.
Note: *If the engine is malfunctioning, do not proceed with the preliminary checks until it has been repaired and runs normally.*
6   Check and adjust the shift cable, if necessary (see Section 4).
7   If hard shifting is experienced, inspect the shift cable under the center console and at the manual lever on the transaxle (see Section 4).

Fluid leak diagnosis

8   Most fluid leaks are easy to locate visually. Repair usually consists of replacing a seal or gasket. If a leak is difficult to find, the following procedure may help.
9   Identify the fluid. Make sure it's transaxle fluid and not engine oil or brake fluid (automatic transaxle fluid is a deep red color).
10   Try to pinpoint the source of the leak. Drive the vehicle several miles, then park it over a large sheet of cardboard. After a minute or two, you should be able to locate the leak by determining the source of the fluid dripping onto the cardboard.
11   Make a careful visual inspection of the suspected component and the area immediately around it. Pay particular attention to gasket mating surfaces. A mirror is often helpful for finding leaks in areas that are hard to see.
12   If the leak still cannot be found, clean the suspected area thoroughly with a degreaser or solvent, then dry it thoroughly.
13   Drive the vehicle for several miles at normal operating temperature and varying speeds. After driving the vehicle, visually inspect the suspected component again.
14   Once the leak has been located, the cause must be determined before it can be properly repaired. If a gasket is replaced but the sealing flange is bent, the new gasket will not stop the leak. The bent flange must be straightened.
15   Before attempting to repair a leak, check to make sure that the following conditions are corrected or they may cause another leak.
Note: *Some of the following conditions cannot be fixed without highly specialized tools and expertise. Such problems must be referred to a qualified transmission shop or a dealer service department.*

Gasket leaks

16   Check the pan periodically. Make sure the bolts are tight, no bolts are missing, the gasket is in good condition and the pan is flat

(dents in the pan may indicate damage to the valve body inside).
17   If the pan gasket is leaking, the fluid level or the fluid pressure may be too high, the vent may be plugged, the pan bolts may be too tight, the pan sealing flange may be warped, the sealing surface of the transaxle housing may be damaged, the gasket may be damaged or the transaxle casting may be cracked or porous. If sealant instead of gasket material has been used to form a seal between the pan and the transaxle housing, it may be the wrong type of sealant.

Seal leaks

18   If a transaxle seal is leaking, the fluid level may be too high, the vent may be plugged, the seal bore may be damaged, the seal itself may be damaged or improperly installed, the surface of the shaft protruding through the seal may be damaged or a loose bearing may be causing excessive shaft movement.
19   Make sure the dipstick tube seal is in good condition and the tube is properly seated. Periodically check the area around the sensors for leakage. If transaxle fluid is evident, check the seals for damage.

Case leaks

20   If the case itself appears to be leaking, the casting is porous and will have to be repaired or replaced.
21   Make sure the oil cooler hose fittings are tight and in good condition.

Fluid comes out vent pipe or fill tube

22   If this condition occurs, the possible causes are: the transaxle is overfilled; there is coolant in the fluid; the dipstick is incorrect; the vent is plugged or the drain-back holes are plugged.

3   Driveaxle oil seals - replacement

Refer to illustrations 3.3 and 3.5

1   The driveaxle oil seals are located on the sides of the transaxle, where the inner ends of the driveaxles are splined into the differential side gears. If you suspect that a driveaxle oil seal is leaking, raise the vehicle and support it securely on jackstands. If the seal is leaking, you'll see lubricant on the side of the transaxle, below the seal.
2   Remove the driveaxle or mid-shaft (see Chapter 8).
3   Using a screwdriver or prybar, carefully pry the oil seal out of the transaxle bore **(see illustration)**.
4   If the oil seal cannot be removed with a screwdriver or prybar, a special oil seal removal tool (available at auto parts stores) will be required.
5   Using a seal installer, install the new oil seal. Drive it into the bore squarely until it bottoms **(see illustration)**.
6   Install the driveaxle (see Chapter 8).

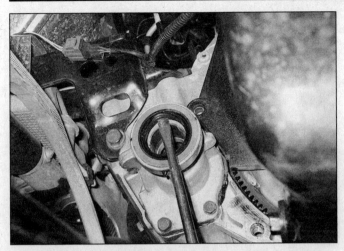

3.3 Using a large screwdriver or prybar, carefully pry the oil seal out of the transaxle (if you can't remove the oil seal with a screwdriver or prybar, you may need to obtain a special seal removal tool, available at most auto parts stores) – left side seal on 42TE transaxle shown, 62TE similar

3.5 Using a seal installer, large section of pipe or a large deep socket as a drift, drive the new seal squarely into the bore and make sure that it's completely seated; lubricate the lip of the new seal with multi-purpose grease (left side seal on 42TE transaxle shown, 62TE similar)

7   Check the fluid level (see Chapter 1) and adjust as necessary.

4   Shift cable - removal, installation and adjustment

Warning: *The models covered by this manual are equipped with Supplemental Restraint systems (SRS), more commonly known as airbags. Always disarm the air-bag system before working in the vicinity of any airbag system component to avoid the possibility of accidental deployment of the airbag, which could cause personal injury (see Chapter 12). Do not use a memory saving device to preserve the PCM's mem-ory when working on or near airbag system components.*
Warning: *Do not attempt this procedure until the vehicle has cooled completely. The*

exhaust system components must be cold to avoid physical harm.

Removal

Refer to illustrations 4.3, 4.4, 4.6a, 4.6b, 4.7 and 4.10

1   Raise the hood and place a blanket over the left (driver's) fender to protect it.
2   Remove the battery and battery tray (see Chapter 5).
3   Working in the engine compartment, disconnect the shift cable from the shift lever **(see illustration)**.
4   Disconnect the shift cable from the bracket **(see illustration)**.

Instrument panel shift models

5   Working inside the vehicle, remove the upper dashpad (see Chapter 11).
6   Remove the fasteners securing the shifter to the dashboard **(see illustrations)**.

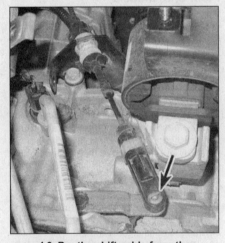

4.3 Pry the shift cable from the manual lever using a trim panel tool or flat-bladed screwdriver

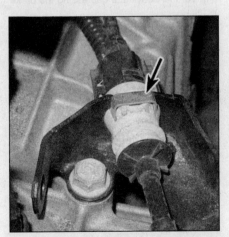

4.4 Pry up the clip then pull the shift cable up off the bracket on the transaxle

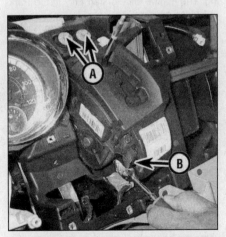

4.6a Remove the upper (A) and lower (B) mounting fasteners for the shifter . . .

4.6b . . . and the very bottom fastener under the dash

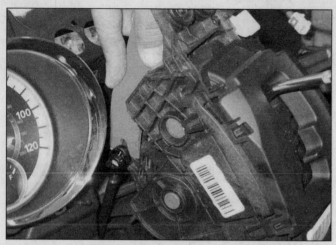

4.7 Carefully pry the shift cable from the stud on the shift lever arm

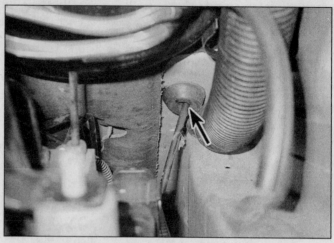

4.10 Remove the grommet from the panel opening

7   Disconnect the shift cable from the gear shift lever stud **(see illustration)**.

Floor shift models

8   Working inside the vehicle, remove the center console (see Chapter 11).
9   Pry the shift cable from the gear shift lever stud and unclip the cable from the bracket.

All models

10   Remove the grommet from the panel opening between the engine compartment and the passenger compartment **(see illustration)**
11   Pull out and remove the cable from the passenger compartment.

Installation

12   Working under the steering column, install the shift cable through the panel opening into the engine compartment.
13   Connect the shift cable onto the shift lever stud. Make sure it snaps into place.
14   Connect the shift cable to the cable bracket.
15   Working in the engine compartment, connect the shift cable to the manual shift lever.

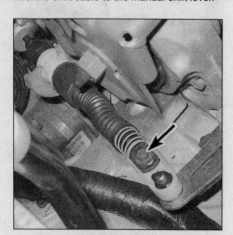

4.20 Shift cable adjustment screw

16   The remainder of installation is the reverse of removal.
17   Adjust the shift cable as described in the following steps.

Adjustment

Refer to illustration 4.20

18   Park the vehicle on a flat surface and set the parking brake.
19   Place the shift lever in the Park position. Remove the key from the ignition.
20   Loosen the shift cable adjustment screw at the transaxle shift lever **(see illustration)**.
21   Make sure the shift lever at the transaxle is in the Park position by pulling it forward all the way. The parking pawl must be engaged when adjusting the cable. If applied, release the parking brake, then rock the vehicle back and forth to ensure that the parking pawl is fully engaged.
22   Tighten the shift cable adjustment screw to the torque listed in this Chapter's Specifications.
23   Check the shift lever for proper operation. It should operate smoothly without binding. The engine should start only in the Park or Neutral positions.
24   Shift the transaxle into all gear positions to make sure the cable is functioning properly. Readjust if necessary.

---

5   Brake Transmission Shift Interlock (BTSI) system - description, check and replacement

---

Description

1   The Brake Transmission Shift Interlock (BTSI) system prevents the shift lever from being moved out of PARK unless the brake pedal is depressed. The BTSI system also prevents the ignition key from being turned to the LOCK or ACCESSORY position unless the shift lever is fully locked into the PARK position.

Check

2   Verify that the ignition key can be removed only when the shift lever is in the PARK position.
3   When the shift lever is in the PARK position, you should be able to rotate the ignition key from OFF to LOCK. But when the shift lever is in any gear position other than PARK (including NEUTRAL), you should not be able to rotate the ignition key to the LOCK position.
4   You should be able to move the shift lever out of the PARK position when the ignition key is turned to the OFF position.
5   You should not be able to move the shift lever out of the PARK position when the ignition key is turned to the RUN or START position until you depress the brake pedal.
6   With the shifter in any gear selection other than Park, you should not be able to turn the key back to the ACC or LOCK position.
7   Once in gear, with the ignition key in the RUN position, you should be able to move the shift lever between gears, or put it into NEUTRAL or PARK, without depressing the brake pedal.
8   If the BTSI system doesn't operate as described, have the system diagnosed by a dealer service department or other qualified auto repair facility.

Replacement

9   Disconnect the negative battery cable (see Chapter 5).

Instrument panel shift models

10   Remove the knee bolster, the defroster panel, the instrument panel center upper cover, the instrument cluster bezel, and the center trim panel (see Chapter 11).
11   Pry out the ignition switch trim bezel from the switch trim cover, and remove the trim cover, if equipped.
12   Loosen the mounting screw on the side of the shift knob, then depress the shift knob button and pull the knob off.

7.17 Location of the torque converter cover bolts

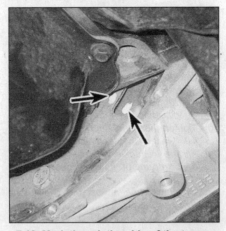

7.18 Mark the relationship of the torque converter to the driveplate

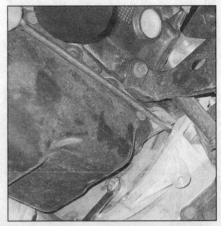

7.19 Wedge a screwdriver between the teeth on the driveplate and the engine block at the transaxle to prevent the engine from turning while loosening the torque converter bolts

13   Unplug the electrical connectors to the ignition switch, the Wireless Ignition Node (WIN) and the shifter.

14   Remove the WIN housing screws and housing.

15   Depress the lock tab at the shifter housing then pull the cable end from the shifter housing **(see illustrations 4.7 and 4.10)**.

16   Remove the shifter mounting bolts and the shifter from the instrument panel.

Floor shift models

17   Remove the center floor console (see Chapter 11).

18   Disconnect the electrical connectors to the shifter.

19   Remove the shift knob from the shifter lever by pulling in straight up and off.

20   Unclip the shift lever "select gate" trim panel and remove the panel from the shifter.

21   Pry the shift lever cable from the shift lever stud and bracket using a screwdriver. Remove the shifter assembly mounting nuts and shifter from the floor.

22   Installation is the reverse of removal.

23   Once the shifter and cable have been installed, adjust the shift cable (see Section 4).

6   Transaxle oil cooler line - removal and installation

Note: *The transaxle oil cooler and air conditioning condenser are serviced as an assembly. See Chapter 3 for the condenser removal procedure.*

1   Disconnect the cable from the negative battery terminal (see Chapter 5).

2   Raise the front of the vehicle and place it securely on jackstands.

3   To remove the lines from the oil cooler end, remove the front bumper cover (see Chapter 11).

4   Put a drain pan underneath the oil cooler line fittings to catch any spilled transaxle fluid.

5   Pull the dust covers from the cooler line fittings then install a quick-disconnect tool over the cooler lines. Push it into the fitting, then pull the lines out of the fittings. Plug the lines and fittings to prevent fluid spills.

6   Once both ends of the lines are disconnected maneuver the lines from the vehicle.

7   Installation is the reverse of removal, making sure the fluid lines click into place in the fittings.

8   Check the transaxle fluid level and add some if necessary (see Chapter 1).

7   Automatic transaxle - removal and installation

Removal

Refer to illustrations 7.17, 7.18 and 7.19

1   Remove the battery and the battery tray (see Chapter 5).

2   Loosen the front wheel lug nuts and the driveaxle/hub nuts (see Chapter 8), then raise the vehicle and support it securely on jackstands. Remove the wheels.

Note: *Depending on the type of wheels installed on the vehicle and the thickness of the socket you are using, you may have to loosen the driveaxle/hub nuts after the wheels have been removed (see Chapter 8).*

3   Remove the lower splash shield (see Chapter 1).

4   On 3.6L engines, remove the vacuum pump (see Chapter 9), if equipped.

5   Remove the air filter housing and air intake duct assembly (see Chapter 4).

6   Remove the coolant reservoir (see Chapter 3).

7   Detach the transaxle oil cooler lines and plug them to prevent fluid from spilling (see Section 6).

8   Remove the heater hose bracket bolts and move the hoses back. Clearly label, and unplug, all electrical connectors from the transaxle.

9   Disconnect the shift cable from the manual lever and bracket (see Section 4).

10   Disconnect and remove the crankshaft sensor (see Chapter 6).

11   Drain the transaxle fluid (see Chapter 1).

12   Remove both driveaxles (see Chapter 8).

13   Support the engine from above with a hoist or engine support fixture, or place a jack and a block of wood under the transaxle.

14   Remove the engine mount subframe (see Chapter 10).

15   Remove the transaxle brace mounting bolts and braces.

16   Remove the starter motor (see Chapter 5).

17   Remove the torque converter cover **(see illustration)**.

18   Mark the relationship of the torque converter to the driveplate so they can be installed in the same position **(see illustration)**.

19   Remove the torque converter-to-driveplate bolts **(see illustration)**. After all the bolts are removed, push the torque converter into the bellhousing so it doesn't stay with the engine when the transaxle is removed.

20   Support the transaxle with a transmission jack, if available, or use a floor jack. Secure the transaxle to the jack using straps or chains so it doesn't fall off during removal.

21   Remove the transaxle upper mount-to-bracket bolts (see Chapter 2A or 2B). Remove the upper transaxle-to-engine bolts.

22   Remove the front transaxle/engine bracket and the rear engine mount and bracket (see Chapter 2A or 2B).

23   Remove the lower transaxle-to-engine bolts.

24   Make a final check that all wires and hoses have been disconnected from the transaxle, then move the transaxle jack toward the side of the vehicle until the transaxle is

clear of the engine locating dowels. Make sure you keep the transaxle level as you do this.

Installation

25 Installation of the transaxle is a reversal of the removal procedure, but note the following points:

a) *As the torque converter is reinstalled, ensure that the drive tangs at the center of the torque converter hub engage with the recesses in the automatic transaxle fluid pump inner gear. This can be confirmed by turning the torque converter while pushing it towards the transaxle. If it isn't fully engaged, it will "clunk" into place.*

b) *When installing the transaxle, make sure the match marks you made on the torque converter and driveplate line up.*

c) *Install all of the driveplate-to-torque converter bolts before tightening any of them.*

d) *Tighten the driveplate-to-torque converter bolts to the torque listed in this Chapter's Specifications.*

e) *Tighten the transaxle mounting bolts to the torque listed in this Chapter's Specifications.*

f) *Tighten the driveaxle/hub nuts to the torque value listed in the Chapter 8 Specifications.*

g) *Tighten the wheel lug nuts to the torque listed in the Chapter 1 Specifications.*

h) *Fill the transaxle with the correct type and amount of fluid as described in Chapter 1.*

i) *On completion, adjust the shift cable (see Section 4).*

8 Automatic transaxle overhaul - general information

In the event of a problem occurring, it will be necessary to establish whether the fault is electrical, mechanical or hydraulic in nature, before repair work can be contemplated. Diagnosis requires detailed knowledge of the transaxle's operation and construction, as well as access to specialized test equipment, and so is deemed to be beyond the scope of this manual. It is therefore essential that problems with the automatic transaxle are referred to a dealer service department or other qualified repair facility for assessment.

Note that a faulty transaxle should not be removed before the vehicle has been diagnosed by a knowledgeable technician equipped with the proper tools, as troubleshooting must be performed with the transaxle installed in the vehicle.

Chapter 8   Driveaxles

Contents

Specifications

Torque specifications	Ft-lbs
Driveaxle/hub nut	
2011 and earlier	118
2012 and later	120
Mid-shaft bearing-to-cylinder block bolts	39
Wheel lug nuts	See Chapter 1

1   Driveaxles - general information and inspection

1   Power is transmitted from the transaxle to the wheels through a pair of driveaxles. The driveaxles are either two equal length halfshafts, consisting of "short" halfshafts on both sides connected to a mid-shaft on the right side, or two unequal length halfshafts with a short halfshaft on the left side and long halfshaft on the right. The inner end of each driveaxle is splined to the differential side gears or the mid-shaft. The driveaxles can be pulled out to replace the oil seals (see Chapter 7). The outer ends of the driveaxles are splined to the front hubs and locked in place by a large nut.

2   Each driveaxle assembly consists of an inner and outer constant velocity (CV) joint connected together by a driveaxle shaft. The inner ends of the driveaxles are equipped with a tri-pot type joint. The design is capable of both angular and axial motion. In other words,

the inner CV joints are free to slide in-and-out as the driveaxle moves up-and-down with the wheel.

3   The outer CV joints use a ball-and-cage design or "Rzeppa" joint, capable of angular but not axial movement.

4   The boots should be inspected periodically for damage and leaking lubricant. Torn CV joint boots must be replaced immediately or the joints can be damaged. Boot replacement involves removal of the driveaxle (see Section 2).

2.2 Loosen the front hub nut before you raise the vehicle and remove the wheel

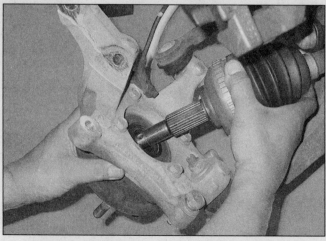

2.8 Pull the steering knuckle away from the outer CV joint

5   The most common symptom of worn or damaged CV joints, besides lubricant leaks, is a clicking noise in turns, a clunk when accelerating after coasting and vibration at highway speeds. To check for wear in the CV joints and driveaxle shafts, grasp each axle (one at a time) and rotate it in both directions while holding the CV joint housings, feeling for play indicating worn splines or sloppy CV joints. Also check the axleshafts for cracks, dents and distortion.

2   Driveaxle - removal and installation

Removal

Refer to illustrations 2.2, 2.8 and 2.9

1   Set the parking brake. Remove the wheel cover or hubcap.
2   Loosen, but do not remove, the driveaxle/hub nut **(see illustration)**.
3   Loosen, but do not remove, the wheel lug nuts.

4   Raise the vehicle and support it securely on jackstands, then remove the lug nuts and the wheel.
5   Remove the brake caliper and disc (see Chapter 9).
6   If equipped with antilock brakes, remove the speed sensor cable routing bracket from the steering knuckle (see Chapter 9).
7   Remove the two steering knuckle-to-strut bracket bolts (see Chapter 10) and separate the strut from the steering knuckle.
Caution: *The steering knuckle-to-strut bolts are serrated and must not be turned during removal.*
Note: *If the strut assembly is attached to the steering knuckle using a cam bolt in the lower slotted hole, mark the relationship of the cam bolt to the strut to preserve the wheel alignment setting on reassembly.*
8   Remove the driveaxle/hub nut and pull the steering knuckle out and away from the outer CV joint of the driveaxle **(see illustration)**. Strike the end of the stub shaft with a soft-faced hammer to separate the splines from the hub and bearing assembly, if necessary.

9   Support the outer end of the driveaxle and insert a prybar between the inner CV joint and the transaxle case **(see illustration)**. Pry out sharply to disengage the inner CV joint from the transaxle. Make sure you have a drain pan under the transaxle, as some oil will leak out.
10   On models equipped with a passenger's side mid-shaft, insert a prybar between the inner CV joint and the mid-shaft bearing housing and pry out sharply to disengage the inner CV joint from the mid-shaft bearing.
11   Carefully withdraw the inner CV joint from the transaxle. Do not let the spline or the snap-ring drag across the sealing lip of the driveaxle oil seal.
12   On models equipped with a mid-shaft bearing on the passenger's side, remove the heat shield fasteners, then remove the mid-shaft bearing mounting bolts and pull the mid-shaft from the transaxle.

Installation

13   Installation is the reverse of removal, noting the following additional points:

a) *Thoroughly clean the splines and bearing shield on the outer CV joint. This is very important, as the bearing shield protects the wheel bearings from water and contamination. Also clean the wheel bearing area of the steering knuckle.*
b) *Thoroughly clean the splines and oil seal sealing surface on the inner CV joint. Apply an even bead of multi-purpose grease around the oil seal sealing surface of the inner CV joint.*
c) *When installing the driveaxle, push it sharply in to seat the snap-ring on the inner CV joint stub shaft into its groove in the differential gears inside the transaxle. Pull out on the inner CV joint housing to ensure it's seated.*

2.9 Using a large pry bar, pry the inner CV joint out sharply to disengage the snap-ring from the differential gears inside the transaxle

3.5 Remove the snap-ring with a pair of snap-ring pliers

3.6 Mark the relationship of the tri-pot bearing assembly to the axleshaft

d) *On models equipped with a passenger's side mid-shaft, insert the splined mid-shaft assembly into the splined differential gears inside the transaxle then install the bearing mounting bolts and tighten the bolts to the torque listed in this Chapter's Specifications. Install the bearing heat shield and tighten the mounting bolts securely.*

e) *Tighten the steering knuckle-to-strut bolts to the torque listed in Chapter 10.*

f) *The steering knuckle-to-balljoint stud clamping bolt and nut should not be reused. A new clamping bolt and nut should always be used; tighten it to the torque listed in the Chapter 10 Specifications.*

g) *Tighten the driveaxle/hub nut to the torque listed in this Chapter's Specifications.*

h) *Tighten the lug nuts to the torque listed in the Chapter 1 Specifications.*

3.7 Drive the tri-pot joint off the axleshaft with a brass punch and hammer; be careful not to damage the bearing surfaces or the splines on the shaft

3 Driveaxle boot replacement

Note: *If the CV joints or boots must be replaced, explore all options before beginning the job. Complete, rebuilt driveaxles are available on an exchange basis, eliminating much time and work. Whichever route you choose to take, check on the cost and availability of parts before disassembling the vehicle.*

1 Remove the driveaxle (see Section 2).

2 Mount the driveaxle in a vise with wood-lined jaws, to prevent damage to the axleshaft. Check the CV joints for excessive play in the radial direction, which indicates worn parts. Check for smooth operation throughout the full range of motion for each CV joint. If a boot is torn, the recommended procedure is to disassemble the joint, clean the components and inspect for damage due to loss of lubrication and possible contamination by foreign matter.

If the CV joint is in good condition, lubricate it with CV joint grease and install a new boot.

Inner CV joint

Disassembly

Refer to illustrations 3.5, 3.6 and 3.7

3 Cut the boot clamps with side-cutters, then remove and discard them.

4 Using a screwdriver, pry up on the edge of the boot, pull it off the CV joint housing and slide it down the axleshaft, exposing the tri-pot spider assembly. Pull the CV joint housing straight off.

Note: *When removing the housing, hold the rollers in place on the spider trunnion to prevent the rollers and the needle bearings from falling free.*

5 Remove the spider assembly snap-ring with a pair of snap-ring pliers **(see illustration)**.

6 Mark the tri-pot to the axleshaft to ensure that they are reassembled properly **(see illustration)**.

7 Use a hammer and a brass drift to drive the spider assembly from the axleshaft **(see illustration)**.

8 Slide the boot off the shaft.

Inspection

9 Thoroughly clean all components with solvent until the old CV joint grease is completely removed. Inspect the bearing surfaces of the inner tri-pots and housings for cracks, pitting, scoring and other signs of wear. If any part of the inner CV joint is worn, you must replace the entire driveaxle assembly (inner tri-pot joint, axleshaft and outer CV joint). The only components that can be purchased separately are the boots themselves and the boot clamps.

Reassembly

Refer to illustrations 3.10a, 3.10b, 3.10c, 3.10d, 3.11, 3.12, 3.14a, 3.14b, 3.14c, 3.14d and 3.14e

10 Wrap the splines on the inner end of the axleshaft with tape to protect the boots from the sharp edges of the splines, then slide the

3.10a Wrap the axleshaft splines with tape to prevent damaging the boot as it's slid onto the shaft

3.10b Install the tri-pot spider on the axleshaft (make sure your match mark is facing out and aligned with the mark on the axleshaft)

3.10c Place grease at the bottom of the CV joint housing

3.10d Install the boot and clamps onto the axleshaft, then insert the tri-pot into the housing, followed by the rest of the grease

3.11 Make sure that the thinnest groove on the axleshaft is the only one showing

3.12 Equalize the pressure inside the boot by inserting a screwdriver between the boot and the CV joint housing

clamps and boot onto the axleshaft **(see illustration)**. Remove the tape and place the tri-pot spider on the axleshaft with the chamfer toward the shaft **(see illustration)**. Tap the spider onto the shaft (aligning the marks made in Step 6) with a brass drift until it's seated, then install the snap-ring. Apply grease to the tri-pot assembly and inside the housing **(see illustration)**. Insert the tri-pot into the housing and pack the remainder of the grease around the tri-pot **(see illustration)**.

11   Slide the boot into place, making sure the raised bead on the inside of the seal boot is positioned in the groove on the interconnecting shaft. If the driveaxle has multiple locating grooves on the shaft, position the boot so only one of the grooves (the thinnest) is exposed **(see illustration)**. Position the sealing boot into the groove on the tri-pot housing retaining groove.

12   Position the CV joint mid-way through its travel, then equalize the pressure in the boot **(see illustration)**.
13   Make sure each end of the boot is seated properly, and the boot is not distorted.
14   Install the boot clamps. There are three types of clamps you're likely to encounter: the band type, which requires a special tightening tool, the crimp type (which also requires a special tool), or the fold-over type **(see illustrations)**.
15   Install the driveaxle (see Section 2).

Outer CV joint
Removal

Refer to illustrations 3.19, 3.23, 3.24, 3.26, 3.27, 3.30a and 3.30b

16   Cut the boot clamps with side-cutters, then remove and discard them.

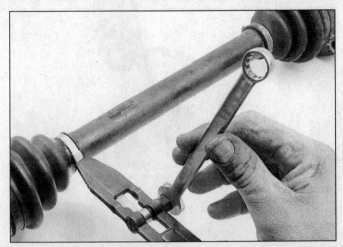

3.14a You'll need a special tightening tool to install "band" type boot clamps: Install the band with its end pointing in the direction of axle rotation and tighten it securely . . .

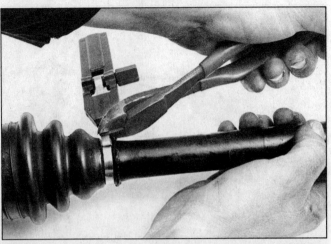

3.14b . . . then bend down the end of the clamp back and cut off the excess

3.14c If you're installing crimp-type boot clamps, you'll need a pair of special crimping pliers (available at most auto parts stores)

3.14d To install fold-over type boot clamps, bend the tang down . . .

3.14e . . . then tap the tabs over to hold it in place

17   Using a screwdriver, pry up on the edge of the boot, pull it off the CV joint housing and slide it down the axleshaft.

18   Wipe the grease from the joint.

19   Using a pair of snap-ring pliers, expand the snap-ring retaining the outer joint to the shaft, then remove the joint (see illustration).

20   Slide the boot off the driveaxle.

21   Clean the axle spline area and inspect for wear, damage, corrosion and broken splines.

22   Clean the outer CV joint bearing assembly with a clean cloth to remove excess grease.

23   Mark the relative position of the bearing cage, inner race and housing (see illustration).

24   Mount the CV joint in the vise with wood blocks to protect the stub shaft. Push down

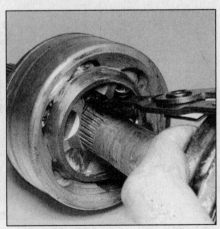

3.19 After expanding the snap-ring, the outer joint assembly can be removed

3.23 Mark the bearing cage, inner race and housing relationship after removing the grease

3.24 With the cage and inner race tilted, the balls can be removed one at a time

3.26 Align one of the elongated windows in the cage with one of the lands on the housing (outer race), then rock the cage and inner race out of the housing

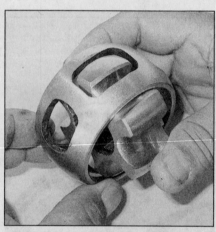

3.27 Tilt the inner race 90-degrees, align the race lands with the windows in the cage, then separate the two components

one side of the cage and remove the ball bearing from the opposite side (**see illustration**). The balls may have to be pried out.

25   Repeat this procedure until all of the balls are removed. If the joint is tight, tap on the inner race (not the cage) with a hammer and brass drift.

26   Remove the bearing assembly from the housing by tilting it vertically and aligning two opposing cage windows in the area between the ball grooves (**see illustration**).

27   Turn the inner race 90-degrees to the cage and align one of the spherical lands with an elongated cage window. Raise the land into the window and swivel the inner race out of the cage (**see illustration**).

28   Clean all of the parts with solvent and dry them with compressed air (if available).

29   Inspect the housing, splines, balls and races for damage, corrosion, wear and cracks.

30   Check the inner race for wear and scoring. If any of the components are not serviceable, the entire CV joint assembly must be replaced with a new one (**see illustrations**).

Assembly

Refer to illustrations 3.36a, 3.36b and 3.37

31   Apply a thin film of oil to all CV joint components before beginning reassembly.

32   Align the marks and install the inner race in the cage so one of the race lands fits into the elongated window (**see illustration 3.27**).

33   Rotate the inner race into position in the cage and install the assembly in the CV joint housing, again using the elongated window for clearance (**see illustration 3.26**).

34   Rotate the inner race into position in the housing. Be sure the large counterbore of the inner race faces out. The marks made during disassembly should face out and be aligned.

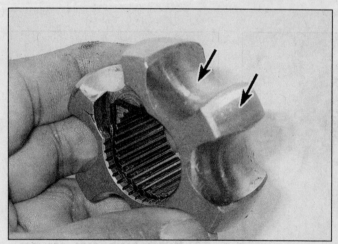

3.30a Check the inner race lands and grooves for pitting and score marks

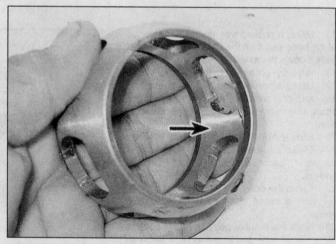

3.30b Check the cage for cracks, pitting and score marks (shiny spots are normal and don't affect operation)

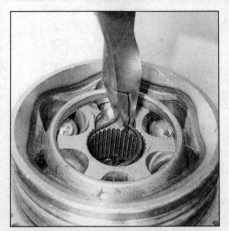

3.36a Use needle-nose pliers to lower the snap-ring into the groove . . .

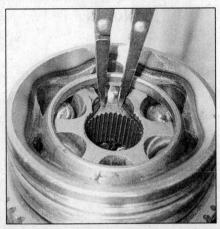

3.36b . . . then seat it into the groove with snap-ring pliers

3.37 Apply grease through the splined hole, then insert a wooden dowel into the hole and push down - the dowel will force the grease into the joint

35   Pack the lubricant from the kit into the ball races and grooves.

36   Install the balls into the holes, one at a time, until they are all in position. Using needle-nose pliers, place the retaining ring into the groove on the outer CV joint housing **(see illustrations)**.

37   Fill the joint with grease through the splined hole, then insert a wooden dowel into the splined hole to force the grease into the joint **(see illustration)**.

38   Place the driveaxle in the vise and slide the inner clamp and boot over it (wrap the shaft splines with tape to prevent damaging the boot) **(see illustration 3.10a)**.

39   Place the CV joint housing in position on the axle, align the splines and push it into place. If necessary, tap it on with a soft-face hammer. Make sure it is seated on the snap-ring by attempting to pull it from the shaft.

40   Install the outer CV joint sealing boot to the axle shaft (see Steps 11 to 14).

41   Install the driveaxle (see Section 2).

Notes

Chapter 9 Brakes

Contents

Specifications

General

Brake fluid type	See Chapter 1

Disc brakes

Brake pad minimum thickness	See Chapter 1
Disc lateral runout limit	0.005 inch
Disc minimum thickness	Cast into disc
Thickness variation (parallelism)	0.0005 inch

Torque specifications

Ft-lbs (unless otherwise indicated)

Note: *One foot-pound (ft-lb) of torque is equivalent to 12 inch-pounds (in-lbs) of torque. Torque values below approximately 15 ft-lbs are expressed in inch-pounds, since most foot-pound torque wrenches are not accurate at these smaller values.*

Brake booster mounting nuts	21
Brake hose banjo bolt-to-caliper	18
Caliper mounting (guide pin) bolts	26
Caliper mounting bracket bolts	
Front	125
Rear	74
Master cylinder-to-brake booster mounting nuts	19
Wheel speed sensor bolt	55 in-lbs
Wheel lug nuts	See Chapter 1

1   General information

The vehicles covered by this manual are equipped with hydraulically operated front and rear brake systems. The front and rear brakes are disc type. Both the front and rear brakes are self adjusting. The disc brakes automatically compensate for pad wear.

Hydraulic system

The hydraulic system consists of two separate circuits. The master cylinder has separate reservoirs for the two circuits, and, in the event of a leak or failure in one hydraulic circuit, the other circuit will remain operative.

Power brake booster

The power brake booster, utilizing engine manifold vacuum and atmospheric pressure to provide assistance to the hydraulically operated brakes, is mounted on the firewall in the engine compartment.

Parking brake

The parking brake operates the rear brakes only, through cable actuation. It's activated by either a foot pedal mounted on the driver's side with a release handle or an electronic parking brake that has a switch in the center console. The switch takes the place of the manual foot pedal and release handle and activates a control module that operates the cable.

Service

After completing any operation involving disassembly of any part of the brake system, always test drive the vehicle to check for proper braking performance before resuming normal driving. When testing the brakes, perform the tests on a clean, dry, flat surface. Conditions other than these can lead to inaccurate test results.

Test the brakes at various speeds with both light and heavy pedal pressure. The vehicle should stop evenly without pulling to one side or the other. Avoid locking the brakes, because this slides the tires and diminishes braking efficiency and control of the vehicle.

Tires, vehicle load and wheel alignment are factors which also affect braking performance.

Precautions

There are some general cautions and warnings involving the brake system on this vehicle:

a) *Use only brake fluid conforming to DOT 3 specifications.*
b) *The brake pads contain fibers which are hazardous to your health if inhaled. Whenever you work on brake system components, clean all parts with brake system cleaner. Do not allow the fine dust to become airborne. Also, wear an approved filtering mask.*
c) *Safety should be paramount whenever any servicing of the brake components is performed. Do not use parts or fasteners which are not in perfect condition, and be sure that all clearances and torque specifications are adhered to. If you are at all unsure about a certain procedure, seek professional advice. Upon completion of any brake system work, test the brakes carefully in a controlled area before putting the vehicle into normal service. If a problem is suspected in the brake system, don't drive the vehicle until it's fixed.*

2   Troubleshooting

PROBABLE CAUSE	CORRECTIVE ACTION

No brakes - pedal travels to floor

1 Low fluid level 2 Air in system	1 and 2 Low fluid level and air in the system are symptoms of another problem - a leak somewhere in the hydraulic system. Locate and repair the leak
3 Defective seals in master cylinder	3 Replace master cylinder
4 Fluid overheated and vaporized due to heavy braking	4 Bleed hydraulic system (temporary fix). Replace brake fluid (proper fix)

Brake pedal slowly travels to floor under braking or at a stop

1 Defective seals in master cylinder	1 Replace master cylinder
2 Leak in a hose, line, caliper or wheel cylinder	2 Locate and repair leak
3 Air in hydraulic system	3 Bleed the system, inspect system for a leak

Brake pedal feels spongy when depressed

1 Air in hydraulic system	1 Bleed the system, inspect system for a leak
2 Master cylinder or power booster loose	2 Tighten fasteners
3 Brake fluid overheated (beginning to boil)	3 Bleed the system (temporary fix). Replace the brake fluid (proper fix)
4 Deteriorated brake hoses (ballooning under pressure)	4 Inspect hoses, replace as necessary (it's a good idea to replace all of them if one hose shows signs of deterioration)

Brake pedal feels hard when depressed and/or excessive effort required to stop vehicle

1 Power booster faulty	1 Replace booster
2 Engine not producing sufficient vacuum, or hose to booster clogged, collapsed or cracked	2 Check vacuum to booster with a vacuum gauge. Replace hose if cracked or clogged, repair engine if vacuum is extremely low
3 Brake linings contaminated by grease or brake fluid	3 Locate and repair source of contamination, replace brake pads or shoes
4 Brake linings glazed	4 Replace brake pads or shoes, check discs and drums for glazing, service as necessary
5 Caliper piston(s) or wheel cylinder(s) binding or frozen	5 Replace calipers or wheel cylinders
6 Brakes wet	6 Apply pedal to boil-off water (this should only be a momentary problem)
7 Kinked, clogged or internally split brake hose or line	7 Inspect lines and hoses, replace as necessary

Excessive brake pedal travel (but will pump up)

1 Drum brakes out of adjustment	1 Adjust brakes
2 Air in hydraulic system	2 Bleed system, inspect system for a leak

Excessive brake pedal travel (but will not pump up)

1 Master cylinder pushrod misadjusted	1 Adjust pushrod
2 Master cylinder seals defective	2 Replace master cylinder
3 Brake linings worn out	3 Inspect brakes, replace pads and/or shoes
4 Hydraulic system leak	4 Locate and repair leak

Brake pedal doesn't return

1 Brake pedal binding	1 Inspect pivot bushing and pushrod, repair or lubricate
2 Defective master cylinder	2 Replace master cylinder

Troubleshooting (continued)

PROBABLE CAUSE	CORRECTIVE ACTION

Brake pedal pulsates during brake application

PROBABLE CAUSE	CORRECTIVE ACTION
1 Brake drums out-of-round	1 Have drums machined by an automotive machine shop
2 Excessive brake disc runout or disc surfaces out-of-parallel	2 Have discs machined by an automotive machine shop
3 Loose or worn wheel bearings	3 Adjust or replace wheel bearings
4 Loose lug nuts	4 Tighten lug nuts

Brakes slow to release

PROBABLE CAUSE	CORRECTIVE ACTION
1 Malfunctioning power booster	1 Replace booster
2 Pedal linkage binding	2 Inspect pedal pivot bushing and pushrod, repair/lubricate
3 Malfunctioning proportioning valve	3 Replace proportioning valve
4 Sticking caliper or wheel cylinder	4 Repair or replace calipers or wheel cylinders
5 Kinked or internally split brake hose	5 Locate and replace faulty brake hose

Brakes grab (one or more wheels)

PROBABLE CAUSE	CORRECTIVE ACTION
1 Grease or brake fluid on brake lining	1 Locate and repair cause of contamination, replace lining
2 Brake lining glazed	2 Replace lining, deglaze disc or drum

Vehicle pulls to one side during braking

PROBABLE CAUSE	CORRECTIVE ACTION
1 Grease or brake fluid on brake lining	1 Locate and repair cause of contamination, replace lining
2 Brake lining glazed	2 Deglaze or replace lining, deglaze disc or drum
3 Restricted brake line or hose	3 Repair line or replace hose
4 Tire pressures incorrect	4 Adjust tire pressures
5 Caliper or wheel cylinder sticking	5 Repair or replace calipers or wheel cylinders
6 Wheels out of alignment	6 Have wheels aligned
7 Weak suspension spring	7 Replace springs
8 Weak or broken shock absorber	8 Replace shock absorbers

Brakes drag (indicated by sluggish engine performance or wheels being very hot after driving)

PROBABLE CAUSE	CORRECTIVE ACTION
1 Brake pedal pushrod incorrectly adjusted	1 Adjust pushrod
2 Master cylinder pushrod (between booster and master cylinder) incorrectly adjusted	2 Adjust pushrod
3 Obstructed compensating port in master cylinder	3 Replace master cylinder
4 Master cylinder piston seized in bore	4 Replace master cylinder
5 Contaminated fluid causing swollen seals throughout system	5 Flush system, replace all hydraulic components
6 Clogged brake lines or internally split brake hose(s)	6 Flush hydraulic system, replace defective hose(s)
7 Sticking caliper(s) or wheel cylinder(s)	7 Replace calipers or wheel cylinders
8 Parking brake not releasing	8 Inspect parking brake linkage and parking brake mechanism, repair as required
9 Improper shoe-to-drum clearance	9 Adjust brake shoes
10 Faulty proportioning valve	10 Replace proportioning valve

Troubleshooting (continued)

PROBABLE CAUSE

CORRECTIVE ACTION

Brakes fade (due to excessive heat)

1 Brake linings excessively worn or glazed	1 Deglaze or replace brake pads and/or shoes
2 Excessive use of brakes	2 Downshift into a lower gear, maintain a constant slower speed (going down hills)
3 Vehicle overloaded	3 Reduce load
4 Brake drums or discs worn too thin	4 Measure drum diameter and disc thickness, replace drums or discs as required
5 Contaminated brake fluid	5 Flush system, replace fluid
6 Brakes drag	6 Repair cause of dragging brakes
7 Driver resting left foot on brake pedal	7 Don't ride the brakes

Brakes noisy (high-pitched squeal)

1 Glazed lining	1 Deglaze or replace lining
2 Contaminated lining (brake fluid, grease, etc.)	2 Repair source of contamination, replace linings
3 Weak or broken brake shoe hold-down or return spring	3 Replace springs
4 Rivets securing lining to shoe or backing plate loose	4 Replace shoes or pads
5 Excessive dust buildup on brake linings	5 Wash brakes off with brake system cleaner
6 Brake drums worn too thin	6 Measure diameter of drums, replace if necessary
7 Wear indicator on disc brake pads contacting disc	7 Replace brake pads
8 Anti-squeal shims missing or installed improperly	8 Install shims correctly

Note: *Other remedies for quieting squealing brakes include the application of an anti-squeal compound to the backing plates of the brake pads, and lightly chamfering the edges of the brake pads with a file. The latter method should only be performed with the brake pads thoroughly wetted with brake system cleaner, so as not to allow any brake dust to become airborne.*

Brakes noisy (scraping sound)

1 Brake pads or shoes worn out; rivets, backing plate or brake shoe metal contacting disc or drum	1 Replace linings, have discs and/or drums machined (or replace)

Brakes chatter

1 Worn brake lining	1 Inspect brakes, replace shoes or pads as necessary
2 Glazed or scored discs or drums	2 Deglaze discs or drums with sandpaper (if glazing is severe, machining will be required)
3 Drums or discs heat checked	3 Check discs and/or drums for hard spots, heat checking, etc. Have discs/drums machined or replace them
4 Disc runout or drum out-of-round excessive	4 Measure disc runout and/or drum out-of-round, have discs or drums machined or replace them
5 Loose or worn wheel bearings	5 Adjust or replace wheel bearings
6 Loose or bent brake backing plate (drum brakes)	6 Tighten or replace backing plate
7 Grooves worn in discs or drums	7 Have discs or drums machined, if within limits (if not, replace them)
8 Brake linings contaminated (brake fluid, grease, etc.)	8 Locate and repair source of contamination, replace pads or shoes
9 Excessive dust buildup on linings	9 Wash brakes with brake system cleaner
10 Surface finish on discs or drums too rough after machining (especially on vehicles with sliding calipers)	10 Have discs or drums properly machined
11 Brake pads or shoes glazed	11 Deglaze or replace brake pads or shoes

Troubleshooting (continued)

PROBABLE CAUSE	CORRECTIVE ACTION

Brake pads or shoes click

PROBABLE CAUSE	CORRECTIVE ACTION
1 Shoe support pads on brake backing plate grooved or excessively worn	1 Replace brake backing plate
2 Brake pads loose in caliper	2 Loose pad retainers or anti-rattle clips
3 Also see items listed under Brakes chatter	

Brakes make groaning noise at end of stop

PROBABLE CAUSE	CORRECTIVE ACTION
1 Brake pads and/or shoes worn out	1 Replace pads and/or shoes
2 Brake linings contaminated (brake fluid, grease, etc.)	2 Locate and repair cause of contamination, replace brake pads or shoes
3 Brake linings glazed	3 Deglaze or replace brake pads or shoes
4 Excessive dust buildup on linings	4 Wash brakes with brake system cleaner
5 Scored or heat-checked discs or drums	5 Inspect discs/drums, have machined if within limits (if not, replace discs or drums)
6 Broken or missing brake shoe attaching hardware	6 Inspect drum brakes, replace missing hardware

Rear brakes lock up under light brake application

PROBABLE CAUSE	CORRECTIVE ACTION
1 Tire pressures too high	1 Adjust tire pressures
2 Tires excessively worn	2 Replace tires
3 Defective proportioning valve	3 Replace proportioning valve

Brake warning light on instrument panel comes on (or stays on)

PROBABLE CAUSE	CORRECTIVE ACTION
1 Low fluid level in master cylinder reservoir (reservoirs with fluid level sensor)	1 Add fluid, inspect system for leak, check the thickness of the brake pads and shoes
2 Failure in one half of the hydraulic system	2 Inspect hydraulic system for a leak
3 Piston in pressure differential warning valve not centered	3 Center piston by bleeding one circuit or the other (close bleeder valve as soon as the light goes out)
4 Defective pressure differential valve or warning switch	4 Replace valve or switch
5 Air in the hydraulic system	5 Bleed the system, check for leaks
6 Brake pads worn out (vehicles with electric wear sensors - small probes that fit into the brake pads and ground out on the disc when the pads get thin)	6 Replace brake pads (and sensors)

Brakes do not self adjust

Disc brakes

PROBABLE CAUSE	CORRECTIVE ACTION
1 Defective caliper piston seals	1 Replace calipers. Also, possible contaminated fluid causing soft or swollen seals (flush system and fill with new fluid if in doubt)
2 Corroded caliper piston(s)	2 Same as above

Rapid brake lining wear

PROBABLE CAUSE	CORRECTIVE ACTION
1 Driver resting left foot on brake pedal	1 Don't ride the brakes
2 Surface finish on discs or drums too rough	2 Have discs or drums properly machined
3 Also see Brakes drag	

3.2 The integrated electronic and hydraulic control unit is located below the brake master cylinder

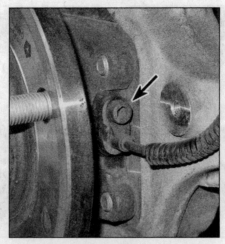

3.9a The front wheel speed sensor is mounted to the steering knuckle

3.9b The rear wheel speed sensor is mounted to the rear hub and bearing assembly

3 Anti-lock Brake System (ABS) - general information

General information

Refer to illustration 3.2

1   The Anti-lock Brake System is designed to maintain vehicle steerability, directional stability and optimum deceleration under severe braking conditions on most road surfaces. It does so by monitoring the rotational speed of each wheel and controlling the brake line pressure to each wheel during braking. This prevents the wheels from locking up.

2   The ABS system has three main components: the wheel speed sensors, an electronic control unit and a hydraulic unit. Four wheel speed sensors - one at each wheel - send a variable voltage signal to the control unit, which monitors these signals, compares them to its program and determines whether a wheel is about to lock up. When a wheel is about to lock up, the control unit signals the hydraulic unit to reduce hydraulic pressure (or not increase it further) at that wheel's brake caliper. Pressure modulation is handled by electrically-operated solenoid valves within the hydraulic control unit **(see illustration)**.

3   If a problem develops within the system, an ABS warning light will glow on the dashboard. Sometimes, a visual inspection of the ABS system can help you locate the problem. Carefully inspect the ABS wiring harness. Pay particularly close attention to the harness and connections near each wheel. Look for signs of chafing and other damage caused by incorrectly routed wires. If a wheel sensor harness is damaged, it must be replaced along with the sensor (if they are assembled together). *Warning: Do NOT try to repair an ABS wiring harness. The ABS system is sensitive to even the smallest changes in resistance. Repairing the harness could alter resistance values and*

cause the system to malfunction. If the ABS wiring harness is damaged in any way, it must be replaced.

Caution: *Make sure the ignition is turned off before unplugging or reattaching any electrical connections.*

Diagnosis and repair

4   If the ABS warning light comes on and stays on while the vehicle is in operation, the ABS system requires attention. Although special electronic ABS diagnostic testing tools are necessary to properly diagnose the system, you can perform a few preliminary checks before taking the vehicle to a dealer service department.

   a) *Check the brake fluid level in the reservoir.*
   b) *Verify that the computer electrical connectors are securely connected.*
   c) *Check the electrical connectors at the hydraulic control unit.*
   d) *Check the fuses.*
   e) *Follow the wiring harness to each wheel and verify that all connections are secure and that the wiring is undamaged.*

5   If the above preliminary checks do not solve the problem, the vehicle should be diagnosed by a dealer service department or other qualified repair shop. Due to the complex nature of the ABS system, all actual repair work must be done by a qualified automotive technician.

Wheel speed sensor - removal and installation

Refer to illustrations 3.9a and 3.9b

6   Loosen the wheel lug nuts, raise the vehicle and support it securely on jackstands. Remove the wheel.

7   Make sure the ignition key is turned to the Off position.

8   Trace the wiring back from the sensor, detaching all brackets and clips while noting its correct routing, then disconnect the electrical connector.

9   Remove the mounting fastener and carefully detach the sensor from the knuckle (front) or hub and bearing assembly (rear) **(see illustrations)**.

10   Installation is the reverse of the removal procedure. Tighten the bolt to the torque listed in this Chapter's Specifications.

11   Install the wheel and lug nuts, lower the vehicle and tighten the lug nuts to the Specifications in Chapter 1.

4 Disc brake pads - replacement

Warning: *Disc brake pads must be replaced on both front or both rear wheels at the same time; never replace the pads on only one side. Also, the dust created by the brake system is harmful to your health. Never blow it out with compressed air and don't inhale any of it. An approved filtering mask should be worn when working on the brakes. Do not, under any circumstances, use petroleum-based solvents to clean brake parts. Use brake system cleaner only!*

Caution: *Don't depress the brake pedal with the caliper removed.*

1   Using a syringe or equivalent, remove approximately two-thirds of the fluid from the master cylinder reservoir and discard it.

Caution: *Brake fluid will damage paint. If any fluid is spilled, wash it off immediately with plenty of clean, cold water.*

2   Loosen the wheel lug nuts, raise the end of the vehicle you will be working on and support it securely on jackstands. Block the wheels that remain on the ground.

3   Remove the wheels. Work on one brake assembly at a time, using the assembled brake for reference if necessary.

4.4 Spray the disc and brake pads with brake cleaner to remove brake dust; DO NOT blow brake dust off with compressed air - collect the contaminated fluid in a suitable container and dispose of it properly!

4.5 Use a C-clamp to press the caliper piston into its bore

Front

Refer to illustrations 4.4, 4.5 and 4.6a through 4.6k

4   Position a drain pan under the brake assembly and clean the caliper and surrounding area with brake system cleaner **(see illustration)**.

5   Push the piston back into its bore using a C-clamp **(see illustration)**. As the piston is depressed to the bottom of the caliper bore, the fluid in the master cylinder will rise as the brake fluid is displaced. Make sure it doesn't overflow. If necessary, remove more of the fluid.

6   To replace the brake pads, follow the accompanying photos, beginning with **illustration 4.6a**. Stay in order and read the caption under each illustration.

4.6a Using two wrenches, hold the guide pin (A) while loosening the caliper mounting bolt (B)

4.6b Remove the lower caliper mounting bolt and rotate the caliper up on the mounting bracket

4.6c Secure the caliper to the suspension with a length of wire

4.6d Remove the inner brake pad

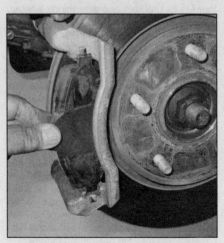

4.6e Remove the outer brake pad

4.6f Remove the brake pad support plates from the caliper bracket

4.6g Slide the guide pin out and remove the caliper from the mounting bracket

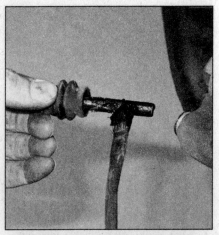

4.6h Pull out the caliper guide pins and clean them, then apply a coat of high-temperature grease to the pins and reinstall the pins in the caliper bracket

4.6i Clean the support plates, lubricate the wear points with high-temp brake grease and reinstall on the caliper mounting bracket then place the pads in the caliper mounting bracket

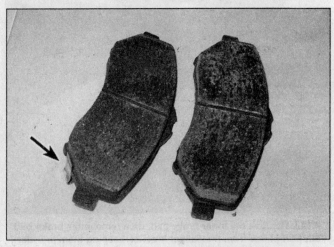

4.6j The inner pad is the one with the wear indicator

7   While the pads are removed, inspect the caliper for brake fluid leaks and ruptures of the piston dust boot. Replace the caliper if necessary (see Section 5). Also inspect the brake disc carefully (see Section 6). If machining is necessary, follow the information in that Section to remove the disc. Inspect the brake hoses for damage and replace if necessary (see Section 8).

8   Before installing the caliper, clean and inspect the guide pin bolts for corrosion and damage. If they're significantly corroded or damaged, replace them. Also check the guide pin rubber bushings for wear. When installing the caliper, Tighten the guide pin bolts to the torque listed in this Chapter's Specifications.

9   Repeat the procedure on the opposite wheel, then install the wheels and lug nuts, lower the vehicle and tighten the lug nuts to the torque listed in the Chapter 1 Specifications.

10   Add the specified type of brake fluid to the reservoir until it's full (see Chapter 1).

11   Pump the brake pedal a few times to bring the pads into contact with the disc. Check the level of the brake fluid, adding some if necessary.

12   Check the operation of the brakes carefully before placing the vehicle into normal service. Try to avoid heavy brake application until the brakes have been applied lightly several times to seat the pads.

Rear

Refer to illustrations 4.14a through 4.14h

13   Position a drain pan under the brake assembly and clean the caliper and surrounding area with brake system cleaner (**see illustration 4.4**).

14   To replace the brake pads, follow the accompanying photos, beginning with **illustration 4.14a**. Stay in order and read the caption under each illustration.

4.6k Install the caliper and tighten the caliper mounting bolts to the torque listed in this Chapter's Specifications

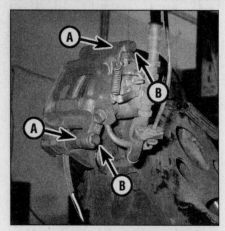

4.14a Using two wrenches, hold the guide pins (A) while loosening the caliper mounting bolts (B)

4.14b Remove the caliper and secure it to the suspension with a length of wire

4.14c Remove the outer brake pad

4.14d Remove the inner brake pad, then remove the brake pad support plates from the caliper bracket, keeping them in order; the support plates are not interchangeable

4.14e To provide room for the new pads, the piston must be retracted – to do this, rotate the piston clockwise while pushing in on it. Piston rotating tools, like this one, are available at most auto parts stores

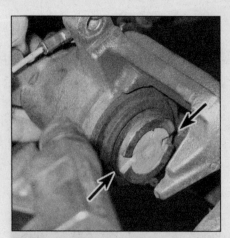

4.14f Once the piston is retracted, the slots in the piston must be aligned at the 6 o'clock and 12 o'clock positions to allow for the inner pad to be installed

4.14g Clean the support plates, lubricate the wear points with a small amount of high-temp brake grease, and reinstall the plates on the caliper mounting bracket. Place the pads in the caliper mounting bracket

4.14h Install the caliper and tighten the caliper mounting bolts to the torque listed in this Chapter's Specifications, then insert the parking brake cable through the bracket and hook the end of the cable onto the parking brake actuator

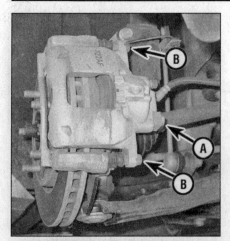

5.2a Remove the banjo bolt (A), then remove the caliper mounting bolts (B) – front caliper shown, rear caliper similar

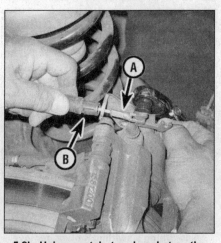

5.2b Using a ratchet and socket on the parking brake actuator, rotate the lever and unhook the parking brake cable (A) from the actuator, then depress the parking brake cable tabs (B) and slide the cable out of the mounting bracket

6.3 The brake pads on this vehicle were obviously neglected - they wore down completely and cut deep grooves into the disc (wear this severe means the disc must be replaced)

15 While the pads are removed, inspect the caliper for brake fluid leaks and ruptures of the piston dust boot. Replace the caliper if necessary (see Section 5). Also inspect the brake disc carefully (see Section 6). If machining is necessary, follow the information in that Section to remove the disc. Inspect the brake hoses for damage and replace if necessary (see Section 8).

16 Before installing the caliper guide pins, clean and inspect them for corrosion and damage. If they're significantly corroded or damaged, replace them. Also check the guide pin rubber bushings for wear. Tighten them to the torque listed in this Chapter's Specifications.

17 Repeat the procedure on the opposite wheel, then install the wheels and lug nuts, lower the vehicle and tighten the lug nuts to the torque specified in Chapter 1.

18 Add the specified type of brake fluid to the reservoir until it's full (see Chapter 1).

19 Pump the brake pedal a few times to bring the pads into contact with the disc. Check the level of the brake fluid, adding some if necessary.

20 Check the operation of the brakes carefully before placing the vehicle into normal service. Try to avoid heavy brake application until the brakes have been applied lightly several times to seat the pads.

5 Disc brake caliper - removal and installation

Warning: *Dust created by the brake system is harmful to your health. Never blow it out with compressed air and don't inhale any of it. An approved filtering mask should be worn when working on the brakes. Do not, under any circumstances, use petroleum-based solvents to clean brake parts. Use brake system cleaner only.*

Note: *If replacement is indicated (usually because of fluid leakage), it is recommended that the calipers be replaced, not overhauled. New and factory rebuilt units are available on an exchange basis. Always replace the calipers in pairs - never replace just one of them.*

Removal

Refer to illustrations 5.2a and 5.2b

1 Loosen the wheel lug nuts, raise the vehicle and support it securely on jackstands. Remove the wheel.

2 Remove the banjo bolt and disconnect the brake hose from the caliper **(see illustration)**. On rear calipers, disconnect the parking brake cable **(see illustration)**. Plug the brake hose to keep contaminants out of the brake system and to prevent losing any more brake fluid than is necessary. Discard the sealing washers - new ones should be used during installation.

Note: *If the caliper is being removed for access to other components, don't disconnect the hose.*

3 Remove the caliper guide pins or pin bolts.

Note: *Hold the guide pins with a wrench while loosening the caliper mounting bolts* **(see illustration 4.6a).**

Installation

4 Install the caliper by reversing the removal procedure. Remember to replace the sealing washers at the brake hose-to-caliper connection. Tighten the caliper guide pins or pin bolts to the torque listed in this Chapter's Specifications.

5 Bleed the brake circuit (see Section 9) (only if the brake hose was disconnected). Make sure there are no leaks from the hose connections. If you didn't disconnect the hose, pump the brake pedal several times to bring the pads into contact with the disc.

6 Test the brakes carefully before returning the vehicle to normal service.

6 Brake disc - inspection, removal and installation

Warning: *Dust created by the brake system is harmful to your health. Never blow it out with compressed air and don't inhale any of it. An approved filtering mask should be worn when working on the brakes. Do not, under any circumstances, use petroleum-based solvents to clean brake parts. Use brake system cleaner only.*

Note: *This procedure applies to both front and rear brake discs.*

Inspection

Refer to illustrations 6.3, 6.4a, 6.4b, 6.5a and 6.5b

1 Loosen the wheel lug nuts, raise the vehicle and support it securely on jackstands. Remove the wheel and reinstall the lug nuts to hold the disc in place (washers may be required). If the rear brake disc is being worked on, release the parking brake.

2 Remove the brake caliper and pads (see Sections 4 and 5). Don't disconnect the brake hose from the caliper, or you'll have to bleed the brakes when everything is reassembled. After removing the caliper, suspend it out of the way with a piece of wire.

3 Visually inspect the disc surface for score marks and other damage. Light scratches and shallow grooves are normal after use and may not always be detrimental to brake operation, but deep scoring requires disc removal and refinishing by an automotive machine shop. Check both sides of the disc **(see illustration)**. If pulsating has been noticed during application of the brakes, suspect excessive disc runout.

4 To check disc runout, place a dial indicator at a point about 1/2-inch from the outer

6.4a Use a dial indicator to measure disc runout - if the reading exceeds the maximum allowable runout limit, the disc will have to be machined or replaced

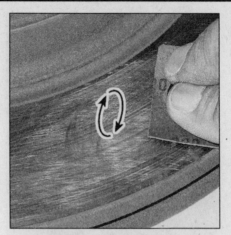

6.4b Using a swirling motion, remove the glaze from the disc surface with sandpaper or emery cloth

6.5a The minimum wear dimension is cast into the back side of the disc (typical)

edge of the disc **(see illustration)**. Set the indicator to zero and turn the disc. The indicator reading should not exceed the specified allowable runout limit. If it does, the disc should be refinished by an automotive machine shop.

6.5b Use a micrometer to measure disc thickness

Note: *The discs should be resurfaced regardless of the dial indicator reading, as this will impart a smooth finish and ensure a perfectly flat surface, eliminating any brake pedal pulsation or other undesirable symptoms related to questionable discs. At the very least, if you elect not to have the discs resurfaced, remove the glaze from the surface with emery cloth using a swirling motion* **(see illustration)**.

5   It's absolutely critical that the disc not be machined to a thickness under the specified minimum allowable thickness. The minimum thickness is cast into the inside of the disc **(see illustration)**. The disc thickness can be checked with a micrometer **(see illustration)**.

Note: *The rear disc has the minimum thickness specification cast into it as well, although the location may vary.*

Removal

Refer to illustrations 6.6a, 6.6b and 6.6c

6   Remove the caliper mounting bracket bolts **(see illustrations)**. Remove the lug nuts which were put on to hold the disc in place

and remove the disc from the hub.

Note: *Remove and discard any retaining clips on the wheel studs that hold the disc to the hub. These clips are not necessary for reinstallation of the brake disc.*

Installation

7   Place the disc in position over the wheel studs. Install the mounting bracket (if you're installing a front disc), tightening the bolts to the torque listed in this Chapter's Specifications.

8   Install the brake pads and caliper (see Sections 4 and 5). Tighten the caliper guide pins or pin bolts to the torque listed in this Chapter's Specifications.

9   Install the wheel, lower the vehicle and tighten the lug nuts to the torque listed in the Chapter 1 Specifications.

10   Pump the brake pedal a few times to bring the brake pads into contact with the disc. Bleeding won't be necessary unless the brake hose was disconnected from the caliper. Check the operation of the brakes carefully before driving the vehicle.

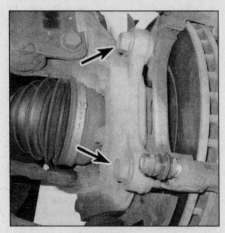

6.6a Remove the caliper mounting bracket bolts and remove the bracket – front calipers

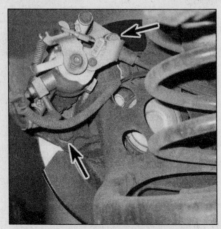

6.6b On rear calipers, remove the caliper mounting bracket bolts . . .

6.6c . . . then remove the caliper assembly off of the disc as a unit

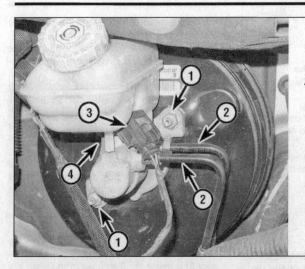

7.6 Master cylinder details:

1 Mounting nut
2 Brake line fitting
3 Brake fluid level sensor connector
4 Reservoir retaining screw (one hidden in this photo)

7.10 The best way to bleed air from the master cylinder before installing it on the vehicle is with a pair of bleeder tubes that direct brake fluid into the reservoir during bleeding

7 Master cylinder - removal and installation

Caution: *Brake fluid will quickly damage paint. Cover all body parts and be careful not to spill fluid during any of the following procedures. Wipe up any spilled fluid immediately and then flush the area thoroughly with water.*

Removal

Refer to illustration 7.6

1   The master cylinder is located in the engine compartment, mounted to the power brake booster.

2   With the engine off, pump the brake pedal several times to relieve the vacuum reserve inside the power brake booster.

Note: *This step will prevent contaminants from being sucked into the power brake booster when the cylinder is removed.*

3   Remove the battery (see Chapter 5).

4   Using a syringe or equivalent, siphon the brake fluid from the master cylinder reservoir and dispose of it properly.

5   Disconnect the brake fluid level switch connector and move the harness out of the way.

6   Place rags under the fluid fittings and prepare caps or plastic bags to cover the ends of the lines once they are disconnected. Loosen the fittings at the ends of the brake lines where they enter the master cylinder **(see illustration)**. Pull the brake lines slightly away from the master cylinder and quickly plug the ends to prevent contamination.

Note: *To prevent rounding off the corners on these nuts, the use of a flare-nut wrench, which wraps around the nut, is preferred.*

7   Thoroughly clean the area where the master cylinder mounts to the power booster. Remove the nuts attaching the master cylinder to the power booster **(see illustration 7.6)**. Pull the master cylinder off the studs and out of the engine compartment. Again, be careful not to spill any fluid as this is done.

8   If necessary, remove the reservoir mounting screw and the old reservoir and

transfer it to the new master cylinder **(see illustration 7.6)**.

Note: *Install new seals between the master cylinder and reservoir.*

Installation

Refer to illustration 7.10

9   Bench bleed the new master cylinder before installing it. Mount the master cylinder in a vise, with the jaws of the vise clamping on the mounting flange.

10   Attach a pair of master cylinder bleeder tubes to the outlet ports of the master cylinder **(see illustration)**.

11   Fill the reservoir with brake fluid of the recommended type (see Chapter 1).

12   Slowly push the pistons into the master cylinder (a large Phillips screwdriver can be used for this) - air will be expelled from the pressure chambers and into the reservoir. Because the tubes are submerged in fluid, air can't be drawn back into the master cylinder when you release the pistons.

13   Repeat the procedure until no more air bubbles are present.

14   Remove the bleed tubes, one at a time, and install plugs in the open ports to prevent fluid leakage and air from entering. Install the reservoir cap.

15   Install a new vacuum seal onto the master cylinder where it mates with the power booster.

Warning: *Do not skip this step or a vacuum leak could occur and render the power booster ineffective; this results in greatly increased pedal effort and longer stopping distances.*

16   Install the master cylinder over the studs on the power brake booster and tighten the attaching nuts only finger tight at this time.

17   Carefully thread the brake line fittings into the master cylinder. Since the master cylinder is still a bit loose, it can be moved slightly in order for the fittings to thread in easily. Do not strip the threads as the fittings are tightened.

18   Fully tighten the mounting nuts, and then the brake line fittings. Tighten the nuts to the torque listed in this Chapter's Specifications.

19   Fill the master cylinder reservoir with

fluid, then bleed the master cylinder and the brake system (see Section 9). To bleed the cylinder on the vehicle, have an assistant depress the brake pedal and hold the pedal to the floor. Loosen the fitting to allow air and fluid to escape. Repeat this procedure on both fittings until the fluid is clear of air bubbles.

Caution: *Have plenty of rags on hand to catch the fluid - brake fluid will ruin painted surfaces. After the bleeding procedure is completed, rinse the area under the master cylinder thoroughly with clean water.*

20   Test the operation of the brake system carefully before placing the vehicle into normal service.

Warning: *Do not operate the vehicle if you are in doubt about the effectiveness of the brake system. It is possible for air to become trapped in the anti-lock brake system hydraulic control unit; if the pedal continues to feel spongy after repeated bleedings or the BRAKE or ANTI-LOCK light stays on, have the vehicle towed to a dealer service department or other qualified shop to be bled with the aid of a scan tool.*

8 Brake hoses and lines - inspection and replacement

Brake hose inspection

1   Whenever the vehicle is raised and supported securely on jackstands, the rubber hoses which connect the steel brake lines with the front and rear brake assemblies should be inspected for cracks, chafing of the outer cover, leaks, blisters and other damage. These are important and vulnerable parts of the brake system and inspection should be thorough. A light and mirror will be helpful for a complete check. If a hose exhibits any of the above conditions, replace it immediately.

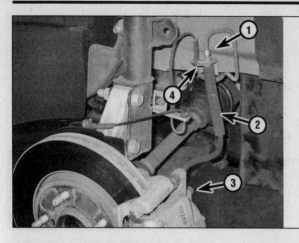

8.3 Front brake hose/line details:

1   Brake line fitting
2   Flexible brake hose
3   Brake line banjo fitting at caliper
4   Brake hose bracket (integral with flexible brake hose)

Flexible hose replacement

Refer to illustration 8.3

2   Clean all dirt away from the hose and line fittings.

3   Using a flare-nut wrench, disconnect the metal brake line from the hose fitting and immediately plug the metal line to prevent excessive leakage and contamination **(see illustration)**. Be careful not to bend the metal line. If the threaded fitting is corroded, spray it with a penetrating oil and allow it to soak in for about 10 minutes, then try again. If you try to break loose a brake tube nut that's stuck, you will kink the metal line, which will then have to be replaced.

4   Remove the brake hose bracket/fitting assembly by removing the bracket's mounting bolt.

5   Unscrew the banjo bolt at the caliper and remove the hose, discarding the sealing washers on either side of the fitting.

6   Attach the new brake hose to the caliper.

Note: *When replacing the brake hoses, always use new sealing washers.*

7   Tighten the banjo bolt to the torque listed this Chapter's Specifications.

8   Attach the brake hose bracket/fitting assembly to the vehicle making sure the hose isn't kinked or twisted. Then connect the metal line to the hose fitting, tightening the hose bracket and brake line fitting securely.

9   Carefully check to make sure the suspension or steering components don't make contact with the hose. Have an assistant push down on the vehicle while you watch to see whether the hose interferes with suspension operation. If you're replacing a front hose, have your assistant turn the steering wheel lock-to-lock while you make sure the hose doesn't interfere with the steering linkage or the steering knuckle.

10   After installation, check the master cylinder fluid level and add fluid as necessary. Bleed the brakes (see Section 9). Carefully test brake operation before resuming normal operation.

Metal brake line replacement

11   When replacing brake lines, be sure to use the correct parts. Do not use copper tub-

ing for any brake system components. Purchase steel brake lines from a dealer parts department or auto parts store.

12   Prefabricated brake lines, with the tube ends already flared and fittings installed, are available at auto parts stores and dealer parts departments. These lines can be bent to the proper shapes using a tubing bender.

13   When installing the new line make sure it's well supported in the brackets and has plenty of clearance between moving or hot components. Make sure you tighten the fittings securely.

14   After installation, check the master cylinder fluid level and add fluid as necessary. Bleed the brakes (see Section 9). Carefully test brake operation before resuming normal operation.

9   Brake system - bleeding

Refer to illustration 9.8

Warning: *The following procedure is a manual bleeding procedure. This is the only bleeding procedure which can be performed at home without special tools. However, if air has found its way into the hydraulic control unit, the entire system must be bled manually, then with a DRB scan tool (or equivalent), then manually a second time. If the brake pedal feels spongy even after bleeding the brakes, or the ABS light on the instrument panel does not go off, or if you have any doubts whatsoever about the effectiveness of the brake system, have the vehicle towed to a dealer service department or other repair shop equipped with the necessary tools for bleeding the system.*

Warning: *Wear eye protection when bleeding the brake system. If the fluid comes in contact with your eyes, immediately rinse them with water and seek medical attention.*

Note: *Bleeding the hydraulic system is necessary to remove any air that manages to find its way into the system when it's been opened during removal and installation of a hydraulic component.*

1   It will be necessary to bleed the complete system if air has entered the system due to

low fluid level, or if the brake lines have been disconnected at the master cylinder.

2   If a brake line was disconnected only at a wheel, then only that caliper or wheel cylinder must be bled.

3   If a brake line is disconnected at a fitting located between the master cylinder and any of the brakes, that part of the system served by the disconnected line must be bled. The following procedure describes bleeding the entire system, however.

4   Remove any residual vacuum from the brake power booster by applying the brake several times with the engine off.

5   Remove the cap from the master cylinder reservoir and fill the reservoir with brake fluid. Reinstall the cap.

Note: *Check the fluid level often during the bleeding operation and add fluid as necessary to prevent the fluid level from falling low enough to allow air bubbles into the master cylinder.*

6   Have an assistant on hand, as well as a supply of new brake fluid, a clear container partially filled with clean brake fluid, a length of clear tubing to fit over the bleeder valve and a wrench to open and close the bleeder valve.

7   Begin the bleeding process by bleeding the first wheel in the bleeding sequence, loosen the bleeder valve slightly, then tighten it to a point where it is snug but can still be loosened quickly and easily. The bleeding sequence is as follows:

   Left rear
   Right front
   Right rear
   Left front

8   Place one end of the hose over the bleeder valve and submerge the other end in brake fluid in the container **(see illustration)**.

9   Have the assistant push the brake pedal slowly to the floor, then hold the pedal firmly depressed.

9.8 When bleeding the brakes, a hose is connected to the bleed screw at the caliper or wheel cylinder and then submerged in clean brake fluid - air will be seen as bubbles exiting the tube (all air must be expelled before moving to the next wheel)

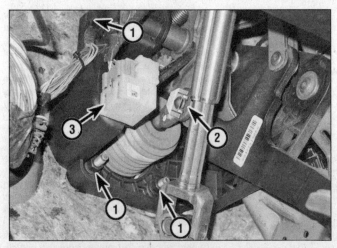

10.12 Power brake booster mounting details:

11.1 Brake light switch location

1 Mounting nuts (3 of 4 shown)
2 Pushrod-to-brake pedal retaining clip (DO NOT reuse)
3 Brake light switch

10   While the pedal is held depressed, open the bleeder valve just enough to allow a flow of fluid to leave the valve. Watch for air bubbles to exit the submerged end of the tube. When the fluid flow slows after a couple of seconds, close the valve and have your assistant release the pedal.

11   Repeat Steps 9 and 10 until no more air is seen leaving the tube, then tighten the bleeder valve and proceed to bleed the other calipers/ wheel cylinders, in the proper sequence, using the same procedure. Check the fluid in the master cylinder reservoir frequently.

Note: *Be careful not to over-tighten the bleeder valve.*

12   Never use old brake fluid. It contains moisture which can boil, rendering the brakes inoperative.

13   Refill the master cylinder with fluid at the end of the operation.

14   Check the operation of the brakes. The pedal should feel solid when depressed, with no sponginess. If necessary, repeat the entire process.

Warning: *If, after bleeding the system, you do not have a firm brake pedal, if the ABS light on the instrument panel does not go off, or if you have any doubts whatsoever about the effectiveness of the brake system, have it towed to a dealer service department or other repair shop to have the system bled.*

10   Power brake booster - check, removal and installation

Operating check

1   Depress the pedal and start the engine. If the pedal goes down slightly, operation is normal.

2   Depress the brake pedal several times with the engine running and make sure that there is no change in the pedal reserve distance.

Airtightness check

3   Start the engine and turn it off after one or two minutes. Depress the brake pedal several times slowly. If the pedal goes down farther the first time but gradually rises after the second or third depression, the booster is airtight.

4   Depress the brake pedal while the engine is running, then stop the engine with the pedal depressed. If there is no change in the pedal reserve travel after holding the pedal for 30 seconds, the booster is airtight.

Removal

Refer to illustration 10.12

5   The power brake booster unit requires no special maintenance apart from periodic inspection of the vacuum hoses and the case. The booster should never be disassembled. If a problem develops, it must be replaced with a new one.

6   Remove any vacuum from the booster by pumping the pedal several times with the engine off, until the pedal feels hard to push.

7   Remove the battery and battery tray (see Chapter 5).

8   Clean the area where the master cylinder attaches to the power brake booster.

9   Detach the master cylinder from the brake booster and carefully move it aside while keeping it supported (see Section 7).

Note: *It is not necessary to disconnect the brake lines from the master cylinder when detaching it from the brake booster. Be careful not to kink or damage the brake lines when placing it aside.*

10   Disconnect the vacuum hose from the check valve that's located on the outside of the brake booster.

Warning: *Do not remove the check valve from the booster.*

11   Working under the dash, disconnect

and remove the brake light switch (see Section 11).

12   Disconnect the brake pedal pushrod from the top of the brake pedal by inserting a small screwdriver into the center of the retaining clip and carefully prying the tang back **(see illustration).** For safety reasons, discard the old pushrod retaining clip and buy a new clip for reassembly.

13   Remove the nuts attaching the booster to the firewall **(see illustration 10.12).**

14   Working inside the engine compartment, carefully withdraw the brake booster unit from the firewall and out of the engine compartment.

Installation

15   To install the booster, place it into position on the firewall, then tighten the retaining nuts to the torque listed in this Chapter's Specifications. Connect the brake pedal to the brake booster pushrod using a new retaining clip.

Warning: *DO NOT reuse the old booster pushrod retaining clip.*

16   The remainder of installation is the reverse of removal. Install a new vacuum seal on the master cylinder before reinstalling it to the power brake booster.

17   Carefully test the operation of the brakes before placing the vehicle into normal operation.

11   Brake light switch - check, replacement and adjustment

Refer to illustration 11.1

1   The brake light switch is located along the arm of the brake pedal and is attached to a bracket near the power brake booster mount **(see illustration).** When the brake pedal is applied, the pedal arm moves away from the

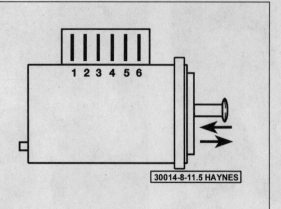

11.5 With the switch closed (plunger extended fully), there should be continuity between terminals 1 and 2 and no continuity between terminals 3 and 4 or 5 and 6. With the switch open (plunger compressed), the opposite should occur

30014-8-11.5 HAYNES

switch and a spring-loaded plunger closes the circuit to the brake lights.

2   Models equipped with cruise control use a dual-purpose brake light switch that also deactivates the cruise control system when the brake pedal is depressed.

Check

Refer to illustration 11.5

Caution: *This switch can only be adjusted once and this occurs when the switch is installed. Do not move the small lever on the switch or remove the switch unless you intend on replacing it. Once the switch is removed, it cannot be reused.*

3   Check the brake light fuse (see Chapter 12). If the fuse has blown, replace it. If it blows again, look for a short in the brake light circuit.

4   If the fuse is okay, use a test light or voltmeter to verify that there's voltage to the switch. If there's no voltage to the switch, look for an open or short in the power wire to the switch. Repair as necessary.

5   If the brake lights still don't come on when the brake pedal is applied, unplug the electrical connector from the brake light switch and, using an ohmmeter, verify that there is continuity between the switch terminals when the brake pedal is applied (the switch is closed). If continuity is not detected, replace the switch **(see illustration)**.

6   If there is continuity between the switch terminals when the brake is applied (it closes the circuit), but the brake lights don't come on when the brake pedal is applied, check for power to the brake light bulb sockets when the pedal is depressed. If voltage is present, replace the bulbs (it isn't very likely that all of them would fail simultaneously, but it is possible that they could be burned out). If voltage is not available, check the wiring between the switch and the brake lights for an open circuit and repair as necessary.

Replacement and adjustment

7   Disconnect the cable from the negative battery terminal (see Chapter 5).

8   Depress and hold the brake pedal, then rotate the brake light switch about 30-degrees in a counterclockwise direction and remove it from the mounting bracket.

9   Unplug the electrical connector from the switch, remove the switch from the vehicle and discard it.

10   Pull the plunger out on the new switch, depress the brake pedal and install the switch into the bracket by aligning the slots, inserting the switch and rotating it about 30-degrees clockwise.

Caution: *Do not move the small lever on the switch before it is fully installed.*

11   Release the brake pedal and gently pull it back to make certain that it is seated against the pedal striker. The switch plunger will ratchet backward to the correct position.

12   Plug the electrical connector into the switch.

13   Reconnect the battery and test the brake lights for proper operation.

Chapter 10
Suspension and steering systems

Contents

Specifications

Torque specifications

Note: *One foot-pound (ft-lb) of torque is equivalent to 12 inch-pounds (in-lbs) of torque. Torque values below approximately 15 ft-lbs are expressed in inch-pounds, since most foot-pound torque wrenches are not accurate at these smaller values.*

Ft-lbs (unless otherwise indicated)

Front suspension

Control arm pivot bolt/nut	114
Hub and bearing-to-steering knuckle bolts	45
Stabilizer bar link nuts	65
Stabilizer bar bushing retainer screws	33
Steering knuckle-to-balljoint stud nut	
Step 1	27
Step 2	Tighten an additional 180-degrees
Strut upper mounting nuts-to-body	21
Strut damper shaft nut	48
Strut-to-steering knuckle nuts	
Step 1	65
Step 2	Tighten an additional 90-degrees
Engine mount subframe	
Forward mounting bolt-to-radiator support	83
Rearward mounting bolts-to-subframe/cradle	41
Subframe/cradle-to-body bolts	120
Subframe support bracket bolts	40

Torque specifications
Ft-lbs (unless otherwise indicated)

Note: *One foot-pound (ft-lb) of torque is equivalent to 12 inch-pounds (in-lbs) of torque. Torque values below approximately 15 ft-lbs are expressed in inch-pounds, since most foot-pound torque wrenches are not accurate at these smaller values.*

Rear suspension

Hub and bearing mounting bolts	41
Shock absorber bolts	55
Trailing arm bracket-to-body bolts	40
Trailing arm through bolt	129
Track bar mounting bolt/nuts	60

Steering system

Airbag module screws	120 in-lbs
Power steering pump mounting bolts	17
Power steering pump mounting bracket bolts (3.6L models)	21
Power steering reservoir mounting bolts	105 in-lbs
Steering column coupler pinch bolt	31
Steering column mounting nuts	21
Steering gear mounting bolts	89
Steering wheel retaining bolt	37
Tie-rod end-to-steering knuckle nut	55
Wheel lug nuts	See Chapter 1

1.1 Front suspension/steering and related components

1	Balljoint	4	Control arm	7	Strut/coil spring assembly
2	Steering knuckle	5	Engine mount subframe	8	Brake caliper
3	Tie-rod end	6	Subframe/cradle		

1.2 Rear suspension components

| 1 | Axle assembly | 3 | Trailing arm |
| 2 | Shock absorber | 4 | Coil spring |

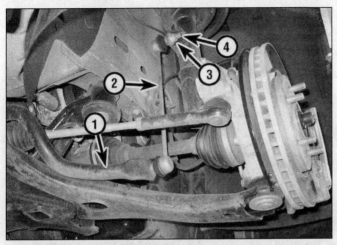

2.3 Stabilizer bar link details

2.7 Stabilizer bar bushing retainer bolt

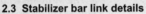

1 *Stabilizer bar*   3 *Link nut*
2 *Stabilizer bar link*   4 *Link stud*

1 General information

Refer to illustrations 1.1 and 1.2

The front suspension **(see illustration)** on these vehicles is a MacPherson strut design. The upper end of each strut is attached to the vehicle's body strut support. The lower end of the strut is connected to the upper end of the steering knuckle. The steering knuckle is attached by a balljoint mounted to the outer end of the suspension control arm. The control arm is held longitudinally by the front suspension subframe/cradle. A stabilizer bar, mounted to the subframe/cradle and connected to the strut, reduces body roll while cornering.

The rear suspension **(see illustration)** on these vehicles is composed of a beam-type axle with integral trailing arms. Side-to-side axle movement is controlled by a rear track bar attached to the top of the axle housing and the frame.

The power-assisted rack-and-pinion steering gear is attached to the front suspension subframe/cradle. The steering gear actuates the tie-rods, which are attached to the steering knuckles. The steering column is designed to collapse in the event of an accident.

Frequently, when working on the suspension or steering system components, you may come across fasteners that seem impossible to loosen. These fasteners on the underside of the vehicle are continually subjected to water, road grime, mud, etc., and can become rusted or frozen, making them extremely difficult to remove. In order to unscrew these stubborn fasteners without damaging them (or other components), Use lots of penetrating oil and allow it to soak in for a while. Using a wire brush to clean exposed threads will also ease removal of the nut or bolt and prevent damage to the threads. Sometimes a sharp blow with a hammer and punch will break the bond between a nut and bolt threads, but care must

be taken to prevent the punch from slipping off the fastener and ruining the threads. Heating the stuck fastener and surrounding area with a torch sometimes helps too, but isn't recommended because of the obvious dangers associated with fire. Long breaker bars and extension, or cheater, pipes will increase leverage, but never use an extension pipe on a ratchet - the ratcheting mechanism could be damaged. Sometimes tightening the nut or bolt first will help to break it loose. Fasteners that require drastic measures to remove should always be replaced with new ones.

Since most of the procedures dealt with in this Chapter involve jacking up the vehicle and working underneath it, a good pair of jackstands will be needed. A hydraulic floor jack is the preferred type of jack to lift the vehicle, and it can also be used to support certain components during various operations.
Warning: *Never, under any circumstances, rely on a jack to support the vehicle while working on it.*

Whenever any of the suspension or steering fasteners are loosened or removed they must be inspected and, if necessary, replaced with new ones of the same part number or of original equipment quality and design. Torque specifications must be followed for proper reassembly and component retention. Never attempt to heat or straighten any suspension or steering components. Instead, replace any bent or damaged part with a new one.

2 Stabilizer bar and bushings (front) - removal and installation

Removal

Refer to illustrations 2.3 and 2.7

1   Loosen the front wheel lug nuts, raise the front of the vehicle and support it securely on jackstands. Apply the parking brake and block

the rear wheels to keep the vehicle from rolling off the stands. Remove the front wheels.
2   Remove the engine mount subframe (see Section 16).
Note: *There is no need to remove the subframe/cradle if you are just replacing the stabilizer bar bushings or links.*
3   Remove the stabilizer bar link nuts to detach the link from the stabilizer bar **(see illustration)**.
Note: *Hold the stud on the link with a Torx bit so that it does not rotate when removing the nut. The link can be detached from the stabilizer bar and the strut assembly entirely if replacement is necessary.*
4   Remove the steering gear heat shield (see Section 20).
5   Remove the power steering hose bracket fasteners from the rear of the subframe/cradle and move the line away from the stabilizer bar.
6   Remove the engine mount (see Chapter 2A or 2B).
7   Remove the stabilizer bar bushing retainers from the subframe/cradle **(see illustration)**.
Note: *Note how the bushing sits in the retainer and where the bushing is slit for reinstallation purposes.*
8   Remove the stabilizer bar and bushings from the vehicle, guiding the bar out from the driver's side wheelwell.

Installation

9   Install the stabilizer bar, bushings and bushing retainers onto the subframe/cradle but do not tighten them yet.
10   Center the stabilizer bar on the subframe/cradle. Attach the bar links to the stabilizer bar and tighten the link nuts to the torque listed in this Chapter's Specifications.
11   Tighten the bushing retainer nuts to the torque listed in this Chapter's Specifications.
12   Install the engine mount and power

3.4 Mark the strut-to-knuckle bolts and strut bracket before removing the bolts

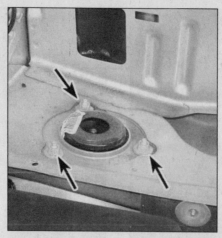

3.6 Strut assembly upper mounting nuts

4.3 The strut assembly is carefully clamped in a vise with necessary components marked for disassembly and with a spring compressor installed

steering line fasteners.

13   Install the engine mount subframe (see Section 16).

14   Install the wheels and lug nuts. Lower the vehicle and tighten the wheel lug nuts to the torque listed in the Chapter 1 Specifications.

3   Strut assembly (front) - removal, inspection and installation

Removal

Refer to illustrations 3.4 and 3.6

Warning: *Always replace the struts and/or coil springs in pairs - never replace just one strut or one coil spring; this could cause dangerous handling peculiarities.*

Note: *If both strut assemblies are going to be removed, mark the assemblies Right and Left so they will be reinstalled on the correct side.*

1   Remove the cowl cover (see Chapter 11).

2   Loosen the wheel lug nuts, raise the vehicle and support it securely on jackstands. Remove the wheels and detach the ABS speed sensor wiring harness from the strut (see Chapter 9).

3   Disconnect the stabilizer bar link from the strut assembly (see Section 2).

4   Mark the position of the strut to the steering knuckle **(see illustration).**

Note: *This is only necessary if special camber adjusting bolts have been installed in place of the regular strut-to-knuckle bolts.*

5   Remove the nuts and bolts, then separate the strut from the steering knuckle. Be careful not to overextend the inner CV joint. Also, don't let the steering knuckle fall outward and strain the brake hose.

Caution: *The bolts are serrated and must not be turned. Hold the bolts with a wrench, then remove the strut-to-knuckle nuts. Knock the bolts out with a hammer and punch, noting which way the bolt heads face.*

6   Secure the steering knuckle safely aside. Have an assistant support the strut and spring assembly, then remove the three strut-to-body nuts **(see illustration).** Remove the assembly from the fenderwell.

Inspection

7   Check the strut body for leaking fluid, dents, cracks and other obvious damage which would warrant repair or replacement.

8   Check the coil spring for chips or cracks in the spring coating (this will cause premature spring failure due to corrosion). Inspect the spring seat for cuts, hardness and general deterioration.

9   If any undesirable conditions exist, proceed to the strut disassembly procedure (see Section 4).

Installation

10   Guide the strut assembly up into the fenderwell and insert the upper mounting studs through the holes in the body. Once the studs protrude, install the nuts so the strut won't fall back through. This is most easily accomplished with the help of an assistant, as the strut is quite heavy and awkward.

11   Tighten the upper mounting nuts to the torque listed in this Chapter's Specifications.

12   Slide the steering knuckle into the strut flange and insert the two bolts. Install the nuts, align the previously made match marks (if applicable) and tighten them to the torque listed in this Chapter's Specifications.

Note: *Make certain that the bolts are installed in their original direction; the direction is different for each side of the vehicle.*

13   If the vehicle is equipped with ABS, install the speed sensor wiring harness bracket.

14   Connect the stabilizer bar link to the strut. Tighten the nut to the torque listed in this Chapter's Specifications.

15   Install the wheel and lug nuts, then lower the vehicle and tighten the lug nuts to the torque listed in the Chapter 1 Specifications.

16   Drive the vehicle to an alignment shop to have the front end alignment checked, and if necessary, adjusted.

4   Strut/coil spring - replacement

Warning: *Struts and/or coil springs must be replaced in pairs - never replace just one of them.*

Note: *You'll need a spring compressor for this procedure. Spring compressors are available on a daily rental basis at most auto parts stores or equipment rental yards.*

1   If the struts or coil springs exhibit the tell-tale signs of wear (leaking fluid, loss of damping capability, chipped, sagging or cracked coil springs) explore all options before beginning any work. The strut body is not serviceable and must be replaced if a problem develops. However, complete strut assemblies (with springs) may be available on an exchange basis; which eliminates much time and work. Whichever route you choose to take, check on the cost and availability of parts before disassembling your vehicle.

Warning: *Disassembling a strut assembly is potentially dangerous and utmost attention must be directed to the job, or serious injury may result. Use only a high-quality spring compressor and carefully follow the manufacturer's instructions furnished with the tool. After removing the coil spring from the strut, set it aside in a safe, isolated area.*

Disassembly

Refer to illustrations 4.3, 4.5 and 4.6

2   Remove the strut and spring assembly (see Section 3).

3   Mount the strut clevis bracket portion of the strut assembly in a vise and mark the components for reassembly **(see illustration).**

Caution: *Do not clamp any other portion of the strut assembly in the vise; it will be dam-*

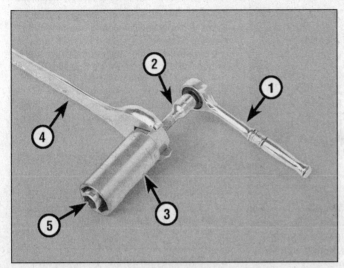

4.5 Here's the setup that can be used to unscrew the damper shaft nut

1 1/4-inch drive ratchet	4 Wrench to turn socket
2 Extension	5 10 mm socket (to hold
3 18 mm deep socket	damper shaft)

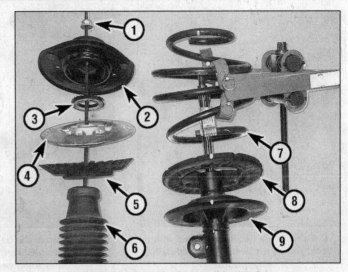

4.6 Front strut/coil assembly details

1 Nut	7	Coil spring (with spring
2 Upper mount		compressor)
3 Pivot bearing	8	Lower spring isolator
4 Upper spring seat	9	Damper unit
5 Upper spring isolator		
6 Dust boot (rubber bumper		
underneath - hidden by		
dust boot)		

aged. Line the vise jaws with wood or rags to prevent damage to the unit and don't tighten the vise excessively.

4   Following the tool manufacturer's instructions, install the spring compressor on the spring and compress it sufficiently to relieve all pressure from the upper mount **(see illustration 4.3)**. This can be verified by wiggling the spring.

5   While holding the damper shaft from turning, loosen the shaft nut with a socket. A special tool is available to do this, but a substitute can be made from a 18 mm socket (with a hex surface at the top), a ratchet, a 1/4-inch drive extension inserted through the hole in the spark plug socket, and a 10 mm socket attached to the extension **(see illustration)**.

6   Remove the nut and upper mount **(see illustration)**. Inspect the pivot bearing for smooth operation. If it doesn't turn smoothly, replace it. Remove the upper spring seat and check the upper spring isolator for cracking and general deterioration. Replace any parts that are damaged or worn.

7   Carefully lift the compressed spring from the assembly.

Warning: When removing the compressed spring, lift it off very carefully and set it in a safe place. Keep the ends of the spring away from your body.

8   Remove the dust boot from the damper shaft.

9   Slide the rubber bumper off the damper shaft. Check the lower spring isolator for cracking and hardness; replace it if necessary **(see illustration 4.6)**.

Reassembly

10   Extend the damper rod to its full length and install the rubber bumper.

11   Install the dust boot onto the damper.

12   Carefully place the coil spring onto the damper. Align the coil spring on the damper using the reference marks made during disassembly. If a new spring or strut damper unit is being installed, use the marks on the old component to help you orient the spring properly.

13   Install the upper spring isolator and seat onto the damper shaft, again, noting reference marks.

14   Install the upper mount to the damper shaft noting its alignment.

15   Install the nut on the damper shaft and tighten it to the torque listed in this Chapter's Specifications.

16   Loosen the coil spring compressor until the top coil is properly seated against the upper spring seat and upper mount. Relieve all tension from the spring compressor and remove the tool from the coil spring.

17   Install the strut/spring assembly (see Section 3).

5   Control arm - removal, inspection, and installation

Removal

Refer to illustration 5.4

1   Loosen the wheel lug nuts, raise the front of the vehicle and support it securely on jackstands. Remove the wheel.

2   Remove the steering knuckle (see Section 8).

3   If you're removing the left control arm on models equipped with a 62TE (6-speed), remove the front and rear engine mount through-bolts (see Section 16) and rotate the lower part of the engine/transaxle slightly to access the bolts.

Note: The pivot bolt cannot clear the transmission without lowering the subframe/cradle.

4   Remove the front bolt attaching the control arm to the subframe/cradle **(see illustration)**.

5   Remove the rear bolt, then remove the control arm.

Inspection

6   Make sure the control arm is straight. If it is bent, replace it. Do not attempt to straighten a bent control arm.

7   Inspect all bushings for cracks, distortion, and tears. If a bushing is torn or worn,

5.4 Control arm-to-subframe bolts

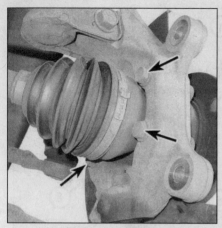

7.5 Remove the hub/bearing mounting bolts (one of the bolts is not visible in this photo)

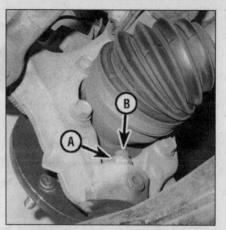

8.8 Remove the balljoint nut (A); if the ballstud (B) turns, hold it with an Allen wrench

take the assembly to an automotive machine shop and have it replaced.

Note: *Rear bushings designed with a slit can be removed and replaced easily without having to take the control arm to a machine shop.*

Installation

8   Position the control arm in the subframe/ cradle and install the rear bolt and nut but do not tighten the bolt yet.

Note: *Make certain that the rear bushing is positioned correctly in the subframe/cradle.*

9   If you're installing the left control arm, pivot the transaxle then install the front bolts and tighten the bolt to the torque listed in this Chapter's Specifications.

10   Reinstall the engine mount subframe (see Section 16) and mount through-bolts.

11   Reinstall the steering knuckle (see Section 8).

12   Place a floor jack under the control arm (as close to the balljoints as possible). Raise the control arm to simulate normal ride height.

13   Tighten the control arm front and rear mounting bolts to the torque listed in this Chapter's Specifications.

14   Install the wheel and lug nuts, lower the vehicle and tighten the lug nuts to the torque listed in the Chapter 1 Specifications.

15   Have the front wheel alignment checked and, if necessary, adjusted.

6   Balljoints - replacement

Note: *This procedure can be done in the vehicle with special tools #C-4212F, 8445-3 and 10140-3, or equivalent. If these tools are available, remove the steering knuckle (see Section 8) to access the balljoint.*

1   Remove the control arm (see Section 5).

2   Take the control arm to a machine shop and have the balljoint pressed out of the and new one pressed in.

3   Install the control arm (see Section 5).

7   Hub and bearing assembly (front) - removal and installation

Removal

Refer to illustration 7.5

Note: *If the hub/bearing assembly cannot be removed easily and appears frozen in the steering knuckle, it will have to be pressed out of the steering knuckle. If this is the case, remove the steering knuckle (see Section 8) and take it to an automotive machine shop or other repair facility for service.*

1   Loosen the driveaxle/hub nut (see Chapter 8).

2   Loosen the wheel lug nuts, raise the vehicle and support it securely on jackstands and remove the wheel.

3   Remove the brake caliper, the caliper mounting bracket, brake disc and the backing plate from the hub (see Chapter 9).

Note: *Be sure to support the brake caliper as described in Chapter 9.*

4   Remove the driveaxle/hub nut.

5   Remove the hub/bearing assembly mounting bolts from the rear of the steering knuckle **(see illustration)**.

6   Remove the hub/bearing assembly from the steering knuckle.

Note: *If the driveaxle splines stick in the hub, push the driveaxle out of the hub with a two-jaw puller. Be careful not to overextend the driveaxle inner CV joint.*

Installation

7   Make sure that the mounting surface inside the steering knuckle and on the driveaxle splines is smooth and free of burrs and nicks prior to installing the hub/bearing assembly.

8   Lubricate the driveaxle splines with multi-purpose grease. Install the hub/bearing assembly onto the driveaxle and into the steering knuckle until it is seated on the steering knuckle.

9   Install the hub/bearing assembly-to-

steering knuckle bolts. Tighten the bolts equally in a criss-cross pattern until the hub/ bearing assembly is seated securely against the steering knuckle. Tighten the bolts to the torque listed in this Chapter's Specifications.

10   Install the driveaxle/hub nut. Do not tighten the nut yet.

11   Install the brake disc, the caliper mounting bracket and the caliper; tighten the fasteners to the torque values listed in the Chapter 9 Specifications.

12   Install the wheel and lug nuts, remove the jackstands, and lower the vehicle.

13   Tighten the driveaxle/hub nut to the torque listed in the Chapter 8 Specifications.

14   Tighten the lug nuts to the torque listed in the Chapter 1 Specifications.

8   Steering knuckle - removal and installation

Note: *The steering knuckle is not a repairable component. It must be replaced if it is damaged in any way.*

Removal

Refer to illustration 8.8

1   Loosen the wheel lug nuts and the driveaxle/hub nut (see Chapter 8), raise the vehicle and support it securely on jackstands.

2   Remove the wheel.

3   Remove the driveaxle/hub nut.

4   Remove the brake disc and, if equipped, the ABS front wheel speed sensor (see Chapter 9).

5   Detach the tie-rod end from the steering knuckle (see Section 18).

6   Remove the two steering knuckle-to-strut bolts, noting their direction (see Section 3).

Caution: *The steering knuckle-to-strut assembly bolts are serrated and must not be turned during removal - turn the nuts only.*

Note: *If the strut assembly is attached to the steering knuckle using a cam bolt in the lower slotted hole, mark the relationship of the cam bolt to the strut to preserve the wheel alignment setting on reassembly (see Section 3).*

7   Separate the driveaxle from the steering knuckle and suspend it safely aside (see Chapter 8).

Note: *By tilting the steering knuckle with the balljoint still attached, the driveaxle can be removed.*

Caution: *Do not separate the inner CV joint during this operation. Do not allow the driveshaft to hang by the inner CV joint. If the driveaxle splines stick in the hub, push the driveaxle out with a two-jaw puller.*

8   Support the steering knuckle, then remove the nut holding the balljoint to the knuckle **(see illustration)**.

9   Separate the knuckle from the balljoint.

Note: *The procedure used in Section 18 for separating the tie-rod end from the steering knuckle can be used for separating the balljoint from the steering knuckle **(see illustration 18.4b)**.*

9.2 Track bar fasteners

11.3 Trailing arm through bolt/nut (A) and bracket
mounting bolts (B)

Installation

10   Installation is the reverse of removal.
When connecting the balljoint with the steering knuckle, insert an Allen wrench into the
ballstud to keep it from turning while tightening the balljoint nut. Tighten all suspension
fasteners to the torque listed in this Chapter's
Specifications.

11   Install the wheel, lower the vehicle and
tighten the lug nuts and driveaxle/hub nut to
the torque listed in the Chapter 1 and 8 Specifications.

12   Have the front end alignment checked
and, if necessary, adjusted.

9   Track bar - removal and installation

Removal

Refer to illustration 9.2

1   Raise the vehicle and support it securely
on jackstands placed under the unibody structure (not the axle). Block the front wheels to
keep the vehicle from moving.

2   Remove the track bar lower bolt and nut
at the axle **(see illustration).**

Note: *The mounting bolts are inserted from
the front to the rear.*

3   Remove the track bar upper bolt and nut,
and remove the track bar.

4   To remove the mount, remove the bolts
retaining the mount to the body.

Note: *It is not necessary to remove the mount
unless it is being replaced.*

Installation

5   Install the track bar mount, if removed.
Tighten the bolts to the torque listed in this
Chapter's Specifications.

6   Install the track bar.

7   Install the track bar bolts with the bolt
heads facing towards the front. Do not tighten
the bolts yet.

8   Lower the vehicle so the weight of the
vehicle is on the tires. Tighten the track bar
bolts to the torque listed in this Chapter's
Specifications.

10   Coil springs - removal and installation

Removal

1   Raise the vehicle and support it securely
on jackstands. Block the front tires to keep the
vehicle from moving.

2   Place a floor jack under the axle and
raise it until the weight is supported by the
jack.

3   Remove the track bar-to-axle housing
bolt (see Section 9).

4   Remove the lower shock absorber
mounting bolt (see Section 12).

5   Remove the rear brake hose bracket
fastener and allow the hose to hang freely.

6   Slowly lower the floor jack until each
spring can be removed from the axle seat.

7   Remove the lower seat isolator and the
jounce bumper.

Installation

8   Install the jounce bumper to the top of
the spring then place the lower seat onto the
end of the spring.

9   Insert the spring between the upper seat
in the body and the lower seat on the axle.

10   Using the jack, raise the axle assembly and compress the spring until the shock
absorber lower through bolts can be installed.
Do not tighten it yet.

11   Connect the track bar to the axle and
install the bolt. Do not tighten them yet.

12   Installation is the reverse of removal.

13   Lower the vehicle to the floor with the full
weight of the vehicle on the wheels. Tighten
the shock absorber bolts and track bar bolt to
the torque listed in this Chapter's Specifications.

11   Trailing arm bracket - removal and installation

Removal

Refer to illustration 11.3

1   Raise the vehicle and support it securely
on jackstands placed under the unibody structure (not the axle).

2   Support the axle under each coil spring
with a floor jack.

3   Remove the trailing arm through-bolt and
nut **(see illustration).**

4   Pull the front of the arm downwards
until the trailing arm is clear of the mounting
bracket.

5   Remove the mounting bracket-to-body
bolts and the brackets.

Installation

6   Install the bracket and mounting bolts
and tighten them to the torque listed in this
Chapter's Specifications.

7   Install the trailing arm through-bolts. Do
not tighten them yet.

8   Lower the vehicle to the floor with the full
weight of the vehicle on the wheels. Tighten
all components to the torque values listed in
this Chapter's Specifications.

12   Shock absorbers (rear) - removal and installation

Removal

Refer to illustration 12.3

1   Raise the vehicle and support it securely
on jackstands placed under the unibody structure (not the axle). Block the front wheels to
keep the vehicle from moving.

2   Support the axle with a floor jack near
the shock absorber to be removed. Raise the
jack just enough to support the weight of the
axle.

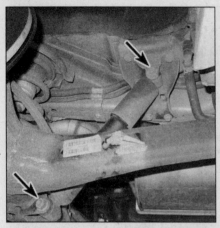

12.3 Shock absorber mounting fasteners

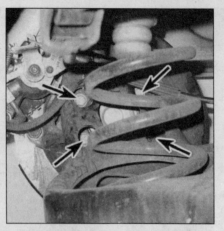

14.4 Rear hub and bearing assembly mounting bolts

3   Remove the lower shock absorber nut and bolt **(see illustration)**.
4   Remove the upper mounting bolt.

Installation

5   Install the upper shock absorber bolt finger tight.
6   Swing the shock absorber into position, and tighten the lower shock absorber bolt finger-tight.
7   Lower the vehicle to the ground and tighten the bolts to the torque listed in this Chapter's Specifications.

13   Rear axle assembly - removal and installation

Removal

1   Loosen the rear wheel lug nuts, raise the vehicle and support it securely on jackstands. Block the front wheels to keep the vehicle from moving.
2   Remove the rear wheels and ABS speed sensors (see Chapter 9).
3   Remove the rear caliper and caliper mounting bracket, and suspend the assembly out of the way. Remove the rear brake disc (see Chapter 9).
4   Remove any brake line and parking brake cable fasteners attached to the axle or trailing arms.
Note: *The rear brake lines and parking brake cables do not have to be disconnected because the brake components they are connected to can be suspended out of the way.*
5   Remove the hub and bearing mounting bolts, then remove the hub assembly (see Section 14).
6   Support the axle with a floor jack.
7   Remove the shock absorber lower bolts.
8   Remove the track bar-to-axle bolt and nut.
9   Carefully lower the axle assembly until the coil springs can be removed.
10   Remove the trailing arm through-bolts

(see illustration 11.3), lower the jack and remove the axle assembly.

Installation

11   Position the axle assembly until the trailing arm through bolts can be installed. Install the trailing arm through-bolts. Do not tighten them yet.
12   Install the coil springs (see Section 10).
13   Carefully raise the axle assembly and install the lower shock absorber bolts, but do not tighten them yet.
14   Install the track bar bolt and nut, but do not tighten them yet.
15   Reattach any brake line or parking brake cable fasteners removed from the axle.
16   Install the hub/bearing assemblies (see Section 14) and all brake components, tightening all fasteners to the torque values listed in the Chapter 9 Specifications.
17   Install the wheel and lug nuts. Lower the vehicle and tighten the lug nuts to the torque listed in the Chapter 1 Specifications.
18   With the vehicle on the ground, tighten the trailing arm, track bar and lower shock absorber fasteners to the torque values listed in this Chapter's Specifications.
19   If any brake lines were disconnected, bleed the rear brakes before placing the vehicle back in service (see Chapter 9).

14   Hub and bearing assembly (rear) - removal and installation

Refer to illustration 14.4

1   Loosen the rear wheel lug nuts, raise the rear of the vehicle, support it securely on jackstands and remove the wheels.
2   Remove the brake disc (see Chapter 9) and parking brake cable bracket fasteners.
3   Remove the rear wheel speed sensor (see Chapter 9).
4   Remove the bolts retaining the hub/bearing assembly to the rear axle **(see illustration)**.
5   Remove the hub/bearing assembly and

brake backing plate from the axle **(see illustration)**.
Caution: *If the hub/bearing assembly sticks in the axle, DO NOT remove it with a slide hammer unless you intend to replace it. The manufacturer recommends the use of a special press tool to remove the hub/bearing assembly without damaging it.*
6   Installation is the reverse of removal. Tighten the hub/bearing mounting bolts to the torque listed in this Chapter's Specifications.
7   Install the wheel and lug nuts. Lower the vehicle and tighten the lug nuts to the torque listed in the Chapter 1 Specifications.

15   Subframe/cradle - removal and installation

Refer to illustration 15.8

1   Apply the parking brake, then raise the front of the vehicle and support it securely on jackstands. Block the rear wheels.
2   Remove the power steering hose fasteners from the subframe/cradle.
3   Remove the ABS ICU mounting bracket fasteners and secure the unit out of the way.
4   Disengage the driveaxles from the steering knuckles (see Chapter 8), then disconnect the lower control arm from the steering knuckle (see Section 5).
5   Disconnect the stabilizer bar links from the stabilizer bar (see Section 2).
6   Remove the engine mount subframe (see Section 16).
7   Remove the steering gear mounting bolts and separate the gear from the subframe. Once the gear is separated, tie it up out of the way.
8   Support the subframe/cradle with a floor jack and remove the mounting bolts **(see illustration)**.
9   Slowly lower the subframe/cradle down, making sure nothing is still attached.
10   If the subframe/cradle is being replaced, separate the control arms once it is on the ground (see Section 5).
11   Installation is the reverse of removal. Tighten all subframe/cradle mounting bolts to the torque listed in this Chapter's Specifications.
Note: *Use the correct torque value for the various sized mounting bolts used to fasten the reinforcement plate to the subframe/cradle and body.*

16   Engine mount subframe - removal and installation

Refer to illustration 16.3

1   Apply the parking brake, then raise the front of the vehicle and support it securely on jackstands. Block the rear wheels.
2   Remove the front engine/transaxle mount through-bolt, or unbolt the mount from the subframe/cradle.
3   Remove the subframe mounting bolts

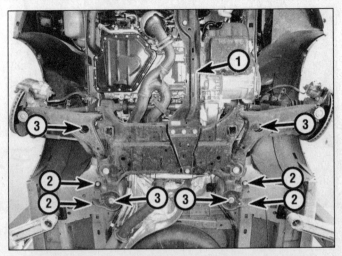

15.8 Subframe/cradle reinforcement plate mounting details

1 Engine mount subframe
2 Subframe/cradle support bracket bolts
3 Subframe/cradle mounting bolts

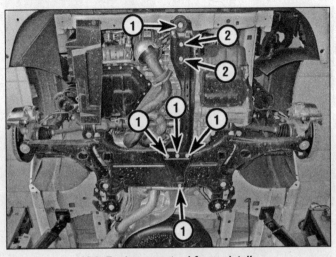

16.3 Engine mount subframe details

1 Engine mount subframe bolts
2 Transaxle front mount bolts

and lower the subframe **(see illustration)**.
Note: *If the engine mount subframe needs to be replaced, remove the front engine mounting bolts and separate the engine mount from the subframe.*
4   Installation is the reverse of removal. Tighten all subframe mounting bolts to the torque listed in this Chapter's Specifications.
Note: *Use the correct torque value for the various sized mounting bolts used to fasten the engine mount subframe to the subframe/ cradle and body.*

17   Steering wheel - removal and installation

Warning: *These models have airbags. Always disarm the airbag system before working in the vicinity of the impact sensors, steering column, or instrument panel to avoid accidental deployment of the airbag, which could cause personal injury (see Chapter 12).*
Warning: *Do not use a memory saving device to preserve the PCM's memory when working on or near airbag system components.*

Removal
1   Park the vehicle with the wheels pointing straight ahead and the steering wheel centered. Disconnect the cable from the negative terminal of the battery (see Chapter 5).
Warning: *Wait at least two minutes before proceeding with the following steps.*

2010 and earlier models
2   Lower the steering wheel. There are three airbag retainer access holes on the back side of the steering wheel hub, located at 2 o'clock, 6 o'clock and 10 o'clock.
Note: *The steering wheel must be rotated to the top or 12 'clock position for each of*

17.5 Pry up the covers to access the airbag module bolts

the access holes to disengage the retaining wires.
3   With an access hole in the 12 o'clock position, insert special tool # 10187(or the tip of a blade screwdriver) into the access hole. Pry the retaining wire loop up until it disengages from the hook of the steering wheel, while carefully pulling the airbag outwards.
4   Repeat Step 3 for all the retainer wires. Once all three retaining wires are free, rotate the steering wheel to the center position.
Note: *The lower retainer wire loop has a V-shape and must always be installed at the bottom hook of the steering wheel.*

2011 and later models
Refer to illustration 17.5
5   Remove the fasteners holding the airbag module to the steering wheel **(see illustration)**.

17.6 Remove the airbag module and disconnect the electrical connectors (to disconnect the airbag connectors, squeeze the tabs on the sides)

All models
Refer to illustrations 17.6 and 17.10
6   Remove the airbag module from the steering wheel and disconnect the electrical connectors **(see illustration)**.
Note: *Squeeze the small tabs on the sides of the airbag connectors to release them from the module. Note that they are color-coded.*
7   Set the module aside in a safe, isolated area, with the airbag side of the module facing UP.
Warning: *When carrying the airbag module, keep the driver's (trim) side facing away from you.*
8   Remove the steering wheel retaining bolt and mark the position of the steering wheel to the shaft, if marks don't already exist or don't line up.
9   Partially reinstall the bolt, leaving a 1/2-

17.10 Use a puller with hooked legs to remove the steering wheel from the steering shaft

18.2 Hold the tie-rod end while breaking loose the jam nut

inch of thread between the bolt head and the steering wheel.

10   Remove the steering wheel using a puller with hooked legs **(see illustration)**. The puller screw must contact the steering wheel bolt.

Caution: *Do not hammer on the steering shaft or the steering wheel in an attempt to free the steering wheel from the shaft. Also, do not use a slide hammer puller to remove the steering wheel from the shaft.*

Caution: *While the steering wheel is removed, DO NOT turn the steering shaft. If you do so, the airbag clockspring could be damaged when the vehicle is put back in service.*

Installation

11   Make sure the clockspring is still centered.

a) *On 2010 and earlier models, if the clockspring has become uncentered, remove it from the steering column, then turn the clockspring rotor clockwise until you feel resistance.*
    Caution: *Do not apply too much force. Now turn the rotor approximately 2-1/2 turns counterclockwise so that the drive pin is at the bottom and the arrow marks on the rotor and housing are aligned.*

b) **Warning:** *On 2011 and later models, if the clockspring becomes uncentered it must be replaced with a new one. The clockspring is installed pre-centered using an indexing pin.*

12   Install the wheel on the steering shaft, making sure to align the shaft splines correctly. Also, engage the slot in the bottom portion of the steering wheel with the pin on the clockspring.

Note: *Make sure the clockspring wires are routed correctly through the steering wheel.*

13   Install the steering wheel retaining bolt and tighten it to the torque listed in this Chapter's Specifications.

14   Reconnect the electrical connectors and place the airbag module on the steering wheel.

15   On 2010 and earlier models, hook the lower retainer wire (6 o'clock position) first, then hook the remaining two retaining wires.

16   On 2011 and later models, install the airbag module fasteners and tighten them to the torque listed in this Chapter's Specifications.

17   Connect the cable to the negative battery terminal (see Chapter 5).

18   Turn the ignition key On and verify that the airbag system is operating properly by watching the airbag warning light in the instrument cluster (see Chapter 12).

Warning: *If the airbag system is not operating properly (as indicated by the airbag warning light), DO NOT drive the vehicle. Have the airbag system repaired at a dealership service department or other qualified repair shop.*

---

18 Tie-rod ends - removal and installation

Removal

Refer to illustrations 18.2, 18.3, 18.4a and 18.4b

1   Loosen the wheel lug nuts, raise the front of the vehicle and support it securely on jackstands. Apply the parking brake and block the rear wheels to keep the vehicle from rolling off the jackstands. Remove the wheel.

2   Loosen the tie-rod end jam nut **(see illustration)**.

3   Mark the relationship of the tie-rod end to the threaded portion of the tie-rod. This will ensure the toe-in setting is restored when reassembled **(see illustration)**.

4   Loosen the nut from the tie-rod end ball-stud a few turns **(see illustration)**. Disconnect the tie-rod end ballstud from the steering

18.3 Back-off the jam nut and mark the exposed threads

18.4a If the tie-rod end stud spins when loosening the nut, hold the stud with a wrench or socket

18.4b Use a two-jaw puller to push the tie-rod end out of the steering knuckle

knuckle arm with a puller **(see illustration)**.

5   Remove the nut from the ballstud, separate the tie-rod end from the steering knuckle, then unscrew the tie-rod end from the tie-rod.

Installation

6   Thread the tie-rod end onto the tie-rod to the marked position and connect the tie-rod end to the steering arm. Install the nut on the ballstud and tighten it to the torque listed in this Chapter's Specifications.

7   Tighten the jam nut securely and install the wheel. Lower the vehicle and tighten the lug nuts to the torque listed in the Chapter 1 Specifications.

8   Have the front end alignment checked and, if necessary, adjusted.

---

19   Steering column - removal and installation

Warning: *These models have airbags. Always disarm the airbag system before working in the vicinity of the impact sensors, steering column, or instrument panel to avoid accidental deployment of the airbag, which could cause personal injury (see Chapter 12).*

Warning: *Do not use a memory saving device to preserve the PCM's memory when working on or near airbag system components.*

Removal

Refer to illustrations 19.5, 19.7 and 19.8

1   Park the vehicle with the wheels pointing straight ahead. Disconnect the cable from the negative terminal of the battery (see Chapter 5).

2   Remove the steering wheel (see Section 17).

Warning: *Do not move the steering shaft after the steering wheel has been removed or damage to the clockspring could occur when the vehicle is put back into service. To ensure this doesn't happen, make sure the steering column is locked.*

3   Remove the steering column covers and

19.5 Disconnect all electrical connectors from the steering column components (not all are shown here)

the lower knee bolster (see Chapter 11).

4   Remove the knee blocker panel and the reinforcement behind it (see Chapter 11), or, on models so equipped, the knee blocker airbag and reinforcement (see Chapter 12).

5   Disconnect all electrical connectors coming from the large harness on the side of the steering column and any ground wires that may be attached to the steering column from the other side **(see illustration)**.

6   Remove the shift cable from the steering column (see Chapter 7).

7   Mark the relationship of the intermediate shaft to the steering column coupler. Remove the pinch bolt and separate the intermediate shaft from the coupler by compressing the shaft **(see illustration)**.

8   Remove the steering column mounting fasteners; carefully lower the column, making sure nothing is still connected, and remove it **(see illustration)**.

Installation

9   Guide the steering column into position, then install the steering column mounting fasteners and tighten them to the torque listed in

19.7 Mark the steering column coupler and intermediate shaft before separation

this Chapter's Specifications.

10   Connect the steering column coupler to the intermediate shaft and install the pinch bolt and nut, tightening it to the torque listed in this Chapter's Specifications.

11   The remainder of installation is the reverse of removal. Reconnect the negative battery cable (see Chapter 5).

---

20   Steering gear - removal and installation

Warning: *Lock the steering wheel to keep it from moving while the steering shaft is disconnected or damage to the airbag system could occur when the vehicle is placed back in service. With the ignition key in the LOCK position, turn the steering wheel just enough to lock it or secure it with the seatbelt.*

Removal

Refer to illustrations 20.8, 20.9 and 20.11

1   Park the vehicle with the wheels pointing directly forward.

2   Remove as much fluid as possible from the power steering pump reservoir.

Note: *Compress the intermediate shaft to separate the coupler from the steering gear, then suspend it aside.*

3   Loosen the wheel lug nuts, raise the vehicle, support it securely on jackstands, and remove the wheels.

4   Remove the engine mount subframe (see Section 16). Remove the rear engine mount (see Chapter 2A or 2B).

5   Remove both tie-rod ends from the steering knuckles (see Section 18).

6   Remove the steering gear heat shield mounting pins and heat shield.

7   Detach the stabilizer bar links from the stabilizer bar (see Section 2).

8   Detach the power steering fluid pressure and return lines from the power steering gear

19.8 Steering column mounting fasteners

using a flare nut wrench **(see illustration)**. Cap or plug all openings to prevent contamination from entering the power steering system.

Note: *Mark the lines so they can be installed in the same position when they are reconnected.*

9   Detach the power steering pressure hose from the subframe/cradle **(see illustration)**.

10   Remove the stabilizer bar bushing retainers, then remove the stabilizer bar out from the driver's side (see Section 2).

11   Remove the steering gear mounting bolts **(see illustration)**.

12   Push up on the steering intermediate shaft rubber boot, mark the shaft to the coupler, then remove the pinch bolt and separate the intermediate shaft extension from the steering gear shaft.

13   Rotate the top of the steering gear towards the rear of the vehicle, then guide it out of the driver's side wheelwell.

Note: *The steering gear will have to be rotated to several different positions to be able to remove it.*

Installation

14   Installation is the reverse of removal, noting the following points:

a)   *If a new steering gear is being installed, center the gear by turning the input shaft clockwise until it stops. Turn the input shaft counterclockwise and count the number of rotations until it stops. Divide that number by two and turn the input shaft clockwise that amount.*

b)   *Install the mounting bolts and tighten them to the torque listed in this Chapter's Specifications.*

c)   *Be sure to align the index marks on the steering gear shaft and intermediate shaft coupler before installing the roll pin in the coupler.*

d)   *Install the fluid lines to the steering gear in the correct position and tighten them securely.*

e)   *Install the engine mount subframe bolts to the torque listed in this Chapter's Specifications.*

20.8 Power steering fluid pressure and return lines at the steering gear

f)   *Install the wheels and lug nuts. Lower the vehicle, then tighten the lug nuts to the torque listed in the Chapter 1 Specifications.*

g)   *Fill the power steering pump reservoir with the recommended fluid (see Chapter 1), then bleed the power steering system (see Section 22).*

h)   *Have the front wheel alignment checked and, if necessary, adjusted.*

21   Power steering pump - removal and installation

Removal

Refer to illustration 21.7

1   Disconnect the cable from the negative terminal of the battery (see Chapter 5).

2   Remove the fluid from the reservoir using a suction pump or equivalent.

Caution: *Be careful not to tear any mesh filter that may be present just under the surface of the fluid.*

3   Raise the vehicle and support it securely on jackstands.

20.9 Remove these fasteners and detach the power steering pressure hose from the subframe/cradle

4   Remove the drivebelt (see Chapter 1).

5   On 3.3L, 3.8L and 4.0L engines, remove the reservoir mounting nut and move the reservoir to the side.

6   On 3.6L engines, remove the heat shield mounting bolts and the heat shield.

7   Remove the power steering fluid pressure line and feed hose from the power steering pump **(see illustration)**. Plug them to avoid fluid loss.

8   Working through the holes in the power steering pulley, remove the three mounting bolts. If you're working on a model with a 3.3L, 3.8L or 4.0L engine, remove the pump out from the top of the engine compartment. If you're working on a model with a 3.6L engine, lower the pump out from the bottom of the vehicle.

Installation

9   Installation is the reverse of removal.

10   Tighten all power steering mounting fasteners to the torque listed in this Chapter's Specifications.

11   Tighten the pressure line-to-pump fitting securely.

12   Make sure the hoses are properly routed

20.11 Steering gear left side mounting bolt

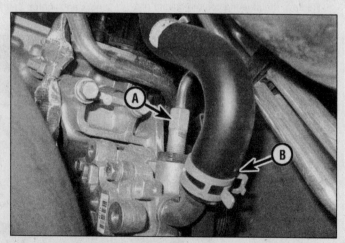

21.7 Power steering pressure line (A) and feed hose (B)

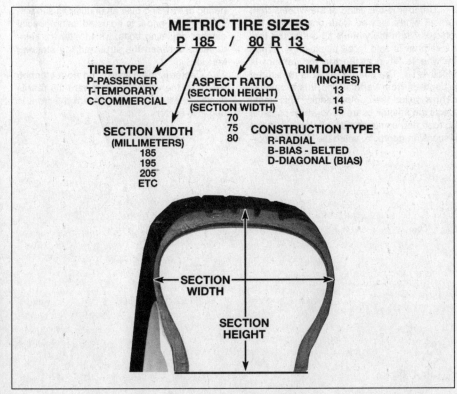

23.1 Metric tire size code

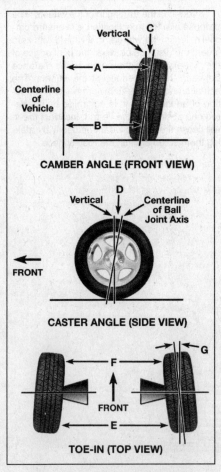

24.1 Front end alignment details

and all hose clamps are tightened securely.

14   Fill the power steering fluid reservoir with the recommended fluid (see Chapter 1).

15   Connect the negative battery cable to the battery (see Chapter 5).

16   Bleed the power steering system (see Section 22). Stop the engine, check the fluid level, and inspect the system for leaks.

22   Power steering system - bleeding

1   Following any operation in which the power steering fluid lines have been disconnected, the power steering system must be bled to remove all air and obtain proper steering performance.

2   With the front wheels in the straight ahead position, check the power steering fluid level (see Chapter 1).

3   Start the engine and allow it to run at fast idle. Recheck the fluid level and add fluid if necessary.

4   Bleed the system by turning the wheels from side to side, without hitting the stops. This will work the air out of the system. Maintain the proper fluid level as this is done.

5   When the air is worked out of the system, return the wheels to the straight ahead position and leave the vehicle running for several more minutes before shutting it off.

6   Road test the vehicle to be sure the steering system is functioning normally and noise free.

7   Recheck the fluid level to be sure it is correct. Add fluid if necessary

23   Wheels and tires - general information

Refer to illustration 23.1

1   All vehicles covered by this manual are equipped with metric-sized fiberglass or steel belted radial tires **(see illustration)**. Use of other size or type of tires may affect the ride and handling of the vehicle. Don't mix different types of tires, such as radials and bias belted, on the same vehicle as handling may be seriously affected. It's recommended that tires be replaced in pairs on the same axle, but if only one tire is being replaced, be sure it's the same size, structure and tread design as the other.

2   Because tire pressure has a substantial effect on handling and wear, the pressure on all tires should be checked at least once a month or before any extended trips (see Chapter 1).

3   Wheels must be replaced if they are bent, dented, leak air, have elongated bolt holes, are heavily rusted, out of vertical symmetry or if the lug nuts won't stay tight. Wheel repairs that use welding or peening are not recommended.

4   Tire and wheel balance is important in the overall handling, braking and performance of the vehicle. Unbalanced wheels can adversely affect handling and ride characteristics as well as tire life. Whenever a tire is installed on a wheel, the tire and wheel should be balanced by a shop with the proper equipment.

24   Wheel alignment - general information

Refer to illustration 24.1

A wheel alignment refers to the adjustments made to the wheels so they are in proper angular relationship to the suspension and the ground. Wheels that are out of proper alignment not only affect vehicle control, but also increase tire wear. The front end angles normally measured are camber, caster and toe-in **(see illustration)**. Toe-in is the only routine adjustment made; camber is adjustable, but only after installing special strut-to-knuckle bolts. If the caster is not correct, check for bent components. There are no adjustments possible to the rear wheels.

Getting the proper wheel alignment is a very exacting process, one in which complicated and expensive machines are necessary to perform the job properly. Because of this, you should have a technician with the proper equipment perform these tasks. We will, however, use this space to give you a basic idea of what is involved with a wheel alignment so you can better understand the process and deal intelligently with the shop that does the work.

Toe-in is the turning in of the wheels. The purpose of a toe specification is to ensure parallel rolling of the wheels. In a vehicle with zero toe-in, the distance between the front edges of the wheels will be the same as the distance between the rear edges of the wheels. The actual amount of toe-in is normally only a fraction of an inch. Toe-in is controlled by the tie-rod end position on the tie-rod. Incorrect toe-in will cause the tires to wear improperly by making them scrub against the road surface.

Camber is the tilting of the wheels from vertical when viewed from one end of the vehicle. When the wheels tilt out at the top, the camber is said to be positive (+). When the wheels tilt in at the top the camber is negative (-). The amount of tilt is measured in degrees from vertical and this measurement is called the camber angle. This angle affects the amount of tire tread which contacts the road and compensates for changes in the suspension geometry when the vehicle is cor-

nering or traveling over an undulating surface. On the front end it is adjusted using special camber adjusting bolts, which alter the relationship between the strut and the steering knuckle.

Caster is the tilting of the front steering axis from the vertical. A tilt toward the rear is positive caster and a tilt toward the front is negative caster.

Chapter 11 Body

Contents

Specifications

Torque specifications

Seat belt mounting bolts .... 29 ft-lbs

1   General information

Warning: *The models covered by this manual are equipped with Supplemental Restraint Systems (SRS), more commonly known as airbags. Always disable the airbag system before working in the vicinity of any airbag system components to avoid the possibility of accidental deployment of the airbags, which could cause personal injury (see Chapter 12).*

Certain body components are particularly vulnerable to accident damage and can be unbolted and repaired or replaced. Among these parts are the hood, doors, tailgate, liftgate, bumpers and front fenders.

Only general body maintenance practices and body panel repair procedures within the scope of the do-it-yourselfer are included in this Chapter.

Make sure the damaged area is perfectly clean and rust free. If the touch-up kit has a wire brush, use it to clean the scratch or chip. Or use fine steel wool wrapped around the end of a pencil. Clean the scratched or chipped surface only, not the good paint surrounding it. Rinse the area with water and allow it to dry thoroughly

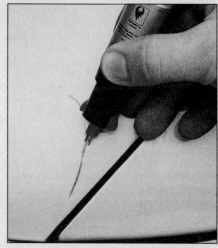

Thoroughly mix the paint, then apply a small amount with the touch-up kit brush or a very fine artist's brush. Brush in one direction as you fill the scratch area. Do not build up the paint higher than the surrounding paint

2   Repair minor paint scratches

No matter how hard you try to keep your vehicle looking like new, it will inevitably be scratched, chipped or dented at some point. If the metal is actually dented, seek the advice of a professional. But you can fix minor scratches and chips yourself. Buy a touch-up paint kit from a dealer parts department or an auto parts store. To ensure that you get the right color, you'll need to have the specific make, model and year of your vehicle and, ideally, the paint code, which is located on a special metal plate under the hood or in the door jamb.

3   Body repair - minor damage

Plastic body panels

The following repair procedures are for minor scratches and gouges. Repair of more serious damage should be left to a dealer service department or qualified auto body shop. Below is a list of the equipment and materials necessary to perform the following repair procedures on plastic body panels.

Wax, grease and silicone removing solvent
Cloth-backed body tape
Sanding discs
Drill motor with three-inch disc holder
Hand sanding block
Rubber squeegees
Sandpaper
Non-porous mixing palette
Wood paddle or putty knife
Curved-tooth body file
Flexible parts repair material

Flexible panels (bumper trim)

1   Remove the damaged panel, if necessary or desirable. In most cases, repairs can be car-

If the vehicle has a two-coat finish, apply the clear coat after the color coat has dried

ried out with the panel installed.
2   Clean the area(s) to be repaired with a wax, grease and silicone removing solvent applied with a water-dampened cloth.
3   If the damage is structural, that is, if it extends through the panel, clean the backside of the panel area to be repaired as well. Wipe dry.
4   Sand the rear surface about 1-1/2 inches beyond the break.
5   Cut two pieces of fiberglass cloth large enough to overlap the break by about 1-1/2 inches. Cut only to the required length.
6   Mix the adhesive from the repair kit according to the instructions included with the kit, and apply a layer of the mixture approximately 1/8-inch thick on the backside of the panel. Overlap the break by at least 1-1/2 inches.
7   Apply one piece of fiberglass cloth to the adhesive and cover the cloth with additional

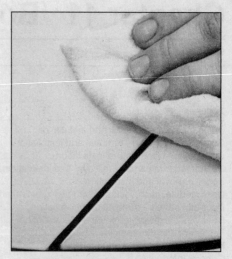

Wait a few days for the paint to dry thoroughly, then rub out the repainted area with a polishing compound to blend the new paint with the surrounding area. When you're happy with your work, wash and polish the area

adhesive. Apply a second piece of fiberglass cloth to the adhesive and immediately cover the cloth with additional adhesive in sufficient quantity to fill the weave.
8   Allow the repair to cure for 20 to 30 minutes at 60-degrees to 80-degrees F.
9   If necessary, trim the excess repair material at the edge.
10   Remove all of the paint film over and around the area(s) to be repaired. The repair material should not overlap the painted surface.
11   With a drill motor and a sanding disc (or a rotary file), cut a "V" along the break line approximately 1/2-inch wide. Remove all dust and loose particles from the repair area.
12   Mix and apply the repair material. Apply a

light coat first over the damaged area; then continue applying material until it reaches a level slightly higher than the surrounding finish.

13 Cure the mixture for 20 to 30 minutes at 60-degrees to 80-degrees F.

14 Roughly establish the contour of the area being repaired with a body file. If low areas or pits remain, mix and apply additional adhesive.

15 Block sand the damaged area with sandpaper to establish the actual contour of the surrounding surface.

16 If desired, the repaired area can be temporarily protected with several light coats of primer. Because of the special paints and techniques required for flexible body panels, it is recommended that the vehicle be taken to a paint shop for completion of the body repair.

Steel body panels

See photo sequence

Repair of dents

17 When repairing dents, the first job is to pull the dent out until the affected area is as close as possible to its original shape. There is no point in trying to restore the original shape completely as the metal in the damaged area will have stretched on impact and cannot be restored to its original contours. It is better to bring the level of the dent up to a point that is about 1/8-inch below the level of the surrounding metal. In cases where the dent is very shallow, it is not worth trying to pull it out at all.

18 If the backside of the dent is accessible, it can be hammered out gently from behind using a soft-face hammer. While doing this, hold a block of wood firmly against the opposite side of the metal to absorb the hammer blows and prevent the metal from being stretched.

19 If the dent is in a section of the body which has double layers, or some other factor makes it inaccessible from behind, a different technique is required. Drill several small holes through the metal inside the damaged area, particularly in the deeper sections. Screw long, self-tapping screws into the holes just enough for them to get a good grip in the metal. Now pulling on the protruding heads of the screws with locking pliers can pull out the dent.

20 The next stage of repair is the removal of paint from the damaged area and from an inch or so of the surrounding metal. This is easily done with a wire brush or sanding disk in a drill motor, although it can be done just as effectively by hand with sandpaper. To complete the preparation for filling, score the surface of the bare metal with a screwdriver or the tang of a file or drill small holes in the affected area. This will provide a good grip for the filler material. To complete the repair, see the Section on filling and painting.

Repair of rust holes or gashes

21 Remove all paint from the affected area and from an inch or so of the surrounding metal using a sanding disk or wire brush mounted in a drill motor. If these are not available, a few sheets of sandpaper will do the job just as effectively.

22 With the paint removed, you will be able to determine the severity of the corrosion and decide whether to replace the whole panel, if possible, or repair the affected area. New body panels are not as expensive as most people think and it is often quicker to install a new panel than to repair large areas of rust.

23 Remove all trim pieces from the affected area except those which will act as a guide to the original shape of the damaged body, such as headlight shells, etc. Using metal snips or a hacksaw blade, remove all loose metal and any other metal that is badly affected by rust. Hammer the edges of the hole in to create a slight depression for the filler material.

24 Wire-brush the affected area to remove the powdery rust from the surface of the metal. If the back of the rusted area is accessible, treat it with rust inhibiting paint.

25 Before filling is done, block the hole in some way. This can be done with sheet metal riveted or screwed into place, or by stuffing the hole with wire mesh.

26 Once the hole is blocked off, the affected area can be filled and painted. See the following subsection on filling and painting.

Filling and painting

27 Many types of body fillers are available, but generally speaking, body repair kits which contain filler paste and a tube of resin hardener are best for this type of repair work. A wide, flexible plastic or nylon applicator will be necessary for imparting a smooth and contoured finish to the surface of the filler material. Mix up a small amount of filler on a clean piece of wood or cardboard (use the hardener sparingly). Follow the manufacturer's instructions on the package, otherwise the filler will set incorrectly.

28 Using the applicator, apply the filler paste to the prepared area. Draw the applicator across the surface of the filler to achieve the desired contour and to level the filler surface. As soon as a contour that approximates the original one is achieved, stop working the paste. If you continue, the paste will begin to stick to the applicator. Continue to add thin layers of paste at 20-minute intervals until the level of the filler is just above the surrounding metal.

29 Once the filler has hardened, the excess can be removed with a body file. From then on, progressively finer grades of sandpaper should be used, starting with a 180-grit paper and finishing with 600-grit wet-or-dry paper. Always wrap the sandpaper around a flat rubber or wooden block, otherwise the surface of the filler will not be completely flat. During the sanding of the filler surface, the wet-or-dry paper should be periodically rinsed in water. This will ensure that a very smooth finish is produced in the final stage.

30 At this point, the repair area should be surrounded by a ring of bare metal, which in turn should be encircled by the finely feathered edge of good paint. Rinse the repair area with clean water until all of the dust produced by the sanding operation is gone.

31 Spray the entire area with a light coat of primer. This will reveal any imperfections in the surface of the filler. Repair the imperfec-

tions with fresh filler paste or glaze filler and once more smooth the surface with sandpaper. Repeat this spray-and-repair procedure until you are satisfied that the surface of the filler and the feathered edge of the paint are perfect. Rinse the area with clean water and allow it to dry completely.

32 The repair area is now ready for painting. Spray painting must be carried out in a warm, dry, windless and dust free atmosphere. These conditions can be created if you have access to a large indoor work area, but if you are forced to work in the open, you will have to pick the day very carefully. If you are working indoors, dousing the floor in the work area with water will help settle the dust that would otherwise be in the air. If the repair area is confined to one body panel, mask off the surrounding panels. This will help minimize the effects of a slight mismatch in paint color. Trim pieces such as chrome strips, door handles, etc., will also need to be masked off or removed. Use masking tape and several thickness of newspaper for the masking operations.

33 Before spraying, shake the paint can thoroughly, then spray a test area until the spray painting technique is mastered. Cover the repair area with a thick coat of primer. The thickness should be built up using several thin layers of primer rather than one thick one. Using 600-grit wet-or-dry sandpaper, rub down the surface of the primer until it is very smooth. While doing this, the work area should be thoroughly rinsed with water and the wet-or-dry sandpaper periodically rinsed as well. Allow the primer to dry before spraying additional coats.

34 Spray on the top coat, again building up the thickness by using several thin layers of paint. Begin spraying in the center of the repair area and then, using a circular motion, work out until the whole repair area and about two inches of the surrounding original paint is covered. Remove all masking material 10 to 15 minutes after spraying on the final coat of paint. Allow the new paint at least two weeks to harden, then use a very fine rubbing compound to blend the edges of the new paint into the existing paint. Finally, apply a coat of wax

4 Body repair - major damage

1 Major damage must be repaired by an auto body shop specifically equipped to perform body and frame repairs. These shops have the specialized equipment required to do the job properly.

2 If the damage is extensive, the frame must be checked for proper alignment or the vehicle's handling characteristics may be adversely affected and other components may wear at an accelerated rate.

3 Due to the fact that all of the major body components (hood, fenders, etc.) are separate and replaceable units, any seriously damaged components should be replaced rather than repaired. Sometimes the components can be found in a wrecking yard that specializes in used vehicle components, often at considerable savings over the cost of new parts.

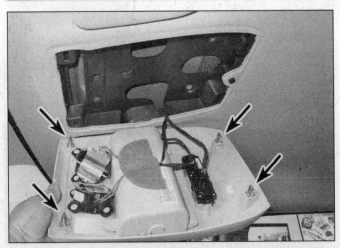

21.1 Grasp the sides of the overhead console and pull straight down to disengage the mounting clips

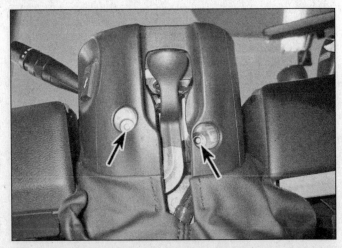

22.3 Remove the two screws from the lower steering column cover

21 Overhead console - removal and installation

Front

Refer to illustration 21.1

1   Insert a plastic trim tool at the front of the overhead console and carefully pry the console from the headliner to disengage the snap clips at the front and rear of the console **(see illustration)**.

2   Lower the overhead console sufficiently to gain access to the electrical connectors. Disconnect the electrical connectors and remove the overhead console.

3   Installation is the reverse of removal.

Rear

4   Insert a plastic trim tool at the front of the overhead console and carefully pry the console trim panel out from the console.

5   Remove the console mounting screws and lower the overhead console sufficiently to gain access to the electrical connectors.

6   Disconnect the electrical connectors and remove the overhead console.

7   Installation is the reverse of removal.

22 Steering column covers - removal and installation

Refer to illustrations 22.3 and 22.4

Warning: *Models covered by this manual are equipped with a Supplemental Restraint System (SRS), more commonly known as airbags. Always disable the airbag system before working in the vicinity of any airbag system component to avoid the possibility of accidental deployment of the airbag, which could cause personal injury (see Chapter 12).*

1   Disconnect the cable from the negative battery terminal (see Chapter 5).

2   Remove the knee bolster panel (see Section 23).

3   Remove the screws from the lower steering column cover **(see illustration)**.

4   Using a trim tool, disengage the dust boot retaining clips around the perimeter of the cover halves **(see illustration)**.

5   Separate the cover halves and detach them from the steering column. On models equipped with adjustable pedals, disconnect the switch electrical connector.

Note: *If the pedal switch needs to be replaced, push the mounting clips in and pull the switch*

out from the front of the lower trim panel.

6   Installation is the reverse of removal.

23 Dashboard trim panels - removal and installation

Warning: *Models covered by this manual are equipped with a Supplemental Restraint System (SRS), more commonly known as airbags. Always disable the airbag system before working in the vicinity of any airbag system component to avoid the possibility of accidental deployment of the airbag, which could cause personal injury (see Chapter 12).*

1   Disconnect the cable from the negative battery terminal (see Chapter 5).

Instrument panel end caps

Refer to illustration 23.2

2   If you're working on the left end cap, remove the attaching screws **(see illustration)**, then detach it from the dashboard.

22.4 Using a small trim tool, disengage the boot retaining clips from the cover halves – upper half shown, lower half similar

23.2 Pry the instrument panel end cap out to disconnect the four mounting clips - left side shown, right side identical

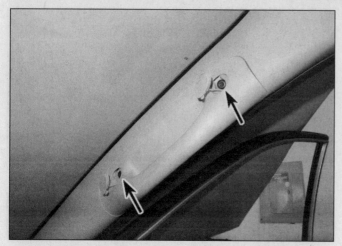

23.5a On the passenger's side, remove the end caps from the A-pillar trim, remove the mounting fasteners and pry the trim panel back

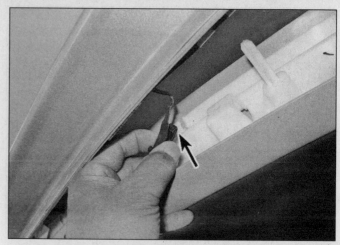

23.5b On the driver's side, pry the trim panel back enough to disengage the tether clip using a small screwdriver, then remove the A-pillar trim

3   If you're working on the right side end cap, grasp the cover securely and pull sharply to remove it.
4   Installation is the reverse of removal.

Instrument panel top cover

Refer to illustrations 23.5a, 23.5b and 23.6

5   Remove the A-pillar trim **(see illustrations)**.
6   Using a trim stick, start from the bottom of the trim panel and work around the perimeter until all the fasteners have been released, then remove the cover **(see illustration)**.
7   Installation is the reverse of removal.

Radio trim panel bezel

Refer to illustration 23.8

8   Using a trim stick, carefully pry around the bezel to release the mounting clips **(see illustration)** and remove the bezel from the instrument panel.
9   Installation is the reverse of removal.

Instrument panel center trim bezel

Refer to illustrations 23.10 and 23.11

10   Open the glove box, remove the inner liner, then remove the bezel fasteners **(see illustration)**.
11   Using a trim tool, pry the center trim

bezel out from the dash **(see illustration)**.
12   Installation is the reverse of removal.

Lower glove box

Refer to illustration 23.13

13   Open the glove box, grasp the sides of the glove box with both hands and push on the sides, then lower the door **(see illustration)**.

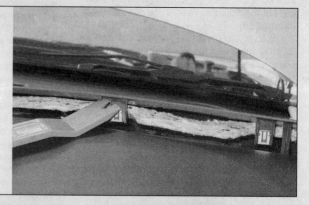

23.6 Using a trim stick, carefully remove the instrument panel top cover

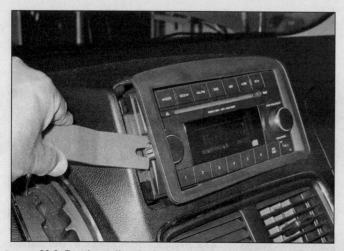

23.8 Pry the radio trim bezel out from around the radio

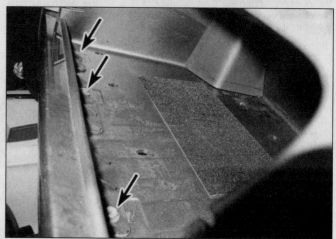

23.10 Remove the bezel fasteners from inside the upper glove box

23.11 Carefully pry the center trim bezel out

23.13 Push on the sides of the glove box then lower the door

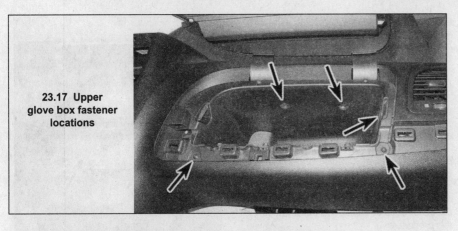

23.17 Upper glove box fastener locations

23.18 Pull the glove box straight out

14   Pivot the glove box in a downward position and disengage the hinge hooks from the instrument panel.
15   Installation is the reverse of removal.

Upper glove box

Refer to illustrations 23.17 and 23.18

16   Remove the center trim bezel as previously described.
17   Remove the glove box mounting screws (see illustration).
18   Pull the glove box out from the instrument panel (see illustration).
19   Installation is the reverse of removal.

Knee bolster

Refer to illustrations 23.20 and 23.21

20   Remove the instrument panel end cap and remove the knee bolster upper fastener (see illustration).

21   Remove the bolster lower mounting fasteners (see illustration).
22   Grasp the cover with both hands and pull straight out to disengage the panel from the instrument panel.
23   Remove the hood release cable (see Section 8).
24   Installation is the reverse of removal.

23.20 Remove the knee bolster upper fastener

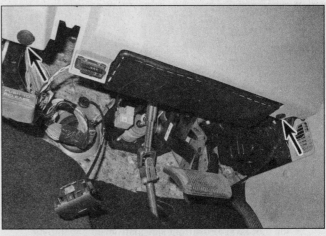

23.21 Remove the knee bolster lower fasteners

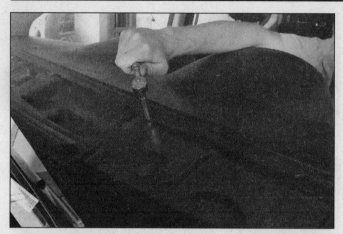

24.5 Remove the seven retaining bolts along the front top of the instrument panel

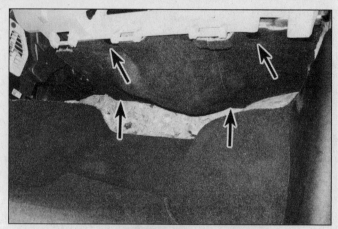

24.7 Location of the lower trim panel fasteners

24 Instrument panel – removal and installation

Refer to illustrations 24.5, 24.7, 24.8, 24.10a, 24.10b, 24.15a, 24.15b, 24.15c and 24.16

Warning: *Models covered by this manual are equipped with a Supplemental Restraint System (SRS), more commonly known as airbags. Always disable the airbag system before working in the vicinity of any airbag system component to avoid the possibility of accidental deployment of the airbag, which could cause personal injury (see Chapter 12).*

1   Disconnect the cable from the negative battery terminal (see Chapter 5).

Note: *This is a difficult procedure for the home mechanic. There are many hidden fasteners, difficult angles to work in and many electrical connectors to tag and disconnect/connect. We recommend that this procedure be done only by an experienced do-it-yourselfer.*

Note: *During removal of the instrument panel, make careful notes of how each piece comes off, where it fits in relation to other pieces and what holds it in place. If you note how each part is installed before removing it, getting the instrument panel back together again will be much easier.*

2   Remove the following parts:
    Steering wheel and column as a unit (see Chapter 10)
    All the dashboard trim panels and the glove boxes (see Section 23)
    Air conditioning and heater control assembly (see Chapter 3)
    Instrument cluster, radio and instrument panel speakers (see Chapter 12)
    Front seats (though not absolutely necessary, removing both front seats allows more room to work and eliminates the possibility of the occurrence of damage to the seats during this procedure)
    Center floor console (see Section 27)

3   Remove the shifter knob and disconnect the shift cable (see Chapter 7).

4   Disconnect the wiring harnesses at each A-pillar.

5   Remove the retaining bolts from the front of the instrument panel **(see illustration)**.

6   Remove the defrost duct-to-instrument panel fasteners.

7   Remove the passenger's side lower trim panel fasteners and panel **(see illustration)**.

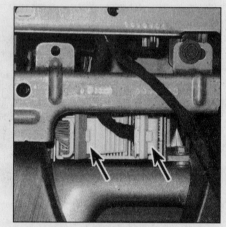

24.8 Depress the lever locks the rotate the levers to release the harness

8   Disconnect the electrical connectors to the occupant restraint controller **(see illustration)**.

9   Disconnect the A/C and heating wiring harness electrical connector.

10   Remove the instrument panel-to-air conditioning/heater housing fasteners **(see illustrations)**.

24.10a Location of the right side instrument panel-to-air conditioning/heater housing . . .

24.10b . . . and left side fasteners

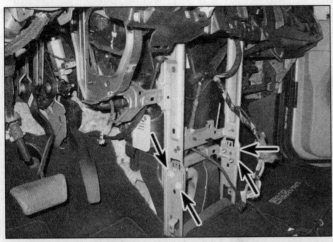

24.15a Remove the instrument panel mounting bolts from the center . . .

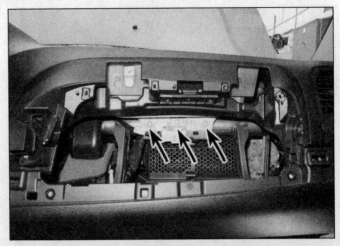

24.15b . . . inside the instrument panel . . .

24.15c . . . and from each corner

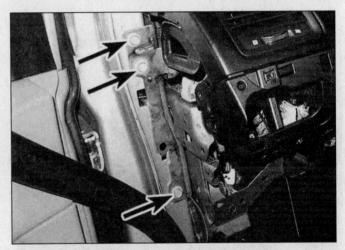

24.16 Remove the bolts from each end of the instrument panel and remove the panel with the help of an assistant

11   Remove the bolts that secure the A/C and heating housing to the bottom of the instrument panel support.

12   Disconnect the antenna harness, main vehicle harnesses, remove the ground wire and separate the data link connector from the instrument panel.

13   Remove the hood release cable handle (see Section 8).

14   Remove the instrument panel support fasteners and support.

15   Remove the instrument panel mounting bolts **(see illustrations)**.

16   Remove the instrument panel mounting bolts from each end of the instrument panel **(see illustration)**.

Caution: *To avoid damage to the instrument panel when removing these last three bolts, have an assistant support the instrument panel. You'll also need an assistant's help when installing the instrument panel and these three bolts.*

17   With an assistant helping you, remove the instrument panel from the vehicle.

18   Installation is the reverse of removal.

25   Rear trim panels - removal and installation

Refer to illustrations 25.4a, 25.4b, 25.4c, 25.4d, 25.4e, 25.4f, 25.4g, 25.4h and 26.4i

1   Disconnect the cable from the negative battery terminal (see Chapter 5).

2   Remove the first and, if equipped, the second rear seat (see Section 26).

3   Remove the plastic plugs from the trim panel that is being removed. Use a flat bladed screwdriver.

4   Separate the trim panels from the body. Remove all mounting screws with a screwdriver and release the mounting clips **(see illustrations)**. Disconnect any wire connectors from accessory power outlets, if so equipped.

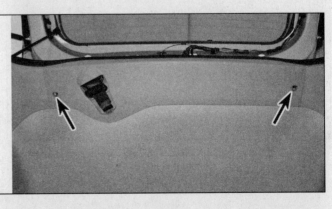

25.4a Pry the trim plugs out, remove the mounting screws and remove the rear header trim . . .

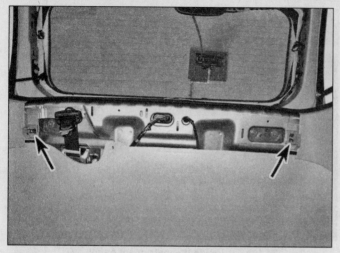

25.4b . . . then remove the D-trim panel upper mounting screw

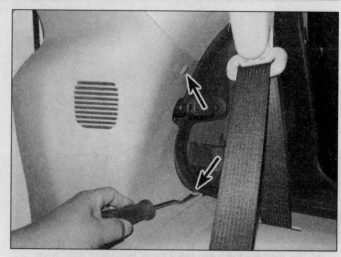

25.4c   Using a trim panel removal tool, remove the fasteners and carefully pry loose the D-pillar trim panel

25.4d Open the rear storage compartment and remove the inner liner . . .

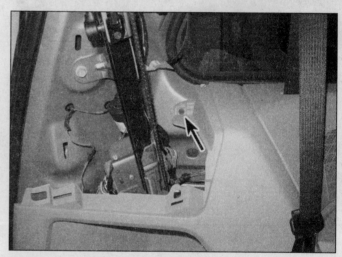

25.4e   . . . remove the quarter panel screw hidden by the D-pillar trim panel

25.4f Using a trim panel removal tool, pry out the speaker cover trim panel . . .

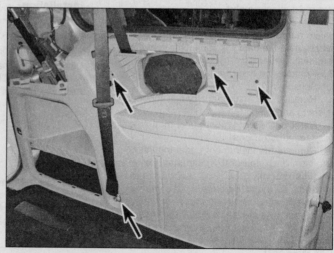

25.4g . . . remove the lower second and third row seat belt mounting bolts and the quarter trim panel mounting screws . . .

25.4h . . . then carefully pull the panel out

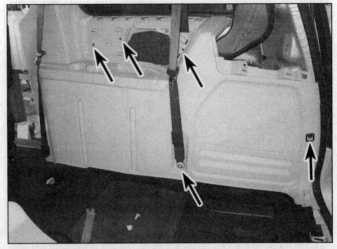

25.4i Passenger's side quarter panel seat belt mounting bolt and quarter trim panel mounting screw locations

5   Installation is the reverse of removal. Tighten the seat belt mounting bolts to the torque listed in this Chapter's Specifications.

26   Seats - removal and installation

Warning: *Models covered by this manual are equipped with a Supplemental Restraint System (SRS), more commonly known as airbags. Always disable the airbag system before working in the vicinity of any airbag system component to avoid the possibility of accidental deployment of the airbag, which could cause personal injury (see Chapter 12).*
1   Disconnect the cable from the negative battery terminal (see Chapter 5).

Front seats

Refer to illustrations 26.2, 26.3 and 26.5
2   Raise the vehicle and support it securely on jackstands, lower the spare tire and remove the tire cover fasteners and cover **(see illustration)**.
3   Working under the vehicle, remove the seat mounting fasteners **(see illustration)**.
4   Working inside the vehicle, tilt the seat forward and disconnect any electrical connectors.
5   Remove the side trim panel **(see illustration)**.
6   Unbolt the seat belt from the side of the seat and remove the seat from the vehicle.
7   Installation is the reverse of removal. Tighten the seat belt mounting bolts to the torque listed in this Chapter's Specifications.

Second row seats

Stow-n-go seat

8   With the seat in the upright position, disengage the release tab at the front of the panel and slide the panel back.
9   Install special tool #9313 on the seat track to prevent the seat from latching.
10   Remove the mounting nuts and seats.

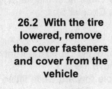

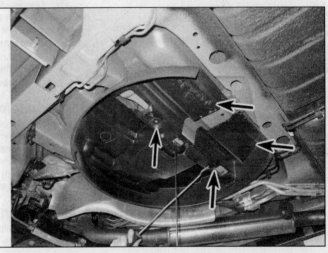

26.2 With the tire lowered, remove the cover fasteners and cover from the vehicle

11   Installation is the reverse of removal.

Non stow-n-go seat
12   Lift the release handle on the lower side of the seat and lift the rear of the seat.

13   Pull the release bar at the bottom of the seat and release the seat from its attachments. Remove the seat from the vehicle.
14   Installation is the reverse of removal.

26.3 Front seat mounting fasteners

26.5 Remove the trim panel then remove the seatbelt fastener

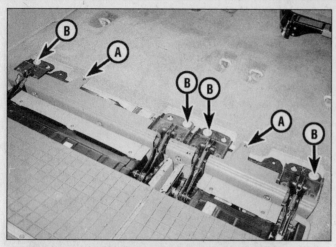

26.15 Remove the two fasteners securing the lower trim (A) and the seat mounting fasteners (B)

26.16 Remove the remaining fasteners securing the lower trim

Third row Stow-n-go seats

Refer to illustrations 26.15 and 26.16

15   With the seats in the downward position, remove the lower trim and seat mounting fasteners **(see illustration)**.

16   Raise the seats to the upright position, then remove the remaining fasteners securing the lower trim and remove the trim **(see illustration)**.

17   Remove the remaining seat mounting fasteners.

18   Installation is the reverse of removal.

27   Center floor console - removal and installation

Warning: *Models covered by this manual are equipped with a Supplemental Restraint System (SRS), commonly known as airbags. Always disable the airbag system before working in the vicinity of any airbag system component to avoid the possibility of accidental deployment of the airbag, which could cause personal injury (see Chapter 12).*

1   Disconnect the cable from the negative battery terminal (see Chapter 5).

Base console

2   Pry the plug out of the clip at the front of the console and remove the clip.

3   Slide the console forward while lifting it up at the same time until the console is free, then remove it from the vehicle.

4   Installation is the reverse of removal.

Premium console

5   Locate the release handle at the bottom front of the console then pull the handle up.

6   While holding the handle up, lift the rear of the console up a few inches.

7   Slide the front edge back to disengage the console from the floor mount.

8   Remove the floor mount retaining screws and mount.

9   Installation is the reverse of removal.

Full console

Refer to illustrations 27.10a, 27.10b, 27.12 and 27.18

10   Carefully pry the console top panel up using a trim tool **(see illustration)**, turn the panel over, then disconnect the electrical connectors and remove the panel **(see illustration)**.

11   Move the front seats all the way to the front.

12   Remove the fasteners at the base of the console on each side **(see illustration)**.

27.10a Pry the console top panel up

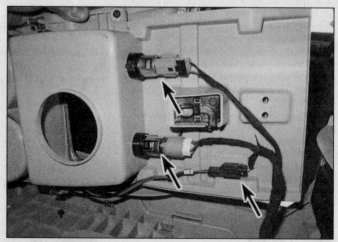

27.10b Disconnect the electrical connectors

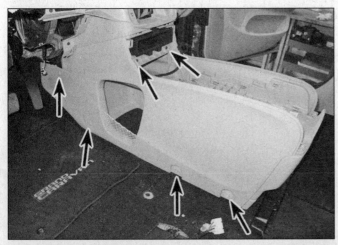

27.12 Remove the fasteners from the sides and top of the console – seats removed for clarity

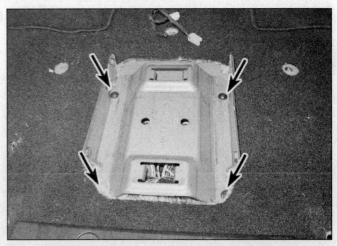

27.17 Location of the floor mount retaining screws

13   Move the front seats all the way to the rear.

14   Remove the fasteners at the base, top and front of the console on each side **(see illustration 27.12)**.

15   On 2012 and earlier models, remove the plastic push-pin connectors on both front sides of the console.

16   Slide the console toward the rear of the vehicle and rotate the back of the console up and out of the vehicle.

17   Remove the floor mount retaining screws and mount **(see illustration)**.

18   Installation is the reverse of removal.

Notes

Chapter 12
Chassis electrical system

Contents

1 General information

The electrical system is a 12-volt, negative ground type. Power for the lights and all electrical accessories is supplied by a lead/acid-type battery that is charged by the alternator.

This Chapter covers repair and service procedures for the various electrical components not associated with the engine. Information on the battery, alternator, ignition system and starter motor can be found in Chapter 5.

It should be noted that when portions of the electrical system are serviced, the negative cable should be disconnected from the battery to prevent electrical shorts and/or fires.

2 Electrical troubleshooting - general information

Refer to illustrations 2.5a, 2.5b, 2.6 and 2.9

A typical electrical circuit consists of an electrical component, any switches, relays, motors, fuses, fusible links or circuit breakers related to that component and the wiring and connectors that link the component to both the battery and the chassis. To help you pinpoint an electrical circuit problem, wiring diagrams are included at the end of this Chapter.

Before tackling any troublesome electrical circuit, first study the appropriate wiring diagrams to get a complete understanding of what makes up that individual circuit.

Trouble spots, for instance, can often be narrowed down by noting if other components related to the circuit are operating properly. If several components or circuits fail at one time, chances are the problem is in a fuse or ground connection, because several circuits are often routed through the same fuse and ground connections.

Electrical problems usually stem from simple causes, such as loose or corroded connections, a blown fuse, a melted fusible link or a failed relay. Visually inspect the condition of all fuses, wires and connections in a problem circuit before troubleshooting the circuit.

If test equipment and instruments are going to be utilized, use the diagrams to plan ahead of time where you will make the nec-

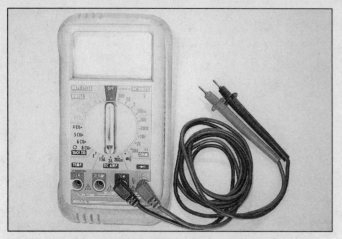

2.5a The most useful tool for electrical troubleshooting is a digital multimeter that can check volts, amps, and test continuity

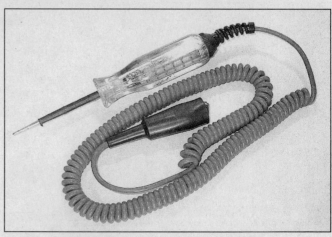

2.5b A simple test light is a very handy tool for testing voltage

essary connections in order to accurately pinpoint the trouble spot.

The basic tools needed for electrical troubleshooting include a circuit tester or voltmeter (a 12-volt bulb with a set of test leads can also be used), a continuity tester, which includes a bulb, battery and set of test leads, and a jumper wire, preferably with a circuit breaker incorporated, which can be used to bypass electrical components **(see illustrations)**. Before attempting to locate a problem with test instruments, use the wiring diagram(s) to decide where to make the connections.

Voltage checks

Voltage checks should be performed if a circuit is not functioning properly. Connect one lead of a circuit tester to either the negative battery terminal or a known good ground. Connect the other lead to a connector in the circuit being tested, preferably nearest to the battery or fuse **(see illustration)**. If the bulb

of the tester lights, voltage is present, which means that the part of the circuit between the connector and the battery is problem free. Continue checking the rest of the circuit in the same fashion. When you reach a point at which no voltage is present, the problem lies between that point and the last test point with voltage. Most of the time the problem can be traced to a loose connection.

Note: *Keep in mind that some circuits receive voltage only when the ignition key is in the Accessory or Run position.*

Finding a short

One method of finding shorts in a circuit is to remove the fuse and connect a test light or voltmeter in place of the fuse terminals. There should be no voltage present in the circuit. Move the wiring harness from side-to-side while watching the test light. If the bulb goes on, there is a short to ground somewhere in that area, probably where the insulation has rubbed through. The same test

can be performed on each component in the circuit, even a switch.

Ground check

Perform a ground test to check whether a component is properly grounded. Disconnect the battery and connect one lead of a continuity tester or multimeter (set to the ohms scale), to a known good ground. Connect the other lead to the wire or ground connection being tested. If the resistance is low (less than 5 ohms), the ground is good. If the bulb on a self-powered test light does not go on, the ground is not good.

Continuity check

A continuity check is done to determine if there are any breaks in a circuit - if it is passing electricity properly. With the circuit off (no power in the circuit), a self-powered continuity tester or multimeter can be used to check the circuit. Connect the test leads to both ends of the circuit (or to the power end and a good

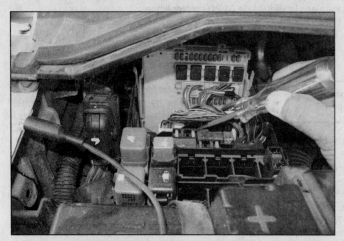

2.6 In use, a basic test light's lead is clipped to a known good ground, then the pointed probe can test connectors, wires or electrical sockets - if the bulb lights, the circuit being tested has battery voltage

2.9 With a multimeter set to the ohm scale, resistance can be checked across two terminals - when checking for continuity, a low reading indicates continuity, a high reading or infinity indicates lack of continuity

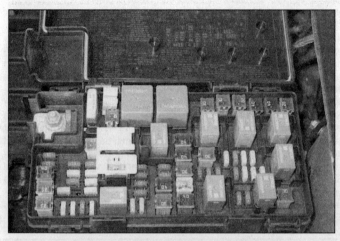

3.1 The engine compartment fuse and relay box

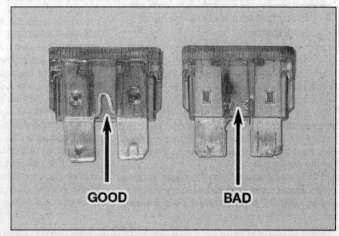

GOOD   BAD

3.3 When a fuse blows, the element between the terminals melts

ground), and if the test light comes on the circuit is passing current properly **(see illustration)**. If the resistance is low (less than 5 ohms), there is continuity; if the reading is 10,000 ohms or higher, there is a break somewhere in the circuit. The same procedure can be used to test a switch, by connecting the continuity tester to the switch terminals. With the switch turned On, the test light should come on (or low resistance should be indicated on a meter).

Finding an open circuit

When diagnosing for possible open circuits, it is often difficult to locate them by sight because the connectors hide oxidation or terminal misalignment. Merely wiggling a connector on a sensor or in the wiring harness may correct the open circuit condition. Remember this when an open circuit is indicated when troubleshooting a circuit. Intermittent problems may also be caused by oxidized or loose connections.

Electrical troubleshooting is simple if you keep in mind that all electrical circuits are basically electricity running from the battery, through the wires, switches, relays, fuses and fusible links to each electrical component (light bulb, motor, etc.) and to ground, from which it is passed back to the battery. Any electrical problem is an interruption in the flow of electricity to and from the battery.

3   Fuses and fusible links - general information

Fuses

Refer to illustrations 3.1 and 3.3

The electrical circuits of the vehicle are protected by a combination of fuses, circuit breakers and fusible links. The main fuse/relay panel is in the engine compartment **(see illustration)**. Each of the fuses is designed to protect a specific circuit, and the various cir-

cuits are identified on the fuse panel itself.

Several sizes of fuses are employed in the fuse blocks. There are small, medium and large sizes of the same design, all with the same blade terminal design. The medium and large fuses can be removed with your fingers, but the small fuses require the use of pliers or the small plastic fuse-puller tool found in most fuse boxes.

If an electrical component fails, always check the fuse first. The best way to check the fuses is with a test light. Check for power at the exposed terminal tips of each fuse. If power is present at one side of the fuse but not the other, the fuse is blown. A blown fuse can also be identified by visually inspecting it **(see illustration)**.

Be sure to replace blown fuses with the correct type. Fuses (of the same physical size) of different ratings may be physically interchangeable, but only fuses of the proper rating should be used. Replacing a fuse with one of a higher or lower value than specified is not recommended. Each electrical circuit needs a specific amount of protection. The amperage value of each fuse is molded into the top of the fuse body.

If the replacement fuse immediately fails, don't replace it again until the cause of the problem is isolated and corrected. In most cases, this will be a short circuit in the wiring caused by a broken or deteriorated wire.

Fusible links

Some circuits are protected by fusible links. The links are used in circuits which are not ordinarily fused, or which carry high current, such as the circuit between the alternator and the battery. Fusible links, which are usually several wire gauges smaller in size than the circuit that they protect, are designed to melt if the circuit is subjected to more current than it was designed to carry. If you have to replace a blown fusible link, make sure that you replace it with one of the same specification. If the replacement fusible link blows in the

same circuit, make sure that you troubleshoot the circuit in which the fusible link melted BEFORE installing another fusible link.

4   Circuit breakers - general information

Circuit breakers protect certain circuits, such as the power windows or heated seats. Depending on the vehicle's accessories, there may be one or two circuit breakers, located in the fuse/relay box in the engine compartment.

Because the circuit breakers reset automatically, an electrical overload in a circuit breaker-protected system will cause the circuit to fail momentarily, then come back on. If the circuit does not come back on, check it immediately.

For a basic check, pull the circuit breaker up out of its socket on the fuse panel, but just far enough to probe with a voltmeter. The breaker should still contact the sockets. With the voltmeter negative lead on a good chassis ground, touch each end prong of the circuit breaker with the positive meter probe. There should be battery voltage at each end. If there is battery voltage only at one end, the circuit breaker must be replaced.

Some circuit breakers must be reset manually.

5   Relays - general information

Several electrical accessories in the vehicle, such as the fuel injection system, horns, starter, and fog lamps use relays to transmit the electrical signal to the component. Relays use a low-current circuit (the control circuit) to open and close a high-current circuit (the power circuit). If the relay is defective, that component will not operate properly. Relays are mounted in the engine compartment fuse/relay box **(see illustration 3.1)**.

6   Electrical connectors - general information

Most electrical connections on these vehicles are made with multiwire plastic connectors. The mating halves of many connectors are secured with locking clips molded into the plastic connector shells. The mating halves of some large connectors, such as some of those under the instrument panel, are held together by a bolt through the center of the connector.

To separate a connector with locking clips, use a small screwdriver to pry the clips apart carefully, then separate the connector halves. Pull only on the shell, never pull on the wiring harness, as you may damage the individual wires and terminals inside the connectors. Look at the connector closely before trying to separate the halves. Often the locking clips are engaged in a way that is not immediately clear. Additionally, many connectors have more than one set of clips.

Each pair of connector terminals has a male half and a female half. When you look at the end view of a connector in a diagram, be sure to understand whether the view shows the harness side or the component side of the connector. Connector halves are mirror images of each other, and a terminal shown on the right side end-view of one half will be on the left side end-view of the other half.

It is often necessary to take circuit voltage measurements with a connector connected. Whenever possible, carefully insert a small straight pin (not your meter probe) into the rear of the connector shell to contact the terminal inside, then clip your meter lead to the pin. This kind of connection is called "backprobing." When inserting a test probe into a terminal, be careful not to distort the terminal opening. Doing so can lead to a poor connection and corrosion at that terminal later. Using the small straight pin instead of a meter probe results in less chance of deforming the terminal connector.

Electrical connectors

Most electrical connectors have a single release tab that you depress to release the connector

Some electrical connectors have a retaining tab which must be pried up to free the connector

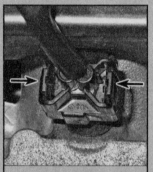

Some connectors have two release tabs that you must squeeze to release the connector

Some connectors use wire retainers that you squeeze to release the connector

Critical connectors often employ a sliding lock (1) that you must pull out before you can depress the release tab (2)

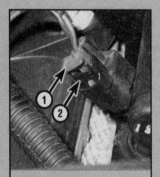

Here's another sliding-lock style connector, with the lock (1) and the release tab (2) on the side of the connector

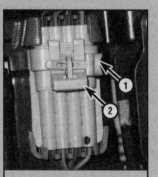

On some connectors the lock (1) must be pulled out to the side and removed before you can lift the release tab (2)

Some critical connectors, like the multi-pin connectors at the Powertrain Control Module employ pivoting locks that must be flipped open

7.3 Press the release tab down until it disengages

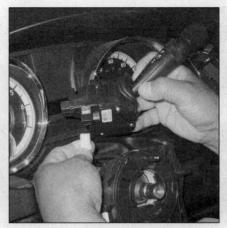

7.4 Disconnect the electrical connector

9.2 Using a trim removal tool, carefully pry the trim panel from the instrument panel

7 Multi-function switch - replacement

Refer to illustrations 7.3 and 7.4

Warning: *The models covered by this manual are equipped with Supplemental Restraint Systems (SRS), more commonly known as airbags. Always disable the airbag system before working in the vicinity of any airbag system components to avoid the possibility of accidental deployment of the airbags, which could cause personal injury (see Section 26).*

Note: *The multi-function switch is located on the steering column. It includes the turn signal switch, the headlight dimmer switch and the windshield wiper/washer switch and is mounted to the side of the clockspring assembly.*

1   Disconnect the cable from the negative terminal of the battery (see Chapter 5).

2   Remove the knee bolster, and the upper and lower steering column covers (see Chapter 11).

3   Press the release tab down until it disengages **(see illustration)**. While holding the tab down, grasp the switch and slide it up and out of the clockspring housing.

4   Disconnect the electrical connector from the back side of the multi-function switch **(see illustration)**.

5   To install the switch, slide the switch down until it clicks in place on the clockspring housing.

6   Installation is the reverse of removal.

8 Wireless Ignition Node (WIN) - replacement

Warning: *The models covered by this manual are equipped with Supplemental Restraint Systems (SRS), more commonly known as airbags. Always disable the airbag system before working in the vicinity of any airbag system components to avoid the possibility of*

accidental deployment of the airbags, which could cause personal injury (see Section 26).

Note: *On all models covered by this manual the key lock cylinder and ignition switch have been replaced by a Wireless Ignition Node (WIN). The WIN is an integrated electronic receiver that is the center of communication for the key transmitter, security system and even the tire pressure monitoring system. If the WIN is damaged it cannot be repaired and must be replaced.*

1   Disconnect the cable from the negative terminal of the battery (see Chapter 5).

2   Remove the knee bolster and the instrument driver's side panel trim (see Chapter 11).

3   Disconnect the coaxial cable connector and the electrical connector to the WIN.

4   Remove the mounting fasteners and WIN from the instrument panel.

5   Installation is the reverse of the removal procedure.

Note: *If a new WIN is installed it must be programmed to the vehicle and the ignition keys. This can only done through a factory scan tool. The vehicle will not operate unless the WIN is programmed to the vehicle.*

9 Instrument panel switches - replacement

Warning: *The models covered by this manual are equipped with Supplemental Restraint Systems (SRS), more commonly known as airbags. Always disable the airbag system before working in the vicinity of any airbag system components to avoid the possibility of accidental deployment of the airbags, which could cause personal injury (see Section 26).*

1   Disconnect the cable from the negative battery terminal (see Chapter 5).

Headlight switch and dimmer control switch

Refer to illustrations 9.2 and 9.5

2   Carefully pry off the trim panel above the headlight switch and rheostat from the instru-

ment panel **(see illustration)**.

3   Remove the end cap and knee bolster panel (see Chapter 11).

4   Remove the switch assembly panel fasteners and pry the panel from the instrument panel.

5   Disconnect the electrical connectors from the headlight and dimmer switches **(see illustration)**.

6   If you're going to replace the headlight switch, carefully pry the switch trim ring back enough to release the locking tabs that secure the switch to the panel, and detach the switch from the panel.

7   If you're going to replace the dimmer switch, remove the mounting screws and detach the switch from the panel.

8   Installation is the reverse of removal.

Instrument cluster POD switch

Refer to illustration 9.12

Note: *The instrument cluster POD switch includes the Hazard switch, the ECON switch and the Traction Control switch. The POD is a single unit or module and the switches cannot be replaced individually. If there is a prob-*

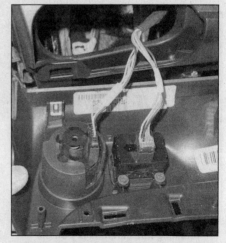

9.5 Disconnect the electrical connectors

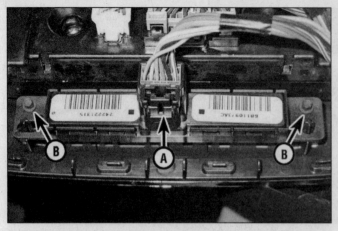

9.12 Disconnect the electrical connector (A) from the POD switch, then remove the mounting screws (B) and the switch

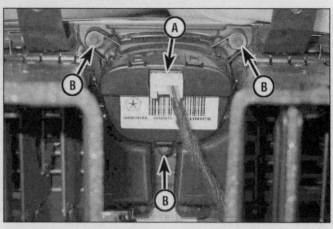

9.18 Disconnect the electrical connector (A) from the clock, then remove the mounting screws (B) and remove the clock

10.3 Instrument cluster mounting screw locations

16   Remove the center instrument panel bezel (see Chapter 11).
17   Remove the heater/air conditioning control assembly (see Chapter 3).
18   Disconnect the electrical connector from the clock **(see illustration)**.
19   Remove the clock mounting screws and remove the clock from the center trim panel/control assembly **(see illustration 9.18)**.
20   Installation is the reverse of removal.

10   Instrument cluster - removal and installation

Refer to illustration 10.3

Warning: *The models covered by this manual are equipped with Supplemental Restraint Systems (SRS), more commonly known as airbags. Always disable the airbag system before working in the vicinity of any airbag system components to avoid the possibility of accidental deployment of the airbags, which could cause personal injury (see Section 26).*

1   Disconnect the cable from the negative terminal of the battery (see Chapter 5).
2   Remove the instrument panel pad and cluster bezel (see Chapter 11).
3   Remove the instrument cluster mounting screws **(see illustration)** and pull the instrument cluster out of the instrument panel just far enough to access the electrical connector on the backside of the cluster.
4   Disconnect the electrical connector and remove the cluster.
5   Installation is the reverse of removal.

11   Wiper motor - replacement

Front wiper motor assembly

Refer to illustrations 11.1, 11.2, 11.5, 11.6, 11.8 and 11.9

1   Pry off the protective caps over the wiper arm nuts **(see illustration)**.
2   Remove the nuts that attach the wiper arms to their splined shafts **(see illustration)**.

lem with any of the switches, the entire POD assembly must be replaced.
9   Remove the radio assembly (see Section 12).
10   Remove the center instrument panel bezel (see Chapter 11).
11   Remove the heater/air conditioning control assembly (see Chapter 3).
12   Disconnect the electrical connector from the POD switch **(see illustration)**.

13   Remove the POD switch mounting screws and remove the switch from the center trim panel/control assembly **(see illustration 9.12)**.
14   Installation is the reverse of removal.

Clock removal and removal

Refer to illustration 9.18

15   Remove the radio assembly (see Section 12).

11.1 To access each front wiper arm retaining nut, carefully pry off the protective cap that covers up the nut

11.2 To detach each front wiper arm from the wiper motor shaft, remove this nut

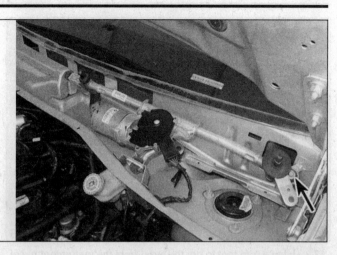

11.6 Wiper assembly mounting fastener location

11.5 To disconnect the front wiper motor electrical connector, push the lock (1) up, then depress the release tab (2) and pull off the connector

3   Mark the position of each wiper arm in relation to its shaft, then remove the wiper arms. If the arm is difficult to remove from the shaft, use a small two-jaw puller.
4   Remove the cowl cover (see Chapter 11).
5   Release the lock on the wiper module electrical connector, then disconnect the connector from the wiper motor **(see illustration)**.
6   Remove the wiper assembly fastener that attaches the wiper assembly to the firewall bracket **(see illustration)**.
7   Lift the wiper assembly from the mounting brackets and place the assembly on a clean workbench.
8   Detach the wiper links from the wiper motor crank arm **(see illustration)**. Do NOT remove the crank arm from the motor.
9   Remove the fasteners that attach the windshield wiper motor assembly to the linkage module **(see illustration)** and remove the motor.
10   Installation is the reverse of removal.

Rear wiper motor

Refer to illustration 11.16
11   Remove the cap that covers up the wiper arm retaining nut **(see illustration 11.1)**.
12   Remove the wiper arm retaining nut.
13   Mark the position of the wiper arm in relation to the wiper motor shaft.
14   Remove the arm from the shaft. If the wiper arm is difficult to remove from the shaft splines, use a small two-jaw puller to detach the arm.
15   Remove the liftgate trim panel (see Chapter 11).
16   Disconnect the electrical connector from the rear wiper motor **(see illustration)**.
17   Remove the rear wiper motor mounting bolts **(see illustration 11.16)** and remove the motor.
18   Installation is the reverse of removal.

12   Radio and speakers - removal and installation

Warning: *The models covered by this manual are equipped with Supplemental Restraint Systems (SRS), more commonly known as*

11.8 Pry off the two link arms from the wiper motor crank arm (do NOT remove the crank arm from the motor)

airbags. Always disable the airbag system before working in the vicinity of any airbag system components to avoid the possibility of accidental deployment of the airbags, which could cause personal injury (see Section 26).
1   Disconnect the cable from the negative terminal of the battery (see Chapter 5).

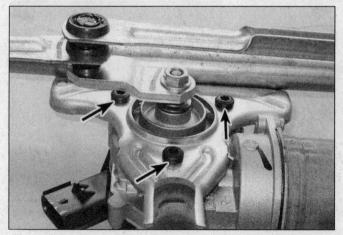

11.9 Wiper motor-to-link assembly fastener locations

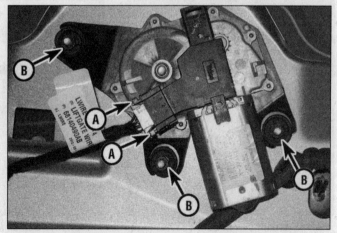

11.16 To disconnect the electrical connector from the rear wiper motor, depress the two release tabs (A) and pull off the connector. To detach the rear wiper motor, remove the mounting bolts (B)

12.2 Using a trim tool to pry the bezel from the instrument panel

12.3 To detach the radio from the instrument panel, remove these four mounting screws

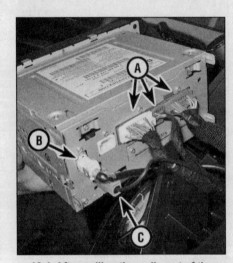

12.4 After pulling the radio out of the instrument panel, depress the release tabs and disconnect the electrical connectors (A), the antenna lead (B) and the coaxial cable (C) from the backside of the radio

Radio

Refer to illustration 12.2, 12.3 and 12.4

Warning: *Do not disassemble the radio. The radios covered by this manual are equipped with invisible laser radiation when the unit is opened and interlock failed or defeated. Avoid direct exposure to the beam, which could cause personal injury.*

2 Using a trim tool, remove the radio trim bezel **(see illustration)**.

3 Remove the radio retaining screws **(see illustration)**, then pull the radio out of the instrument panel.

4 Disconnect the electrical connectors and the antenna lead from the backside of the radio **(see illustration)** and remove the radio.

5 Installation is the reverse of removal.

Speakers

Front door speakers

Refer to illustration 12.7

6 Remove the front door trim panel (see Chapter 11).

7 Remove the speaker mounting screws **(see illustration)**.

8 Pull out the speaker, disconnect the electrical connector from the speaker and remove the speaker.

9 Installation is the reverse of removal.

Instrument panel speakers

Refer to illustration 12.11

10 Remove the A-pillar trim and the instrument panel top pad (see Chapter 11).

11 Remove the speaker mounting screws **(see illustration)**.

12 Pull out the speaker, disconnect the electrical connector and remove the speaker.

13 Installation is the reverse of removal.

Quarter-panel speakers

Refer to illustration 12.15

14 Remove the quarter trim panel armrest/trim bolster (see Chapter 11).

15 Remove the four speaker retaining screws **(see illustration)**.

16 Pull out the speaker, disconnect the elec-

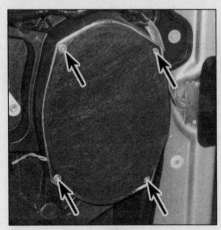

12.7 To detach a front door speaker from the door, remove these four screws

12.11 To detach a speaker from the instrument panel, remove these screws and pull the speaker out of the instrument panel

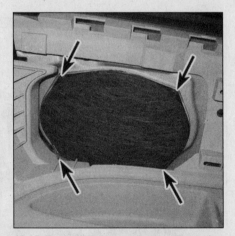

12.15 To detach the quarter-panel speaker from the trim panel, remove these screws

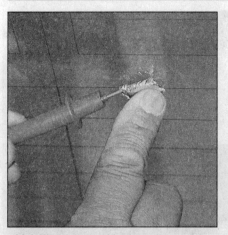

14.4 When measuring the voltage at the rear window defogger grid, wrap a piece of aluminum foil around the positive probe of the voltmeter and press the foil against the wire with your finger

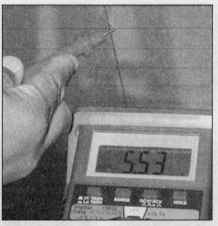

14.5 To determine if a heating element has broken, check the voltage at the center of each element. If the voltage is 5 or 6-volts, the element is unbroken; if the voltage is 10 or 12-volts, the element is broken between the center and the ground side; if there is no voltage, the element is broken between the center and the positive side

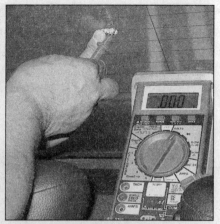

14.7 To find the break, touch the voltmeter negative lead to the defogger ground terminal, place the voltmeter positive lead with the foil strip against the heating element at the positive terminal end and slide it toward the negative terminal end. The point at which the voltmeter reading changes abruptly is the point at which the element is broken

trical connector and remove the speaker.

17   Installation is the reverse of removal.

D-pillar speakers

18   Remove the D-pillar trim panel (see Chapter 11).

19   Slide the speaker out of its retainer, then disconnect the electrical connector from the speaker and remove the speaker.

20   Installation is the reverse of removal.

---

13   Antenna and cable - replacement

Warning: *The models covered by this manual are equipped with Supplemental Restraint Systems (SRS), more commonly known as airbags. Always disable the airbag system before working in the vicinity of any airbag system components to avoid the possibility of accidental deployment of the airbags, which could cause personal injury (see Section 26).*

Antenna mast

1   Use a small open end wrench to unscrew the antenna mast from the base.

2   Installation is the reverse of removal.

Antenna base and antenna cable

3   Remove the antenna mast.

4   Remove the glove box (see Chapter 11).

5   Remove the radio (see Section 12) and disconnect the antenna cable **(see illustration 12.4)**.

6   Remove the right kick panel.

7   Loosen the right front wheel lug nuts, raise the vehicle and support it securely on jackstands, and remove the right front wheel.

Remove the splash shield from the right front wheelwell (see Chapter 11).

8   From inside the wheelwell, locate the rubber grommet insulator (in the upper left corner of the wheelwell) that insulates the hole where the antenna cable goes through into the cabin. Remove the antenna cable grommet, then pull the cable through the grommet hole into the wheelwell.

9   Using an antenna wrench or a special cap nut socket, unscrew the cap nut that secures the antenna base to the front fender. A pair of needle-nose or snap-ring pliers will also work, but be very careful not to let the pliers slip off the nut and scratch the paint.

10   Pull the antenna assembly down into the wheelwell and remove it.

11   Installation is the reverse of removal.

---

14   Rear window defogger - check and repair

---

1   The rear window defogger consists of a number of horizontal elements baked onto the glass surface.

2   Small breaks in the element can be repaired without removing the rear window.

Check

Refer to illustrations 14.4, 14.5 and 14.7

3   Turn the ignition switch and defogger system switches to the ON position. Using a voltmeter, place the positive probe against the defogger grid positive terminal and the negative probe against the ground terminal. If battery voltage is not indicated, check the fuse, defogger switch and related wiring. If voltage is indicated, but all or part of the defogger doesn't heat, proceed with the following tests.

4   When measuring voltage during these tests, wrap a piece of aluminum foil around the tip of the voltmeter positive probe and press the foil against the heating element with your finger **(see illustration)**. Place the negative probe on the defogger grid ground terminal.

5   Check the voltage at the center of each heating element **(see illustration)**. If the voltage is 5 or 6-volts, the element is okay (there is no break). If there is not voltage, the element is broken between the center of the element and the positive end. If the voltage is 10 to 12 volts the element is broken between the center of the element and ground. Check each heating element.

6   Connect the negative lead to a good body ground. The reading should stay the same. If it doesn't, the ground connection is bad.

7   To find the break, place the voltmeter negative probe against the defogger ground terminal. Place the voltmeter positive probe with the foil strip against the heating element at the positive terminal end and slide it toward the negative terminal end. The point at which the voltmeter deflects from several volts to zero is the point at which the heating element is broken **(see illustration)**.

Repair

Refer to illustration 14.13

8   Repair the break in the element using a repair kit specifically recommended for this purpose, available at most auto parts stores. Included in this kit is plastic conductive epoxy.

9   Prior to repairing a break, turn off the system and allow it to cool off for a few minutes.

10   Lightly buff the element area with fine steel wool, then clean it thoroughly with rubbing alcohol.

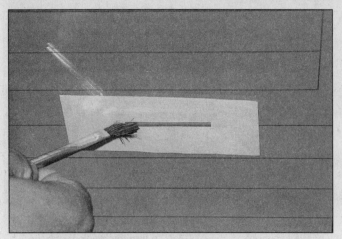

14.13 To use a defogger repair kit, apply masking tape to the inside of the window at the damaged area, then brush on the special conductive coating

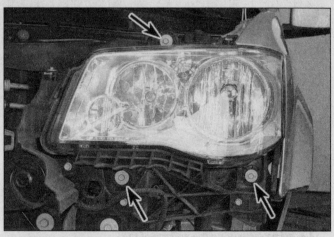

15.3 To detach the headlight housing from the radiator crossmember, remove these bolts

11   Use masking tape to mask off the area being repaired.

12   Thoroughly mix the epoxy, following the instructions provided with the repair kit.

13   Apply the epoxy material to the slit in the masking tape, overlapping the undamaged area about 3/4-inch on either end **(see illustration)**.

14   Allow the repair to cure for 24 hours before removing the tape and using the system.

---

15   Headlight housing - replacement

Refer to illustrations 15.3 and 15.4

Warning: *These vehicles are equipped with halogen gas-filled headlight bulbs, which are under pressure and may shatter if the surface is damaged or the bulb is dropped. Wear eye protection and handle the bulbs carefully, grasping only the base whenever possible. Do not touch the surface of the bulb with your fingers because the oil from your skin could cause it to overheat and fail prematurely. If you do touch the bulb surface, clean it with rubbing alcohol.*

1   Disconnect the cable from the negative battery terminal (see Chapter 5).

2   Remove the front bumper cover (see Chapter 11).

3   Remove the headlight housing mounting screws **(see illustration).**

4   Pull the headlight housing forward enough to disconnect the electrical connectors from the bulbs **(see illustration)**, then remove the housing.

5   Installation is the reverse of removal. Adjust the headlights (see Section 17).

---

16   Headlight bulb - replacement

Warning: *Halogen bulbs are gas-filled and under pressure and might shatter if the surface is scratched or the bulb is dropped. Wear eye protection and handle the bulbs carefully, grasping only the base whenever possible. Don't touch the surface of the bulb with your fingers because the oil from your skin could cause it to overheat and fail prematurely. If you do touch the bulb surface, clean it with rubbing alcohol.*

Halogen headlight

Refer to illustration 16.3

Note: *On Dodge models, the headlights use a dual headlamp bulb; on Chrysler models, a "quad system" is used, with one bulb for high beam and one bulb for low beam.*

1   Disconnect the cable from the negative battery terminal (see Chapter 5).

2   Open the hood and, working from inside the engine compartment, disconnect the electrical connector(s) from the back side of the housing **(see illustration 15.4).**

3   Rotate the headlight bulb counterclockwise and pull the bulb from the headlight housing **(see illustration)**.

4   When installing the new bulb, align the three slots on the circumference of the bulb socket's mounting flange with the three bosses on the inside edge of the mounting hole in the headlight assembly. Install the bulb into the housing then rotate the bulb clockwise to lock it in place.

15.4 Pull out the headlight housing assembly, disconnect the electrical connectors from the front park and turn signal bulb holders (A), then disconnect the electrical connector from the headlight bulbs (B)

16.3 Rotate the headlight bulb counterclockwise and remove it

17.1 Vertical adjustment screw location (right headlight shown, left headlight identical)

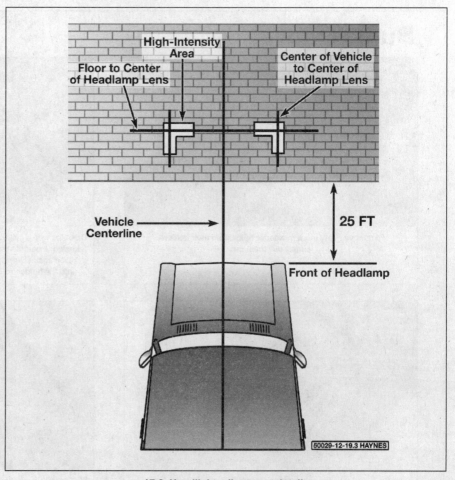

17.2 Headlight adjustment details

Caution: *Don't touch the surface of the bulb with your fingers because the oil from your skin could cause it to overheat and fail prematurely. If you accidentally touch the bulb surface, clean it with rubbing alcohol.*
5   Installation is otherwise the reverse of removal.

Xenon (HID) headlights

Warning: *Some models use High Intensity Discharge (HID) bulbs instead of conventional halogen bulbs. According to the manufacturer, the high voltages produced by this system can be fatal in the event of shock. Also, the voltage can remain in circuit even after the headlight switch has been turned to OFF and the ignition key has been removed. Therefore, for your safety, we don't recommend that you try to replace one of these bulbs yourself Instead, have this service performed by a dealer service department or other qualified repair shop.*

17 Headlights - adjustment

Refer to illustrations 17.1 and 17.2
Warning: *The headlights must be aimed correctly. If adjusted incorrectly, they could temporarily blind the driver of an oncoming vehicle and cause an accident or seriously reduce your ability to see the road. The headlights should be checked for proper aim every 12 months and any time a new headlight is installed or front-end bodywork is performed. The following procedure is only an interim step to provide temporary adjustment until the headlights can be adjusted by a properly equipped shop.*
1   The headlight adjustment screw, located on the inside corner of the housing **(see illustration)**, controls up-and-down movement. The adjustment screw on the outside corner controls the left-and-right movement.
Note: *Only adjust the left-and-right movement if absolutely necessary.*
2   There are several methods of adjusting

the headlights. The simplest method requires a blank wall 25 feet in front of the vehicle and a level floor **(see illustration)**.
3   Position masking tape on the wall in reference to the vehicle centerline and the centerlines of both headlights.
4   Measure the height of the headlight reference marks (in the centers of the headlight lenses) from the ground. Position a horizontal tape line on the wall at the same height as the headlight reference marks.
Note: *It may be easier to position the tape on the wall with the vehicle parked only a few inches away.*
5   Adjustment should be made with the vehicle sitting level, the gas tank half-full and no unusually heavy load in the vehicle.
6   Turn on the low beams. Turn the adjusting screw to position the high intensity zone so it is two inches below the horizontal line.
7   Have the headlights adjusted by a dealer service department at the earliest opportunity.

18 Bulb replacement

Exterior light bulbs
Front park and turn signal bulbs
1   Remove the headlight housing (see Sec-

tion 15), and disconnect the electrical connectors from the headlight and the front park and turn signal bulb.
2   Rotate the park and turn signal bulb socket counterclockwise and remove it from the headlight housing.
3   Remove the front park and turn signal bulb from the socket.
4   Install the new bulb in the socket.
5   The remainder of installation is the reverse of removal.

Front fog light bulbs
Warning: *Halogen bulbs are gas-filled and under pressure and might shatter if the surface is scratched or the bulb is dropped. Wear eye protection and handle the bulbs carefully, grasping only the base whenever possible. Don't touch the surface of the bulb with your fingers because the oil from your skin could cause it to overheat and fail prematurely. If you do touch the bulb surface, clean it with rubbing alcohol.*
6   Raise the front of the vehicle and place it securely on jackstands.
7   Disconnect the bulb electrical connector.
8   Rotate the bulb socket counterclockwise and pull it out of the fog light housing.
9   Replace the bulb and socket as a unit.
10   Installation is the reverse of removal.

Bulb removal

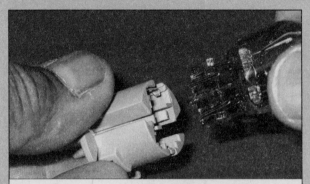

To remove many modern exterior bulbs from their holders, simply pull them out

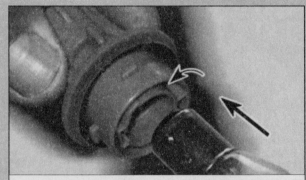

On bulbs with a cylindrical base ("bayonet" bulbs), the socket is spring-loaded; a pair of small posts on the side of the base hold the bulb in place against spring pressure. To remove this type of bulb, push it into the holder, rotate it 1/4-turn counterclockwise, then pull it out

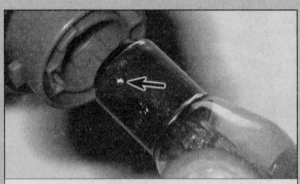

If a bayonet bulb has dual filaments, the posts are staggered, so the bulb can only be installed one way

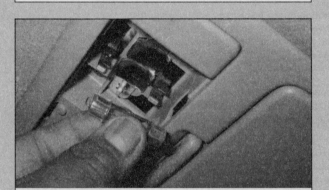

To remove most overhead interior light bulbs, simply unclip them

Center high-mounted brake light bulb

Refer to illustration 18.11

Note: *The high-mounted brake light LEDs are an integral part of the housing, and not separately serviceable.*

11   Remove the liftgate spoiler **(see illustration).**

12   Remove the two high-mount brake light retaining screws, pull the assembly from the rear spoiler, then disconnect the electrical connector.

13   Installation is the reverse of removal.

Taillight bulbs

Refer to illustrations 18.14 and 18.15

14   Open the liftgate and remove the two taillight housing retaining screws **(see illustration).**

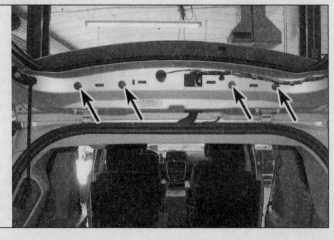

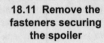
18.11 Remove the fasteners securing the spoiler

18.14 Remove the two taillight housing fasteners

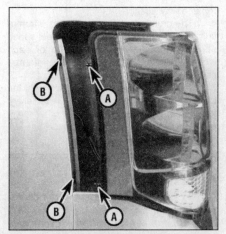

18.15 Pull the taillight away from the vehicle body to disengage the pins (A) from the rubber grommets (B) in the quarter-panel opening. Be sure to inspect the condition of each grommet. If it's cracked, torn or otherwise damaged, replace it

15   To remove the taillight assembly from the vehicle, pull the taillight away from the vehicle body to disengage the pins from the rubber grommets in the quarter-panel opening **(see illustration)**.
16   Disconnect the electrical connectors from the taillight sockets and remove the housing.
17   Remove the bulb socket by turning it counterclockwise and pulling it out from the taillight housing.
18   Remove the bulb from the socket.
19   Installation is the reverse of removal.

License plate light bulbs
20   Open the liftgate.
21   Insert a small screwdriver into the slot in the lens, press the release tab, then remove the lens.
22   Pull the bulb from the socket.
23   Installation is the reverse of removal.

Interior lights
Instrument cluster illumination bulbs
24   The instrument cluster LED lamps are an integral part of the cluster, and not separately serviceable. If the lamps stop working, the cluster must be replaced (see Section 10).

Courtesy light
Note: *The courtesy light LEDs are an integral part of the housing, and not separately serviceable.*
25   Using a trim stick or panel removal tool, pry the courtesy light from the door trim panel.
26   Disconnect the electrical connector from the courtesy light.
27   Installation is the reverse of removal.

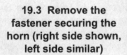

19.3 Remove the fastener securing the horn (right side shown, left side similar)

Dome/cargo light
28   Using a trim panel removal tool or a screwdriver, pry off the dome/cargo light lens.
29   Remove the bulb from the dome/cargo light assembly.
30   Installation is the reverse of removal.

Liftgate light bulb
31   Using a flat-bladed tool, pry the liftgate light lens from the liftgate trim panel.
32   Remove the liftgate light bulb.
33   Installation is the reverse of removal.

Overhead console reading lights
Note: *The overhead console reading LEDs are an integral part of the light pod and are not separately serviceable. If the light is not working, the light pod must be replaced*
34   Remove the front or rear overhead console (see Chapter 11).
35   Disconnect the electrical connector to the lamp(s).
36   From the back side of the housing, use a flat-bladed tool to carefully pry the light assembly or pod out from the console.
Caution: *The console and light pods are easily damaged and care should be taken not to damage them during this procedure.*
37   Installation is the reverse of removal.

Vanity light
Note: *The vanity LED lamps are an integral part of the visor, and not separately serviceable. If the lamps stop working, the visor must be replaced.*
38   Remove the visor mounting screws.
39   Lower the visor and disconnect the electrical connector then remove the visor.
40   Installation is the reverse of removal.

19   Horn - replacement

Refer to illustration 19.3
Warning: *The models covered by this manual are equipped with Supplemental Restraint Systems (SRS), more commonly known as*

airbags. Always disable the airbag system before working in the vicinity of any airbag system components to avoid the possibility of accidental deployment of the airbags, which could cause personal injury (see Section 26).
Note: *The horn is located behind the front bumper cover.*
1   Remove the front bumper cover (see Chapter 11).
2   Disconnect the electrical connector from the horn.
3   Remove the horn mounting fastener and the horn assembly **(see illustration).**
4   Installation is the reverse of removal.

20   Power sliding door drive assembly - removal and installation

Warning: *The models covered by this manual are equipped with Supplemental Restraint Systems (SRS), more commonly known as airbags. Always disable the airbag system before working in the vicinity of any airbag system components to avoid the possibility of accidental deployment of the airbags, which could cause personal injury (see Section 26).*
Note: *The power sliding door drive motor cannot be replaced separately. If the motor does not work or has been damaged, the complete power sliding door drive assembly must be replaced.*
1   Disconnect the cable from the negative battery terminal (see Chapter 5).
2   Using a trim tool, remove the sill plate from the sliding door opening and front door opening, then disengage the B-pillar trim panel clips and pull the panel back (see Chapter 11).
3   Disconnect the electrical connector to the sliding door switch and remove the B-pillar trim panel.
4   Disconnect the electrical connector from the bottom of the sliding door. Using a trim tool or equivalent, disengage the wiring harness mounting clips from the sliding door.

Note: *Use extreme care not to damage the harness mounting clips; if one is broken or damaged, the clips will need to be replaced to properly secure the harness to the door.*

5   After the harness is free from the door, locate the release tab on the bottom of the chain link. Pull the locking tab forward and remove the wire harness by pulling the chain link off of the mounting pin on the lower hinge.

6   Disconnect the side impact sensor electrical connector, then remove the sensor mounting screw. Pull the sensor straight up to un clip the anti-rotational pin on the bottom of the sensor from the hole in the door channel, then remove the sensor.

7   Using a trim tool, disengage any remaining sliding door electrical harness mounting clips and remove the harness assembly from the channel.

8   Remove the sliding door tensioner mounting bolt and tensioner from the lower hinge.

9   Remove the "hold-open" striker mounting bolts and remove the striker.

10   Pull the bottom of the rubber stop bumper outwards then pull the stop out of the upper track.

Caution: *Do not remove the door hinges during this procedure; if they are removed, the door will not open and close properly.*

11   Place a block of wood onto a floor jack, then place a pad or towel on top of the wood and support the sliding door with the jack. With the help of an assistant, carefully slide the door to the rear of the vehicle until the upper hinge sliding roller comes out of the end of the upper track. Continue sliding the door back until the lower roller comes out of the bottom track, while balancing the door on the jack.

12   With the door secured and out of the way, remove the power sliding door drive assembly mounting nuts.

13   Disengage the assembly electrical harness retaining clips and disconnect the electrical connector from the B-pillar connector.

14   Carefully remove the power sliding door drive assembly from the vehicle.

15   Installation is the reverse of removal.

16   Once the power sliding door drive assembly is installed, the assembly must go through the power sliding door learn cycle before it will properly operate. The learn cycle enables the power sliding door control module to learn or relearn critical information such as opening and closing force, open and closed positions and all stops which allows the door system to operate properly and safely. The power sliding door learn cycle requires a factory type scan tool. This procedure is recommend to be performed by a dealership or authorized repair shop after the assembly been serviced.

21   Electric side view mirrors - general information

Note: *On these models, the outside mirrors are controlled by the Front Door Power Switch Assembly (FDPSA), which houses the mirror control switches and the Front Door Control Module (FDCM). The FDPSA interprets the mirror control switch movements, while the FDCM supplies the battery voltage and ground to the motors to move the mirrors.*

1   The electric rear view mirrors use two motors to move the glass; one for up and down adjustments and one for left-right adjustments.

2   The control switch has a selector portion which sends voltage to the left or right side mirror. With the ignition in the ACC position and the engine OFF, roll down the windows and operate the mirror control switch through all functions (left-right and up-down) for both the left and right side mirrors.

3   Listen carefully for the sound of the electric motors running in the mirrors.

4   If the motors can be heard but the mirror glass doesn't move, there's probably a problem with the drive mechanism inside the mirror. Power mirrors have no user-serviceable parts inside - a defective mirror must be replaced as a unit (see Chapter 11).

5   If the mirrors don't operate and no sound comes from the mirrors, check the fuses (see Section 3).

6   If the fuses are OK, remove the mirror control switch. Have the switch continuity checked by a dealer service department or other qualified shop.

7   Check the ground connections.

8   If the mirror still doesn't work, remove the mirror and check the wires at the mirror for voltage.

9   If there's not voltage in each switch position, check the circuit between the mirror and control switch for opens and shorts.

10   If there's voltage, remove the mirror and test it off the vehicle with jumper wires. Replace the mirror if it fails this test.

22   Cruise control system – description and check

1   The cruise control system maintains vehicle speed with the Antilock Brake Module (ABM), Powertrain Control Module (PCM), throttle actuator control motor, Brake Pedal Position (BPP) sensor, wheel speed sensors, control switches and associated wiring. There is no mechanical connection, such as a vacuum servo or cable. Some features of the system require special testers and diagnostic procedures that are beyond the scope of the home mechanic. Listed below are some general procedures that may be used to locate common problems.

2   Check the fuses (see Section 3).

3   The BPP switch (or brake light switch) deactivates the cruise control system. Have an assistant press the brake pedal while you check the brake light operation.

4   If the brake lights do not operate properly, correct the problem and retest the cruise control.

5   Check the wiring between the PCM and throttle actuator motor for opens or shorts and repair as necessary.

6   The cruise control system uses information from the PCM, including the wheel speed sensors, located on the knuckle of each wheel. Refer to Chapter 9 for more information on the wheel speed sensors.

7   Test drive the vehicle to determine if the cruise control is now working. If it isn't, take it to a dealer service department or other qualified repair shop for further diagnosis.

23   Power window system - description and check

Note: *These models are equipped with a Body Control Module (BCM). Several systems are linked to this centralized control module, which allows simple and accurate troubleshooting, but only with a professional-grade scan tool. The BCM governs the door locks, the power windows, the ignition lock and security system, the interior lights, the Daytime Running Lights system, the horn, the windshield wipers, the heating/air conditioning system and the power mirrors. In the event of a malfunction with this system, have the vehicle diagnosed by a dealership service department or other qualified automotive repair facility.*

1   The power window system operates electric motors, mounted in the doors, which lower and raise the windows. The system consists of the control switches, the motors, regulators, glass mechanisms, the Body Control Module (BCM) and associated wiring.

2   The power windows can be lowered and raised from the master control switch by the driver or by remote switches located at the individual windows. Each window has a separate motor that is reversible. The position of the control switch determines the polarity and therefore the direction of operation.

3   The circuit is protected by a fuse and a circuit breaker. Each motor is also equipped with an internal circuit breaker; this prevents one stuck window from disabling the whole system.

4   The power window system will only operate when the ignition switch is ON, and for a period of time after the ignition key has been turned Off (unless one of the doors is opened). In addition, many models have a window lockout switch at the master control switch which, when activated, disables the switches at the rear windows and, sometimes, the switch at the passenger's window also. Always check these items before troubleshooting a window problem.

5   These procedures are general in nature, so if you can't find the problem using them, take the vehicle to a dealer service department or other properly equipped repair facility.

6   If the power windows won't operate, always check the fuse and circuit breaker first.

7   If only the rear windows are inoperative, or if the windows only operate from the master control switch, check the rear window lockout switch for continuity in the unlocked position.

24.14 Using the emergency key or small screwdriver, carefully pry the halves apart

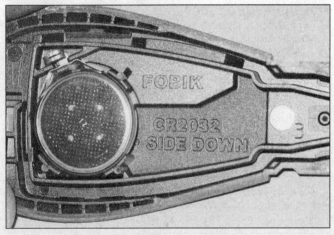

24.15 Remove the battery making sure to note the direction the battery faces

Replace it if it doesn't have continuity.

8   Check the wiring between the switches and fuse panel for continuity. Repair the wiring, if necessary.

9   If only one window is inoperative from the master control switch, try the other control switch at the window.

Note: *This doesn't apply to the driver's door window.*

10   If the same window works from one switch, but not the other, check the switch for continuity.

11   If the switch tests OK, check for a short or open in the circuit between the affected switch and the window motor.

12   If one window is inoperative from both switches, remove the switch panel from the affected door. Check for voltage at the switch and at the motor (refer to Chapter 11 for door panel removal) while the switch is operated.

13   If voltage is reaching the motor, disconnect the glass from the regulator (see Chapter 11). Move the window up and down by hand while checking for binding and damage. Also check for binding and damage to the regulator. If the regulator is not damaged and the window moves up and down smoothly, replace the motor. If there's binding or damage, lubricate, repair or replace parts, as necessary.

14   If voltage isn't reaching the motor, check the wiring in the circuit for continuity between the switches and the body control module, and between the body control module and the motors. You'll need to consult the wiring diagram at the end of this Chapter. If the circuit is equipped with a relay, check that the relay is grounded properly and receiving voltage.

15   Test the windows after you are done to confirm proper repairs.

24   Power door lock and keyless entry system - description and check

Note: *These models are equipped with a Body Control Module (BCM). Several sys-* *tems are linked to this centralized control module, which allows simple and accurate troubleshooting, but only with a professional-grade scan tool. The BCM governs the door locks, the power windows, the ignition lock and security system, the interior lights, the Daytime Running Lights system, the horn, the windshield wipers, the heating/air conditioning system and the power mirrors. In the event of a malfunction with this system, have the vehicle diagnosed by a dealership service department or other qualified automotive repair facility.*

1   The power door lock system operates the door lock actuators mounted in each door. The system consists of the switches, actuators, BCM and associated wiring. Diagnosis can usually be limited to simple checks of the wiring connections and actuators for minor faults that can be easily repaired.

2   Power door lock systems are operated by bi-directional solenoids located in the doors. The lock switches have two operating positions: Lock and Unlock. These switches send a signal to the BCM, which in turn sends a signal to the door lock solenoids.

3   If you are unable to locate the trouble using the following general steps, consult your dealer service department.

4   Always check the circuit protection first. Some vehicles use a combination of circuit breakers and fuses. Refer to the wiring diagrams at the end of this Chapter.

5   Check for voltage at the switches. If no voltage is present, check the wiring between the fuse panel and the switches for shorts and opens.

6   If voltage is present, test the switch for continuity. Replace it if there's not continuity in both switch positions. To remove the switch, use a flat-bladed trim tool to pry out the door/window switch assembly (see Chapter 11).

7   If the switch has continuity, check the wiring between the switch and door lock solenoid.

8   If all but one lock solenoids operate, remove the trim panel from the affected door (see Chapter 11) and check for voltage at the solenoid while the lock switch is operated. One of the wires should have voltage in the Lock position; the other should have voltage in the Unlock position.

9   If the inoperative solenoid is receiving voltage, replace the solenoid.

10   If the inoperative solenoid isn't receiving voltage, check for an open or short in the wire between the lock solenoid and the relay.

11   On the models covered by this manual, power door lock system communication goes through the Body Control Module (BCM). If the above tests do not pinpoint a problem, take the vehicle to a dealer or qualified shop with the proper scan tool to retrieve trouble codes from the BCM.

Keyless entry system

12   The keyless entry system consists of a remote control transmitter that sends a coded infrared signal to a receiver, which then operates the door lock system.

13   Replace the battery when the transmitter doesn't operate the locks at a distance of ten feet. Normal range should be about 30 feet.

Key remote control battery replacement

Refer to illustrations 24.14 and 24.15

Note: *The key remote control replacement battery is a "CR2032" battery*

14   Use the tip of the emergency key, a plastic trim tool or coin to carefully separate the case halves **(see illustration)**.

Caution: *Do not touch the battery terminals that are on the back of the transmitter housing or the printed circuit board. The transmitter also contains "perchlorate material" that may require special handling for disposal. See www.dtsc.ca.gov/hazardouswaste/perchlorate for more information.*

15   Replace the battery **(see illustration)**.

16   Snap the case halves together.

Transmitter programming

17 Programming replacement transmitters requires the use of a specialized scan tool. Take the vehicle and the transmitter(s) to a dealer service department or other qualified repair shop equipped with the necessary tool to have the transmitter(s) programmed to the vehicle.

25 Daytime Running Lights (DRL) - general information

The Daytime Running Lights (DRL) system, which is required on new Canadian models and an option on models made for the United States, illuminates the headlights when the engine is running. The DRL system supplies reduced power to the headlights so they won't be too bright for daytime use, which also prolongs headlight life.

26 Airbag system - general information and precautions

General information

1 All models are equipped with a frontal-impact airbag system, which is referred to as the Supplemental Restraint System (SRS). The SRS is designed to protect the driver and the front seat passenger from serious injury in the event of a head-on or frontal collision. The SRS is controlled by the Occupant Restraint Controller (ORC), also referred to as the Airbag Control Module (ACM), which is mounted in the center of the vehicle, on the floor transmission tunnel, below the center of the instrument panel. The SRS uses an array of airbags to protect the front-seat occupants (and on models equipped with side curtain airbags, the rear seat passengers, too): the driver's airbag in the steering wheel; the knee blocker airbag, which is located below the steering column; the passenger airbag, which is located in the right end of the instrument panel, beneath the instrument panel top pad and above the glove box; and, on models so equipped, the side curtain airbags, which are located above the side windows, in the outer edges of the headliner, between the A- and D-pillars. The SRS is activated by a pair of front impact sensors located on the front of the frame, just behind the bumper attachments. Other important components in the SRS include the clockspring, a wind-up coil that delivers battery voltage to the steering wheel airbag, and the AIRBAG readiness light on the instrument cluster.

In addition to the airbags, seat belt pretensioners are incorporated into the front seat belt retractor mechanisms. These are pyrotechnic (explosive) devices which retract the seat belts up to four inches when the airbag system is activated.

Driver airbag

2 The airbag inflator module contains a housing incorporating the cushion (airbag) and inflator unit, mounted in the center of the steering wheel. The inflator assembly is mounted on the back of the housing over a hole through which gas is expelled, inflating the bag almost instantaneously when an electrical signal is sent from the system. The clockspring assembly on the steering column under the steering wheel carries this signal to the module. The clockspring assembly can transmit an electrical signal regardless of steering wheel position. The igniter in the airbag converts the electrical signal to heat and ignites the powder, which inflates the bag.

3 In the event of a frontal collision serious enough to trigger SRS deployment, the knee blocker airbag inflates toward the driver's knees to help protect them and to help put the driver in the optimal position for deployment of the driver's airbag. The knee blocker airbag deploys in about 50 milliseconds.

Passenger airbag

4 The airbag is mounted in the right end of the instrument panel, beneath the instrument panel top pad and above the glove box. It consists of an inflator containing an igniter, a bag assembly, a reaction housing and a trim cover. The passenger airbag is considerably larger than the steering wheel-mounted unit and is supported by the steel reaction housing. The trim cover is textured and painted to match the instrument panel and has a molded seam that splits when the bag inflates.

5 Unlike the inflatable airbag knee blocker on the driver's side, the passenger knee blocker is simply a structural reinforcement that's an integral part of the glove box. But it does the same thing as the driver's inflatable knee blocker: it offers a degree of protection for the passenger's knees in a frontal impact and it positions the passenger for deployment of the passenger airbag.

Side-impact window airbags

6 Optional side-impact window airbags protect vehicle occupants in the event of a side impact. The side-impact window airbags are located above the windows, between the A- and D-pillars. If you're not sure whether your vehicle is equipped with side-impact window airbags, look for the words "SRS AIRBAG" imprinted on a small identification trim button located above the B- and C-pillars.

7 Vehicles equipped with side-impact window airbags use six side-impact sensors, three on the left side of the vehicle and three more on the right side. The front row side-impact sensors are located inside the B-pillars, above the front seatbelt retractors. The second-row side-impact sensors are located in the sliding door track openings, just ahead of the C-pillars. The third-row sensors are located behind the quarter-trim panels, between the C- and D-pillars, above the rear wheelwells.

Occupant Restraint Controller (ORC) or Airbag Control Module (ACM)

8 The ORC or ACM supplies current to the SRS in the event of a collision, even if battery power is cut off. The ORC/ACM checks the SRS every time the vehicle is started, and indicates that it is doing so by turning on the AIRBAG readiness light. If the SRS is operating properly, the ORC/ACM turns off the AIRBAG readiness light. If it detects a fault in the system, the AIRBAG readiness light will remain on. If this condition occurs, take the vehicle to your dealer immediately for service.

Disarming the system and other precautions

Warning: *Failure to follow these precautions could result in accidental deployment of the airbag and personal injury.*

9 Whenever you are working in the vicinity of the driver airbag in the steering wheel or any of the other airbags on your vehicle, DISARM THE SYSTEM. To disarm the system:

a) *Point the wheels straight ahead and turn the ignition key to the LOCK position.*

b) *Disconnect the cable from the negative battery terminal. Isolate the cable terminal so it won't accidentally contact the battery post.*

c) *Wait at least two minutes for the back-up power supply to be depleted. Back-up power is supplied by a capacitor that takes about two minutes to fully discharge. During this two-minute interval, the SRS is still capable of deploying.*

10 Whenever handling an airbag, always keep the airbag opening (the trim side) pointed away from your body. Never place the airbag on a bench or other surface with the airbag opening facing the surface. Always place the airbag module in a safe location with the airbag opening facing up.

11 Never measure the resistance of any SRS component. An ohmmeter has a built-in battery supply that could accidentally deploy the airbag.

12 Never dispose of a live airbag. Return it to a dealer service department or other qualified repair shop for safe deployment and disposal.

Component removal and installation

Driver airbag and clockspring

13 Refer to Chapter 10, *Steering wheel - removal and installation*, for the driver's side airbag module and clockspring removal and installation procedures.

Driver knee blocker airbag

Refer to illustrations 26.16 and 26.17

14 Disarm the airbag system (see Step 9).

15 Remove the knee bolster and the instrument panel left end cover (see Chapter 11).

16 Disconnect the knee blocker airbag elec-

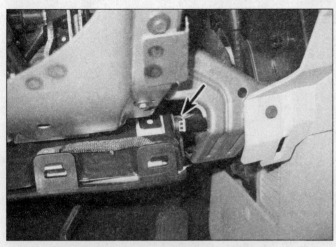

26.16 Location of the electrical connector for the driver's knee blocker airbag

26.17 To detach the driver knee blocker airbag, remove these fasteners

trical connector **(see illustration)**.

17   Remove the knee blocker airbag mounting fasteners **(see illustration)** and remove the knee blocker airbag. Be sure to heed the precautions outlined previously in this Section.

18   Installation is the reverse of removal.

27 Wiring diagrams - general information

Since it isn't possible to include all wiring diagrams for every year covered by this manual, the following diagrams are those that are typical and most commonly needed.

Prior to troubleshooting any circuits, check the fuse and circuit breakers (if equipped) to make sure they're in good condition. Make sure the battery is properly charged and check the cable connections (see Chapters 1 and 5).

When checking a circuit, make sure that all connectors are clean, with no broken or loose terminals. When unplugging a connector, do not pull on the wires. Pull only on the connector housings.

Notes

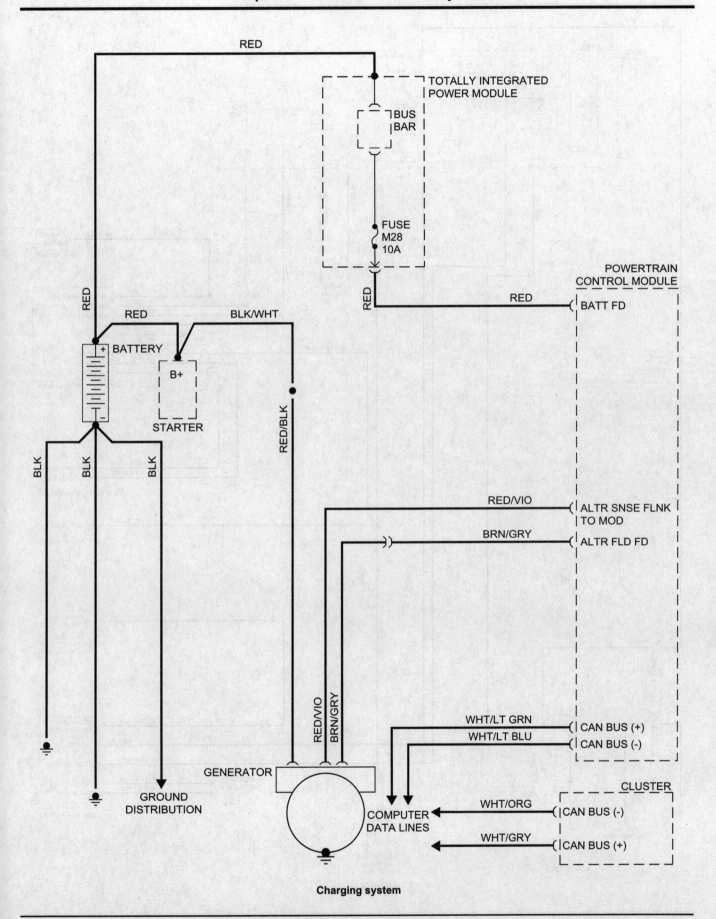

Charging system

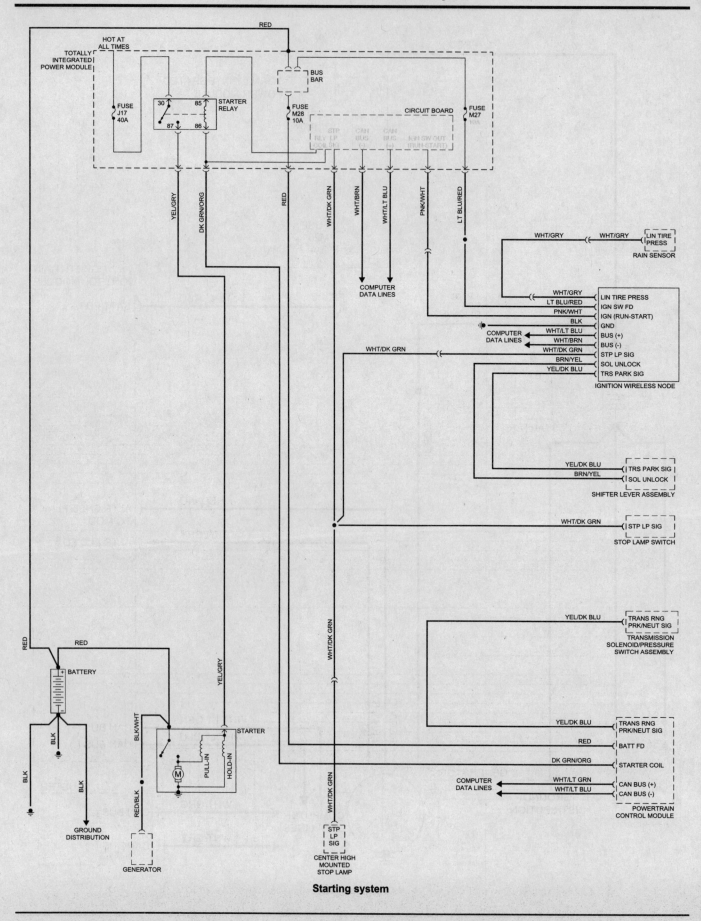

Starting system

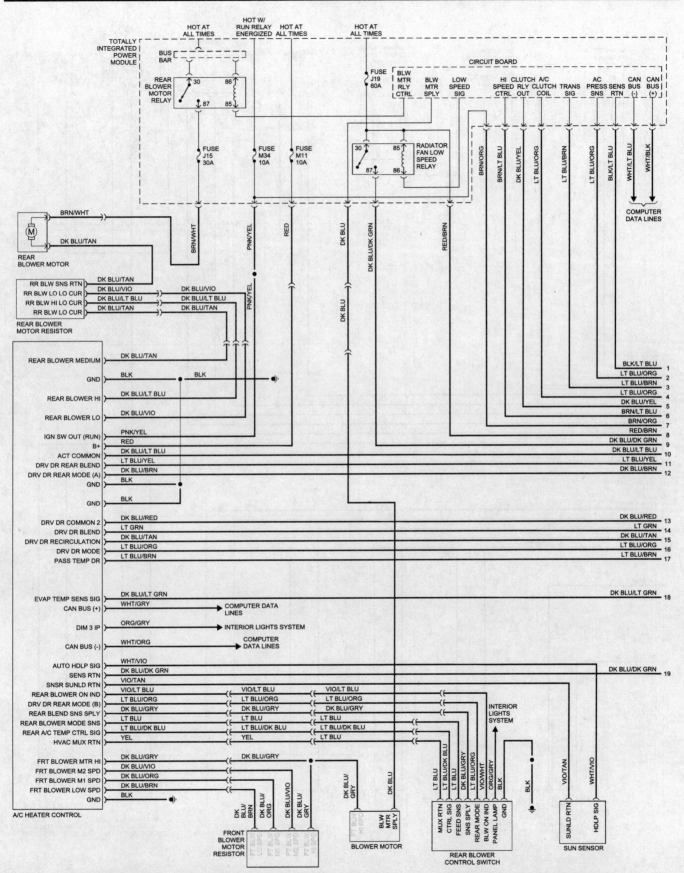

Heating, air conditioning (manual) and engine cooling fan systems - 2010 and earlier models (1 of 2)

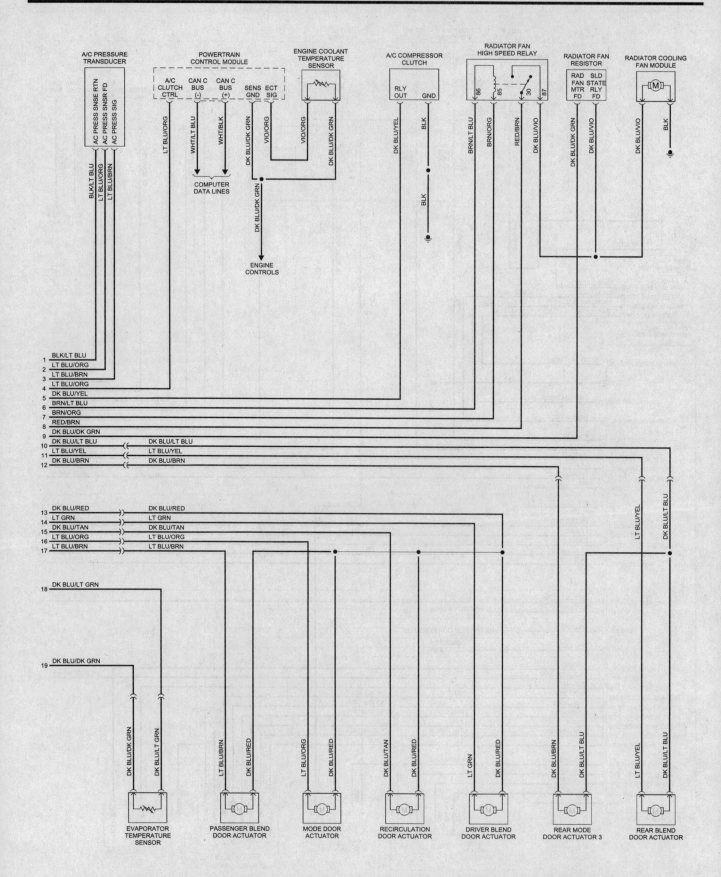

Heating, air conditioning (manual) and engine cooling fan systems - 2010 and earlier models (2 of 2)

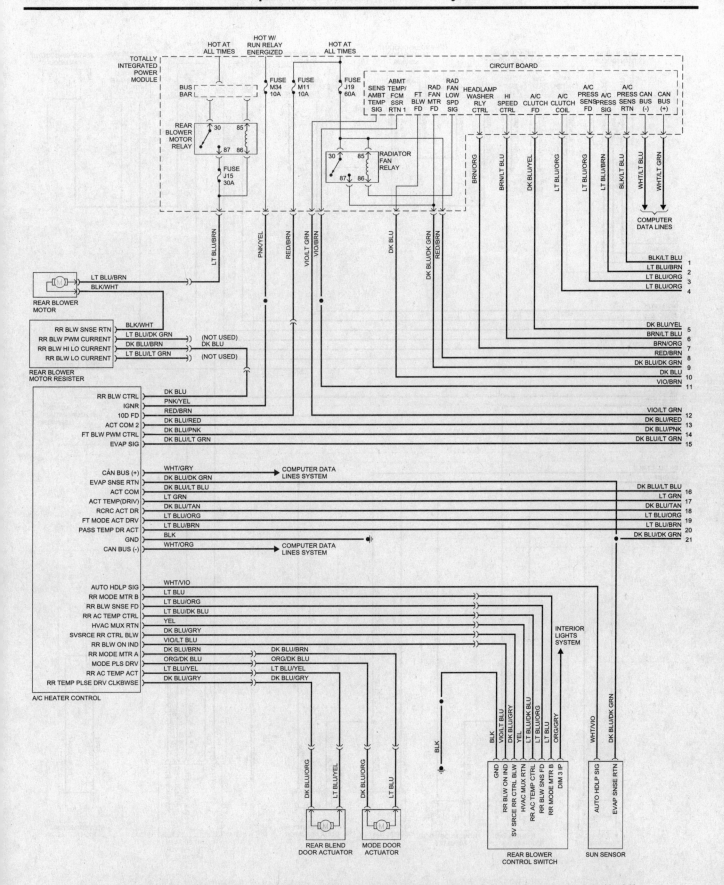

Heating, air conditioning (manual) and engine cooling fan systems - 2011 and later Grand Caravan models (1 of 2)

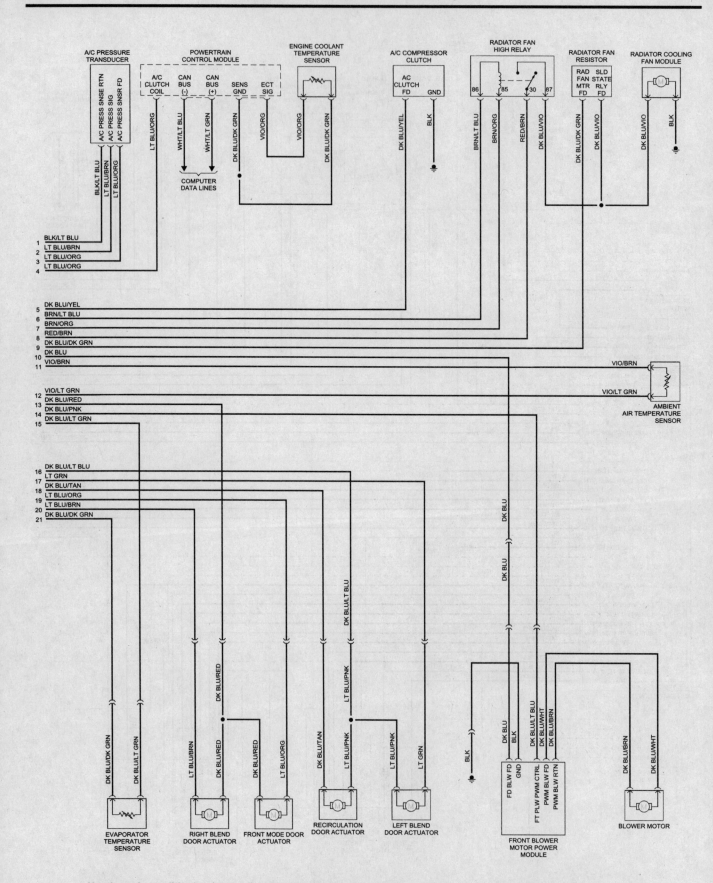

Heating, air conditioning (manual) and engine cooling fan systems - 2011 and later Grand Caravan models (2 of 2)

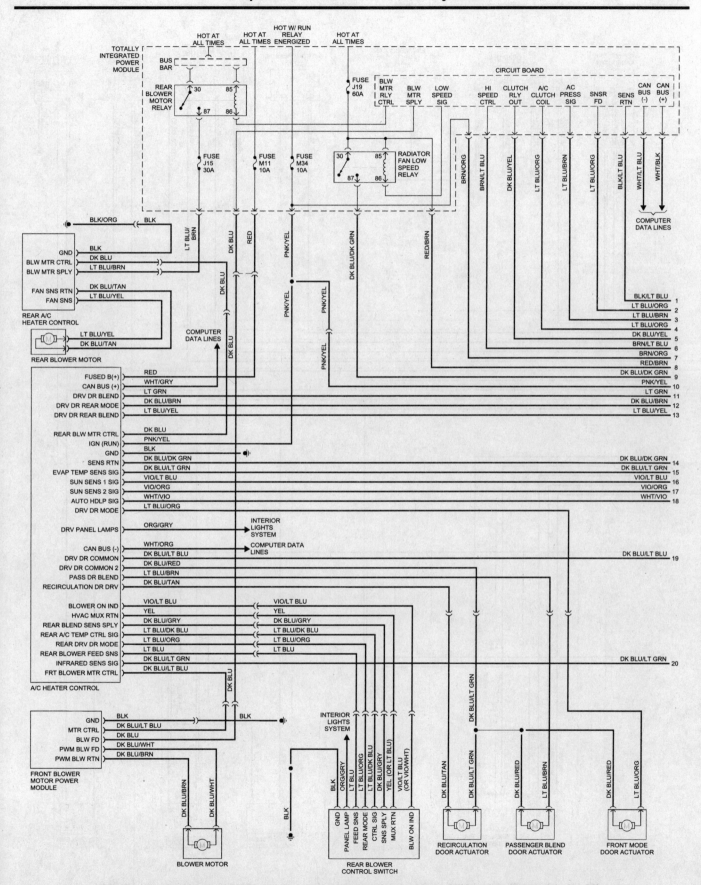

Heating, air conditioning (automatic) and engine cooling fan systems - 2010 and earlier models (1 of 2)

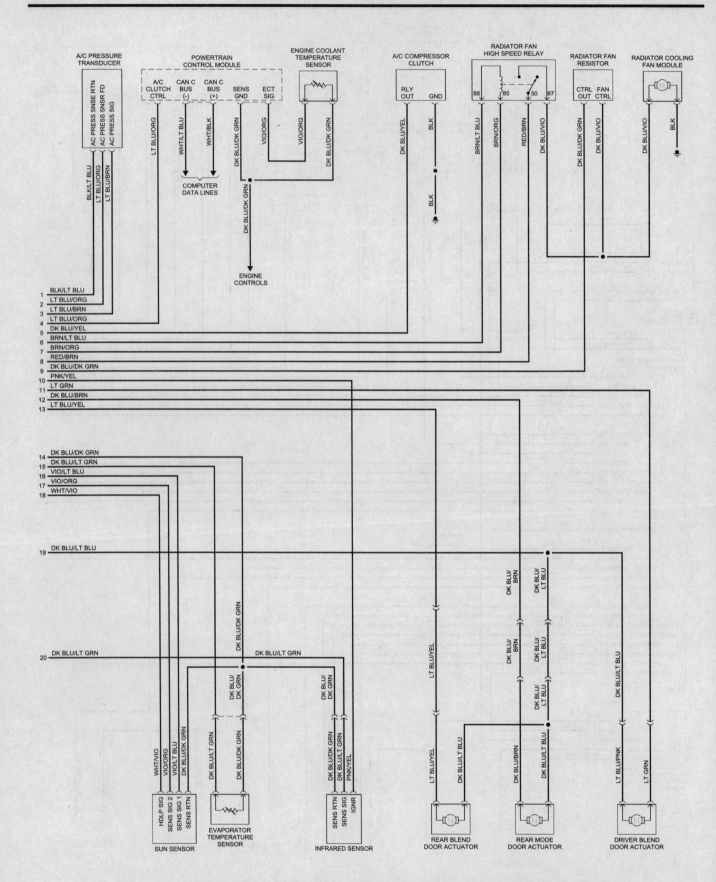

Heating, air conditioning (automatic) and engine cooling fan systems - 2010 and earlier models (2 of 2)

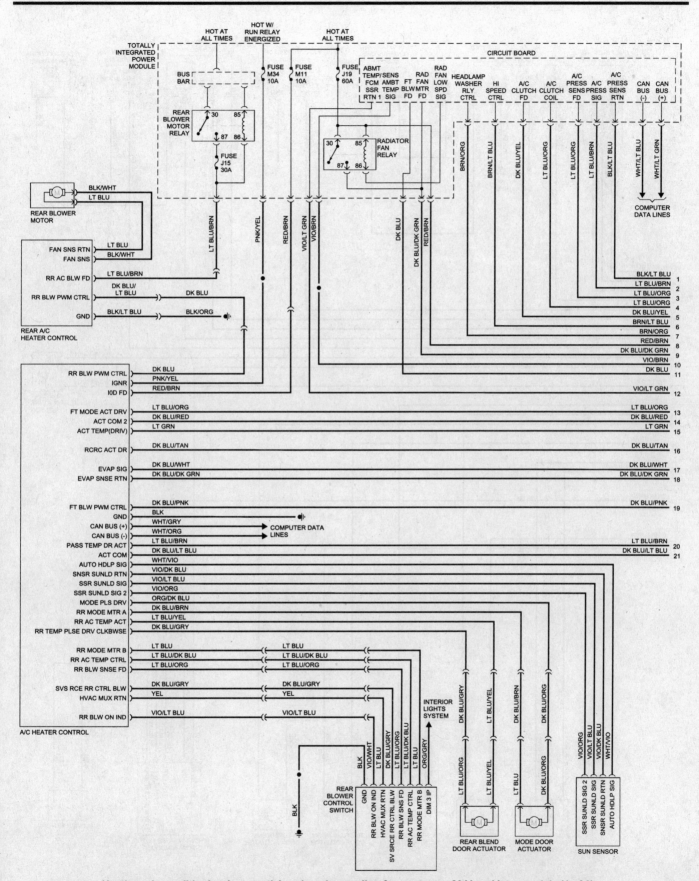

Heating, air conditioning (automatic) and engine cooling fan systems - 2011 and later models (1 of 2)

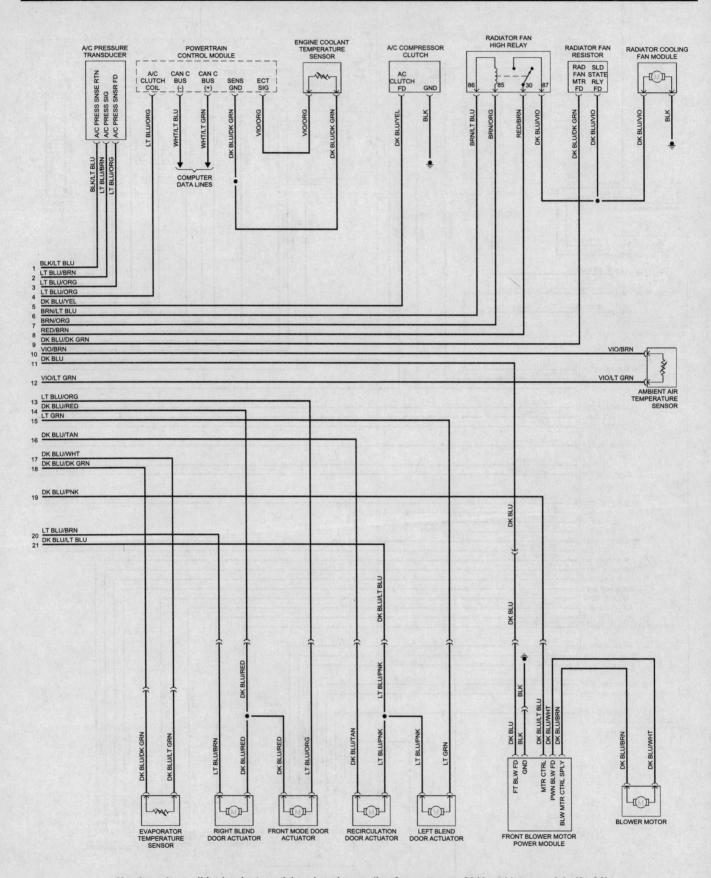

Heating, air conditioning (automatic) and engine cooling fan systems - 2011 and later models (2 of 2)

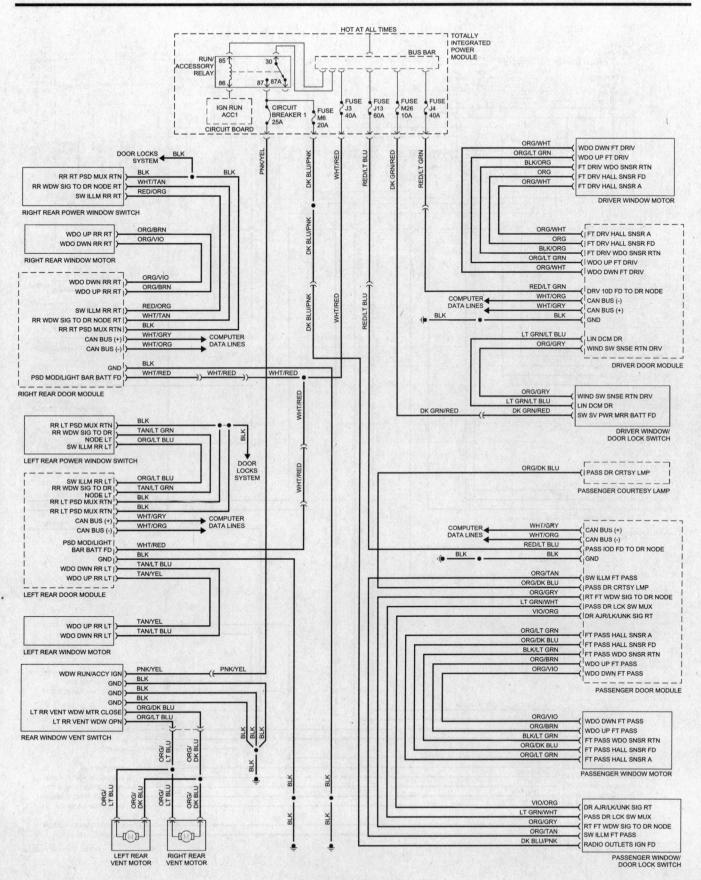

Power window system

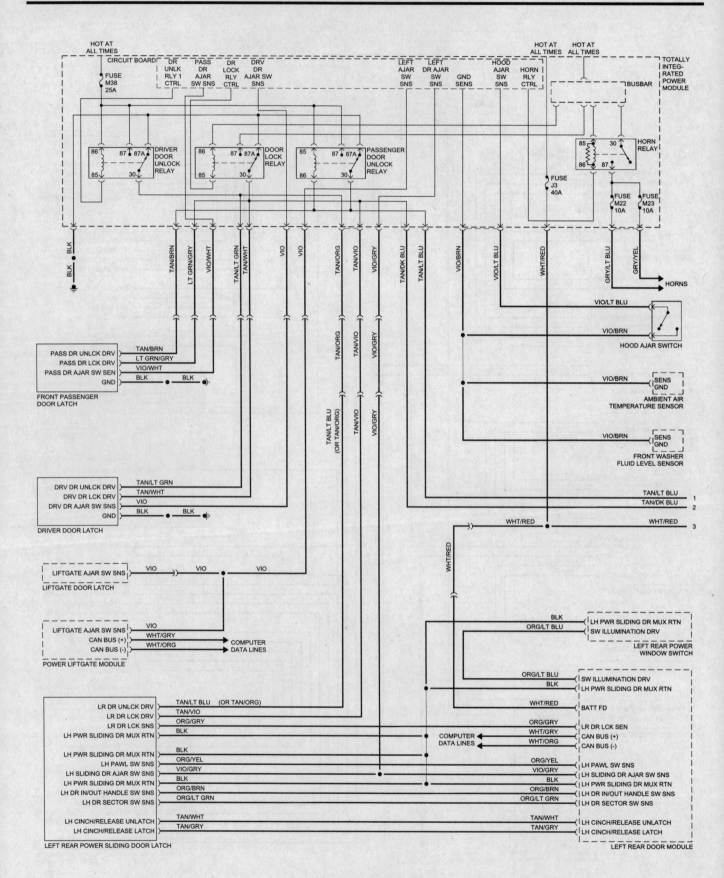

Power door lock system (1 of 2)

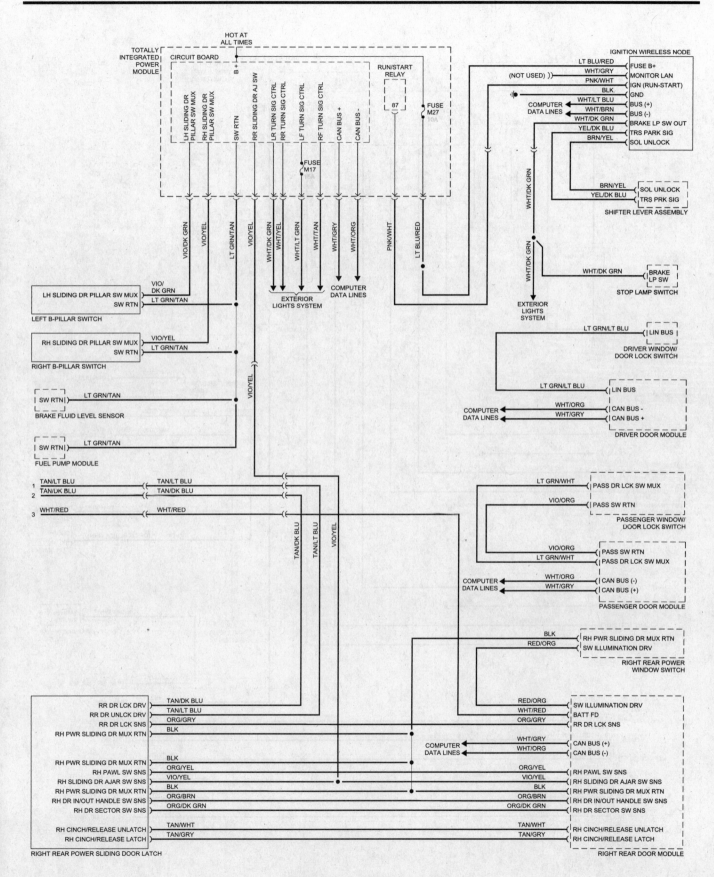

Power door lock system (2 of 2)

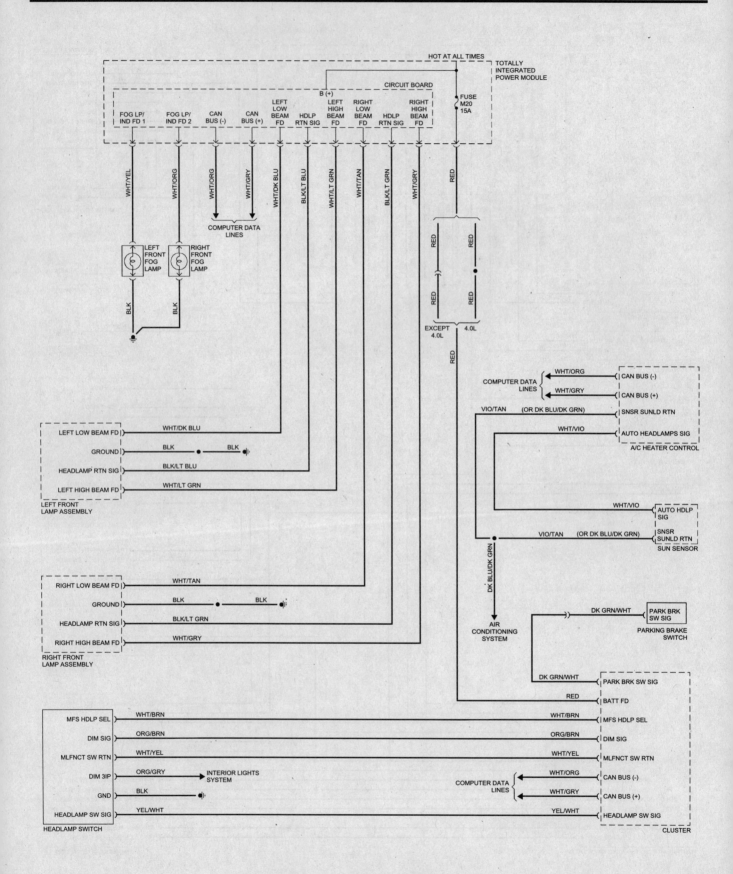

Headlight system - 2010 and earlier models

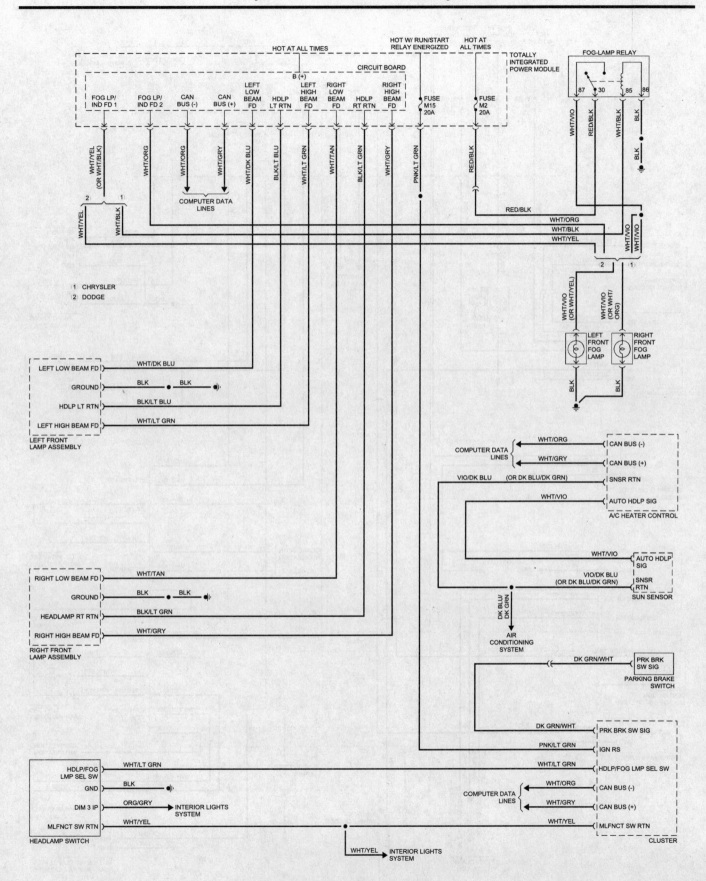

Headlight system - 2011 and later models

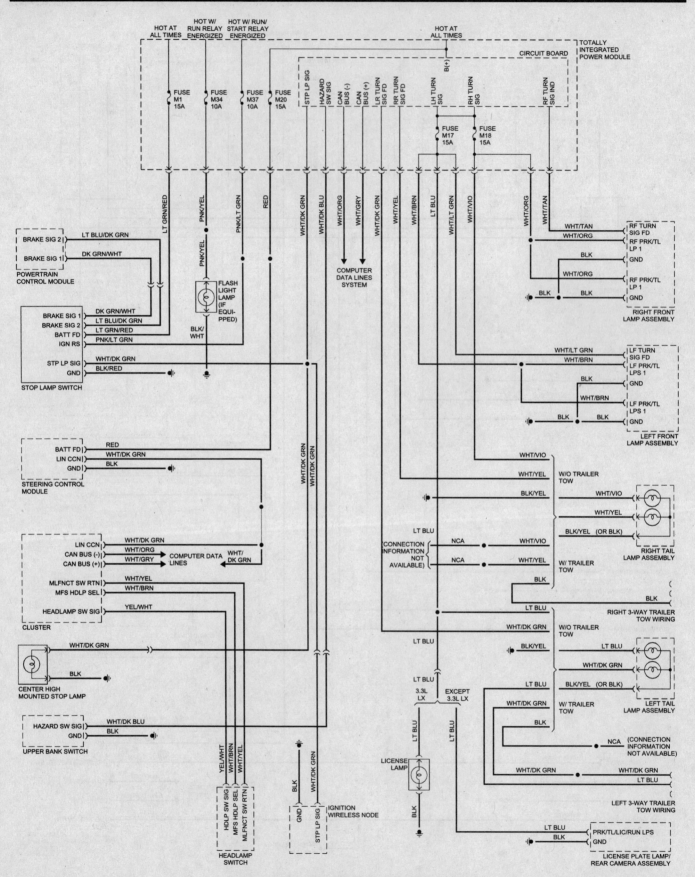

Exterior lighting system - 2010 and earlier models

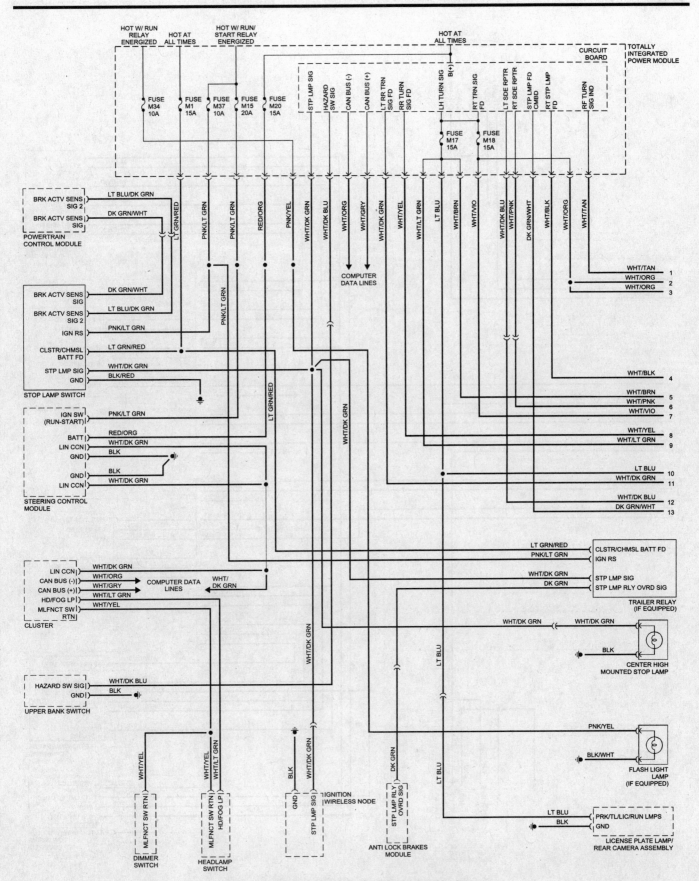

Exterior lighting system - 2011 and later models (1of 2)

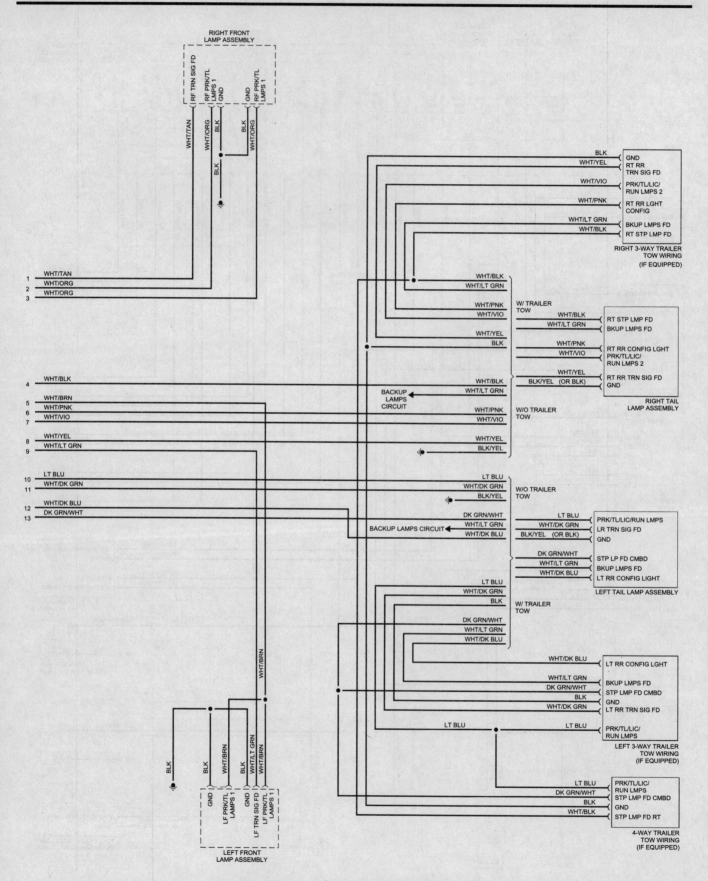

Exterior lighting system - 2011 and later models (2of 2)

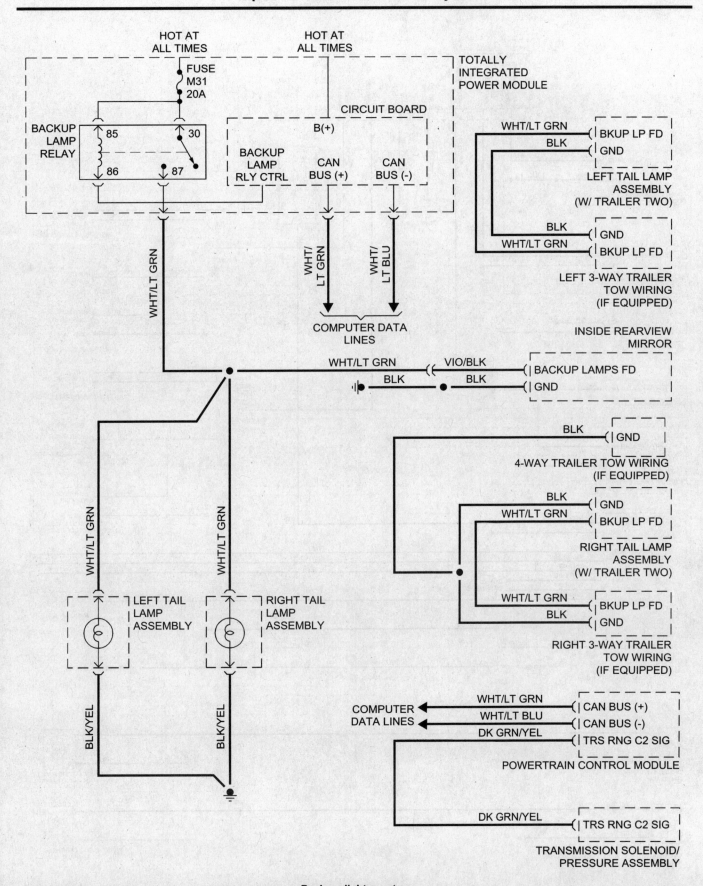

Back-up lights system

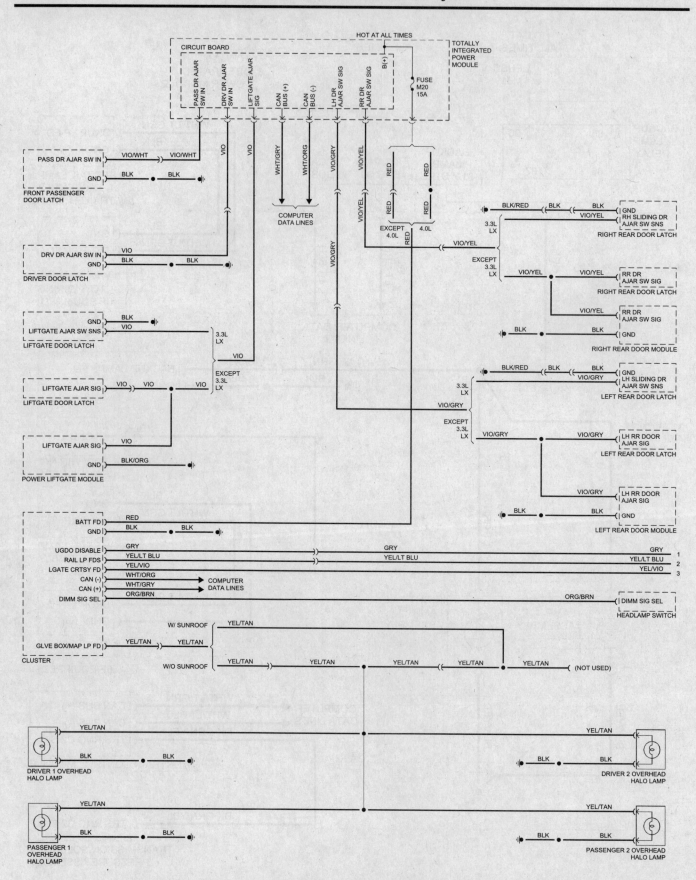

Courtesy lights system - 2010 and earlier models (1 of 2)

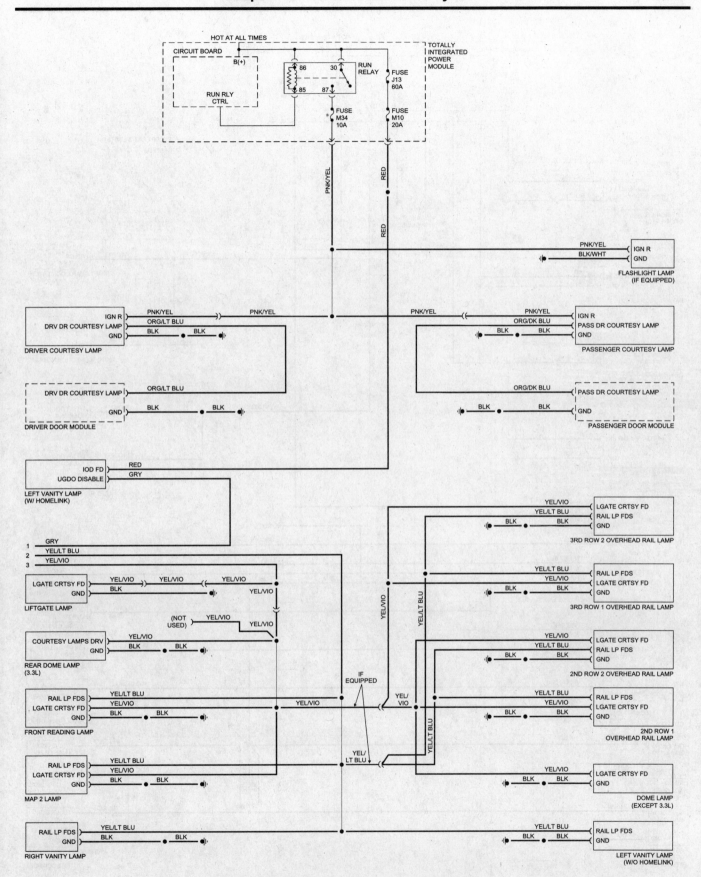

Courtesy lights system - 2010 and earlier models (2 of 2)

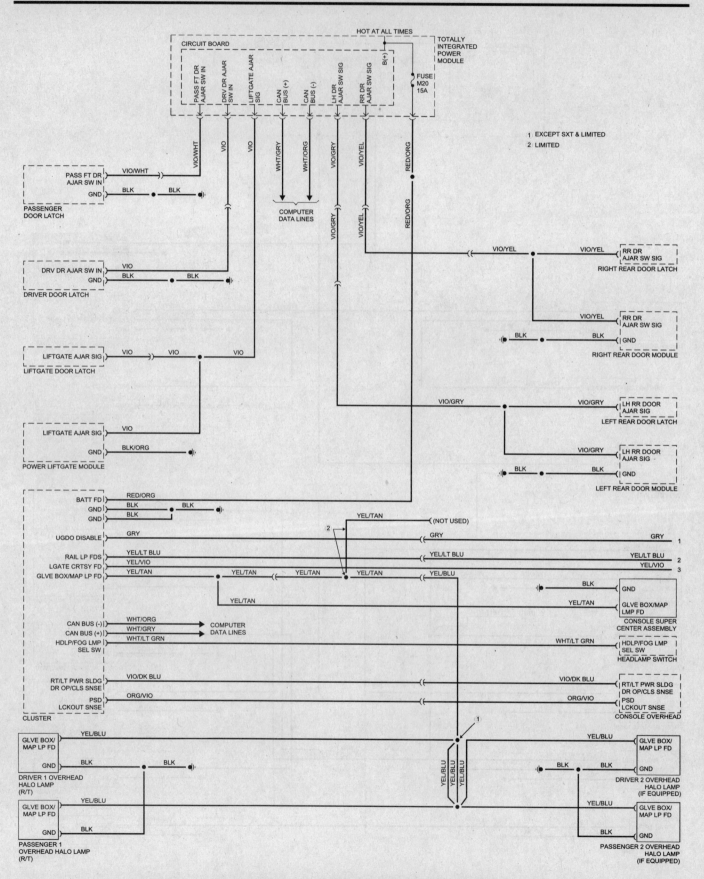

Courtesy lights system - 2011 and earlier models (1 of 2)

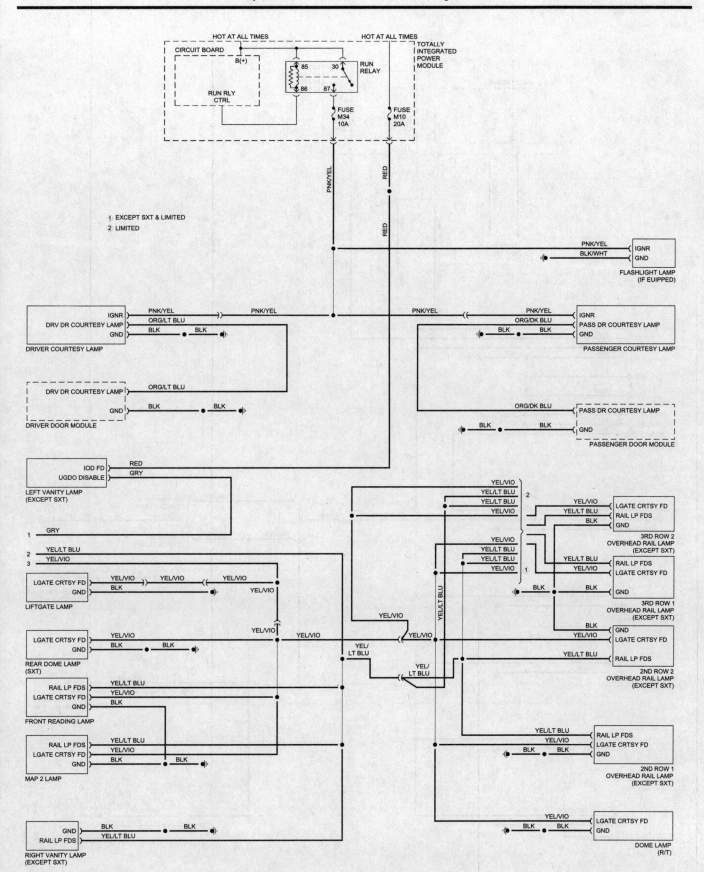

Courtesy lights system - 2011 and earlier models (2 of 2)

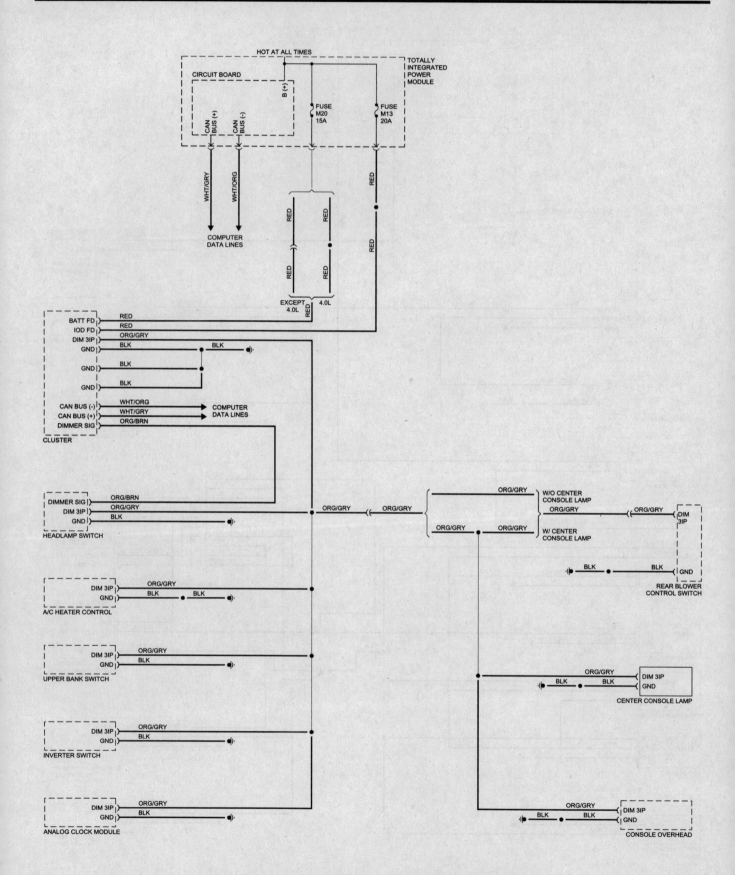

Instrument and switch illumination system - 2010 and earlier models

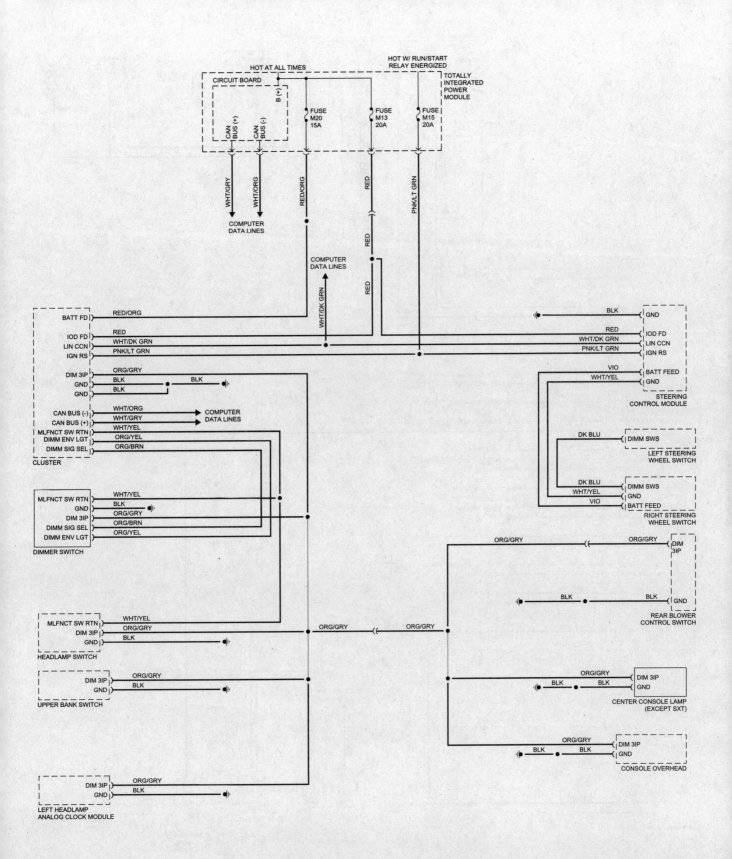

Instrument and switch illumination system - 2011 and later models

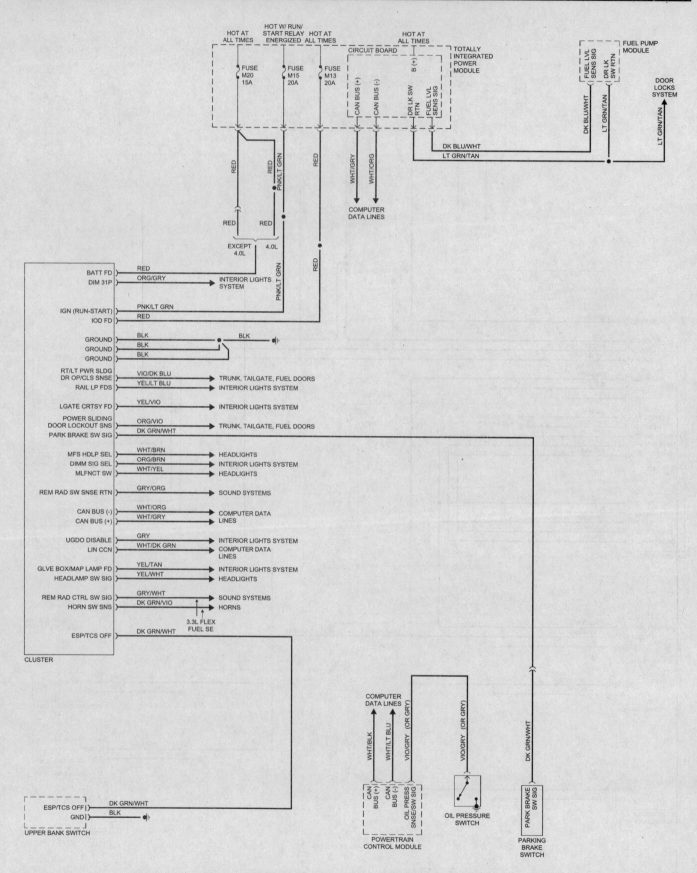

Warning lights and gauges system - 2010 and earlier models

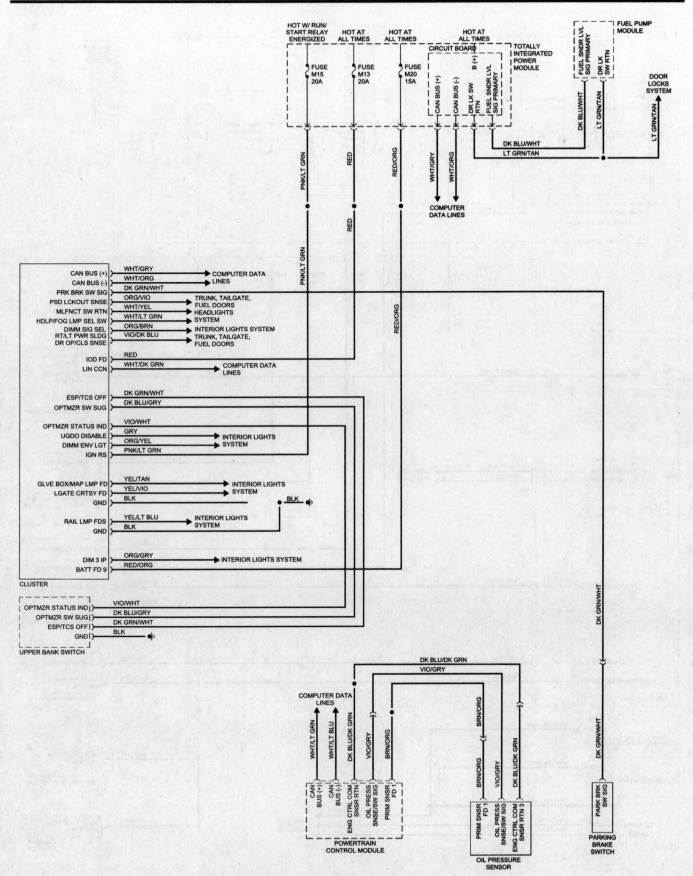

Warning lights and gauges system - 2011 and later models

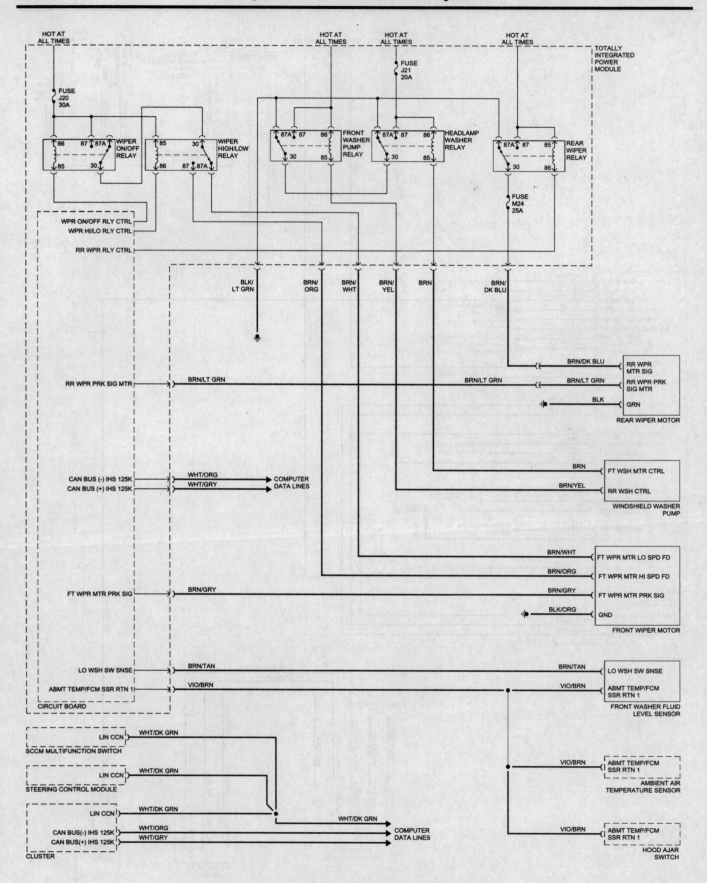

Windshield wiper/washer system - 2010 and earlier models

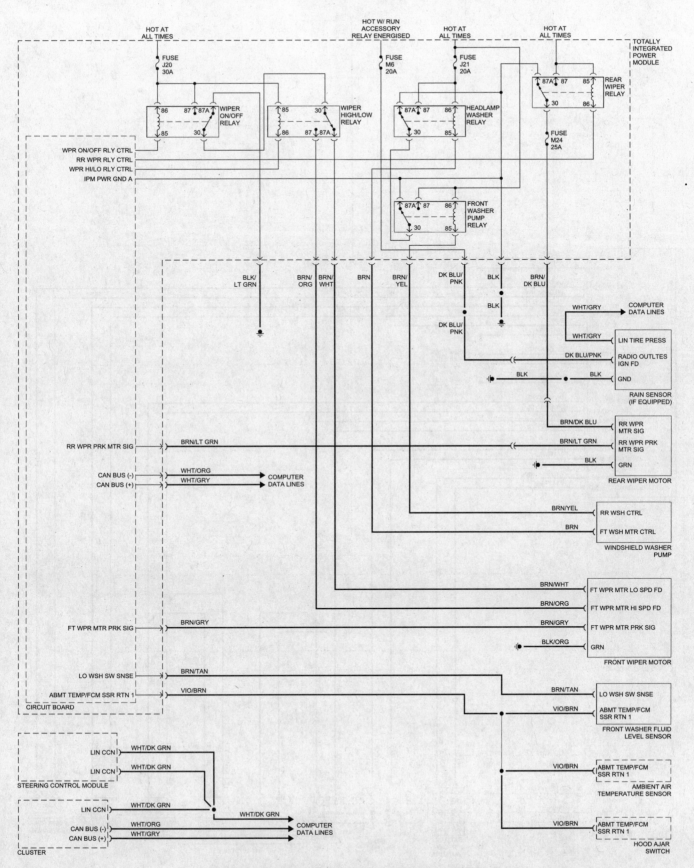

Windshield wiper/washer system - 2011 and later models

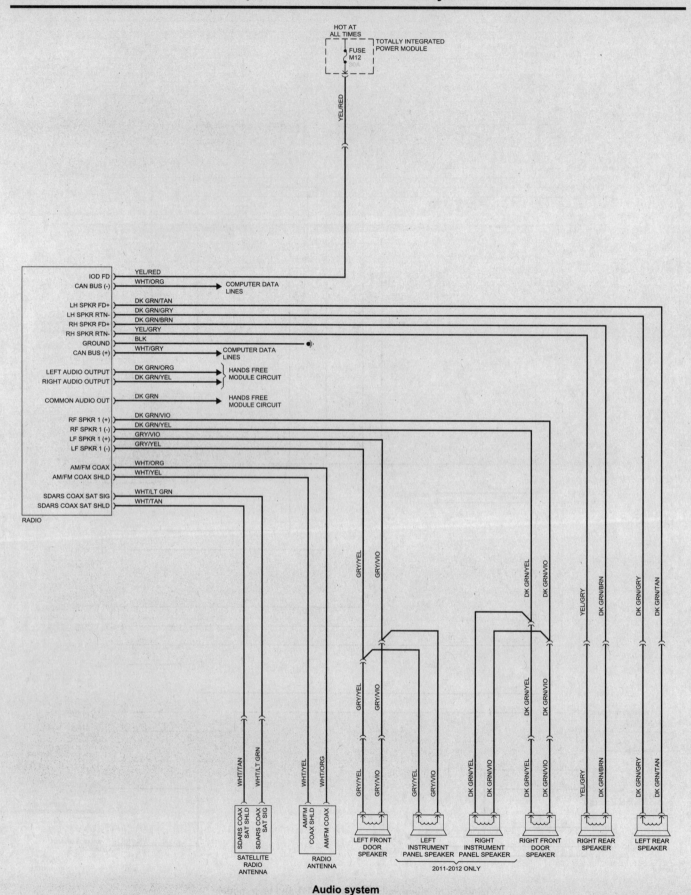

Audio system

Index

Notes

Haynes Automotive Manuals

NOTE: If you do not see a listing for your vehicle, consult your local Haynes dealer for the latest product information.

ACURA
12020 Integra '86 thru '89 & Legend '86 thru '90
12021 Integra '90 thru '93 & Legend '91 thru '95
Integra '94 thru '00 - see HONDA Civic (42025)
MDX '01 thru '07 - see HONDA Pilot (42037)
12050 Acura TL all models '99 thru '08

AMC
Jeep CJ - see JEEP (50020)
14020 Mid-size models '70 thru '83
14025 (Renault) Alliance & Encore '83 thru '87

AUDI
15020 4000 all models '80 thru '87
15025 5000 all models '77 thru '83
15026 5000 all models '84 thru '88
Audi A4 '96 thru '01 - see VW Passat (96023)
15030 Audi A4 '02 thru '08

AUSTIN-HEALEY
Sprite - see MG Midget (66015)

BMW
18020 3/5 Series '82 thru '92
18021 3-Series incl. Z3 models '92 thru '98
18022 3-Series incl. Z4 models '99 thru '05
18023 3-Series '06 thru '10
18025 320i all 4 cyl models '75 thru '83
18050 1500 thru 2002 except Turbo '59 thru '77

BUICK
19010 Buick Century '97 thru '05
Century (front-wheel drive) - see GM (38005)
19020 Buick, Oldsmobile & Pontiac Full-size (Front-wheel drive) '85 thru '05
Buick Electra, LeSabre and Park Avenue; Oldsmobile Delta 88 Royale, Ninety Eight and Regency; Pontiac Bonneville
19025 Buick, Oldsmobile & Pontiac Full-size (Rear wheel drive) '70 thru '90
Buick Estate, Electra, LeSabre, Limited, Oldsmobile Custom Cruiser, Delta 88, Ninety-eight, Pontiac Bonneville, Catalina, Grandville, Parisienne
19030 Mid-size Regal & Century all rear-drive models with V6, V8 and Turbo '74 thru '87
Regal - see GENERAL MOTORS (38010)
Riviera - see GENERAL MOTORS (38030)
Roadmaster - see CHEVROLET (24046)
Skyhawk - see GENERAL MOTORS (38015)
Skylark - see GM (38020, 38025)
Somerset - see GENERAL MOTORS (38025)

CADILLAC
21015 CTS & CTS-V '03 thru '12
21030 Cadillac Rear Wheel Drive '70 thru '93
Cimarron - see GENERAL MOTORS (38015)
DeVille - see GM (38031 & 38032)
Eldorado - see GM (38030 & 38031)
Fleetwood - see GM (38031)
Seville - see GM (38030, 38031 & 38032)

CHEVROLET
10305 Chevrolet Engine Overhaul Manual
24010 Astro & GMC Safari Mini-vans '85 thru '05
24015 Camaro V8 all models '70 thru '81
24016 Camaro all models '82 thru '92
24017 Camaro & Firebird '93 thru '02
Cavalier - see GENERAL MOTORS (38016)
Celebrity - see GENERAL MOTORS (38005)
24020 Chevelle, Malibu & El Camino '69 thru '87
24024 Chevette & Pontiac T1000 '76 thru '87
Citation - see GENERAL MOTORS (38020)
24027 Colorado & GMC Canyon '04 thru '10
24032 Corsica/Beretta all models '87 thru '96
24040 Corvette all V8 models '68 thru '82
24041 Corvette all models '84 thru '96
24045 Full-size Sedans Caprice, Impala, Biscayne, Bel Air & Wagons '69 thru '90
24046 Impala SS & Caprice and Buick Roadmaster '91 thru '96
Impala '00 thru '05 - see LUMINA (24048)
24047 Impala & Monte Carlo all models '06 thru '11
Lumina '90 thru '94 - see GM (38010)
24048 Lumina & Monte Carlo '95 thru '05
Lumina APV - see GM (38035)
24050 Luv Pick-up all 2WD & 4WD '72 thru '82
Malibu '97 thru '00 - see GM (38026)
24055 Monte Carlo all models '70 thru '88
Monte Carlo '95 thru '01 - see LUMINA (24048)
24059 Nova all V8 models '69 thru '79
24060 Nova and Geo Prizm '85 thru '92
24064 Pick-ups '67 thru '87 - Chevrolet & GMC
24065 Pick-ups '88 thru '98 - Chevrolet & GMC

24066 Pick-ups '99 thru '06 - Chevrolet & GMC
24067 Chevrolet Silverado & GMC Sierra '07 thru '12
24070 S-10 & S-15 Pick-ups '82 thru '93, Blazer & Jimmy '83 thru '94,
24071 S-10 & Sonoma Pick-ups '94 thru '04, including Blazer, Jimmy & Hombre
24072 Chevrolet TrailBlazer, GMC Envoy & Oldsmobile Bravada '02 thru '09
24075 Sprint '85 thru '88 & Geo Metro '89 thru '01
24080 Vans - Chevrolet & GMC '68 thru '96
24081 Chevrolet Express & GMC Savana Full-size Vans '96 thru '10

CHRYSLER
10310 Chrysler Engine Overhaul Manual
25015 Chrysler Cirrus, Dodge Stratus, Plymouth Breeze '95 thru '00
25020 Full-size Front-Wheel Drive '88 thru '93
K-Cars - see DODGE Aries (30008)
Laser - see DODGE Daytona (30030)
25025 Chrysler LHS, Concorde, New Yorker, Dodge Intrepid, Eagle Vision, '93 thru '97
25026 Chrysler LHS, Concorde, 300M, Dodge Intrepid, '98 thru '04
25027 Chrysler 300, Dodge Charger & Magnum '05 thru '09
25030 Chrysler & Plymouth Mid-size front wheel drive '82 thru '95
Rear-wheel Drive - see Dodge (30050)
25035 PT Cruiser all models '01 thru '10
25040 Chrysler Sebring '95 thru '06, Dodge Stratus '01 thru '06, Dodge Avenger '95 thru '00

DATSUN
28005 200SX all models '80 thru '83
28007 B-210 all models '73 thru '78
28009 210 all models '79 thru '82
28012 240Z, 260Z & 280Z Coupe '70 thru '78
28014 280ZX Coupe & 2+2 '79 thru '83
300ZX - see NISSAN (72010)
28018 510 & PL521 Pick-up '68 thru '73
28020 510 all models '78 thru '81
28022 620 Series Pick-up all models '73 thru '79
720 Series Pick-up - see NISSAN (72030)
28025 810/Maxima all gasoline models '77 thru '84

DODGE
400 & 600 - see CHRYSLER (25030)
30008 Aries & Plymouth Reliant '81 thru '89
30010 Caravan & Plymouth Voyager '84 thru '95
30011 Caravan & Plymouth Voyager '96 thru '02
30012 Challenger/Plymouth Saporro '78 thru '83
30013 Caravan, Chrysler Voyager, Town & Country '03 thru '07
30016 Colt & Plymouth Champ '78 thru '87
30020 Dakota Pick-ups all models '87 thru '96
30021 Durango '98 & '99, Dakota '97 thru '99
30022 Durango '00 thru '03 Dakota '00 thru '04
30023 Durango '04 thru '09, Dakota '05 thru '11
30025 Dart, Demon, Plymouth Barracuda, Duster & Valiant 6 cyl models '67 thru '76
30030 Daytona & Chrysler Laser '84 thru '89
Intrepid - see CHRYSLER (25025, 25026)
30034 Neon all models '95 thru '99
30035 Omni & Plymouth Horizon '78 thru '90
30036 Dodge and Plymouth Neon '00 thru '05
30040 Pick-ups all full-size models '74 thru '93
30041 Pick-ups all full-size models '94 thru '01
30042 Pick-ups full-size models '02 thru '08
30045 Ram 50/D50 Pick-ups & Raider and Plymouth Arrow Pick-ups '79 thru '93
30050 Dodge/Plymouth/Chrysler RWD '71 thru '89
30055 Shadow & Plymouth Sundance '87 thru '94
30060 Spirit & Plymouth Acclaim '89 thru '95
30065 Vans - Dodge & Plymouth '71 thru '03

EAGLE
Talon - see MITSUBISHI (68030, 68031)
Vision - see CHRYSLER (25025)

FIAT
34010 124 Sport Coupe & Spider '68 thru '78
34025 X1/9 all models '74 thru '80

FORD
10320 Ford Engine Overhaul Manual
10355 Ford Automatic Transmission Overhaul
11500 Mustang '64-1/2 thru '70 Restoration Guide
36004 Aerostar Mini-vans all models '86 thru '97
36006 Contour & Mercury Mystique '95 thru '00
36008 Courier Pick-up all models '72 thru '82
36012 Crown Victoria & Mercury Grand Marquis '88 thru '10
36016 Escort/Mercury Lynx all models '81 thru '90
36020 Escort/Mercury Tracer '91 thru '02

36022 Escape & Mazda Tribute '01 thru '11
36024 Explorer & Mazda Navajo '91 thru '01
36025 Explorer/Mercury Mountaineer '02 thru '10
36028 Fairmont & Mercury Zephyr '78 thru '83
36030 Festiva & Aspire '88 thru '97
36032 Fiesta all models '77 thru '80
36034 Focus all models '00 thru '11
36036 Ford & Mercury Full-size '75 thru '87
36044 Ford & Mercury Mid-size '75 thru '86
36045 Fusion & Mercury Milan '06 thru '10
36048 Mustang V8 all models '64-1/2 thru '73
36049 Mustang II 4 cyl, V6 & V8 models '74 thru '78
36050 Mustang & Mercury Capri '79 thru '93
36051 Mustang all models '94 thru '04
36052 Mustang '05 thru '10
36054 Pick-ups & Bronco '73 thru '79
36058 Pick-ups & Bronco '80 thru '96
36059 F-150 & Expedition '97 thru '09, F-250 '97 thru '99 & Lincoln Navigator '98 thru '09
36060 Super Duty Pick-ups, Excursion '99 thru '10
36061 F-150 full-size '04 thru '10
36062 Pinto & Mercury Bobcat '75 thru '80
36066 Probe all models '89 thru '92
Probe '93 thru '97 - see MAZDA 626 (61042)
36070 Ranger/Bronco II gasoline models '83 thru '92
36071 Ranger '93 thru '10 & Mazda Pick-ups '94 thru '09
36074 Taurus & Mercury Sable '86 thru '95
36075 Taurus & Mercury Sable '96 thru '05
36078 Tempo & Mercury Topaz '84 thru '94
36082 Thunderbird/Mercury Cougar '83 thru '88
36086 Thunderbird/Mercury Cougar '89 thru '97
36090 Vans all V8 Econoline models '69 thru '91
36094 Vans full size '92 thru '10
36097 Windstar Mini-van '95 thru '07

GENERAL MOTORS
10360 GM Automatic Transmission Overhaul
38005 Buick Century, Chevrolet Celebrity, Oldsmobile Cutlass Ciera & Pontiac 6000 all models '82 thru '96
38010 Buick Regal, Chevrolet Lumina, Oldsmobile Cutlass Supreme & Pontiac Grand Prix (FWD) '88 thru '07
38015 Buick Skyhawk, Cadillac Cimarron, Chevrolet Cavalier, Oldsmobile Firenza & Pontiac J-2000 & Sunbird '82 thru '94
38016 Chevrolet Cavalier & Pontiac Sunfire '95 thru '05
38017 Chevrolet Cobalt & Pontiac G5 '05 thru '11
38020 Buick Skylark, Chevrolet Citation, Olds Omega, Pontiac Phoenix '80 thru '85
38025 Buick Skylark & Somerset, Oldsmobile Achieva & Calais and Pontiac Grand Am all models '85 thru '98
38026 Chevrolet Malibu, Olds Alero & Cutlass, Pontiac Grand Am '97 thru '03
38027 Chevrolet Malibu '04 thru '10
38030 Cadillac Eldorado, Seville, Oldsmobile Toronado, Buick Riviera '71 thru '85
38031 Cadillac Eldorado & Seville, DeVille, Fleetwood & Olds Toronado, Buick Riviera '86 thru '93
38032 Cadillac DeVille '94 thru '05 & Seville '92 thru '04 Cadillac DTS '06 thru '10
38035 Chevrolet Lumina APV, Olds Silhouette & Pontiac Trans Sport all models '90 thru '96
38036 Chevrolet Venture, Olds Silhouette, Pontiac Trans Sport & Montana '97 thru '05
General Motors Full-size Rear-wheel Drive - see BUICK (19025)
38040 Chevrolet Equinox '05 thru '09 Pontiac Torrent '06 thru '09
38070 Chevrolet HHR '06 thru '11

GEO
Metro - see CHEVROLET Sprint (24075)
Prizm - '85 thru '92 see CHEVY (24060), '93 thru '02 see TOYOTA Corolla (92036)
40030 Storm all models '90 thru '93
Tracker - see SUZUKI Samurai (90010)

GMC
Vans & Pick-ups - see CHEVROLET

HONDA
42010 Accord CVCC all models '76 thru '83
42011 Accord all models '84 thru '89
42012 Accord all models '90 thru '93
42013 Accord all models '94 thru '97
42014 Accord all models '98 thru '02
42015 Accord '03 thru '07
42020 Civic 1200 all models '73 thru '79
42021 Civic 1300 & 1500 CVCC '80 thru '83
42022 Civic 1500 CVCC all models '75 thru '79

(Continued on other side)

Haynes North America, Inc., 861 Lawrence Drive, Newbury Park, CA 91320-1514 • (805) 498-6703 • http://www.haynes.com

Haynes Automotive Manuals (continued)

NOTE: If you do not see a listing for your vehicle, consult your local Haynes dealer for the latest product information.

42023 Civic all models '84 thru '91
42024 Civic & del Sol '92 thru '95
42025 Civic '96 thru '00, CR-V '97 thru '01, Acura Integra '94 thru '00
42026 Civic '01 thru '10, CR-V '02 thru '09
42035 Odyssey all models '99 thru '10
Passport - *see ISUZU Rodeo (47017)*
42037 Honda Pilot '03 thru '07, Acura MDX '01 thru '07
42040 Prelude CVCC all models '79 thru '89

HYUNDAI
43010 Elantra all models '96 thru '10
43015 Excel & Accent all models '86 thru '09
43050 Santa Fe all models '01 thru '06
43055 Sonata all models '99 thru '08

INFINITI
G35 '03 thru '08 - *see NISSAN 350Z (72011)*

ISUZU
Hombre - *see CHEVROLET S-10 (24071)*
47017 Rodeo, Amigo & Honda Passport '89 thru '02
47020 Trooper & Pick-up '81 thru '93

JAGUAR
49010 XJ6 all 6 cyl models '68 thru '86
49011 XJ6 all models '88 thru '94
49015 XJ12 & XJS all 12 cyl models '72 thru '85

JEEP
50010 Cherokee, Comanche & Wagoneer Limited all models '84 thru '01
50020 CJ all models '49 thru '86
50025 Grand Cherokee all models '93 thru '04
50026 Grand Cherokee '05 thru '09
50029 Grand Wagoneer & Pick-up '72 thru '91 Grand Wagoneer '84 thru '91, Cherokee & Wagoneer '72 thru '83, Pick-up '72 thru '88
50030 Wrangler all models '87 thru '11
50035 Liberty '02 thru '07

KIA
54050 Optima '01 thru '10
54070 Sephia '94 thru '01, Spectra '00 thru '09, Sportage '05 thru '10

LEXUS
ES 300/330 - *see TOYOTA Camry (92007) (92008)*
RX 330 - *see TOYOTA Highlander (92095)*

LINCOLN
Navigator - *see FORD Pick-up (36059)*
59010 Rear-Wheel Drive all models '70 thru '10

MAZDA
61010 GLC Hatchback (rear-wheel drive) '77 thru '83
61011 GLC (front-wheel drive) '81 thru '85
61012 Mazda3 '04 thru '11
61015 323 & Protogé '90 thru '03
61016 MX-5 Miata '90 thru '09
61020 MPV all models '89 thru '98
Navajo - *see Ford Explorer (36024)*
61030 Pick-ups '72 thru '93
Pick-ups '94 thru '00 - *see Ford Ranger (36071)*
61035 RX-7 all models '79 thru '85
61036 RX-7 all models '86 thru '91
61040 626 (rear-wheel drive) all models '79 thru '82
61041 626/MX-6 (front-wheel drive) '83 thru '92
61042 626, MX-6/Ford Probe '93 thru '02
61043 Mazda6 '03 thru '11

MERCEDES-BENZ
63012 123 Series Diesel '76 thru '85
63015 190 Series four-cyl gas models, '84 thru '88
63020 230/250/280 6 cyl sohc models '68 thru '72
63025 280 123 Series gasoline models '77 thru '81
63030 350 & 450 all models '71 thru '80
63040 C-Class: C230/C240/C280/C320/C350 '01 thru '07

MERCURY
64200 Villager & Nissan Quest '93 thru '01
All other titles, see FORD Listing.

MG
66010 MGB Roadster & GT Coupe '62 thru '80
66015 MG Midget, Austin Healey Sprite '58 thru '80

MINI
67020 Mini '02 thru '11

MITSUBISHI
68020 Cordia, Tredia, Galant, Precis & Mirage '83 thru '93
68030 Eclipse, Eagle Talon & Ply. Laser '90 thru '94
68031 Eclipse '95 thru '05, Eagle Talon '95 thru '98
68035 Galant '94 thru '10
68040 Pick-up '83 thru '96 & Montero '83 thru '93

NISSAN
72010 300ZX all models including Turbo '84 thru '89
72011 350Z & Infiniti G35 all models '03 thru '08
72015 Altima all models '93 thru '06
72016 Altima '07 thru '10
72020 Maxima all models '85 thru '92
72021 Maxima all models '93 thru '04
72025 Murano '03 thru '10
72030 Pick-ups '80 thru '97 Pathfinder '87 thru '95
72031 Frontier Pick-up, Xterra, Pathfinder '96 thru '04
72032 Frontier & Xterra '05 thru '11
72040 Pulsar all models '83 thru '86
Quest - *see MERCURY Villager (64200)*
72050 Sentra all models '82 thru '94
72051 Sentra & 200SX all models '95 thru '06
72060 Stanza all models '82 thru '90
72070 Titan pick-ups '04 thru '10 Armada '05 thru '10

OLDSMOBILE
73015 Cutlass V6 & V8 gas models '74 thru '88
For other OLDSMOBILE titles, see BUICK, CHEVROLET or GENERAL MOTORS listing.

PLYMOUTH
For PLYMOUTH titles, see DODGE listing.

PONTIAC
79008 Fiero all models '84 thru '88
79018 Firebird V8 models except Turbo '70 thru '81
79019 Firebird all models '82 thru '92
79025 G6 all models '05 thru '09
79040 Mid-size Rear-wheel Drive '70 thru '87
Vibe '03 thru '11 - *see TOYOTA Matrix (92060)*
For other PONTIAC titles, see BUICK, CHEVROLET or GENERAL MOTORS listing.

PORSCHE
80020 911 except Turbo & Carrera 4 '65 thru '89
80025 914 all 4 cyl models '69 thru '76
80030 924 all models including Turbo '76 thru '82
80035 944 all models including Turbo '83 thru '89

RENAULT
Alliance & Encore - *see AMC (14020)*

SAAB
84010 900 all models including Turbo '79 thru '88

SATURN
87010 Saturn all S-series models '91 thru '02
87011 Saturn Ion '03 thru '07
87020 Saturn all L-series models '00 thru '04
87040 Saturn VUE '02 thru '07

SUBARU
89002 1100, 1300, 1400 & 1600 '71 thru '79
89003 1600 & 1800 2WD & 4WD '80 thru '94
89100 Legacy all models '90 thru '99
89101 Legacy & Forester '00 thru '06

SUZUKI
90010 Samurai/Sidekick & Geo Tracker '86 thru '01

TOYOTA
92005 Camry all models '83 thru '91
92006 Camry all models '92 thru '96
92007 Camry, Avalon, Solara, Lexus ES 300 '97 thru '01
92008 Toyota Camry, Avalon and Solara and Lexus ES 300/330 all models '02 thru '06
92009 Camry '07 thru '11
92015 Celica Rear Wheel Drive '71 thru '85
92020 Celica Front Wheel Drive '86 thru '99
92025 Celica Supra all models '79 thru '92
92030 Corolla all models '75 thru '79
92032 Corolla all rear wheel drive models '80 thru '87
92035 Corolla all front wheel drive models '84 thru '92
92036 Corolla & Geo Prizm '93 thru '02
92037 Corolla models '03 thru '11
92040 Corolla Tercel all models '80 thru '82
92045 Corona all models '74 thru '82
92050 Cressida all models '78 thru '82
92055 Land Cruiser FJ40, 43, 45, 55 '68 thru '82
92056 Land Cruiser FJ60, 62, 80, FZJ80 '80 thru '96
92060 Matrix & Pontiac Vibe '03 thru '11
92065 MR2 all models '85 thru '87
92070 Pick-up all models '69 thru '78
92075 Pick-up all models '79 thru '95
92076 Tacoma, 4Runner, & T100 '93 thru '04
92077 Tacoma all models '05 thru '09
92078 Tundra '00 thru '06 & Sequoia '01 thru '07
92079 4Runner all models '03 thru '09
92080 Previa all models '91 thru '95
92081 Prius all models '01 thru '08
92082 RAV4 all models '96 thru '10
92085 Tercel all models '87 thru '94
92090 Sienna all models '98 thru '09
92095 Highlander & Lexus RX-330 '99 thru '07

TRIUMPH
94007 Spitfire all models '62 thru '81
94010 TR7 all models '75 thru '81

VW
96008 Beetle & Karmann Ghia '54 thru '79
96009 New Beetle '98 thru '11
96016 Rabbit, Jetta, Scirocco & Pick-up gas models '75 thru '92 & Convertible '80 thru '92
96017 Golf, GTI & Jetta '93 thru '98, Cabrio '95 thru '02
96018 Golf, GTI, Jetta '99 thru '05
96019 Jetta, Rabbit, GTI & Golf '05 thru '11
96020 Rabbit, Jetta & Pick-up diesel '77 thru '84
96023 Passat '98 thru '05, Audi A4 '96 thru '01
96030 Transporter 1600 all models '68 thru '79
96035 Transporter 1700, 1800 & 2000 '72 thru '79
96040 Type 3 1500 & 1600 all models '63 thru '73
96045 Vanagon all air-cooled models '80 thru '83

VOLVO
97010 120, 130 Series & 1800 Sports '61 thru '73
97015 140 Series all models '66 thru '74
97020 240 Series all models '76 thru '93
97040 740 & 760 Series all models '82 thru '88
97050 850 Series all models '93 thru '97

TECHBOOK MANUALS
10205 Automotive Computer Codes
10206 OBD-II & Electronic Engine Management
10210 Automotive Emissions Control Manual
10215 Fuel Injection Manual '78 thru '85
10220 Fuel Injection Manual '86 thru '99
10225 Holley Carburetor Manual
10230 Rochester Carburetor Manual
10240 Weber/Zenith/Stromberg/SU Carburetors
10305 Chevrolet Engine Overhaul Manual
10310 Chrysler Engine Overhaul Manual
10320 Ford Engine Overhaul Manual
10330 GM and Ford Diesel Engine Repair Manual
10333 Engine Performance Manual
10340 Small Engine Repair Manual, 5 HP & Less
10341 Small Engine Repair Manual, 5.5 - 20 HP
10345 Suspension, Steering & Driveline Manual
10355 Ford Automatic Transmission Overhaul
10360 GM Automatic Transmission Overhaul
10405 Automotive Body Repair & Painting
10410 Automotive Brake Manual
10411 Automotive Anti-lock Brake (ABS) Systems
10415 Automotive Detailing Manual
10420 Automotive Electrical Manual
10425 Automotive Heating & Air Conditioning
10430 Automotive Reference Manual & Dictionary
10435 Automotive Tools Manual
10440 Used Car Buying Guide
10445 Welding Manual
10450 ATV Basics
10452 Scooters 50cc to 250cc

SPANISH MANUALS
98903 Reparación de Carrocería & Pintura
98904 Manual de Carburador Modelos Holley & Rochester
98905 Códigos Automotrices de la Computadora
98906 OBD-II & Sistemas de Control Electrónico del Motor
98910 Frenos Automotriz
98913 Electricidad Automotriz
98915 Inyección de Combustible '86 al '99
99040 Chevrolet & GMC Camionetas '67 al '87
99041 Chevrolet & GMC Camionetas '88 al '98
99042 Chevrolet & GMC Camionetas Cerradas '68 al '95
99043 Chevrolet/GMC Camionetas '94 al '04
99048 Chevrolet/GMC Camionetas '94 al '06
99055 Dodge Caravan & Plymouth Voyager '84 al '95
99075 Ford Camionetas y Bronco '80 al '94
99076 Ford F-150 '97 al '09
99077 Ford Camionetas Cerradas '69 al '91
99088 Ford Modelos de Tamaño Mediano '75 al '86
99089 Ford Camionetas Ranger '93 al '10
99091 Ford Taurus & Mercury Sable '86 al '95
99095 GM Modelos de Tamaño Grande '70 al '90
99100 GM Modelos de Tamaño Mediano '70 al '88
99106 Jeep Cherokee, Wagoneer & Comanche '84 al '00
99110 Nissan Camioneta '80 al '96, Pathfinder '87 al '95
99118 Nissan Sentra '82 al '94
99125 Toyota Camionetas y 4Runner '79 al '95

Over 100 Haynes motorcycle manuals also available

7-12